M000106861

TIMELY REFLECTIONS

A MINUTE A DAY WITH DALE MEYER

TRI-PILLAR PUBLISHING

TIMELY REFLECTIONS

Copyright © 2014 by Dale A. Meyer

Tri-Pillar Publishing
Anaheim Hills, California
Website: www.TriPillarPublishing.com
e-mail: tripillarpublishing@cox.net

ALL RIGHTS RESERVED. This book or parts thereof may not be reproduced in any form without prior written permission of the publisher.

International   Standard   Book   Number   --13:   978-1-942654-00-1

International   Standard   Book   Number   --10:   1-942654-00-6

Library of Congress Control Number: 2015930002

Unless otherwise indicated, all Scripture is from the *ESV® Bible* (*The Holy Bible, English Standard Version®*), copyright © 2001 by Crossway Bibles, a publishing ministry of Good News Publishers. Used by permission. All rights reserved.

Scripture quotations marked (NIV) are taken from the Holy Bible, New International Version®, NIV®. Copyright © 1973, 1978, 1984, 2011 by Biblica, Inc.™ Used by permission of Zondervan. All rights reserved worldwide. www.zondervan.com The "NIV" and "New International Version" are trademarks registered in the United States Patent and Trademark Office by Biblica, Inc.™

The Scripture quotation marked (CEV) is from the Contemporary English Version Copyright © 1991, 1992, 1995 by American Bible Society. Used by Permission.

The Scripture quotation marked (NASB) is taken from the New American Standard Bible®, Copyright © 1960, 1962, 1963, 1968, 1971, 1972, 1973, 1975, 1977, 1995 by The Lockman Foundation. Used by permission.

Scripture quotations marked (KJV) are taken from the Holy Bible, King James Version, which is in the public domain.

First edition, December, 2014
Printed in the United States of America

Front cover location: Reflection Lake, Mount Rainier National Park, WA
Front cover photograph: Peggy Boerneke, Vista, CA
Back cover photograph of Dr. Meyer courtesy of Concordia Seminary, St. Louis
Cover design: Peter Dibble, Wilsonville, OR

YOU CAN BLESS
PRESENT AND FUTURE GENERATIONS

The prayers and gifts of caring Christians like you are essential to Concordia Seminary's mission of preparing the church's future pastors, missionaries, deaconesses, scholars, and leaders.

With your partnership, Concordia Seminary will continue to prepare servants of Christ who are rock solid in their theology and fully prepared to lead and serve congregations now and for generations to come. You are providing faithful pastors just as sainted Christians supported Concordia Seminary to prepare the pastors who blessed you.

To give by phone or ask questions
1-800-822-5287

For more information
www.csl.edu

To give now
www.csl.edu/give

...tell to the coming generation the glorious deeds of the LORD, and his might, and the wonders that he has done.

(PSALM 78:4)

Concordia Seminary
801 Seminary Place
St. Louis, MO 63105
1-800-822-5287
www.csl.edu

Diane, your persistent love for our family and your untiring service to community, church, and Seminary are a blessing to many, most especially to your devoted husband. Dale

Contents

Acknowledgments

The *Meyer Minute* began in November, 2000 with the goal of sharing short spiritual thoughts with my coworkers at Lutheran Hour Ministries. That it has continued is a credit to many dear people. My wife Diane distributes the *Minute* every day via e-mail and Internet, things about which I know almost nothing and therefore owe her yet another debt of gratitude. The name *Meyer Minute* was suggested by Michelle Christ, my faithful assistant at *The Lutheran Hour* and now at Concordia Seminary. For many years, Paul Clayton and Gary Duncan recorded the *Minute* every day so it could be broadcast on radio station KFUO-AM. Josephine and Andy Dibble, the founders and directors of Tri-Pillar Publishing, have been great to work with. They even let me split a few infinitives! Tri-Pillar is unique and refreshing in its approach; check out their website to learn more about their ministry and other publications. Dr. Hummert, President Friedrich, and Congressman Shimkus, thank you for writing forewords. I learned things about myself from what you wrote. The faculty, staff, and students of Concordia Seminary paradoxically have nothing and have everything to do with the *Minute*. It's not their project, but they are the people with whom I am privileged to work. Their mantra is "the vigorous life of the mind in the service of the Gospel," and they continually stimulate my thinking.

To you who have read the *Minute* over the years and to you who will use this book, I express my sincere appreciation. When you write something, advised the Roman poet Horace, put it in a drawer for nine years and only then take it out and revise it. Doing that with old *Meyer Minutes* has been an interesting exercise in self-reflection. Each *Minute* has been enlarged and revised, hopefully sharpening the thought and improving its expression. *Timely Reflections* has also made me reflect on my own piety, a piety formed by my family, parents Art and Norma, and siblings Bruce and Pam, and by St. Paul's Lutheran Church and School in Chicago Heights, Illinois. I've gotten older and learned a whale of a lot since then, but my piety is pretty much the piety formed in my youth. In the *Anaphora* of Divine Service, we say to God, "not as we ought, but as we are able."[1] That is how I offer this work to Him and to you.

Forewords

To Capture the Mind (Foreword 1 of 3)

It happened again, just the other day! I wonder: *Can Dale read my mind?* I've known him for thirty years as professor, professional colleague, and friend. He's interviewed me and I him. He knows my parents and my brother – by name – and even remembers his time with my parents and the World's Largest Buffalo in Jamestown, ND. Sure, he knows me, but can he read my mind? Sometimes I think so. At least I do when I read *The Meyer Minute*.

Just last week, in my early morning read of the local paper, the president of the flagship university of our state touted all "his university" was doing to expand the diversity of the staff and student body. Humph, I said to myself as another swig of dark roast Folgers® hit my throat. I wish *we* had funds to do what *they* are doing. Then off to work I went, and before the day's first appointment arrived there was *The Meyer Minute* in my Outlook® in-box. *Hurry: read and delete*, I thought.

Not so fast! Dale read my mind that morning. The *Minute* was about "Statistics," overwhelming statistics. "Try these, President Brian."

> Outside the United States: 1 million Japanese live in Sao Paulo, Brazil. 50 million Chinese live outside China. The British Empire has 52 nations, and all are represented in London. There are 46 French-speaking countries, all represented in Paris.
>
> Inside the United States: One New York City zip code has 123 ethnic groups. The borough of Queens has 600 Korean churches. There are 400,000 Arabs in Chicago, 50,000 Serbs in Pittsburg, and 1 million international students in the USA. The USA is the largest Jewish, Scandinavian, and Irish nation in the world. Our country is the second largest "African" nation after Nigeria and the third largest Spanish speaking nation after Mexico and Spain. All these statistics are only the tip of the iceberg.[1]

In just a minute, Dale had done it again. He jolted me from my envy and complacency, and reminded me that God calls us to serve Him and proclaim the Gospel right now with all we have and are. There is no time to dismiss what we think we can't do because of what we don't have. Rather, every day is a day in which God calls us to listen more carefully, act more boldly, and proclaim more zealously the Good News of Jesus Christ – the one and only Savior of the world – to all people everywhere.

If you are looking for a devotional that will capture (and sometimes read) your mind for a minute but fire your heart for a lifetime, this book is for you. In it, by God's grace, the truth of God's Holy Word is revealed, proclaimed, and applied through the thoughts and words of one who, throughout the minutes of his lifetime, has searched the Scriptures and lived their truths in humble, honest, and humorous ways. I am thrilled Dale has taken the time to chronicle the many gems contained in this book because they point always to the Savior. As they do, they also reveal a warm, witty, winsome man, precious and chosen in God's sight, who throughout his ministry has been "Jesus with skin on" to parishioners, pupils, politicians, pastors, professors, presidents, and people aplenty!

Brian L. Friedrich, M.Div., Ph.D.
President, Concordia University, Nebraska
Seward, Nebraska

An Invitation to Pause Each Day (Foreword 2 of 3)

As a consulting psychologist, I am dedicated to helping individuals, families, groups, and organizations improve their situations, maximize their strengths, and push through adversity and the day-to-day barriers that confront us all. The "daily" aspect of these challenges and struggles is important to note. While it is helpful, and healthy, to set long-term goals and strive forward, our journeys are still traveled one day at a time. I have found, and psychological research supports this, that we perform better and achieve more when we pause each day to remind ourselves of what is important in our lives, what values should guide us, and how we want to use our talents and gifts. Some people do this through prayer, some by meditation, perhaps a personal reflection during the commute to work, others by a personal pep talk, many not at all.

Through some consulting work I have done at Concordia Seminary in St. Louis, I met Dr. Dale Meyer, and then became a reader of *The Meyer Minute*. Each *Meyer Minute* is a succinct commentary that draws upon a Scripture passage, explores the implications and messages from this reading, and invites the reader to reflect upon these messages and perhaps discover their own interpretation and meaning for their daily lives, along with further suggested readings that carry similar themes.

I realized that each *Meyer Minute* could provide that opportunity to pause and reflect that I think is important and energizing. It is like developing a positive daily habit that contributes to a healthy emotional and spiritual balance. By design, these *Minutes* are brief and can be quickly absorbed even as we go about our frequently very busy days and schedules.

Dr. Meyer helps you feel good – not by platitudes or self-congratulation, but by inviting you to do the right thing, make the proper moral choice, and find the personal satisfaction that comes from getting outside of yourself and into the lives of others. His daily reflections are inspiring, motivating, and challenging. He translates a Scripture passage or parable into a practical guidepost for your day. He has a distinctive knack for taking the spiritual and transcendent and making it very human and accessible. This is a great accomplishment and a worthwhile read.

A *Meyer Minute* can enrich your day, and motivate you to become better than you were yesterday. It certainly helps me, and I expect it will do the same for you if you include it in your day.

Henry J. Hummert, Ph.D.
Consulting Psychologist
Senior Consultant, Colarelli, Meyer & Associates (CMA)
St. Louis, Missouri

Christ into Every Aspect of Our Lives (Foreword 3 of 3)

I have had the pleasure of knowing Dale Meyer for over 30 years. We are members of the same church and live in the same small town of Collinsville, Illinois. We've seen each other's families grow up and watched our community and church weather changes and cycles. Dale and I also share the experience of being occasionally separated from our families – myself in Washington, D.C. as a Congressman and Dale as he travels representing the Seminary. We both understand the importance of building relationships with people in the vocations in which we find ourselves, and appreciate the strain and joys those relationships can bring.

Sometimes dubbed "The Irreverent Reverend," Dale Meyer has always used God's Word to address our human condition. Years ago, Dale's conversational style was evident as his Bible class back at my home church of Holy Cross in Collinsville, Illinois, was broadcast over KFUO-AM radio and on his *On Main Street* television show. Many more Christians came to appreciate his friendly and accessible manner, and were able to grow in the Word when he left Holy Cross and was called to be *The Lutheran Hour* speaker. After *The Lutheran Hour*, Dale received the call to be the tenth President of Concordia Seminary in St. Louis. From this position he has helped develop the next generation of called ministers of the Word. Dale continues to be a sincere preacher and popular speaker throughout our synod.

I typically spend half of my week in Washington, D.C. and the other half in Illinois, often traveling throughout the lower half of the state as I connect with my constituents. My family lives in Illinois full time. I am home almost every weekend, however, and attend church almost every Sunday at Holy Cross in Collinsville, leading a Bible class when I am able. Likewise, Dale is often away from his wife Diane and from their home as he preaches and speaks around our synod. We see Diane regularly at Holy Cross without Dale, in the same pew their family has long occupied. It is truly good to have a home church that supports our families, even when we are apart.

Many times leadership can be a lonely position to hold – whether it's in government or the church. I have said that being a politician is the only "honest" profession because we at least acknowledge that we truly practice politics! Even in the church and at the Seminary, "politics" can abound. Being on friendly terms with the people involved in difficult decisions can go a long way toward diffusing uncomfortable and unproductive situations. (How often have we heard that Washington is too divided?) What a joy it is to watch a true "people person" like Dale Meyer build relationships among the staff and friends of the Seminary and thus further the work of the Lord to which he is called.

Even with his many other duties and positions, Dr. Dale still has a burden on his heart to speak truth to a fallen world, hence *The Meyer Minute*. Using the World Wide Web and being aware of the short attention span and busy schedules of many Americans, *The Meyer Minute* has fit the bill for thousands. Whether the topic is the liturgical calendar, current events, the family, or the myriad other things that bombard us in our daily lives, the topics Dale addresses are those which we all find ourselves dealing with regularly. Applying God's Word to these events and stressors encourages us to bring Christ into every aspect of our life from the mundane to the enormous and challenging.

I have been reading and using *The Meyer Minute* for many years. It is part of my morning devotions. During the Bible class I have the privilege to lead at Holy Cross, we always start our discussion with conversation and prayer about current events and issues. As I read *The Meyer Minute*, I find that Dale has been following those same events with commentary from a biblical perspective.

The Bible is God's Word and a living document for us to follow and learn from. It speaks to all regardless of their condition. Anyone who doubts this would do well to subscribe to *The Meyer Minute*.

This book is a compilation from thousands of *Meyer Minutes* boiled down into a collection of one per day used as a daily devotional for one full year. I challenge you to recommit yourself to spend some time daily with God. You will find this book of short, minute-long devotions stimulating and intriguing in your everyday walk with our Lord.

Thank you, Dale and Diane. Joshua 1:8.

John Shimkus
Member of Congress, 15th District
Collinsville, Illinois

Introduction

Timely Resources

Timely Reflections is designed to lead you into daily reflection on your life and piety as a follower of Jesus Christ. *Timely Reflections* is also designed to provide you "Timely Resources" for various purposes.

The indexes, calendars for 2015-2017, and symbols at the top of each page throughout Lent and Advent will help you "time" your reading. For example, Ash Wednesday, Easter, and some other church holidays fall on different dates each year. Using these resources, you can find an appropriate *Timely Reflection* for special days for years to come.

When something is weighing on your mind and your heart is heavy, the topical and Scripture passage indexes will lead you to relevant thoughts and prayer. The same is true for happy times: for birthdays, baptisms, confirmation, graduations, weddings. And I hope you'll enjoy the several *Minutes* that are written from the unique perspective of our grandsons. For these and many other themes, simply scan the topical index.

When you are invited to lead a devotion for a group, the indexes can direct you to a *Reflection* that can stimulate your thinking as you prepare.

Pastors, you'll find that many of these daily thoughts can be starting points as you plan and craft your sermons. Besides the Scripture passage index that I hope you'll find useful, the Endnotes section identifies the sources of hymns and quotations used in the *Reflections*.

How to use this book? In various ways, but always under this prayer: "Teach us to number our days that we may get a heart of wisdom" (Psalm 90:12).

Talking to Jesus

Taking time to reflect has always been important to me, but I find it occupying more and more of my time as I get older. What's driving me, and at least in this aspect of life I am a driven person, is this question: *How do I talk to*

Jesus? My question isn't especially about prayer, although talking to Jesus is obviously an act of prayer, whether the talking is formal or informal or even thoughts and sighs. I'm focused on *how* I approach Him, *how* I think of myself in contrast to Him. We approach different people in different ways, depending upon who they are. You approach a TSA agent far differently than you approach a trusted pastor or teacher. You speak to a bill collector differently than a dear longtime friend, and so on. How do I approach Jesus as He truly is and not how I might falsely imagine Him to be? We are, after all, prone to project our own opinions upon God, to fashion Him after our image, and so we're tempted to approach Jesus as we'd like Him to be or, for some of us, as we dread Him to be, at any given time. However, when you read the Gospels, you're surprised to find that Jesus often didn't act as people expected. Most of my life is over, so sooner rather than later I'll be coming before Jesus in judgment. How I talk to Him now is in some measure how I will talk to Him when I enter eternity. I want to know him aright, and I know many of you share this desire. Do we expect to meet a gentle Savior, but then will be shocked to see Him as a stern judge? Do we anticipate hearing, "Come, you who are blessed by my Father" but then will hear Him say, "I never knew you" (Matthew 25:34; 7:23)? How do we approach Jesus in a way that is not self-delusion but rather Spirit-led?

My own reflections have led me to realize that I'm a modern Pharisee. Did that get your attention? You probably know enough of the New Testament to know that Jesus wasn't the best of buddies with the Pharisees. Reflecting over the years has persuaded me that I probably would have been a Pharisee had I lived in Israel in the first century A.D. You might have been one too, because the Pharisees were an attractive religious group. In Matthew chapter 23, Jesus pronounces seven woes upon the Pharisees. Jesus had "X-ray vision," as it were; I don't. He looked into their hearts but I would have been impressed by what I saw in the Pharisees. Jesus' woes upon the Pharisees show us why they were outwardly attractive. They were preachers and teachers. They were visible in the community – probably would have used social media. They were into missions and evangelism. "You travel across sea and land to make a single proselyte" (Matthew 23:15), Jesus said, and we recall that the Pharisee Saul was on a religious mission to Damascus when Jesus appeared to him (Acts 9:2). The Pharisees were masters at theological distinctions, and so are ministers and professors today. Pharisees had an active and very well-defined stewardship program. Liturgical practice was one of their hallmarks, as was reverence for the fathers of their faith. Yes, had I lived then, I suspect I would have been a Pharisee and I have seen many of their attributes in my own life and outlook on religion. That's why *how* I approach Jesus really is an issue; I don't want to hear Him pronounce "woe" upon me.

You and I are living in a time of profound transition in culture and thought. Born and shaped in the mid-twentieth century, I was blessed with a wonderful Christian home, parochial education, and was taken every week to a church that believed that the Word of God is revealed absolute truth. It is, and I still believe that. Our congregation wasn't unique; in those years American culture was a churched culture and people more or less knew the Bible. That was the setting that formed my personal piety, and you'll see in page after page of this book that I remain an old-time believer. Some things are different today; many preachers are more transparent and will talk about their own faith struggles. They'll use humor to help their teaching, and I certainly love humor. That said, at heart I remain an old-time believer and it wouldn't surprise me if you are too. But the world and American culture have changed drastically over the decades of our lives. Academics describe it as a shift from modernism to post-modernism. For centuries, the mind-set of western civilization was the Enlightenment, the Age of Reason. The Enlightenment exalted reason above all else, and looked to reason for human progress. The Enlightenment had no use for sectarian religion, to which the church took strong exception. Reason cannot determine the truth of God's Word. But that aside, believers used reason to present and advance the faith. Church and culture more or less had reason in common, and reason promised progress. Progress in science, progress in learning, progress in culture, progress in philosophy – in every way you had "to admit it's getting better … getting better all the time," as the Beatles sang.[1] However, popular belief in reason and progress was undermined in the last century from wars and genocides and failures in science, technology, and economy on an unprecedented scale. Trust in reason and progress had been weakening for some time, but in the twentieth century it gave way to the relativism that dominates our present time. That change has had a profound impact upon the faith of individual people and upon the institutional church. While there are millions and millions of Americans who still believe that the

Bible is true, the popular culture presented and promoted by media, universities, and opinion shapers would lead us to believe that there is no objective truth. The Bible is ignored, misquoted, or despised. *You have your opinion; I have mine. Who are you to tell me that I'm wrong?* Philipp Melanchthon, Martin Luther's colleague in the Reformation, called that "Epicurean indifference,"[2] after the teachings of the Greek philosopher Epicurus. *Don't worry about what the gods think.* That's where you and I find ourselves today – believers in the truth of God's Word but living amidst Epicurean indifference. Or to compare our present situation with ancient Israel, "Everyone did what was right in his own eyes" (Judges 17:6).

Now I ask that you follow this paragraph closely. I hope to show why my Pharisaic tendencies are dangerous, potentially dangerous eternally. Maybe you'll see yourself in this predicament by the end of the paragraph. Melanchthon said that the opposite of Epicurean indifference is "Pharisaic pride."[2] Keep in mind that we believe that the Bible is God's revealed Word; it's absolute, objective truth, "the power of God for salvation to everyone who believes" (Romans 1:16). In 2 Corinthians 5:7, the converted Pharisee Paul says, "we walk by faith, not by sight." Now that line isn't as black-and-white as it sounds. If you walk by faith and not by sight across a busy highway, you'll quickly find yourself in heaven. In fact, heaven is the ultimate destination Paul had in mind when he sharply distinguished between faith and sight. A few verses later Paul wrote, "we must all appear before the judgment seat of Christ, so that each one may receive what is due for what he has done in the body, whether good or evil" (2 Corinthians 5:10). How I handle the truth of God's Word, what some theologians call the "body of doctrine," is ultimately a question of walking by faith or walking by sight. Taking it by faith means we receive the teaching of truth as an unmerited gift from God and we obediently trust what it says, and this is by the gracious working of the Holy Spirit. Taking the doctrine by sight means that our reason makes it an object, a holy object that we handle. We see it, we study it, we ruminate on it, we write about it, we publish our thoughts about it, we talk about it amongst ourselves, we use it to substantiate our own positions, and through it all we say: *We have the Word of God in its truth and purity*. But now it is no longer a matter of faith seeking understanding, as St. Augustine taught us – rather by our understanding we presume to own the true faith. Reason that was created to be a servant of God's revealed truth is now trying to lord it over God's truth. First century Pharisees felt they owned religious doctrine, and that is the temptation for Bible-believing Christians today: to puff ourselves up, to think more highly of ourselves than we should. We wouldn't know diddly-squat if God hadn't graciously revealed it to us. Jesus said to the ancient Pharisees, "you are wrong, because you know neither the Scriptures nor the power of God" (Mark 12:24). His seven woes upon the Pharisees were not so much about what they taught but about the way they handled and lived out their body of doctrine.

How can we resist this subtle temptation to imagine that it's "our doctrine?" The answer, I think, is the fear of God. "Fear" in the Bible describes a wide range of feelings. At one extreme is the feeling that overtakes you when someone or something comes at you that is bigger than you are, more powerful than you are, and poses an imminent threat. A terminal diagnosis from your doctor, your spouse leaving you, imminent collapse of your financial house, a terrorist attack... these evoke a feeling of dread and helplessness. Death produces this fear. Dr. C.F.W. Walther, the first president of Concordia Seminary, said that it's a very rare Christian who doesn't fear death.[3] I'm certainly not that rare Christian; there are many things about death that scare me – hence my reflection on *how* I approach Jesus. I add that I'm suspicious of people who brush death off. So, that's one extreme of the word "fear" in the Bible. At the other extreme is a similar feeling. Something or someone comes at you that is bigger than you are, more powerful than you are, but is coming to help you. This is the power of God, God for us and not against us, Jesus, Gospel, the saving doctrine, totally beyond us but coming to help us. The feeling that this should evoke in us is, *Wow!* This is awe, this is reverence, and this is what the Bible calls the "fear of God." I've been traveling around the country for some 25 years, preaching in churches, speaking at conferences, staying in homes and hotels, getting a sense of what's going on. What I sense is lacking today, certainly absent in contemporary American culture but also little spoken of in church, is the fear of God. "If you call on him as Father who judges impartially according to each one's deeds, conduct yourselves with fear throughout the time of your exile" (1 Peter 1:17). The body of doctrine is a good thing, but woe upon us if we handle it like we own it, handle it without fear of God who is our Judge, and without awe for Jesus our only Savior. In 1518, Martin Luther presented his eleventh thesis at the Heidelberg

Disputation: "Arrogance cannot be avoided or true hope be present unless the judgment of condemnation is fear in every work."[4] "Fear in every work" includes how we handle the truths of the Bible. "Not many of you should become teachers, my brothers, for you know that we who teach will be judged with greater strictness" (James 3:1). "We must all appear before the judgment seat of Christ, so that each one may receive what is due for what he has done in the body" (2 Corinthians 5:10). How shall I talk to Jesus? *Oh, dear God! Be merciful to me, a sinner* (cf. Luke 18:13).

In conclusion, I'm maturing in *how* to approach and talk to Jesus. Our cultural shift to postmodernism is not without blessing. For us who believe the Bible is God's revealed Word, the Reformation truth "by faith alone," *sola fide*, shines more clearly than ever.

> Our reason cannot fathom / The truth of God profound;
> Who trusts in human wisdom / Relies on shifting ground.
> God's Word is all sufficient, / It makes divinely sure;
> And trusting in its wisdom, / My faith shall rest secure.[5]

The Spirit of God uses that Word to bless our reflections in faith and to grow our trust in Jesus as loving Savior. Jesus brought some Pharisees around to get it right. "Now there was a man of the Pharisees named Nicodemus … This man came to Jesus by night" (John 3:1-2). Jesus said to him, "Are you the teacher of Israel [a professor of theology and Seminary president!] and yet you do not understand these things?" (John 3:10). I'm coming to Jesus in the darkness of my understanding, so much tinged by Pharisaic pride. Jesus led that Pharisee to this truth, "God did not send his Son into the world to condemn the world, but in order that the world might be saved through him" (John 3:17). That is the salutary (spiritually healthful) fear of God, and it's known by faith. "Whoever believes in him should not perish but have eternal life" (John 3:16).

Jesus got faith through the thick head and into the heart of another Pharisee who had thought he "owned" the truth. Paul is a model for us all.

> If anyone else thinks he has reason for confidence in the flesh, I
> have more: circumcised on the eighth day, of the people of
> Israel, of the tribe of Benjamin, a Hebrew of Hebrews; as to the
> law, a Pharisee. … But whatever gain I had, I counted as loss for
> the sake of Christ. Indeed, I count everything as loss because of
> the surpassing worth of knowing Christ Jesus my Lord. For his

sake I have suffered the loss of all things and count them as rubbish, in order that I may gain Christ and be found in him, not having a righteousness of my own that comes from the law, but that which comes through faith in Christ, the righteousness from God that depends on faith – that I may know him and the power of his resurrection. (Philippians 3:4-5, 7-10)

I suggest we stop talking about "doctrines," plural. The Reformers talked about the *corpus doctrinae*, the one body of doctrine. That is the evangelical doctrine: Jesus Christ come as Lord to save us in this world of hurt for an eternity with Him in heaven. The doctrine has its parts, what the Reformers called "articles" or "topics," but the fear of God leads us to see that it's all bound together in the one evangelical doctrine. "Whoever comes to me I will never cast out" (John 6:37). That's timely now and for eternity. That's why the Bible not only teaches us to fear God but also to love Him, "that I may know him and the power of his resurrection." I hope these humble reflections will in some small way help us all to know Jesus better. Remember, you and I are staking our lives on His Good News.

Rev. Dale A. Meyer, Ph.D.
St. Louis, Missouri
December, 2014

Timely Reflections

January 1

Time with Jesus

Happy New Year! Let's compare Christmas to New Year's Day. Christmas is dominated by things. Yes, we tried to keep Christ in Christmas but presents were piled all around the manger of little Lord Jesus. New Year's Day is not about things but about time. Our new things have been put away and we celebrate – is that the right word? – time. No, "celebrate" isn't right because we're not at peace with time. You might have plenty of things but your time is limited. Nicholas Berdyaev wrote, "The passage of time strikes a man's heart with despair, and fills his gaze with sadness."[1] So we begin with a dose of reality. Happy New Year?

People act as if Christmas is religious but New Year's is secular. Resolve to think more spiritually! The Creator put us into time, and into time put our Redeemer. "When the fullness of time had come, God sent forth his Son" (Galatians 4:4). And on the eighth day He was circumcised and given the name "Jesus" (cf. Luke 2:21). We dominate things but we can't dominate time. It terrorizes us… unless we invite Jesus the Lord of time into our swiftly-fleeting times. "Jesus is Lord" (1 Corinthians 12:3). "Here we have no lasting city but we seek the city that is to come" (Hebrews 13:14). A profoundly spiritual Happy New Year to you!

> Crown Him the Lord of years, / The potentate of time,
> Creator of the rolling spheres, / Ineffably sublime.
> All hail, Redeemer, hail! / For Thou hast died for me;
> Thy praise and glory shall not fail / Throughout eternity.[2]

For further reflection: Psalm 90 – "Teach us to number our days"

Dear Jesus, give me joy from knowing that "my times are in Your hand" (Psalm 31:15). Amen!

January 2

"Oh, That the Lord Would Guide My Ways"!

Did you make any resolutions for the New Year? If so, do they acknowledge that you are a child of the heavenly Father? Will you more gladly put out your hand for His guidance? Some Bible passages to integrate into goal setting:

"A man's steps are from the LORD; how then can man understand his way?" (Proverbs 20:24).

"I know, O LORD, that the way of man is not in himself, that it is not in man who walks to direct his steps. / Correct me, O LORD, but in justice; not in your anger, lest you bring me to nothing" (Jeremiah 10:23-24).

"Search me, O God, and know my heart! Try me and know my thoughts! / And see if there be any grievous way in me, and lead me in the way everlasting!" (Psalm 139:23-24).

"Give me understanding, that I may keep your law and observe it with my whole heart" (Psalm 119:34).

"A person cannot receive even one thing unless it is given him from heaven" (John 3:27).

And if you made no New Year's resolutions, fine, but please don't be satisfied with your sanctification status quo. We are saved "Just as I am, without one plea, / But that Thy blood was shed for me"[1] but God loves you too much to leave you just as you are. As you step into the new year, and encounter people and issues before you, horizontally, discipline yourself to think vertically – to heaven!

For further reflection: Psalm 73:23-28 – Living life heavenly-minded

Oh, that the Lord would guide my ways / To keep His statutes still!
Oh, that my God would grant me grace / To know and do His will![2]

January 3

God's Word Changes Things

"In the beginning, God created the heavens and the earth" (Genesis 1:1). If God created life in the beginning, it's helpful in these first days of January to remember that your life is forever a gift from your Creator.

"The earth," Genesis reports, "was without form and void, and darkness was over the face of the deep" (Genesis 1:2). What will the next 12 months bring you? Health and happiness, or illness and sadness? Prosperity, or struggling to make ends meet? Will light illuminate what comes your way, or will you fear the darkness of the unknown?

"And the Spirit of God was hovering over the face of the waters. And God said…" His Word changes things. "And God said, 'Let there be light' and there was light" (Genesis 1:2-3). Who better to illumine your year than the Creator of light? "In your light do we see light" (Psalm 36:9). God speaks and light comes to our lives. Will we discipline ourselves to listen to the Word that helps us understand?

"And God saw that the light was good. And God separated the light from the darkness. God called the light Day, and the darkness he called Night. And there was evening and there was morning, the first day" (Genesis 1:4-5). God give light to the days of your New Year!

> [God] saved us and called us to a holy calling, not because of our works but because of his own purpose and grace, which he gave us in Christ Jesus before the ages began, and which now has been manifested through the appearing of our Savior Christ Jesus, who abolished death and brought life and immortality to light through the gospel. (2 Timothy 1:9-10)

For further reflection: 2 Corinthians 4:1-6 – Jesus, God's Word of light

O Holy Spirit, Spirit of our Lord Jesus, through Your Word radiate His light and immortality throughout my life. Amen.

January 4

Getting It All Together – in His Grace

Things can get pretty intense in January. Take house cleaning, for example. It's not just tidying up after all the clutter of Christmas, but it's cleaning with determination. There's a place for everything, and by golly we're going to get everything in its place. Another example is family finances. We start putting in order all the financial records for the past year and are doggedly determined this new year will be better. Our intensity can easily erupt in anger – anger at the world and outbursts of anger at family and friends. Why all this intensity in January? Sometimes it's fear – fear that our nicely decorated holiday house is about to crash down.

Jesus told a parable about a man who had done well, had his house in order, but the poor guy died suddenly. "So is the one who lays up treasure for himself and is not rich toward God" (Luke 12:21). Notice that Jesus doesn't have a problem with things; nothing wrong with your dogged determination to get your physical and financial house in better shape. Just do it "toward God." Is the weight of the world making your chest tight and your outlook fearful? There's nothing wrong with intensity, but pray God to take your fear-inspired intensity into His intense grace. Through that richness toward God, He will calm you and lovingly serve others through you.

> Fear not! I am with you, O be not dismayed,
> For I am your God and will still give you aid;
> I'll strengthen you, help you, and cause you to stand,
> Upheld by My righteous, omnipotent hand.[1]

For further reflection: Isaiah 26:3-4 – Peace of mind

Lord, help me not to fret and to know that "better is the little that the righteous has than the abundance of many wicked" (Psalm 37:16). Let me hear Your promise that You will not abandon me. Give Your child peace. Amen.

January 5

Our Common Life Together

Back to the grind after the holidays. Ugh!

The ancient philosopher Seneca wrote to a man named Lucilius: "You asked what I think ought to be especially avoided. The crowd! You'll never safely entrust yourself to a crowd. I never come out with the character I took in. Any peace that I had gained for myself is upset."[1] After a holiday, I often fantasize about ways to keep the calm feeling, but I know from experience it'll turn out just like Seneca said.

Fifteen centuries later, another thinker, Martin Chemnitz, offered a positive view about the upset that people can bring.

> Many people in all ages have given great approval to the solitary life … [but] in the Second Table [of the Ten Commandments] not even one word calls attention to the solitary life. God has carefully established the various duties in which individuals in mutual love serve other individuals, share their tasks, and bear together the common burdens of their entire life. … No greater praise for man's life in society can be imagined than that God by so many glorious and marvelous testimonies on Mt. Sinai, gave the entire Second Table of the Law dealing with the duties of our common life together.[2]

"For everything there is a season" (Ecclesiastes 3:1), times to rest and times to plunge back into work. Our Lord knew the press of the crowd. "When the great crowd heard all that he was doing they came to him. And he told his disciples to have a boat ready for him, because of the crowd, lest they crush him" (Mark 3:8-9). Plunging into people and their problems is the good work of the Second Table, good works appointed for us to do. The fact that there's always more work to do than time to do it is a reminder of the supremacy of God's grace in Christ over works. "Come to me, all who labor and are heavy laden, and I will give you rest" (Matthew 11:28).

"The shepherds returned" to their work, "glorifying and praising God" (Luke 2:20). So may we!

For further reflection: Ephesians 2:8-10 – Graced for works

Spirit of God, guide me to worship not only in the Sunday sanctuary but also in daily service to others. Amen.

January 6

Get Over the Baby?

If grief is a feeling of loss, then December 26th was the day I began to feel grief. The few radio stations that carried quality Christmas music on the 25th dropped it on the 26th. TV reports Christmas trees going to recycling stations, analysts judge whether the holidays were an economic boom or bust, and the news has become the same old news – the wearying world too much with us! Now that world is pressuring us, "Get on with it; get over the Baby!"

So this day, Epiphany, helps us deal with the grief of putting Christmas away. In eastern Christianity, January 6th is the day Christ's coming is celebrated. For western traditions, today recalls the story of the Magi (Matthew 2:1-12) and reminds us that Christ not only came for Jews but also for Gentiles, which includes me and probably you. But there's another reason why I value Epiphany.

As a kid I was impressed that our church left its two huge Christmas trees up several weeks into January. The reason was – and still is – that Epiphany is more than a day; it's a season designed to continue Christmas. Through Scripture and hymns, the Epiphany season plays out the ramifications of the Savior's coming for our lives. So I protest our culture telling me to get over the Baby. Our tree and decorations are defiantly still up!

Mary and Joseph never got over the Baby. When the Magi left, the world went back to its terrible ways. Herod was about to kill all the male children in Bethlehem, so God warned Joseph and the Holy Family fled to Egypt. When Herod died, they brought Jesus back to Judea, but hearing that another tyrant ruled there, they took the baby to Nazareth in Galilee. Angels glorifying God in the heavens, shepherds and Wise Men: those all became past events, but they still had the Baby – and so do we!

For further reflection: Matthew 2 – Magi and refugees in the world

O God, by the leading of a star You once made known to all nations Your only-begotten Son; now lead us, who know You by faith, to know in heaven the fullness of Your divine goodness; through Jesus Christ, our Lord.[1] Amen.

January 7

Are You Heeding God's Warnings?

"Warned in a dream not to return to Herod, they departed to their own country by another way" (Matthew 2:12).

God gives us warnings that we should change our way. The Wise Men had taken the logical route – they went to Herod and asked about the newborn king. When Herod's scholars said the child was to be born in Bethlehem, Herod asked the Wise Men to go visit but then return and report to him what they had found. That seemed innocent enough, but they didn't know that Herod was treacherous and a murderer.

Things may seem harmless to us but in fact can threaten our lives, our physical lives, our lives in family and community, and our lives with God. So God warns us. Perhaps He warns us by a sleepless night of worry. Perhaps someone is courageous enough to tell you, "Be careful." Certainly the Bible warns us. Read, for example, all that Jesus teaches us in the Sermon on the Mount about how to walk in life (Matthew 5-7). "Whatever was written in former days was written for our instruction, that through endurance and through the encouragement of the Scriptures we might have hope" (Romans 15:4). What warning from God's words are you heeding today? Your heavenly Father cares about the paths your heart and life will take today. It's *now* for you to follow Him home.

"Receive with meekness the implanted word, which is able to save your souls. Be doers of the word, and not hearers only, deceiving yourselves" (James 1:21-22).

For further reflection: Psalm 119:105-112 – "I incline my heart to perform your statutes"

Oh, what blessing to be near You / And to listen to Your voice;
Let me ever love and hear You, / Let Your Word be now my choice![1]

January 8

What Started You toward Jesus?

What led you to Jesus? It's helpful this Epiphany season to notice that the star didn't lead the Wise Men to Jesus as much as it set them to seek the newborn king of the Jews. What started you toward Jesus? Was it parents, family, friends, or some circumstance in life that led you to search for something more? When the Wise Men got to Jerusalem, the star disappeared, just as the initial impulses of Christian faith can also fade. At that point, the harder work begins – the work of trusting the Word of God. The Holy Spirit brought the blessings of justification into your life with a purpose, "for obedience to Jesus Christ" (1 Peter 1:2). That obedience is faith, trusting God's Word (see Romans 1:5). The Wise Men got their starting word from Herod's theologians, that the Christ was to be born in Bethlehem. When something has started us toward Christ, we must shift and trust His Word for guidance. Whatever we experience is important, and testimonies from others are not to be rejected out of hand, but in the last analysis it's to be His Word. "We walk by faith, not by sight" (2 Corinthians 5:7).

Still, stars and sights and significant testimonies do sometimes come as we journey by faith. When the Wise Men headed to Bethlehem, the star reappeared and "they rejoiced exceedingly with great joy" (Matthew 2:10). Living by faith, today's experiences can be added joys from God, but our fullness of joy comes from His underlying Word. "These things I have spoken to you, that my joy may be in you, and that your joy may be full" (John 15:11).

For further reflection: Mark 4:1-20 – Faith springs up and then what?

Holy Spirit, let not Satan or troubles or riches or desires choke out the Word of faith You have planted in me. For my Savior's sake I pray that You work in me the obedience of faith. Amen.

January 9

The Tedium of Routine Days

Our living room seems so empty now. Our family tradition is to keep the Christmas tree up until after Epiphany, January 6th. Now that the Wise Men have left and taken the day of Epiphany with them, the tree is gone and the empty space tells us that life reverts to its normal routine.

Routine is the place of spiritual growth or deterioration. As a parish pastor, I discovered that the folks who best weathered the tough times, and who had the deepest appreciation of the good times, were the people who had nurtured their spiritual development during the routine times. For example, when that enemy death would come into a home, especially come suddenly, the grief was noticeably different between families who had spiritual routines, especially faithful Sunday worship, and those who did not. All grieved, but those who had used the time of grace to grow closer to their Savior grieved with a glisten of hope in their tears.

It's interesting that the Gospel writers tell us almost nothing about Jesus' first 30 years except this: "Jesus increased in wisdom and stature and in favor with God and man" (Luke 2:52). Routine stuff... and it prepared Him for ministry, cross, and resurrection. It's not the holidays that grow you as much as following Jesus on the humdrum days. It's in the tedium of daily life the Spirit teaches us to sing *"Te Deum Laudamus."* Tedium, te-dium, *Te Deum!* "We praise Thee, O God!"

For further reflection: Colossians 3:12-17 – God, help us live like that!

Spirit of Jesus, motivate us to approach every day but especially this day as a time of grace.

 Help us that we Thy saving Word / In faithful hearts may treasure;
 Let e'er that Bread of Life afford / New grace in richest measure.
 O make us die to ev'ry sin, / Each day create new life within,
 That fruits of faith may flourish.[1]
Amen.

January 10

Reflection… and Another Candle on the Cake

Today is a special day for me – comes only once a year. You have this once-a-year day too, and you've noticed that they seem to come faster and faster than when we were kids. It's a day to reflect back. For whatever it's worth, here's what I've learned over the years.

About bodily life…

1.   I can't eat like I used to.
2.   I have to stretch.
3.   Sleeping through the night is no longer automatic.
4.   I can't burn both ends of the candle… and don't have to!

About the institutional church…

5.   The church is in a time of profound societal change, and most people are clueless.
6.   People don't want the church's opinion, unless church people have earned their trust.
7.   Church people need other people's opinions, whether we agree with them or not. That helps us search Scripture to know why we believe what we believe.
8.   Religious people got Jesus crucified back then, and some religious people today pursue their agendas, not His.
9.   Jesus is alive and present with us. No Gospel is preached without the resurrection.

About the stewardship of my remaining time…

10. Everything can be outsourced, except face-to-face caring contact.
11. God puts people before me. I can't ignore them because I have something else planned.
12. God will strip away everything dear, either slowly, one thing at a time, or with one fell blow.
13. Older doesn't necessarily mean wiser. "No fool like an old fool."
14. We don't fully realize how much we need Jesus until we realize Jesus is all we've got.
15. Just wait. The best is yet to come!

For further reflection: What have you learned during your years?

The Lord hath helped me hitherto by His surpassing favor; / His mercies ev'ry morn were new, His kindness did not waver / God hitherto hath been my Guide, hath pleasures hitherto supplied, / And hitherto hath helped me. / Help me henceforth, O God of grace, help me on each occasion, / Help me in each and every place, help me through Jesus' Passion; / Help me in life and death, O God, help me through Jesus' dying blood; / Help me as Thou hast helped me.[1]   Amen.

January 11

Submit to the Word!

Many churchgoers will hear these words about Jesus' Baptism. Matthew 3:13-17 begins: "Jesus came from Galilee to the Jordan to John, to be baptized by him. John would have prevented Him, saying, 'I need to be baptized by you, and do you come to me?'" John's resistance makes sense. Since the Bible teaches that Baptism saves us, 1 Peter 3:21, why should the Savior be baptized? John knew just enough to resist Jesus' word. Jesus could have compelled John, the way a lord would do, but instead He took a gentler way. "Let it be so now, for thus it is fitting for us to fulfill all righteousness." Jesus sought Baptism so that He would show Himself truly one with us. He hadn't come as a compelling Lord but gently as our brother. Hence Jesus desired Baptism and John "consented."

Does your relationship with Jesus continually move from objection to consent? Jesus has something to say to you every day. Often our instinctive reaction is, *Jesus, I know more about this than You do. What You say is too simple, too weak for what is needed here.* Jesus doesn't compel. He has given you the terrible ability to say "no" to God but He does keep pleading with you. John submitted to the Word. Submission to the Word is our constant struggle. Do you know just enough of the Word to object until the Spirit leads you deeper and you consent?

For further reflection: Isaiah 42:1-4 – Gentle Jesus

Oh, Son of God, by being baptized You placed Yourself with us under the Law of Your Father. Give us Your Spirit that we will hear and obey Your gentle pleadings and know Your Gospel. Amen.

January 12

Retreat with Jesus

Jesus says, "'Come away by yourselves to a desolate place and rest a while.' For many were coming and going, and they had no leisure even to eat" (Mark 6:31).

That's a sweet invitation to us Christians, but how sad, almost inexplicable, that we don't retreat more often with Jesus. "Oh, what peace we often forfeit; oh, what needless pain we bear – all because we do not carry everything to God in prayer."[1] Life weighs on us: work and problems dominate our minds; anger, grief, worry, and so many unhealthy emotions can fester within us; the busyness of our digital age consumes our time; and we get caught up in the "coming and going" of people. Whew! No wonder we're so stressed. You'd think we'd spend more time with Him in whom "we live and move and have our being" (Acts 17:28). Do weak devotional lives reflect some illusion that our sufficiency is of ourselves? (See 2 Corinthians 3:5.)

Our God waits and watches with fatherly patience for us to come. "He knows our frame; he remembers that we are dust" (Psalm 103:14). Yes, there are justifiable occasions when we skip devotion but, if you're like me, many days we are out-and-out delinquent. Martin Luther:

> Yet we must be careful not to break the habit of true prayer and imagine other works to be necessary which, after all, are nothing of the kind. Thus at the end we become lax and lazy, cool and listless toward prayer. The devil who besets us is not lazy or careless, and our flesh is too ready and eager to sin and is disinclined to the spirit of prayer.[2]

Are you a disciple today and into eternity? An answer comes from our quiet, unpublicized time with Jesus.

"Come unto Me, ye weary, / And I will give you rest."
O blessed voice of Jesus, / Which comes to hearts oppressed!
It tells of benediction, / Of pardon, grace, and peace,
Of joy that hath no ending, / Of love that cannot cease.[3]

For further reflection: Isaiah 30:8-18 – Rebellious people won't rest in God

Dear Jesus, You invite me to come and be with You. I have learned from experience that You do keep Your promise and give me rest. Help me keep coming to You. Amen.

January 13

We Are Accountable

On this date in 2012, the *Costa Concordia* cruise ship was wrecked off the coast of Italy. Thirty-two people died; 64 were injured. In 1708, another *Concordia* ran into bad weather and disappeared off the coast of Africa in the Indian Ocean; 130 people were lost. In 2010, still another *Concordia* sank off the coast of Brazil; all 64 people were saved. I cut out the newspaper account of that 2010 *Concordia* disaster and taped it to my office door as a reminder that poor leadership can be disastrous when you're steering a ship… or a seminary named "Concordia." The captain was the focus of attention in the most recent *Concordia* tragedy. He was placed under arrest on charges of manslaughter, shipwreck, and abandoning ship with passengers aboard.

Christians who believe that God forgives our sins for Jesus' sake often slough off accountability. God forgives me, we may reason, so let's just overlook this sin I've committed. That kind of thinking leads many people to view us believers as naïve. The Bible, in fact, teaches that we will be judged by our works (2 Corinthians 5:10). Understanding that we are accountable in work and life, that we can be punished or rewarded on this side of eternity for our attitudes and actions toward others, makes God's forgiveness a most precious gift. But what does forgiveness mean if you don't take accountability seriously? Dietrich Bonhoeffer called it "cheap grace."[1]

For further reflection: 1 Peter 1:15-19 – You'll be judged!

Thy works, not mine, O Christ, / Speak gladness to this heart;
They tell me all is done, / They bid my fear depart.
To whom, save Thee,
Who canst alone / For sin atone,
Lord, shall I flee?[2]

January 14

Hold on to Hope

"I consider that the sufferings of this present time are not worth comparing with the glory that is to be revealed to us" (Romans 8:18). That was true for Paul almost 2,000 years ago; today that's still true for you and me as we follow Jesus.

On January 14, 1948, Peter Marshall opened the United States Senate by praying, "We are glad, our Father, that troubles are cannibals – the big ones eat up the little ones."[1] He's talking about *the other shoe dropping*, about *trouble comes in threes*, about *this is only going to get worse*. But Peter Marshall also prayed, "In all things, big and little, reveal to us Thy wisdom and Thy love."[1]

It's in our sufferings, the little ones and the big cannibal ones, that God invites you to the hope that does not disappoint because this hope comes from God Himself. It is sure and certain because God poured His love into our hearts (cf. Romans 5:5). The Spirit breathes that hope to your beaten-down soul from the resurrection of Jesus Christ and His ascension to glory, where He prays for you now. "Christ Jesus is the one who died – more than that, who was raised – who is at the right hand of God, who indeed is interceding for us" (Romans 8:34). It's like ripples in the water. Baptized into the resurrection of Christ, the joy of His resurrection ripples out with hope to your problems today. Therefore, as Chaplain Marshall prayed, "We are glad."

"May the God of hope fill you with all joy and peace in believing, so that by the power of the Holy Spirit you may abound in hope" (Romans 15:13).

For further reflection: 1 Peter 1:18-21 – The reason for your faith and hope

Almighty, everlasting God, Your Son has assured forgiveness of sins and deliverance from eternal death. Strengthen us by Your Holy Spirit that our faith in Christ may increase daily and that we may hold fast to the hope that on the Last Day we shall be raised in glory to eternal life; through Jesus Christ, our Lord.[2]   Amen.

January 15

"A Helper Fit for Him" (and Her!)

"It is not good that the man should be alone; I will make him a helper fit for him" (Genesis 2:18). Over the weekend I tried to reverse that, to help Diane. "I'll go with you to the grocery store."

First she sent me off to get Philadelphia® Cream Cheese. After a lot of staring at the cheese case, I came back with a proud smile. "That's not it," Diane said, and sent me back to try again.

Next she sent me to get lunch meat, but this time didn't let me out of her sight. "No, not there!" she called. "Go to the deli." So I went to the counter and asked for some turkey. "What kind of turkey?" the clerk asked. "Huh? How many kinds are there?"

I saw some pickles nearby. I love pickles, so I picked a jar up, all on my own. "No, not from there," Diane said. "Get it from the pickle aisle." I put it back but said nothing, a defeated man.

When we checked out, I got to pay. That was the first thing I did correctly the whole shopping trip!

Finally at home, a tired Diane said, "I've had it," to which I innocently said, "I've had it with you." If looks could kill! "I mean, I'm worn out just like you are." In reflection, I wonder how many husbands are like me; we try to help our wives when it's convenient for us, but since it's not our daily habit, we can't help to their satisfaction. Yes, a husband could say, "I've tried; I've had it with you; don't expect any help from me," but that's not what we heard when we stood before the altar on our wedding day. "The union of husband and wife in heart, body, and mind is intended by God for the mutual companionship, help, and support that each person ought to receive from the other, both in prosperity and adversity."[1] Notice the words "ought to." More shopping trips ahead!

For further reflection: 2 Corinthians 9:6-15 – Charity begins at home

Heavenly Father, as a husband and wife stand side-by-side before Your altar, help them live side-by-side in mutual companionship, help, and support throughout all the years You give them. Inspired by Your Son, help them lovingly serve one another. Amen.

January 16

Out of Controversy, Blessing

James woke up one Friday morning with things on his mind, James being King James I of England and the date January 16, 1604. He had called a conference to deal with religious strife in England and today was the day to hear the Puritans complain about the Church of England. They had written:

> We, to the number of more than a thousand, of your Majesty's subjects and ministers, all groaning as under a common burden of human rites and ceremonies, do with one joint consent humble ourselves at your Majesty's feet to be eased and relieved in this behalf.[1]

So they proposed improving the clergy, eliminating some ceremonies, more strictly keeping the Sabbath, and writing a new catechism. Of course, the establishment bishops thought differently, and James was caught in the middle of it all. Some years later Dr. Myles Smith wrote:

> His Majesty ... was well aware that whoever attempts anything for the public, especially if it has to do with religion or with making the Word of God accessible and understandable, sets himself up to be frowned upon by every evil eye, and casts himself headlong on a row of pikes, to be stabbed by every sharp tongue.[2]

Many people dismiss the church because they see how Christians squabble. Many in the church disdain theological arguments; I certainly do. But when we read the Gospels, we see Jesus Himself at loggerheads with the religious establishment. Often it's out of controversy that truth becomes clearer. It certainly did when James presided that January 16th over 400 years ago. When the flustered Puritans off-handedly mentioned a new translation of the Bible, James seized on the suggestion. The result was the King James Bible, an eternal blessing to the lives and salvation of millions upon millions of people. Out of controversy, blessing.

For further reflection: Romans 8:18-30 – In all things...

O Spirit who brooded over the chaos, hover over our controversies and by Your holy inspiration bring forth good for the edification and salvation of precious souls. Amen.

January 17

Pride Goes Before a Fall

I've only gone downhill skiing once in my life, about 30 years ago. After taking lessons, I tried the bunny hill… and fell down repeatedly. One time when I was down, our little daughter Katie flew past me and said, "Why are you on the ground, Dad?" Humiliating! Eventually I got the hang of it, enough that my friend Robert said, "Let's try the advanced slope." I resisted but eventually my ego got the best of me. I was persuaded. By the way, Robert's an undertaker!

I started down that steep advanced slope and to my delight, I didn't fall. Finally, very near the end of the run, a skier wiped out ahead of me. *Aha*, I thought, *you wiped out and I, the beginner, am still up*. No kidding, the very moment I thought that, I wiped out, taking the fall of my life.

Pride goes before a fall (cf. Proverbs 16:18), also spiritually. Pay constant attention to your soul and your eternal destiny, and God will see you through. "He who began a good work in you will bring it to completion at the day of Jesus Christ" (Philippians 1:6). But if you puff yourself up when others fall, if you don't focus on the one thing needful, then sooner or later you'll go down. "Therefore let anyone who thinks that he stands take heed lest he fall" (1 Corinthians 10:12).

> I walk in danger all the way; / The thought shall never leave me
> That Satan, who has marked his prey, / Is plotting to deceive me.
> This foe with hidden snares / May seize me unawares
> If e'er I fail to watch and pray. / I walk in danger all the way.[1]

For further reflection: Proverbs 11:2; 16:18 – Pride

O keep me watchful, then, and humble; / Permit me nevermore to stray.
Uphold me when my feet would stumble, / And keep me on the narrow way.
Fill all my nature with Thy light, / O Radiance strong and bright![2]   *Amen.*

January 18

"Who Do You Say That I Am?"

I remember the moment well – the moment it dawned on me that an uninformed person can still have a knack for asking critical questions, thereby looking thoughtful, engaged… and impeding progress. My job has me with Ph.D.s every day, super-informed people who can pick anything to pieces. You know from your own experiences what I'm talking about. It's not rearranging deck chairs on the Titanic; it's *talking* about rearranging the deck chairs.

Today the church observes "The Confession of St. Peter." Jesus called an impromptu meeting to ask the disciples what people were saying about Him, a polling meeting. After the disciples gave their reports, Jesus put it to them. "Who do you say that I am?" Peter spoke up, "You are the Christ" (Mark 8:29). Peter was led to make the right confession, to act, but he sure didn't know all that was involved. Self-denial, suffering, martyrdom came to him after that "meeting."

Jesus asks the most important question you'll ever hear: "Who do *you* say that I am?" (italics mine). People in meetings want to know and discuss all the details before committing to a proposal – paralysis by analysis – but the call to faith doesn't come with a full report. Jesus called to Peter and his brother Andrew, "Follow me … And immediately they left their nets and followed him" (Mark 1:17-18). Immediately! You confess, and find out the rest of your life what that all means. You're staking your life on it. Really, think about it. You're staking your life on Jesus!

For further reflection: Luke 9:57-62 – The leap of faith

Living or dying, Lord, / I ask but to be Thine;
My life in Thee, Thy life in me, / Makes heav'n forever mine.[1]   *Amen.*

January 19

God Will Be at Your Side

Each year in mid-January, we remember the legacy of Martin Luther King, Jr. Here's how he reacted to a late night, threatening phone call.

> I got out of bed and began to walk the floor. Finally I went to the kitchen and heated a pot of coffee. In this state of exhaustion, when my courage had almost gone, I determined to take my problem to God. *I am afraid ... I am at the end of my powers. I've come to the point where I can't face it alone.*
>
> At that moment I experienced the presence of the Divine as I had never before experienced Him. It seemed as though I could hear the quiet assurance of an inner voice saying, *Stand up for righteousness, stand up for truth. God will be at your side forever.* Almost at once my fears began to pass from me...[1]

Jesus doesn't call you to die for Him as much as He calls you to live for Him. Be a living sacrifice today, deny yourself, and heed the servant call of Christ. When we're brought low, we can best hope in the promise, "My grace is sufficient for you, for my power is made perfect in weakness" (2 Corinthians 12:9).

"Out of my distress I called on the LORD; the LORD answered me and set me free. / The LORD is on my side; I will not fear" (Psalm 118:5-6).

For further reflection: 2 Corinthians 11:16-30 – Paul's sufferings

"The LORD is my light and my salvation; whom shall I fear?" (Psalm 27:1). Lord, there's much I fear! Adversity, confrontation, hostile people. Lord, be "the stronghold of my life" (ibid.) so I will not be afraid. Amen.

January 20

Sunday Promises – Weekday Actions?

This line in a prayer caught my attention: "Our deeds do not perform what our words promise." Do you include yourself in that confession, your Sunday professions not matched by your sanctified life during the week? "Although we know that we are weak and our deeds do not perform what our words promise," the prayer adds, "give us faith's courage and hope to try anew."[1]

That gap between Sunday promises and weekday actions is forgiven by God for Jesus' sake. That's forgiveness, but that's not full repentance. Repentance becomes full when you change your behavior. For that amendment of life, since "we are weak and our deeds do not perform what our words promise," we put biblical words of life direction into our heads and hearts, and ask the Spirit of God to enable us to live by them.

When the Ten Commandments had been given, the people of Israel said, "All that the LORD has spoken we will do, and we will be obedient" (Exodus 24:7). How did that turn out? They gave the right liturgical response but it didn't take long for their lives to fall far short of their profession. Amendment of life: "Lord Jesus, think on me / And purge away my sin"![2]

For further reflection: Romans 7:18-25 – Not easy, not easy at all!

O Holy Spirit, help me hear the Word and not harden my heart as ancient Israel did and so many still do today. For Jesus' sake! Amen.

January 21

Sink the Word into Your Heart

One Sunday, some words from the Collect for Grace set me thinking. "Defend us … with Your mighty power and grant that this day we fall into no sin."[1] How does God's power keep us from sinning? Is it a leash to yank you back when you want to go someplace you shouldn't? Is it a muzzle to shut your mouth against your will?

A chaplain back from Iraq told me how his safety depended upon armed soldiers. Chaplains are not armed; they need another power to protect them. God's power in your life is the weaponry of His Word. If you want to do your own thing, you can – no leash or muzzle will stop you. The Creator lets people do what they want, at least for the time being; see Romans 1:26. On the other hand, when you sink the Word into your heart by memory and intentional recall during the day, the Word of God enables you to resist temptation. St. Peter says, "Through faith [you] are shielded by God's power" (1 Peter 1:5 NIV). The Greek word translated "shielded" suggests a military fort. The Word in your heart puts protective walls around you. "A mighty fortress is our God."[2]

Don't have time? Have you ever offered advice to a young person, advice tested and proved true in your own experience, but the advice was brushed off? Is our Father ever saddened that we leave His protection?

> I walk in danger all the way; / The thought shall never leave me
>
> That Satan, who has marked his prey, / Is plotting to deceive me.
>
> This foe with hidden snares / May seize me unawares
>
> If e'er I fail to watch and pray. / I walk in danger all the way.[3]

Come into the Word and prayer. Garrison yourself!

For further reflection: Psalm 48 – In fortress Zion

O Lord, our heavenly Father, almighty and everlasting God, You have safely brought us to the beginning of this day. Defend us in the same with Your mighty power and grant that this day we fall into no sin, neither run into any kind of danger, but that all our doings, being ordered by Your governance, may be righteous in Your sight; through Jesus Christ, Your Son, our Lord, who lives and reigns with You and the Holy Spirit, one God, now and forever.[1]   *Amen.*

January 22

A Prayer for Today's Challenges

Thank You, O Lord, for the problems I'll wrestle with today. May they remind me that I'm Your dependent, sometimes helpless, child.

Thank You for letting me fret over paying bills. "Man does not live by bread alone" (Deuteronomy 8:3), but still we need our daily bread. When wherewithal is scant, help me trust that You are merciful to help in unexpected ways.

Thank You for any infirmities of body I may feel today. What a strange blessing to come to terms with my mortality. Ouch! It drives me to You, who do not change (Malachi 3:6; Hebrews 13:8).

Thank You for disappointments. People and problems will disappoint me. Of course! They are not God; only You are. Disappointments direct me back to You (Psalm 42:11).

Thank You for the difficult people who will get under my skin today. Remind me it's not them versus me, but Your patient love through me to them (Romans 12:21). Since Jesus is my best friend, I can be calm with people.

Thank You, O Lord, for all the work that won't get done today, try as I might. In that, You teach that we live by grace, not by works (Ephesians 2:8-9).

It's going to be a good day. Amen!

For further reflection: Psalm 131 – A calm and quiet soul

> *God gives me my days of gladness, / And I will / Trust Him still / When He sends me sadness.*
>
> *God is good; / His love attends me / Day by day, / Come what may, / Guides me and defends me.*[1]

January 23

God at Work through Our Cross-carrying

I didn't sleep well last night – was awake for several hours when I should have been blissfully asleep. My mind was churning about our students. Some of them are feeling beat up by the demands of classes. Some are worried about student debt. Some are battling the flu. Others are just carrying the heavy load of school, work, and family. Is it the moon, the alignment of the stars, cold sunless January, or maybe just life?

What bothers me most is that they seem to think these crosses shouldn't come our way, especially when we dedicate ourselves to serve the Lord Jesus. In fact, these are the times when God Himself is breaking us, remaking us, and fitting us for His service in this world. I want to hear seminarians pour out their problems with an appreciation that God is at work through their cross-carrying. These are our future pastors. They will have parishioners share problems with them just as they have shared with me. They will find that they can't fix everyone's problem, just as I can't fix theirs, much as I might like to. They will need to teach and preach how God is most at work when the cross is heaviest on our shoulders. Truth is, they probably won't truly own the great themes of the Bible – cross, resurrection, faith, hope, and love – until life beats them up. I think that's the truth for all of us.

Oswald Chambers: "The Bible has been so many words to us – clouds and darkness – then all of a sudden the words become spirit and life because Jesus re-speaks them to us in a particular condition."[1]

When I can't sleep, I sometimes get up and pour a glass of milk. Last night, as I sat in the darkness, I heard the Spirit: *Instead of crying in your beer, or milk, see this day's problems and worries as your Father's gift of growing up into Christ.* I pray our students learn that, and hope you appreciate it too. "Give thanks in all circumstances" (1 Thessalonians 5:18).

For further reflection: Jeremiah 18:1-6; 2 Corinthians 4:7 – The Potter and His clay pots

Holy Spirit, "With our spirit bear Thou witness / That we are the sons of God / Who rely upon Him solely / When we pass beneath the rod; / For we know, as children should, / That the cross is for our good."[2] Amen.

January 24

Pick Up the Script and Learn Your Lines!

Would you like God to make a dramatic appearance on the stage of your life, perhaps as Jesus appeared to Paul? "Suddenly a light from heaven flashed around him. … I am Jesus whom you are persecuting" (Acts 9:3, 5). No one I know has ever gotten such a revelation of Jesus and, truth be told, God's appearances to people in the Bible were rare. God won't play supporting actor in some fantasy script where you're the star.

Supporting actors to God, that's our role. God told Ananias:

> Rise and go to the street called Straight, and at the house of Judas look for a man of Tarsus named Saul … But Ananias answered, "Lord, I have heard from many about this man, how much evil he has done to your saints at Jerusalem. And here he has authority from the chief priests to bind all who call on your name." (Acts 9:11, 13-14)

I get that. *Lord, I'm not too keen about doing this! I feel comfy with my role in the Sunday sanctuary. Let me deliver Your lines when and where I want!* No, "You shall love your neighbor as yourself" (Matthew 22:39). That neighbor, the Good Samaritan teaches us, could be anyone (Luke 10:25-37). "But the Lord said to him, 'Go'" (Acts 9:15). So Ananias went and welcomed Paul, and showed himself a great supporting actor in the spread of the Good News.

Does God speak directly to us today? We might say "no," or we might confuse our feelings with the will of God, but ask yourself, *How many Bible passages are in my memory? How much is my conscience informed by Bible passages I've taken to heart?* "These words that I command you today [and that was a rare revelation thousands of years ago] shall be on your heart" (Deuteronomy 6:6). Supporting actor: pick up the script and learn your lines. The Spirit will use you!

For further reflection: Mark 13:9-13 – Maybe the words will be given you from your memory

"If you cannot speak like angels, / If you cannot preach like Paul…"[1] *Lord, I'm not Paul and I'm certainly not an angel, but I can be a modern Ananias and play my part in the spread of Your Good News. Help me learn the lines You've given me so Your Spirit can direct more people to Jesus. Amen.*

January 25

Hang onto Forgiveness in Christ

Being in a public position, I get my share of criticism. What strikes me is that critics, both the kind and the mean-spirited, don't have a clue. I know more against myself than they can imagine!

Today the church calendar remembers the conversion of St. Paul. You can read about his Damascus Road experience in Acts 9. Despite his conversion, some people kept doubting him, even reproaching him, for the rest of his life because he had persecuted the Church. But Paul's conscience was cleaned, not by the opinion of people but by God's forgiveness in Jesus Christ. "I received mercy for this reason, that in me, as the foremost, Jesus Christ might display his perfect patience as an example to those who were to believe in him for eternal life" (1 Timothy 1:16).

Martin Luther:

> Even the holiest of saints must confess: I have done what I could, perhaps, but I have failed far oftener than I know. So our conscience stands against us all, accusing us and declaring us unclean, even though we have passed with highest honors before the world or even now are passing.[1]

So when critics pound you, hang your conscience on God's sign of forgiveness. Jesus hung on the cross to make your conscience clean; now you hang onto Jesus! "By this we know love, that he laid down his life for us … Whenever our heart condemns us, God is greater than our heart, and he knows everything" (1 John 3:16, 20). Only in Jesus do you have a "good conscience" before God (1 Peter 3:21).

For further reflection: Acts 9:19-31 – Wary of Saul's conversion

"Blessed is the one whose transgression is forgiven, whose sin is covered" (Psalm 32:1). Jesus, You make that true for me! Help me to trust that against all my critics – and against my conscience when it condemns me – You make me clean! Amen.

January 26

Once Is Enough!

"My name is Connor. Bubby and I were taking our bath. Bubby poured water on me. He said he was baptizing me."

"That's right, Opa. At church pastor baptizes people. So I baptized Connor in the tub."

"Interesting. For being three- and one-year-olds, you give us older people a lot to think about. A long time ago, this time of year, winter, Epiphany, Martin Luther preached about Baptism. He talked about how many times you should be baptized. Some people get baptized but then fall away from God. When they realize they've gotten away from God, they think they need to start all over and get baptized again."

"Like I did to Connor?"

"Sort of. Dr. Luther says it's like taking a trip. If you get lost, you don't go back home and start all over again. You just admit you got lost and get back on the right way. No need to get baptized again. Just repent and get back to God's way of living. After all, God did His part of Baptism correctly. He gave forgiveness. He doesn't have to do His part over. We need to get back on the straight and narrow."

"Opa, you're turning our bath into a sermon!"

"It was on my mind. I was baptized on this date a long time ago."

"Opa, did you know Dr. Luther?"

For further reflection: 2 Timothy 2:11-13 – God is faithful to the promises He made when you were baptized

I have been washed; I have been sanctified; I have been justified in the name of the Lord Jesus Christ and by the Spirit of God! (cf. 1 Corinthians 6:11). Lord, help me always to know that, to live that, and when I get off Your path, to get right by repentance. Amen.

January 27

Raising Children for Eternity

I opened our strong box the other day and found a somewhat yellowed, small envelope with a 3 cent stamp, canceled on January 23, 1947. Inside the envelope were a bill and three receipts. The bill was from Ingalls Memorial Hospital in Harvey, Illinois. Five days in the hospital at $6 a day, $10 for maternity, $10 for "care of baby," and some other charges to bring the grand total to $61.10. There also were two receipts from Dr.'s Helge and Herbert Jansen for $135. For less than $200, my parents took home a ten pound baby.

In that strong box I also came across the certificate of my Baptism, January 26, 1947. That's a receipt of sorts, a spiritual receipt worth keeping. "You are not your own, for you were bought at a price. So glorify God in your body" (1 Corinthians 6:20). Because my parents understood that Baptism needs to be lived out, there followed years of Christian family life with Sunday worship and religious education during the week.

While the costs of bearing children have gone way up, the cost of training up a child for eternity is unchanged. It still costs the time, commitment, and example of parents, and absolutely needs the help of the Spirit of God who is ready and willing. Raising children for their life in this world … and … raising children for eternity. Which of the two is your most important investment?

> Oh, blest the parents who give heed
> Unto their children's foremost need
> And weary not of care or cost.
> May none to them and heav'n be lost![1]

For further reflection: Psalm 127 – "Unless the LORD builds the house…"

"Wisdom's highest, noblest treasure, Jesus, is revealed in You."[2] *Amen.*

January 28

The Value of Christian Education

It's that time of year when Roman Catholics and Lutherans celebrate and promote their parochial schools. Are Christian schools worth the cost?

I may not remember this accurately, but it's close enough to reflect how American culture has changed religiously. It seems that an on-the-street reporter asked a passerby what Easter is about. "That's when Jesus comes out. If he see his shadow, we have six more weeks of…"

Lifelong educator Daniel Aleshire wrote, "Our culture is less than convinced that religion is a cultural asset" and more and more people "do not know the tradition or understand it."[1] Parochial grade school wasn't just a positive influence in my life; it formed me into the person I am. The teachers, the parents, the church… all joined in a purpose-filled community of faith and learning. And when we went on to public high school and university, surprise! We had been holistically prepared.

Of course, these schools take effort above and beyond taxes. Aleshire says, "The question about cost is really a question about value." No parochial school close to you? People of faith teach and learn and serve in public schools as well. Parochial or public school, the question necessarily comes home. Do you value Christian education in your home? Do you prioritize it where you worship? Are you yourself a lifelong learner? Your answers are "yes," "yes," and "yes," if you know what Easter is truly about…

For further reflection: 2 Timothy 1:3-7 – Lois and Eunice valued religious education

Lord, bless all the schools in our country and those who support them. May Christian schools prove themselves Your special blessing to our communities and nation. May Your people who teach and learn and serve in public schools radiate the blessings that come from You. For Your sake! Amen.

January 29

Thank God for Teachers!

Their gratifications are small, often delayed. They're caught between idealism and the realities of long hours, low pay, and less time with their own families. They are teachers.

Many years ago a family friend died. Diane and I took daughters Elizabeth and Katie to the visitation. Katie was maybe five or six at the time, Elizabeth ten or so. On our way home, the girls were talking very quietly in the back seat. I butted in. "What are you talking about?"

Elizabeth answered, "Katie is wondering how Alfred (our friend) can be in heaven and the funeral home at the same time."

Well, faster than Clark Kent slipping into a phone booth, I slipped into my super pastor role and explained that his soul is in heaven and his body is waiting here until the Last Day and the resurrection of all people.

I thought I did a marvelous job of explaining it so a child could understand, but there was no immediate reaction from the back seat, only silence. Finally, Katie said, "I think I will ask my teacher."

Thank God for all our wonderful teachers!

For further reflection: 1 Samuel 3:1-10 – A child who trusted his "teacher"

Our sons and daughters we shall tell / And they again to theirs
That generations yet unborn / May teach them to their heirs.[1]
Lord, help us so to do! Amen.

January 30

Seeing God in Hindsight

Every year Concordia Seminary recognizes ordination anniversaries in a chapel service. Ordination is the rite by which the church places a candidate into the pastoral ministry. Time marches on, so the 40th year of my ordination was recognized in 2014. It was a time for looking back, and I hope today's *Reflection* will encourage you to look back as well.

A college professor taught me that we see God in hindsight. That is, we can't know the details of what God is doing in our lives today or the specifics of what He will do tomorrow. Moses had led the Israelites out of Egypt, received the Ten Commandments, and dealt with the Golden Calf idolatry – no small ministry! Moses asked, "Please show me your glory" (Exodus 33:18). The LORD said,

> I will be gracious to whom I will be gracious, and will show mercy on whom I will show mercy. But,' he said, 'you cannot see my face, for man shall not see me and live.' And the LORD said, 'Behold there is a place by me where you shall stand on the rock, and while my glory passes by I will put you in a cleft of the rock, and I will cover you with my hand until I have passed by. Then I will take away my hand, and you shall see my back, but my face shall not be seen. (Exodus 33:19-23)

It's only in hindsight that we see how God was present with His grace and mercy, how He took up the experiences of the years and wove us into the person we are today. And hindsight kindly frees us to be more honest about our need for forgiveness. Sometimes it takes time to realize we were wrong. Sitting in the chapel, thinking back, those thoughts were a pleasant release from so much.

If the past is forgiven, tomorrow is filled with hope. Frankly we shouldn't get too worried about tomorrow, although we should make provision for our loved ones and church. Tomorrow is in God's hands. All you and I have is now, today, what the old theologians called "the time of grace." "His grace has brought me safe thus far, / His grace will lead me home."[1] You too?

For further reflection: 2 Corinthians 4:1-6 – Where to see the glory

Rock of Ages, cleft for me, / Let me hide myself in Thee[2]

January 31

Nevertheless

One of the most memorable sermons I've heard was preached by Professor Waldemar Degner. That was back in the mid-60s when I was a student at Concordia College in Milwaukee. Fifty years ago? It must have been a good sermon to stick with me so long, and indeed it was. Dr. Degner preached the word "nevertheless" deep down into my heart.

He spoke on Luke chapter five. Fisherman Peter had spent the night on the Sea of Galilee but caught nothing. Jesus told him to go out and try once more. *Why?* Peter must have thought; after all, he did this for a living, but because he had heard Jesus teach and knew of His miracles, Peter agreed. "Master, we have toiled all the night, and have taken nothing: nevertheless at thy word I will let down the net" (Luke 5:5 KJV).

The Bible is filled with promises that God is good to you. Sometimes, sadly for you, the evidence suggests that is not true. Try as you might to succeed and be godly in your work, there are times your effort seems futile, and even times when you think God has forgotten you. "We have toiled all the night," tried as hard as we could, and have nothing to show. "Nevertheless at thy word," because I take Your teachings to heart, I persevere in hope.

One reason why Dr. Degner's sermon was so memorable is because he repeated the word "nevertheless" many times. Sometimes we imagine preaching is a mysterious, spiritual event, and yes, it is an occasion for the unseen Spirit of God to work on our spirits. But preaching is also a simple physical transaction. The preacher speaks, the air carries the sound waves, they physically enter our ears, and the Spirit takes them down into our hearts. "Repetition is the mother of learning."[1] Repeat "nevertheless" over and over today; sink it down into your heart. "In the Lord your labor is not in vain" (1 Corinthians 15:58).

For further reflection: Psalm 37:3-8 – Fretting over work?

Forth in Thy name, O Lord, I go, / My daily labor to pursue,
Thee, only Thee, resolved to know / In all I think or speak or do.
The task Thy wisdom has assigned, / O let me cheerfully fulfill;
In all my works Thy presence find, / And prove Thy good and perfect will.[2]
Amen.

February 1

Front-Row Seats Still Available!

Go to church? Boring! Super Bowl party? Exciting!

That's the way many young people raised in the church size up their options for football weekends. Some years ago, 31% of 18- to 29-year-olds told the Barna Group, "Church is boring;" 24% said, "Faith is not relevant to my career or interests;" and 23% said, "My church does not prepare me for real life."[1] These are young people raised in many of our churches. Are your children or grandchildren among them?

So what's a pastor and church to do? From Dietrich Bonhoeffer:

> Every day brings to the Christian many hours in which he will be alone in an unchristian environment. These are the times of testing. This is the test of true meditation and true Christian community. Has the fellowship … transported him for a moment into a spiritual ecstasy that vanishes when everyday life returns, or has it lodged the Word of God so securely and deeply in his heart that it holds and fortifies him?[2]

Two more stats affirm what Bonhoeffer wrote: 23% said, "The Bible is not taught clearly or often enough;" and 20% said, "God seems missing from my experience of church." It makes you wonder if the church is just trying to provide a nice hour, instead of being a passionate gathering of transparent people on a quest to know more about God and to be known by Him in Jesus Christ. Think about that… as you watch the crowds throng to football.

For further reflection: Deuteronomy 6:1-15 – "Teach your children well"[3]

Dear Jesus, people of all ages knew they could come to You. By Your Spirit make me a winsome person and make our church a safe place where people of all ages will say, "I was glad when they said to me, 'Let us go to the house of the LORD'" (Psalm 122:1). Amen.

February 2

Bearing with One Another

What is it in marriage? "We" or "Me?"

Dr. Dale Lefever tells this story. A wife stopped at the grocery store on her way home from work. When she got home, she was putting the groceries on the counter when she realized she had locked her keys in the car. Knowing how her husband would react, she decided not to call him. In due time he came home, found out about her keys, and exploded. "How could God make anyone so beautiful and so stupid at the same time?" he asked. After fuming a while, he started to walk away.

"Wait," she said. "I want to answer your question. God made me beautiful so you'd love me and God made me stupid so I'd love you."

Sometimes it's easier to be nice to strangers than to family. I hope this husband had enough sense to seek forgiveness … and it sounds like the wife had enough grace to give it. "Breathe, O breathe Thy loving Spirit / Into ev'ry troubled breast."[1]

> Put on then, as God's chosen ones, holy and beloved, compassionate hearts, kindness, humility, meekness, and patience, bearing with one another and, if one has a complaint against another, forgiving each other; as the Lord has forgiven you, so you also must forgive. And above all these put on love, which binds everything together in perfect harmony. And let the peace of Christ rule in your hearts, to which indeed you were called in one body. (Colossians 3:12-15)

We, not me.

For further reflection: 1 Peter 3:7 – Man up and read this!

Almighty, everlasting God, our heavenly Father, grant that by Your blessing husbands and wives may continue to live together according to Your Word and promise. Strengthen them in faithfulness and love toward each other. Sustain and defend them in every trial and temptation. Help them to live in faith toward You, in the communion of Your holy Church, and in loving service to each other that they may ever enjoy Your heavenly blessing; through Jesus Christ, Your Son, our Lord, who lives and reigns with You and the Holy Spirit, one God, now and forever.[2]   Amen.

February 3

Crossing the Line

How is it with you and Jesus?

His ministry just launched in Capernaum, Jesus now travels throughout Galilee, preaching and casting out demons. A leper comes up and asks to be healed. That was wrong on many counts, at least by the rules of that time. Lepers were outcasts, not supposed to approach "normal" people. No bother to this leper. This untouchable crosses the line, kneels right before Jesus and says, "If you will, you can make me clean" (Mark 1:40).

Do you cross the lines to go to Jesus? "Conventional wisdom" tells us what lines not to cross. Don't talk about your church with people at work. Don't bring Christian morality into office intrigues. Oh, you can believe in Jesus – just be private and personal about it. If that's what you do, then how is it with you and Jesus, really?

"Moved with pity, he stretched out his hand and touched him and said to him, 'I will; be clean.' And immediately the leprosy left him, and he was made clean" (Mark 1:41-42). Jesus Himself crosses the line. The clean touches the unclean; the Son of God touches a hurting brother, hurting sister.

> Come in poverty and meanness, / Come defiled, without, within;
>
> From infection and uncleanness, / From the leprosy of sin,
>
> Wash your robes and make them white; / Ye shall walk with God in light.[1]

Do you know His touch? When you kneel at the Communion table, do you know that you have been restored to community, unclean made clean because Jesus willed your deliverance? How is it with you and Jesus?

Cleansed, cross the line to go to places dominated by conventional wisdom. First, go; let words of witness follow your presence. Jesus told the leper, "See that you say nothing to anyone, but go, show yourself to the priest and offer for your cleansing what Moses commanded, for a proof to them" (Mark 1:44). Jesus tells you, "Present your bodies as a living sacrifice, holy and acceptable to God, which is your spiritual worship" (Romans 12:1).

For further reflection: 1 Peter 2:9-17 – Now that you have received mercy, let it show in the places of daily life

I, a sinner, come to Thee / With a penitent confession. / Savior, mercy show to me; / Grant for all my sins remission. / Let these words my soul relieve: / Jesus sinners doth receive.[2]

February 4

Lives Cut Short in the Line of Duty

Much of the grief poured out at the funerals of our fallen soldiers comes from the fact, the bitter fact, that their hopes and dreams will never be realized. "The joy of our hearts has ceased; our dancing has been turned to mourning" (Lamentations 5:15). What historian Ronald White, Jr. wrote of Civil War casualties, is true again. They died "just as they were preparing to harvest the fruits of their young lives."[1]

Their lives did yield fruit as they played their roles in combating our nation's enemies and terrorists, but the harvest will be ours to enjoy, not theirs. We have our careers, our families, and so many experiences. They had similar expectations but their hopes will never be realized. Because of their sacrifices, you and I harvest the benefits of living in a civilized society. "My heart goes out to the commanders of Israel who offered themselves willingly among the people. Bless the LORD" (Judges 5:9).

In grief for our fallen, followers of Jesus remember His sacrifice for us and His call for us to sacrifice ourselves for others. "By this we know love, that he laid down his life for us, and we ought to lay down our lives for the brothers. Little children, let us not love in word or talk but in deed and in truth" (1 John 3:16, 18).

Let us continually express our deep gratitude for our fallen young heroes and our sympathies to their families.

For further reflection: 2 Samuel 1 – David laments the deaths of Saul and Jonathan in battle

To give all peoples concord and peace; to preserve our land from discord and strife; to give our country Your protection in every time of need:

To direct and defend our president and all in authority; to bless and protect our magistrates and all our people:

To watch over and help all who are in danger, necessity, and tribulation ... to defend all orphans and widows and provide for them:

To strengthen and keep all sick persons and young children; to free those in bondage; and to have mercy on us all:

We implore You to hear us, good Lord.[2]

February 5

Reverence, Please

Every February, early in the month, the National Prayer Breakfast is held in Washington, D.C. People praise prayer, and rightly so, but do we contemplate what we're about to do when we bow our heads? That's why I like a practice I've seen especially in black preachers… significant silence before they say the first words of the prayer.

Prayer proceeds on the assumption that your words will be heard by the mysterious Almighty. That's a breathtaking assumption. The content of our prayers is even more amazing because most of our requests to the Eternal are small in the cosmic scheme of things. That's fine; His eye is on the sparrow.

Thou art coming to a King, / Large petitions with thee bring;

For His grace and pow'r are such / None can ever ask too much.[1]

But doesn't it follow that God can respond to us with His specifics? If we speak words to Him, can't He speak words to us? We don't talk to God with visions and emotions but words. When we pray, aren't we taking on the obligation to get into biblical words, "the Word of God" as it's called… and is?

Read the Hebrew prophets and you often come across their complaint that ancient Israel prayed the right words but their heart wasn't receptive to God's words and ways. So let the pray-er understand and beware. When you bow your head, you're humbling yourself before the Almighty. When you fold your hands, you're making the sign of the cross, the only way we have access to the heavenly Father. … Reverence, please. God Himself is present.

For further reflection: Habakkuk 2:20; Luke 11:1 – "Sweet hour of prayer"[2]

Speak, O God, and I will hear Thee; / Let Thy will be done indeed.
May I undisturbed draw near Thee / While Thou dost Thy people feed.
Here of life the fountain flows; / Here is balm for all our woes.[3]   Amen.

February 6

The Father's Loving Discipline

The state of the American economy is sometimes good, other times not good, but that's irrelevant when you and your family are feeling the economic pinch. Blame tough times on whomever you want; the Bible puts our troubles in a larger context. "Does disaster come to a city, unless the LORD has done it?" (Amos 3:6). Somehow God's behind it all. That doesn't mean that God maliciously sends national recessions or your own personal recession. As with so many other troubles we have, it's our self-centeredness, the undisciplined stewardship of our lives and resources, our prodigal ways, even our unknown faults (Psalm 19:12) – in short, our sinfulness – that brings troubles upon us. As a nation we do it to ourselves, and personally, best efforts notwithstanding, our sinfulness catches up to us. "He [God] himself tempts no one" (James 1:13).

God could use His omnipotence to remove our problems, but He doesn't. Instead He shows Himself a Father – not a doting grandfather – but a loving Father, who uses our troubles to mature us. The pain of our lives, economic or whatever your personal pain happens to be, is part of the Father's loving discipline to lead you to acknowledge the dead end of your own ways. This draws you more closely to the unending blessing of going the way of His commandments, in dependent trust upon His promises. "For the moment all discipline seems painful rather than pleasant, but later it yields the peaceful fruit of righteousness to those who have been trained by it" (Hebrews 12:11). That'll take patience, looking beyond today, and praying for greater trust in your heavenly Father. "Take not your Holy Spirit from me" (Psalm 51:11)!

For further reflection: Job 1 – I can't begin to imagine

Almighty God, You make us both to will and to do those things that are good and acceptable in Your sight. Let Your fatherly hand ever guide us and Your Holy Spirit ever be with us to direct us in the knowledge and obedience of Your Word that we may obtain everlasting life; through Jesus Christ, our Lord.[1] *Amen.*

February 7

Wherever You Stand, Speak the Truth in Love

Here's a question I'm often asked: "Does the Seminary teach students to preach in or out of the pulpit?" This ranks right up there with the other great questions of the universe. Why does God hide Himself from us? Why does God permit suffering? How can Christianity claim to be the only true religion and only way to heaven? Catch my sarcasm?

We have chapel services on campus every weekday. Most chapel sermons are delivered from the pulpit, but it's not unusual for the preacher to stand in the center of the chancel or even down in the aisle. I teach preaching classes and always get the question, "What about preaching out of the pulpit?" There are, I answer, logistical considerations. For example, if you're standing in the aisle, can the people on the sides or in the balcony see you? There are deeper considerations. What is the congregation used to? If they're used to one way or the other, is this an issue worthy of controversy? Ask the Elders, I tell them. But going farther – my cynicism getting the better of me – why do you ask? I've learned that many imagine that standing out of the pulpit somehow means being relevant. I also hear laypeople say, "We love our pastor. He preaches out of the pulpit." Huh? The real issue is what he's preaching! A compelling sermon from God's Word will be compelling wherever it's delivered from. A sermon of theological jargon that doesn't speak to life will be irrelevant wherever it comes from.

In my mind, it comes down to this. To congregation members: Are we so at home with one worship style that we get upset by something different? Aren't we driven to come to church by this question, "Lord, to whom shall we go? You have the words of eternal life" (John 6:68). To students: Don't make the pulpit the hill you'll die on, or off. Instead, make God's Word so compelling to people's lives that they'll listen intently wherever you are. In or out? Sounds like a belly button question – naval-gazing. I'm desperate to know more about God, wherever the preacher stands.

For further reflection: Matthew 5:1; Luke 4:16-21 – Jesus sat!

You are the truth; Your Word alone / True wisdom can impart;
You only can inform the mind / And purify the heart.[1]

February 8

"A Great Multitude … from Every Nation"

Consider this your invitation to visit the campus of Concordia Seminary and attend daily chapel. Chapel services are usually brief, about 25 minutes, but almost always edifying and uplifting; sometimes they are challenging. That was the case when Pastor Ron Rall preached about mission and shared some interesting facts from urban missiologist Ray Bakke.

One New York City zip code has 123 ethnic groups. The borough of Queens has 600 Korean churches. There are 400,000 Arabs in Chicago, 50,000 Serbs in Pittsburg, and 1 million international students in the USA. The United States is the largest Jewish, Scandinavian, and Irish "nation" in the world. Our country is the second largest African "nation" after Nigeria and the third largest Spanish speaking nation after Mexico and Spain. That's only the tip of the iceberg.

To afflict the comfortable: What's the ethnic look of the church where you worship? 95% of the Christian churches in the United States are monoethnic.

Concordia Seminary reflects both diversity and lack of diversity. The Seminary has residential and distance programs that lead to pastoral and diaconal ministry. The 600-plus students in all programs are ethnically diverse but – this is telling – our largest program, the residential program, is almost all white. That's because these students come from the monoethnic, predominantly white congregations of our denomination. It's not going to be easy to recruit a more diverse residential enrollment, but the mission of Jesus Christ challenges us to do just that. And it's not easy or soon that many of our monoethnic congregations will reflect the mission of God to all people, but the vision of heaven calls us to do just that.

"After this I looked, and behold, a great multitude that no one could number, from every nation, from all tribes and peoples and languages, standing before the throne and before the Lamb" (Revelation 7:9). Are we doing a disservice to the spiritual formation of our children and their generations by not striving for congregations that represent heaven's coming diversity?

For further reflection: Micah 4:1-5 – "Many nations shall come"

Almighty God, You have called Your Church to witness that in Christ You have reconciled us to Yourself. Grant that by Your Holy Spirit we may proclaim the good news of Your salvation so that all who hear it may receive the gift of salvation; through Jesus Christ, our Lord.[1] *Amen.*

February 9

"I Hurt!"

"Hi, Christian here. I feel bad. I hurt. Mommy and Daddy are tired out because I'm crying all the time. I keep them awake at night. They talk about me. Mommy says I have a feber. They talk about getting a tooth. What's a tooth? I don't know what's happening to me. All I know is I hurt.

"Do you big people ever hurt? Do you ever cry because it hurts so bad? Do you wonder, why do I hurt so much? Nobody explains it. What's happening to me?

"Opa and Oma are at my house. The old people came to visit. Opa said, 'Christian, you're one year old. Don't try to figure it out.' Opa thinks some people try to find God in every little event of life. Opa says don't. God is always with us but Opa says we can't explain God's every way. Opa says, 'Trust God and don't try to explain it.'

"I wonder. If God did tell me why I hurt, would it make any difference? Maybe someday I will know why I hurt now. Now I don't know why. It hurts. I know Daddy and Mommy love me. That helps."

> I am Jesus' little lamb,
> Ever glad at heart I am;
> For my Shepherd gently guides me,
> Knows my need, and well provides me,
> Loves me ev'ry day the same,
> Even calls me by my name.[1]

For further reflection: Psalm 103:11-14 – Our Father knows His children

Early let us seek Your favor, / Early let us do Your will;
Blessed Lord and only Savior, / With Your love our bosoms fill.
Blessed Jesus, blessed Jesus, / You have loved us, love us still.
Blessed Jesus, blessed Jesus, / You have loved us, love us still.[2]

February 10

Disappointed with Jesus?

Get into the Gospels and you'll meet people disappointed with Jesus. Religious leaders were disappointed to the point of hatred because Jesus challenged their self-righteousness. People who didn't get a quick fix to their problems, e.g., did not experience a physical healing, were probably disappointed too.

Have you ever been disappointed by someone – a spouse, a child, a parent? Disappointed by a doctor, a hospital? Have you been disappointed by a pastor, a church member, a denomination, a seminary? Of course, we all have. No offense intended now, but duh! What did you expect? People are guaranteed to disappoint you because they're fallible sinners full of foibles and faults. We all are. So we shouldn't be surprised at all when people disappoint us, and we shouldn't let it fester into anger and bitterness.

Have you ever been disappointed with Jesus? Didn't get the answer to prayer you wanted? Felt abandoned? He pulls alongside us and says, "O foolish ones, and slow of heart to believe all that the prophets have spoken!" (Luke 24:25). He came to proclaim an eternal kingdom, help and hope now and, a longer perspective, for eternity (Mark 1:14-15, 38). "The vision awaits its appointed time; it hastens to the end – it will not lie. / If it seems slow, wait for it; it will surely come; it will not delay" (Habakkuk 2:3). Give Jesus time and He'll show you that He did not fail you or forsake you (cf. Deuteronomy 31:6).

My heart with joy is springing; / I am no longer sad.
My soul is filled with singing; / Your sunshine makes me glad.
The sun that cheers my spirit / Is Jesus Christ, my King;
The heav'n I shall inherit / Makes me rejoice and sing.[1]

For further reflection: Psalm 27 – Amidst disappointing people, seek His face

Thine forever! Oh, how blest / They who find in Thee their rest!
Savior, guardian, heav'nly friend, / O defend us to the end!
Thine forever! Thou our guide, / All our wants by Thee supplied,
All our sins by Thee forgiv'n; / Lead us, Lord, from earth to heav'n.[2]
Amen.

February 11

Inch Closer to Jesus

"Though you have not seen Him, you love Him" (1 Peter 1:8).

Is that true? I don't mean do you know about Jesus Christ in your head. Of course you do. I'm not asking if you know things about His life. Sure you do. No, the question is this: Do you love Him? Years ago I heard a story about a married couple in their car; the husband was driving. The wife was lamenting that the romance of their youth had gone out of their marriage. "When we were first married," she said, "we used to sit close together in the front seat." The husband smiled and said, "I haven't moved away." Do you love Jesus? I can't answer for you but can only answer for myself. I often move away from Him. You'll probably admit the same.

Lent… Instead of giving something up, consider doing something more. Consider taking on some practice that inches you closer to Jesus: worship, of course, including mid-week Lenten services – renewed energy in your discipline of private devotion – ponder quietly the inevitable march of time. "Whom have I in heaven but you? And there is nothing on earth that I desire besides you" (Psalm 73:25). "You shall love the Lord your God with all your heart and with all your soul and with all your mind. This is the great and first commandment" (Matthew 22:37-38).

> Jesus, may our hearts be burning
> With more fervent love for You![1]

For further reflection: John 21:15-18 – "Do you love Me?"

Lord, Thee I love with all my heart; / I pray Thee, ne'er from me depart,
With tender mercy cheer me. / Earth has no pleasure I would share,
Yea, heav'n itself were void and bare / If Thou, Lord, were not near me.
And should my heart for sorrow break, / My trust in Thee no one could shake.
Thou art the portion I have sought; / Thy precious blood my soul has bought.
Lord Jesus Christ, my God and Lord, my God and Lord,
Forsake me not! I trust Thy Word.[2]

February 12

How Deep Do Your Waters Run?

Abraham Lincoln was born in Hardin County, Kentucky, on February 12, 1809. I'm no Lincoln scholar but as best as I can tell he was a "still waters run deep" person. And deep down in his still waters ran the Bible.

James Humes passes along this story.

> At a White House reception where the guests were ushered past the President and not allowed to come too close, an old man, disappointed at not having shaken hands with the President, waved his hat and called out, "Mr. President, I'm from up in New York State where we believe that God Almighty and Abraham Lincoln are going to save our country." Hearing that remark, Lincoln smiled and nodded. "My friend," he said, "you're half right."[1]

Here's a second story from Humes's book, *The Wit and Wisdom of Abraham Lincoln.*

> During the Civil War, a delegation of Methodist clergymen called on the White House. The spokesman of the group intoned, "Mr. President, our cause will prevail because the Lord is on our side." "Gentlemen, the question we should always ask ourselves is: 'Are we on His side?'"[2]

In our day, we go to the Christian bookstore and may be tempted by a catchy title on a theologically shallow book, imagining that it will help us in life. Lincoln would probably offer a wry smile. How deep do your waters run?

For further reflection: Psalm 23 – "Still waters"

O Lord, "When the cares of my heart are many, your consolations cheer my soul" (Psalm 94:19). Amen.

February 13

The Hands of Love

The *Letter of Aristeas*, perhaps from the first or second century before Christ, says, "All activity takes place by means of the hands." Over two thousand years later, that's still largely true. As Valentine's Day approaches, think of the activities that love shows by means of the hands.

A doctor places a newborn baby into the hands of the mother and father. The hands of the parents will be in almost constant motion for years to come, from changing diapers to writing checks and swiping credit cards for their child.

The child grows, and if so blessed, stands before the altar to exchange marriage vows. Rings are placed on fingers, hands are joined, and they are pronounced husband and wife.

Hands do work around the house. They run the vacuum, they clean out the gutters, they warm up the car in the cold, they fix the closet door, they build a shelf… because love is about doing for others.

Hands care for an older person. They open doors, they run errands, they deliver meals on wheels… because our understanding of love gets deeper as we live through more and more Valentine's Days.

And when we bury our sobbing face in our hands because we have lost a loved one, we know how blessed we are to have been given God's gift of love.

> Let your work be shown to your servants, and your glorious power to their children.
>
> Let the favor of the Lord our God be upon us, and establish the work of our hands upon us; yes, establish the work of our hands! (Psalm 90:16-17)

For further reflection: Mark 1:40-42 – "He stretched out His hand"

O be our great deliverer still, / O Lord of life and death;
Restore and quicken, soothe and bless, / With Your almighty breath.
To hands that work and eyes that see / Give wisdom's healing pow'r
That whole and sick and weak and strong / May praise You evermore.[1]
Amen.

February 14

Every Day, the Greatest Love

Love! What other word would you expect on Valentine's Day? But let's be honest, isn't Valentine's Day really a manufactured holiday?

Today may leave you bitter, if you don't have a romantic interest in your life. Today may leave you broke, if you imagine that a big purchase will prove your love. And this manufactured holiday will leave you full of disappointment when the expectations of the "perfect" romantic evening fail.

So, act on what you know. Real love isn't industry created, nor is it confined to a solitary day. Christians are able to experience the most powerful love of all, God's love, 365 days a year! "A new commandment I give to you, that you love one another: just as I have loved you, you also are to love one another. By this all people will know that you are my disciples" (John 13:34-35).

Love in Christ is strong and living, / Binding faithful hearts in one;
Love in Christ is strong and giving, / May His will in us be done![1]
Amen.

P.S. This Minute was written in 2001 by our daughter. Thanks, Katie!

For further reflection: 1 Corinthians 13 – Why is love the greatest?

O God, You manifested Your love for us by sending Your Son into the world that we might live through Him. Since You have so loved us, help us love one another (cf. 1 John 4:9, 11). Amen.

February 15

"Yet We May Not Remain"

Your circumstances sometimes change and you may find the change unwelcome. One of the great transition stories in the Bible is the Transfiguration, literally a "mountaintop experience." Jesus took Peter, James, and John up a mountain and "was transfigured before them, and his clothes became radiant, intensely white … And there appeared to them Elijah with Moses, and they were talking with Jesus."

You enjoy sitting in an easy chair before a big screen TV, surrounded by loving family, enjoying health, and feeling secure because there's money in the bank, right? The Transfiguration was far better – glory, heavenly viewing, surround sound included. God spoke from a cloud, "This is my beloved Son; listen to him!" No wonder "Peter said to Jesus, 'Rabbi, it is good that we are here.'" But transitions come and often God causes them. "Suddenly, looking around, they no longer saw anyone with them but Jesus only" (Mark 9:2-9). Moses and Elijah disappeared, Jesus went back to normal and said – my words – "Boys, time to leave the mountaintop. We're going down, down to the plain, down to the cross. Good-bye, great room! No cross, no glory."

Only God sees the end of our transitions, but see them He does. What we should see is only Jesus.

> Change and decay in all around I see;
> O Thou, who changest not, abide with me![1]

For further reflection: Hebrews 12:1-3 – Your focus

'Tis good, Lord, to be here! / Yet we may not remain;
But since You bidst us leave the mount, / Come with us to the plain.[2]
Amen.

February 16

Give Thanks for Our Leaders

No precedent existed for the inauguration of George Washington. The new constitution called for a "President of the United States" but what would that entail? John Adams wanted to address Washington as "His Most Benign Highness." In the end it was simply, "President of the United States."

Washington was inaugurated in Federal Hall in New York on April 30, 1789. After some preliminaries, he said, "I am ready to proceed" and all went to a porch so the public could see. Washington repeated the oath, bowed and kissed the Bible. Going into the Senate chamber, he spoke for about 20 minutes. "I was summoned by my country, whose voice I can never hear but with veneration and love." Fisher Ames observed, "His aspect was grave, almost to sadness." Washington could not know what was ahead of him but felt the weight of leadership.[1]

The shepherd boy David had no clue what was ahead when Samuel anointed him King of Israel (1 Samuel 16). Solomon sensed the burden and so he prayed to the Lord for wisdom (1 Kings 3). Rehoboam presumed he knew and civil war followed (1 Kings 12). Today we thank God for presidents who are willing to carry the heavy weight of leadership, and we pray that they will humbly seek the wisdom that comes from above.

"I urge that supplications, prayers, intercessions, and thanksgivings be made for all people, for kings and all who are in high positions, that we may lead a peaceful and quiet life, godly and dignified in every way" (1 Timothy 2:1-2). Leadership above partisanship.

For further reflection: Romans 13:1-7 – God has given duties to the leaders of our government

O God, You have instituted government for the protection of all people and the promotion of good. We pray that You give insight and wisdom to the President of the United States and to all who advise him so "that we may lead a peaceful and quiet life, godly and dignified in every way." Amen.

February 17

Disconnect for Lent

Traditionally Shrove Tuesday, or the more familiar *Mardi Gras* ("Fat Tuesday"), is the last fling before Lent. Many religious people will party but the next day give up something for Lent. Do they give up something important, or just something?

> "If I give up clams, which I hate, I'm not really doing anything," says Kevin Shine, a 39-year-old electrical contractor from Philadelphia. But abstain from posting "status updates" on his every move? That's a worthy struggle. "It's my candy," he explains, noting that he logs on as much as 20 times a day. "That's pathological." … [Whitley Leiss] abstained from Facebook for Lent [a Facebook Fast]. When Lent ended, she logged on to find dozens of messages waiting and strangely little desire to answer them. "I saw all that I had missed and I realized I hadn't missed anything." … [Lisandrea Wentland is] hopeful putting her renunciation of Facebook in the spiritual context of Lent will help. She plans to use some of the time she would have spent online in prayerful reflection.[1]

Lenten self-restraint and fasting recalls Jesus' 40 days of fasting in the desert, tempted by the devil and communing with His Father. No food, but Jesus must have been in a Wi-Fi hot zone, right? What's getting in the way of your communing with your God and Savior? Certainly not clams, but perhaps being always connected? Jesus says to His disciples, "Come away by yourselves to a desolate place and rest a while" (Mark 6:31). "'In repentance and rest you shall be saved; in quietness and in trust shall be your strength,' / But you were unwilling" (Isaiah 30:15).

For further reflection: Luke 10:38-42 – While Jesus spoke, did Mary keep looking at her cell phone?

Lord Jesus, You fasted to draw closer to Your Father. By Your Spirit may our Lenten disciplines draw us closer to our Father through You. Amen.

February 18

Don't Assume They Know

James Voelz, a professor of New Testament at Concordia Seminary, likes to remind his colleagues that we should not forget what it is like not to know. Ponder that. We easily forget what it is like not to know. Put another way, we easily assume other people know what we know.

Ash Wednesday begins Lent, and all the weeks of Lent culminate in Holy Week, the solemn observance of the passion, death, and resurrection of the Son of God.

Huh? There we go again, assuming everyone knows what we're talking about. We forget what it is like not to know… and by such forgetting we easily scare people off from eternal truths. Seek out someone in your church, someone who was raised outside of the church, and then ask what it was like to come into all the ritual and all the strange language of the church. Or just imagine yourself entering a foreign environment, where you're not sure what to do, how to act. Welcome to the cryptic club of many Christian churches!

Samuel Moor Shoemaker wrote in *I Stand by the Door*: "The door is the most important door in the world – It is the door through which men walk when they find God." Then he contrasts those who go so deeply into theology and church life that they forget those who are outside the door, who don't truly know God. "I stand by the door. I admire the people who go way in. But I wish they would not forget how it was before they got in. Then they would be able to help the people who have not yet even found the door."[1]

Come Ash Wednesday, if the imposition of ashes is your habit, don't forget what it's like for people to look at your forehead and not know. And in the weeks to come, any self-denial you practice, any church jargon you use, don't forget what it's like not to know. Engage the person who doesn't know. Explain. Lead them to the Door.

For further reflection: Mark 4:33-34 – Remember Who is teaching you

Dear Jesus, You continually taught Your disciples! Forgive us for any presumption that we have the inside track on knowing You. Through our Lenten disciplines, teach us that we know precious little about You but the little we know is precious. Make us helpful to those who do not yet know You. Amen.

February 19

Get Your Will Out of the Way

What do you do when your emotions have been brought low, when you're not happy, not whole, but feel like your life is scattered in your own debris field? A natural desire is to ask God to reconstitute your life, to put together what has been shattered in a new and better way. "All things work together for good" we intone (Romans 8:28). But whose good do we instinctively seek? Isn't it usually our own?

"The sacrifices of God are a broken spirit; a broken and contrite heart, O God, you will not despise" (Psalm 51:17). Unwelcome as it certainly is, broken and contrite is where the Spirit of God does some of His best work on us. It's not that God is malicious; God is good. When we're broken and hit bottom, then the promise of our ability to rise up is exposed as a myth. It's people of humble estate that God exalts (Luke 1:52).

In 2008 and 2009, the United States suffered through the "Great Recession." It may well have been a hard time for you; it was extremely hard on Concordia Seminary and its leadership. Looking back, though, it was a time of great spiritual growth for me personally because the emotional anguish left me no resort but to look up for help. He helped indeed; we see His blessings in hindsight.

A vital, breathing relationship with God cannot be focused solely on what you want for yourself. Jesus didn't say, "I'll follow you," but rather "Follow Me." He didn't teach us to pray for our will to be done, but His example in Gethsemane teaches us to put His Father's will above our own (Mark 14:36). So offer the pieces of your life to God, unconditionally, so He can create you anew after His own heart. Get your will out of the way.

For further reflection: Psalm 51 – In verse 13, the psalmist says witness comes out of the broken heart of his repentance

When peace, like a river, attendeth my way,
When sorrows, like sea billows, roll;
Whatever my lot, Thou has taught me to say,
"It is well, it is well with my soul."[1]   *Amen.*

February 20

70 × 7, Learning to Multiply

"Forgive us our trespasses as we forgive those who trespass against us." Why is it so hard to forgive others? I don't mean forgiving someone for something slight – that's easy enough. I mean forgiving someone who has seriously hurt you, hurt you in some way physical, emotional, reputational, financial, or marital – hurt you so that you will never be quite the same again. Why is it so hard to forgive the person who so seriously wronged you?

When God made humanity, He put into us a natural knowledge of how to live in a way pleasing to Him (see Romans 2:14-15). A subtle but disastrous shift came when sin entered the world. Our instincts have been corrupted. Even repentant Christians feel a war within ourselves when we are called upon to forgive someone who has seriously hurt us. "I have the desire to do what is right, but not the ability to carry it out" (Romans 7:18). The god of self who lurks in my heart corrupts everything. Do I cling to my rightness lest I, all important I, be slighted, or do I let my God be Judge of the person who hurt me? Will I honor God by giving over to Him the judgment upon the person who wronged me, or will I steal judgment of sinners from God and make it my own business? Do we seriously believe that God is God and we are not?

Forgiveness does not mean condoning the wrong that was done. Forgiveness does not mean no arrests, no trials, and emptying jails. Forgiveness does mean that you won't let the other person continue to have control over your emotions and life. You lift the weight off your soul by giving judgment to God. "Let those who suffer according to God's will entrust their souls to a faithful Creator while doing good" (1 Peter 4:19). "Father, forgive them, for they know not what they do" (Luke 23:34).

For further reflection: Matthew 18:21-35 – 70 × 7

Jesus, in Your dying woes, / Even while Your lifeblood flows,
Craving pardon for Your foes; / Hear us, holy Jesus.
Savior, for our pardon sue / When our sins Your pangs renew,
For we know not what to do: / Hear us, holy Jesus.
Oh, may we, who mercy need, / Be like You in heart and deed,
When with wrong our spirits bleed: / Hear us, holy Jesus.[1]

February 21

What Should You Ask from God?

When you pray, what do you ask God for? Should you ask Him for anything?

Should you seek great things for yourself? Do not seek them (cf. Jeremiah 45:5). Commenting on this verse, Oswald Chambers wrote, "There is nothing easier than getting into a right relationship with God except when it is not God Whom you want but only what He gives."[1]

That quotation prompted a discussion in my Seminary class about our requests to God. Students tried to find that line between a "God gimme" attitude and "Aw, shucks, I can't ask God for anything." There is a line and Jesus gives it to us. "Seek first the kingdom of God and his righteousness, and all these things will be added to you" (Matthew 6:33). So Dietrich Bonhoeffer wrote, "The disciples always see only Christ. They do not see Christ and the law, Christ and piety, Christ and the world. They do not even begin to reflect that; they just follow Christ in everything."[2]

To follow that line, God's Son gave us actual words and a model for prayer. "Our Father who art in heaven…" Take that whole prayer as your daily companion and use its pattern for the words of your own prayers. Do that and the Spirit will bring you to the greatest thing – your Father in heaven.

For further reflection: Romans 8:26-27 – Help in your prayer life

Our heavenly Father, You teach us to pray to You without ceasing (1 Thessalonians 5:17). How can we possibly do that? Only by seeking Your reign and rule in our lives, seeking first Your kingdom. From our first conscious thought in the morning until our eyes close again in sleep, put our heart and mind on the One who teaches us how to pray – Jesus. Those petitions will be granted; it is Your will, and we will be at peace. Amen.

February 22

Do You Recognize Temptation?

Martin Luther said it's the devil who makes the best teacher of theology. Since few of you aspire to be professional theologians, for sake of talk let's say it's the devil who makes you a truly believing Christian... Luther often made provocative statements such as this, but his point is well-taken. It's through temptations to sin that we realize our spiritual weakness and call upon God who alone can help us.

Many churches on the first Sunday in Lent will hear the story of Jesus' temptation. Jesus "was led by the Spirit in the wilderness for forty days, being tempted by the devil." With three different temptations the devil tried to lure the Son of God from faithfulness to His Father, but each time Jesus resisted with a word of Scripture. Then, "when the devil had ended every temptation, he departed from him until an opportune time" (Luke 4:1-13). Serious about God? Then you need to live in the Word.

Do you recognize temptation when it comes? Generic preaching about temptation and sin and repentance goes into one ear and out the other, at least in my head. Jesus warns that the devil "is a liar and the father of lies," a snake, "more crafty than any other beast of the field" (John 8:44; Genesis 3:1). Sanctified living depends upon exposing the subtle ways the devil tries to lure us away from childlike dependence upon our Father. Better than giving something up for Lent would be to read the Bible, talk with other Christians, and discover the subtleties of temptation – laying bare the insidious nature of evil. Can you name the sins you are struggling to conquer?

"In the world will foes assail me, crafty, stronger far than I; and the strife will never fail me, well I know, before I die. Therefore, Lord, I come, believing Thou canst give the power I need, through the prayer of faith receiving strength – the Spirit's strength, indeed. Amen."[1]

For further reflection: 2 Samuel 12:1-7 – Others help us identify temptation

Grant that I Your passion view / With repentant grieving,
Let me not bring shame to You / By unholy living.
How could I refuse to shun / Ev'ry sinful pleasure
Since for me God's only Son / Suffered without measure?[2]   *Amen.*

February 23

Every Thought Captive to Christ

"We ... take every thought captive to obey Christ" (2 Corinthians 10:5).

How many thoughts we have every day! Our minds seldom slow down; that is a great temptation of our times. Our modern communication devices are wonderful in many ways, but let's not forget that the devil understands technology and uses it for his purposes too. Our phones and tablets and computers keep us constantly connected, bringing the thoughts of others to us all day long and demanding that we reply with our own thinking. So busy receiving, so busy reacting, how easily Jesus slips out of most of our thoughts!

Will we take every one of today's thoughts captive to what Jesus tells us? St. Paul did. We consider Jesus often enough, hear the stories of long ago and wonder what it may mean for today, but pondering the words of God is not the same as obeying it. "And as he reasoned about righteousness and self-control and the coming judgment, Felix was alarmed and said (to Paul), 'Go away for the present. When I get an opportunity I will summon you'" (Acts 24:25). To only *consider* Jesus' words is idolatry, essentially saying to yourself: *I will judge when I'll follow Jesus.*

The Spirit struggles to put lenses on our eyes and aids in our ears so that everything coming to us is intercepted by the Word of Christ. "As for me, I will meditate on your precepts. ... May my heart be blameless in your statutes" (Psalm 119:78, 80). Imagine that every e-mail and every post, everything you see and hear, would be filtered by obedience to Jesus Christ. You would be transformed!

"You keep him in perfect peace whose mind is stayed on you" (Isaiah 26:3).

For further reflection: Romans 12:1-3 – The app of transformation

Therefore You alone, my Savior, / Shall be all in all to me;
Search my heart and my behavior, / Root out all hypocrisy.
Through all my life's pilgrimage, guard and uphold,
In loving forgiveness, O Jesus, enfold me.
This one thing is needful; all others are vain –
I count all but loss that I Christ may obtain![1]   *Amen.*

February 24

Cold Blasts of Reality

I'm sick and tired of cold weather and snow. There was a time when Diane and I fantasized about retiring up in Michigan, sitting in a toasty little house, looking out at the glistening snow, reading our books with no pressure to get anything done. But sometime in these last few years we pitched that fantasy. We're tired of putting on layers of clothes, tired of slipping and sliding on sidewalks and streets, tired of being chilled to the bone – tired, tired, tired.

Some of my faculty colleagues were talking the other day about how we've become insulated from the world of nature. We have so many things to shield us from the realities of nature that we don't regularly ponder our creaturely status in the great creation of God. Heating and air conditioning instead of nature's cold or heat, cars and trucks instead of being exposed in horse and wagon, instant communication instead of walking to talk to someone… On and on goes the list. It's quite easy to miss the realities of nature, the reminders of the real world God made, not man made.

In the creed we confess, "I believe in God, the Father Almighty, maker of heaven and earth." "Earth" includes mankind; we are made by God. How many people today think of themselves as creatures made by a great, unseen Creator? That's one of the effects of the theory of evolution; people think that we just came to be. Aha! Again we've insulated ourselves from our creaturely status. Result: less awe before God.

God said to Job, "Where were you when I laid the foundation of the earth? Have you entered the storehouses of the snow?" (Job 38:4, 22). So thank God for the nuisance of cold and snow and ice! Sinclair Lewis said, "Winter is not a season; it's an occupation."[1] Don't you southerners envy us up north?

For further reflection: Genesis 2:4-7 – "Man became a living *creature*" (italics mine)

The Lord, my God, be praised, / My light, my life from heaven;
My maker, who to me / Has soul and body given;
My Father, who will shield / And keep me day by day,
And make each moment yield / New blessings on my way.[2]

February 25

Ashes: Style or Substance?

Reflecting on Ash Wednesday, I'm reminded of a time when our grandson Christian was a toddler. He was taken forward to have ashes put on his forehead, but the boy wouldn't have any of it. What should have been ashes in the shape of a cross ended up as a smudge.

Something deep within religious people struggles against repentance. After all, we do the church thing many Sundays, if not every Sunday. We live outwardly upright and moral lives. We try to do right by our family. We take God seriously. We get the point about the tax collector in the back of the temple but our outer lives tempt us to identify us with the Pharisee up front (Luke 18:9-14). But, God "saved us and called us to a holy calling, not because of our works but because of his own purpose and grace" (2 Timothy 1:9).

Some years ago on Ash Wednesday, I sat in St. Thomas church on 5th Avenue in New York City. When ashes were offered, a young woman in the pew ahead of me went forward. She returned to the pew, took out her compact and looked at the ashes on her forehead. Was she checking her Ash Wednesday style?

Presenting a superficial religious face to the world can be as telltale as struggling against a ritual of repentance. "Beware of practicing your righteousness before other people in order to be seen by them, for then you will have no reward from your Father who is in heaven" (Matthew 6:1).

When the ashes are off, are you still repenting without any external sign?

For further reflection: Matthew 11:20-24 – The danger of familiarity with Jesus

On my heart imprint Your image, / Blessed Jesus, King of Grace,
That life's riches, cares, and pleasures / Never may Your work erase;
Let the clear inscription be: / Jesus, crucified for me,
Is my life, my hope's foundation, / And my glory and salvation![1]   *Amen.*

February 26

All Scripture, Not Just Sound Bites

It was the worst time of my life. The recession's severe impact on the Seminary had me desperately clinging to some of God's promises, especially this one: "Call upon me in the day of trouble; I will deliver you, and you shall glorify me" (Psalm 50:15).

When I read that entire psalm, not just the one verse, I got a better perspective on my troubles. The preceding verse says, "Offer to God a sacrifice of thanksgiving, and perform your vows to the Most High." Give thanks in the recession? Give thanks in serious, even terminal illness? Give thanks when you're beside yourself because of relationship problems? Give thanks in the day of trouble?

Read the psalm yourself. There are godly and godless people. The godless may pay lip service to the deity but take care of themselves. You, on the other hand, really trust your loving Father to take care of you, and sometimes you trust despite the evidence. Really – read the psalm. The whole psalm says so much, including this: How can you give God mindless worship on Sunday when you realize He doesn't need you but still He loves you? So you're in the day of trouble? First thank Him, then call on Him with confidence that He will deliver you.

> What we call our life, our troubles, our guilt, is by no means all of reality; there in the Scriptures is our life, our need, our guilt, and our salvation. Because it pleased God to act for us there, it is only there that we shall be saved. Only in the Holy Scriptures do we learn to know our own history. (Dietrich Bonhoeffer)[1]

We miss so much when we just hang onto single, unconnected Bible verses. The more verses you meditate upon, the better for you.

For further reflection: Psalm 50 – Get the context!

"Blessed Lord, You have caused all Holy Scriptures to be written for our learning." Lord, that's what the familiar church prayer says: "all Holy Scriptures." In this sound-bite era, lead me into a broader and wider knowledge of the Bible. Make me a lifetime student of Your Word, from Genesis to Revelation. By Your Spirit, help me to see my story in Scripture. Amen.

February 27

As Deep as Our Sin

Sweet! We sin; God forgives. True? After writing about trusting God's gift of forgiveness from Jesus' cross, St. Paul asks, "What shall we say then? Are we to continue in sin that grace may abound? By no means!" (Romans 6:1-2).

So don't sin, don't kill, don't commit adultery, don't steal, and don't lie. OK, you haven't. Now put on your church clothes, hear about grace and forgiveness (which you really don't need as much as other people)… and be numb to the war within you. Dumb too.

"The LORD saw … that every intention of the thoughts of (man's) heart was only evil continually" (Genesis 6:5). Jesus says, "evil things come from within" (Mark 7:23). Our first feelings, our first thoughts are so often sinful. Your emotions are not neutral. Your first feelings are either sinful, coming from the corruption of original sin, or sometimes your first feelings are sanctified, evidence of the work of the Holy Spirit upon your heart.

Martin Chemnitz, a sixteenth century theologian, wrote about emotions. "The first emotion or feeling cannot be stopped or avoided, but see to it that this does not continue on to become sin by which 'the Holy Spirit is grieved' and 'place is given to the devil,'" quoting Ephesians 4:30, 27.[1] It's commendable, godly, when we don't act on a sinful impulse, but the impulse itself is still sin. Paul called himself "captive to the law of sin that dwells in my members" (Romans 7:23).

Only God can get His grace and forgiveness as deep into us as our sin. "The great mystical work of the Holy Spirit is in the dim regions of our personality which we cannot get to" (Oswald Chambers).[2]

For further reflection: Mark 7:14-23 – Heart disease

Lord, I my vows to Thee renew; / Disperse my sins as morning dew;
Guard my first springs of thought and will / And with Thyself my spirit fill.
Direct, control, suggest this day / All I design or do or say
That all my pow'rs with all their might, / In Thy sole glory may unite.[3]
Amen.

February 28

"See You Later, Guys!"

"Hi, Christian here! I am becoming very verbal. I make little sentences. I speak my mind. Last Sunday in church I was restless. So I hopped off the pew, stepped into the aisle, and said to Daddy, Mommy, and Connor, 'See you later, guys.' Opa will tell you this is true. I am not making this up. Well, I didn't see anything wrong with leaving church but Mommy grabbed me and plopped me back in the pew. A plop in the pew is a hard thing, especially when you don't want to be there.

"Do you big people ever walk away from church and say, 'See you later, guys?' Big people can get away with that. Do you like having the time to do what you want to do? Do you think you make your life simpler by not listening to God? Do you ever come back to church? When I grow up, I wonder if I'll say to church, 'See you later, guys.'

"Well, after my hard landing on the pew, it came time for the children's message. I went to the front. Pastor John told me about Jesus. I was glad I was there. If I had still been away from church, I would have missed something good."

For further reflection: Colossians 4:14; Philemon 24; 2 Timothy 4:10 – The example of Demas

Oh, to grace how great a debtor / Daily I'm constrained to be;
Let that grace now, like a fetter / Bind my wand'ring heart to Thee:
Prone to wander, Lord, I feel it; / Prone to leave the God I love.
Here's my heart, O take and seal it, / Seal it for Thy courts above.[1]   *Amen.*

March 1

Who Crucified Jesus?

We're likely to hear someone say during Lent that the Jews killed Jesus. Besides being historically simplistic (the Romans actually carried out the execution, and most Jews lived outside of Palestine and didn't know what was going on), blaming Jews is wrong. A number of years ago I wrote that it was self-righteousness, not ethnicity that killed Jesus. Some people questioned me. Aren't we the true executioners? Wasn't Christ really killed by all us sinners? I once heard of a woman who said it was nice Jesus died but He really didn't have to do that for her. She didn't think she killed Jesus. Who did?

Is my name Pontius Pilate or Caiaphas? Am I a Roman soldier who tortured Jesus? No. So in that sense, I didn't crucify Jesus.

Did my sins force Jesus to die? No. "No one takes it (my life) from me," Jesus once said. Nothing about us, including our sin, forces God to do anything. Jesus could have let us sinners get the just desserts of our sin… a hellish prospect. So, who caused the crucifixion?

"No one takes it from me, but I lay it down of my own accord" (John 10:18). The "who?" is God, whose unconstrained love was willing to lay down His life for us otherwise lost sinners. "One will scarcely die for a righteous person … but God shows his love for us in that while we were still sinners, Christ died for us" (Romans 5:7-8).

It's a figure of speech to say that I killed, you killed Jesus. It's not wrong; it's very effective in laying guilt on us for our sins. That the Father sent Jesus to suffer, that He willingly laid down His life for us… now that's Gospel. Thinking it through… amazing grace!

For further reflection: Isaiah 53 – "It was the will of the LORD"

Almighty God, graciously behold this Your family for whom our Lord Jesus Christ was willing to be betrayed and delivered into the hands of sinful men to suffer death upon the cross; through the same Jesus Christ, Your Son, our Lord, who lives and reigns with You and the Holy Spirit, one God, now and forever.[1] *Amen.*

March 2

The Christian Community – God's Orchestra

In grade school our daughter Katie took cello lessons. But time marched on. When she went off to college and life, the cello sat unused until we finally gave it to Katie's sister-in-law. Cellist Avram Lavin said, "The cello is a solo instrument, though not as popular as the violin or piano. It would be hard to rate instruments in terms of importance, because if you take any of them away, you have no orchestra."[1]

That's a good description of Christian life. Individualism is rampant in America but Christianity is about community, God's people, about each of us as a member of the Body of Christ. When you were baptized, all heaven fixed its loving gaze on you. When you come to the Lord's Supper, it's a Holy Communion. Members of the Body gather as one to receive the heavenly gifts of Christ's body and blood. And then we go forth from the Sacrament and, as poet Omer Westendorf put it, "the tasks of our everyday life we will face."[2]

Whatever your duties may be, play your individual part attuned to Jesus Christ – and together we will be God's orchestra, blessing those around us. As Martin Franzmann taught us to pray, "That in these gray and latter days there may be those whose life is praise, each life a high doxology unto the holy Trinity."[3] In different hands, Katie's cello still serves its music. "Through the Church the song goes on!"[4]

For further reflection: Romans 12:3-8 – The church orchestra

Lord God Almighty, even as You bless Your servants with various and unique gifts of the Holy Spirit, continue to grant us the grace to use them always to Your honor and glory; through Jesus Christ, our Lord.[5]   Amen.

March 3

The Refiner's Fire

My friend Bill shared an e-mail about a woman who visited the shop of a silversmith. The silversmith held a piece of silver over the fire, explaining that the silver had to be held in the *very* middle of the fire to burn away any impurities. The woman, a Bible student, thought of Malachi 3:3: "He [God] will sit as a refiner and purifier of silver."

She asked the silversmith if he had to be there the whole time, and he answered, "Yes." He had to hold and keep his eye on the silver. Otherwise, the silver might be in the fire too long and be destroyed.

"How do you know when the silver is fully refined?" she asked. "Oh, that's easy," he answered. "When I see my image in it."

That anonymous e-mail helps us understand tough days. "The LORD is your keeper" (Psalm 121:5). And the refining of Christians will achieve its goal. "He who began a good work in you will bring it to completion at the day of Jesus Christ" (Philippians 1:6). On that day, fully refined, you will see Him face to face (cf. 1 Corinthians 13:12).

How else can we understand this strange statement of James: "Count it all joy … when you meet trials of various kinds" (James 1:2)?

> When through fiery trials your pathway will lie,
> My grace, all-sufficient, will be your supply.
> The flames will not hurt you; I only design
> Your dross to consume and your gold to refine.[1]

For further reflection: 1 Peter 1:3-9 – Your faith is more precious than gold

From evil, Lord, deliver us; / The times and days are perilous.
Redeem us from eternal death, / And, when we yield our dying breath.
Console us, grant us calm release, / And take our souls to You in peace.[2]
Amen.

March 4

Rocky's Way

In the midst of your workweek, some words about perseverance from *Rocky Balboa*:

> Let me tell you something you already know. The world ain't all sunshine and rainbows. It's a very mean and nasty place and I don't care how tough you are, it will beat you to your knees and keep you there permanently if you let it. You, me, or nobody is gonna hit as hard as life. But it ain't about how hard you hit. It's about how hard you can get hit and keep moving forward. That's how winning is done![1]

In contrast to Rocky's hard, fight-the-world philosophy, here is a grander view, a heavenly view for every workday:

> We rejoice in hope of the glory of God. Not only that, but we rejoice in our sufferings, knowing that suffering produces endurance, and endurance produces character, and character produces hope, and hope does not put us to shame, because God's love has been poured into our hearts through the Holy Spirit who has been given to us. (Romans 5:2-5)

The two quotations show the different impact of the Law and the Gospel. God's Law tells us what to do and what not to do. It tells us what reward we'll get when we do right and what punishment comes when we fail to do right. God put that Law in every heart, and Rocky's tough philosophy reflects it (see Romans 2:14-15). But Rocky's way isn't lasting. Your toughness might achieve some success but eventually someone tougher, savvier, will hit you harder than you can hit back. And Rocky's philosophy won't give you inner peace. That comes only from the Gospel, from the Good News that God in Jesus removes the condemnation of the Law. So while your job lays on you the grind of Law, your inner peace on the job comes from the Gospel. Go today with Paul's approach!

For further reflection: Matthew 6:25-34 – The way of the "Gentiles" is not your way

Lord, I work and I work hard. I try my best to meet expectations but the grind can be so hard! Fill me with joy, endurance, character, hope, and above all love, Your love which the Holy Spirit gives through faith. Amen.

March 5

Recalls and Repentance

Automobile recalls have become regular business stories. I haven't kept up with how many models have been recalled, but it's enough to give carmakers headaches and big-time financial losses.

Has our Maker thought about recalling us? The first page of the Bible says, "God saw everything that he had made, and behold, it was very good" (Genesis 1:31). But soon sin came, sin accelerated – any brakes that may have been applied failed – and, yes, God did a "recall" of what He had made. "The LORD saw that the wickedness of man was great in the earth, and that every intention of the thoughts of his heart was only evil continually. … So the LORD said, 'I will blot out man whom I have created from the face of the land'" (Genesis 6:5-7). Only Noah and his family survived that cataclysmic "recall."

Another "recall" is promised – the final judgment. So here we are, traveling between creation and that Last Day, and we should be like the driver who is concerned that something is wrong. How can we not notice that something is indeed wrong in our world, wrong with people, wrong with you, with me? But rather than be shocked when that final "recall" comes, we should voluntarily recall ourselves every day to the Maker's ways. The design for mankind wasn't defective; remember everything God made was good. Adam's sin, original sin, and our sin has flawed the good design. Only the Spirit of God can fix our fatally defective being. He does it in His shop, the place called "repentance." Bring yourself in this Lent.

For further reflection: Romans 5:12-21 – Two sources for our humanity

From hearts depraved, to evil prone,
Flow thoughts and deeds of sin alone;
God's image lost, the darkened soul
Nor seeks nor finds its heav'nly goal.
We thank Thee, Christ; new life is ours,
New light, new hope, new strength, new pow'rs:
May grace our ev'ry way attend
Until we reach our journey's end![1]   *Amen.*

March 6

God's Forgiveness – the Final Word?

Forgiveness is the heart of the Christian message. In Jesus Christ "we have redemption, the forgiveness of sins" (Colossians 1:14). God's gracious justification of the sinner through faith has been called the article on which the Church stands or falls. So we say, but do we in the Church act as if God's forgiveness truly is the final word?

Think about your own sins. Think especially about what you did, that something that can keep you awake at night, that thing about which your conscience says: *Look what you did! That can never be made right!* You'd like to turn the clock back and do it right but – and oh, this is so big – you can't turn the clock back and do it again. So when you hear that God has forgiven you for Jesus' sake, is that word final? Or does your sin keep coming back to haunt you? It probably keeps coming back, and so you need to hear God's final word over and over again: "your sins are forgiven" (1 John 2:12).

How about your husband, wife, child, a friend, someone who has done you wrong? How about someone in your church whose past sin is known but who comes and hears and believes the word of forgiveness week after week along with you? Do you try to put that wrong out of your mind, or is it something you hang onto and sometimes talk about? If God's word of forgiveness to you for your sins is final but you keep needing to hear it so that you live in forgiveness, isn't God's word of forgiveness for others also final and you need to keep hearing His decision about them so that you can extend His forgiveness?

"Forgive us our debts, as we also have forgiven our debtors" (Matthew 6:12). (Also see Matthew 6:14-15.) Is the Church standing or falling?

For further reflection: 1 Corinthians 6:1-11 – A congregation that wasn't practicing forgiveness

Lord Jesus, so often I feel guilty. Thank You for coming to me again and again with Your words of forgiveness. I confess it's sometimes hard for me to forgive others. Please keep coming at me, get into my head, with Your words that I should forgive as I have been forgiven. Help all of us in our church to forgive. For Your sake, Amen.

March 7

You're Not the First; Be Encouraged!

"No temptation has overtaken you that is not common to man. God is faithful, and he will not let you be tempted beyond your ability, but with the temptation he will also provide the way of escape, that you may be able to endure it" (1 Corinthians 10:13).

Whatever trouble you face today, temptation comes with it. Unseen forces of evil use your troubles to lead you into despair and convince you that God won't bring you through. The first word of good news is that your situation is quite common. As the Contemporary English Version (CEV) translation puts it, "You are tempted in the same way that everyone else is tempted."

The second word of good news is that there's more encouragement than any of us realize. When troubles come, friends come forward with encouragement. But your support is more than your circle of friends. J.S. Bach wrote, "God has always stood by us in every moment of cross and woe. / Let praise arise to God in every land! Let praise arise!"[1] All those who have struggled in their own lives before we were born – prophets, apostles, confessors, all who penned their trust in God – now speak through the centuries to encourage us. "God is faithful … he will also provide the way of escape." Fellow followers of Jesus, the Church through the ages, encourage us toward the better day. "Let praise arise!"

For further reflection: Hebrews 11 – "Through the encouragement of the Scriptures we might have hope" (Romans 15:4)

In faith, Lord, let me serve You; / Though persecution, grief, and pain
Should seek to overwhelm me, / Let me a steadfast trust retain;
And then at my departure / Lord, take me home to You,
Your riches to inherit / As all You said holds true,
In life and death, Lord, keep me / Until Your heav'n I gain,
Where I by Your great mercy / The end of faith attain.[2] Amen.

March 8

The Testimony of Our Sins

"Though our iniquities testify against us…" (Jeremiah 14:7). Do they? Do our sins really testify against us?

Sensitivities change from era to era. There have been times when people were very conscientious about obeying the commandments but there also have been times when, as Jeremiah said to God: "You are near in their mouth and far from their heart" (12:2). How is it today? Do you consciously set out each day to obey God? Is God so great and mysterious to us that we stand in fear before Him because of our sins? Many Americans are indifferent to the commandments because – heh – a God of love wouldn't punish us, would He?

If we're not thinking about the commandments, the testimony of our sins is not muted. What are our feelings of guilt, of shame, of fear, of loneliness? They are the evidence from our deepest being that we're not what the Creator intended, that I do sin against the commandments. If we understand our unpleasant feelings as symptoms of sin, our rational thoughts can find focus for help. "Act, O LORD, for your name's sake; for our backslidings are many; we have sinned against you. … Yet you, O LORD, are in the midst of us, and we are called by your name; do not leave us" (Jeremiah 14:7b, 9b).

Immanuel, God with us. In the midst of a crowd, Jesus asked the Pharisees, "Why do you question these things in your hearts?" (Mark 2:8). Jesus looks past the face you present to the world and looks into your soul. The emotions that stir, the sins that may never see the light of day, He sees them all. The fear of God is not simply cowering in terror because He knows; it is awe because He acts. Jesus is the answer to Jeremiah's prayer, "Act, O Lord" and you, Christian, are called by His name.

For further reflection: Exodus 20:1-17 – Ten words to lead us to Jesus

Come down, O Love divine; / Seek Thou this soul of mine,
And visit it with Thine own ardor glowing …
O let it freely burn, / Till earthly passions turn
To dust and ashes in its heat consuming.[1]   *Amen.*

March 9

Time Is Place

It's the time of year when we turn the clocks forward.

Michael Downing in *Spring Forward: The Annual Madness of Daylight Saving Time*, tells us it was Englishman William Willett who first promoted this change in 1907 so people could exercise more in the evening.[1] In 1966 Congress encouraged Daylight Saving Time for all the United States. Today, Arizona and Hawaii are the only states that don't change their clocks.

"Fall back; spring forward;" we've "lost" an hour. We talk about time as a commodity, a thing. "I'm running short on time." "Can you spare me a minute?" "How much time do you have?" Time as a thing.

The Bible suggests that time is not a commodity but the places of your life. The first commandment tells us to have no false god in our heart. Your heart is a place. The second or third commandment, depending on how you number the commandments, says to revere God with our lips. Your lips are also a place. Heart… lips… what's next? "Remember the Sabbath day to keep it holy." That is, after heart and lips, worship God in the places of your week. Time is not so much a thing; it's places, places one after another where your heart and lips show your faith. The distinction of days does not confine worship and witness to an hour on Sunday. If the God of the Gospel is in your heart and on your lips, you will be His worshipping witness in every place, in time.

The question is not, "How much time do you have?" The question is, "Where are you?" You are in a place, someplace in God's great cathedral of creation. Wherever you find yourself is a place to offer Him thanks and service. Spring forward… to deeper spirituality!

For further reflection: Colossians 3:12-17 – It all happens in the places of your life

O God, our help in ages past, / Our hope for years to come,
Our shelter from the stormy blast, / And our eternal home:
Time, like an ever-rolling stream, / Soon bears us all away;
We fly forgotten as a dream / Dies at the op'ning day.
O God, our help in ages past, / Our hope for years to come,
Be Thou our guard while life shall last / And our eternal home![2]   *Amen.*

March 10

Awesome!

I've often been asked about the fear of God. That's a common phrase in the Bible. "Fear God and keep his commandments" (Ecclesiastes 12:13).

It's also a troublesome phrase. After all, isn't He a God of love? (1 John 4:8)

Fear comes when we encounter something vastly different than ourselves, something that threatens to overwhelm us. So we fear the future, fear cancer, fear financial ruin, fear a failed marriage, fear for our children, fear terrorists, fear, fear, fear.

But you can also encounter something vastly greater than yourself that does not overwhelm you with terror but comes to help you. That results in awe and is what the Bible calls "the fear of God." When one thief on the cross asked the other criminal, "Do you not fear God?" (Luke 23:40), there was more going on than terror of death and judgment. There was awe, awe that God who could overwhelm them with condemnation was offering a chance to repent and receive forgiveness.

What are you afraid of? Let your natural fears drive you to Someone greater than yourself or the people you know, Someone who will not overwhelm you but who promises to care for you with His forgiveness and providence. Awesome! That's what it means to fear God.

> Fear not! I am with you, O be not dismayed,
> For I am your God and will still give you aid;
> I'll strengthen you, help you, and cause you to stand,
> Upheld by My righteous, omnipotent hand.[1]

For further reflection: Mark 6:45-52 – The Law says, "Do not be afraid." The Gospel tells us why: "It is I."

I thank You, my heavenly Father, through Jesus Christ, Your dear Son, that You have kept me this night from all harm and danger; and I pray that You would keep me this day also from sin and every evil, that all my doings and life may please You. For into Your hands I commend myself, my body and soul, and all things. Let Your holy angel be with me, that the evil foe may have no power over me. Amen.[2]

March 11

Anxious? Reflect on This!

Susan Wales wrote a book called *Standing on the Promises*. In it she quotes Vicki Baum who said, "You don't get ulcers from what you eat. You get them from what's eating you."[1]

What's eating you today? Use the passages below as "Timely Reflections" to apply some promises from God to your anxieties and agitations. And look long at the cover of this book. It's peaceful, just as you want to be... and can be.

"Cast your burden on the LORD, and he will sustain you; / he will never permit the righteous to be moved" (Psalm 55:22).

"Blessed be the Lord, who daily bears us up; God is our salvation" (Psalm 68:19).

"When the cares of my heart are many, your consolations cheer my soul" (Psalm 94:19).

"Fear not, for I am with you; be not dismayed, for I am your God; / I will strengthen you, I will help you, I will uphold you with my righteous right hand" (Isaiah 41:10).

"Jesus came and touched them, saying, 'Rise, and have no fear'" (Matthew 17:7).

"My God will supply every need of yours according to his riches in glory in Christ Jesus" (Philippians 4:19).

And a familiar hymn sings it this way: "What need or grief / Ever has failed of relief? / Wings of His mercy did shade you."[2]

"What more can He say than to you He has said, / Who unto the Savior for refuge have fled?"[3]

For further reflection: Matthew 10:26-33 – Remember Who is speaking to you!

Lord Jesus, sometimes my anxieties and agitations consume me. As You told Martha, tell me now: One thing is needful, Your Word of promise (Luke 10:38-42). Remind me that all the comforting promises of God are "Yes" and "Amen" in You (2 Corinthians 1:20).

March 12

A Special Delivery

"Hi! The whole writing team is assembled: Christian, Connor, Drew, and Jacob. We're here to announce a new member to our writing team, Nicholas Bauer Pittman. Nick joined the team March 12, 2013, all 7 pounds, 15 ounces, and 20 inches. And like all of us writers, he uses the English language a lot like Opa. Welcome, Nick!"

"Glad to be here!"

"What was it like to be born?"

"I'm still trying to figure it all out. Everything had seemed perfect to me, all dark and cozy in the womb. Everything I needed delivered right to me. Then, whoosh! Like it or not, I came out. I'm in a new world and not sure what to make of it. There's light. There's color. There are shapes. There are people. Who are these two old people?"

"Oh, that's Oma and Opa. When you want something, go to Oma. She'll take care of you. Opa just sits there and thinks of Bible things. What are you thinking of now, Opa?"

"I'm thinking about how Nick being born is like what big people experience. We big people get comfy here. Sooner or later we're going to be delivered into a whole new life – eternity. Big people can get scared about eternity, but Jesus tells us to trust Him. He'll deliver us into something wonderful – heaven. That will be even more wonderful than being born into this world. ' 'What no eye has seen, nor ear heard, nor the heart of man imagined, / what God has prepared for those who love him' – these things God has revealed to us through the Spirit' (1 Corinthians 2:9-10; and see Isaiah 64:4)."

"Opa, huh? What are you talking about?"

"Boys, just keep what I said in the back of your mind. The time will come when you'll understand. For now, welcome, Nicholas!"

For further reflection: Revelation 21:1-4 – "Jerusalem the golden"[1]

O sweet and blessèd country, / The home of God's elect!
O sweet and blessèd country / That faithful hearts expect!
In mercy, Jesus, bring us / To that eternal rest
With You and God the Father / And Spirit, ever blest.[2]

March 13

God's Deliverance – Today

As I think about my friends with cancer, and for that matter all the various problems we all face in our lives, the words "salvation" and "savior" become filled with meaning.

Kathleen Norris wrote about an acquaintance who thought he could make some good money dealing drugs but got out when he discovered that drug dealers would kill you if you got in their way. "'I decided to get out,' he said. 'This was over my head.'" And Kathleen Norris writes, "And that is salvation, or at least the beginning of it."[1]

Christians often talk about salvation as if it were some kind of airy, non-body experience, but that robs the Good News of its help when we're hurting. The word "salvation" generally means preservation in danger and deliverance from impending death. The "savior" is the deliverer (Greek-English Lexicon).[2] "In Scripture, salvation often has the connotation of restoring a person to good health. Salvation also is used, however, in the sense of snatching someone from peril. It denotes deliverance from danger or removal of a person from a life-threatening situation."[3]

Out of that basic use comes the Bible's description of Jesus rescuing us from sin, death, and Satan, and winning for us forgiveness and eternal life. However, don't let the eternal dimension of salvation cause us to forget salvation's here-and-now implications. God so wants you to be His forever, that His Spirit comes to be with you in whatever problems this sinful and broken world throws your way now.

In "A Mighty Fortress is Our God," Martin Luther wrote, "He helps us free from every need that hath us now o'ertaken."[4] Salvation isn't escaping problems; it's the Savior's presence in them.

For further reflection: Luke 15:11-32 – Slowly realizing you need help, deliverance, salvation

I walk with Jesus all the way; / His guidance never fails me;
Within His wounds I find a stay / When Satan's pow'r assails me;
And by His footsteps led, / My path I safely tread.
No evil leads my soul astray; / I walk with Jesus all the way.[5]   *Amen.*

March 14

Called to Holiness

How can you follow Jesus today? Simply heed His call.

"As he who called you is holy, you also be holy in all your conduct" (1 Peter 1:15). Jesus' sacrifice covers our sin with forgiveness, but let's also seek the Spirit's help to root sin out of our hearts. Name the sins with which you struggle. "You shall be holy, for I the LORD your God am holy" (Leviticus 19:2).

Striving for holiness may bring you some kind of suffering today, but that is the call to you. "For to this you have been called, because Christ also suffered for you, leaving you an example, so that you might follow in his steps" (1 Peter 2:21). Should holiness bring you suffering, it is not without a promise. "Blessed are those who are persecuted for righteousness' sake" (Matthew 5:10). "For to this you were called, that you may obtain a blessing" (1 Peter 3:9). The word translated "obtain" is literally "inherit," pointing you to the future, to the eternal dimension in His call. "The God of all grace ... has called you to his eternal glory in Christ" (1 Peter 5:10).

We're not the normal run of people, you and I. Followers of Jesus are peculiar people, and today we'll show it. By your holy conduct amidst the people of the world, "Proclaim the excellencies of him who called you out of darkness into his marvelous light" (1 Peter 2:9).

"How clear is our vocation, Lord, when once we heed Your call: To live according to Your Word and daily learn, refreshed, restored, that You are Lord of all and will not let us fall."[1]

For further reflection: Mark 10:23-31 – Not easy!

I will sing of steadfast love and justice; to you, O LORD, I will make music. / I will ponder the way that is blameless. Oh when will you come to me? / I will walk with integrity of heart within my house; / I will not set before my eyes anything that is worthless. / I hate the work of those who fall away; it shall not cling to me. / A perverse heart shall be far from me; I will know nothing of evil. (Psalm 101:1-4)   Amen.

March 15

It's Really Him!

Barbara Brown Taylor writes about a friend whose father, a mechanic, died from a heart attack.

> He kept a clean shop, and before he went home at night he scrubbed his hands with a boar's bristle brush, washing away the grime of the day. But as careful as he was, his hands stayed stained in places, and it was that my friend was looking for. Turning his father's big hand over in his own, he saw the motor oil in the fingerprints, the calluses dark from years of hauling engines, and he smiled. "It's him," he said. "They tried to clean him up, but look, they couldn't. It's my daddy. It's really him."[1]

Morticians try to make us look good in death – just as we try to make ourselves look good to others in life – but we are what we are. Only God makes us clean in the grime, in the uncleanness of life in this sinful world. "You were washed, you were sanctified, you were justified in the name of the Lord Jesus Christ and by the Spirit of our God" (1 Corinthians 6:11). And only cleansing by the Spirit of Christ will bring us into eternal life. "Nothing unclean will ever enter it [heaven] … but only those who are written in the Lamb's book of life" (Revelation 21:27).

The grime of your work day after day, the wrinkles from worrying and from laughing, the calluses and age spots that testify to the years – these make you a witness of God's steadfast love, they remind you of sin and grace, and they speak to others. "It's really him." You're really a dear child of God.

> Why not, then, with a faith unbounded / Forever in His love confide?
> Why not, with earthly griefs surrounded, / Rejoicing still in hope abide,
> Until I reach that blissful home / Where doubt and sorrow never come?[2]

For further reflection: Psalm 39 – "My hope is in You"

Swift to its close ebbs out life's little day;
Earth's joys grow dim, its glories pass away;
Change and decay in all around I see;
O Thou who changest not, abide with me.[3]

March 16

"…But One Thing Is Necessary"

Jesus said, "one's life does not consist in the abundance of his possessions" (Luke 12:15). Thank You, Lord, for that reminder! Somehow I suspect I'm not the only one working on income taxes… or stalling on that dread job. April 15th – only one month away! For me the task is worse this year because I've fallen behind – way, way behind – keeping up with my financial records. Over the last months, piles proliferated around my desk at home. The Quakers sing, "'Tis the gift to be simple,"[1] and I believe it, but the mess of papers, each one a reminder of my poor record keeping… not simple!

The day of rest commanded to Old Testament people says, "six days you shall labor, and do all your work" (Exodus 20:9). But what if all your work isn't done? No matter, was the Old Testament judgment. Stop work anyway. It's a great paradox but true: Stop some work and put devotion and prayer into your daily life and you'll accomplish more. About those who put God first in their schedules, a psalm about the Sabbath promises, "the righteous flourish" (Psalm 92:12). "You are anxious and troubled about many things," Jesus says, "but one thing is necessary" (Luke 10:41-42).

He also says, "do not lay up for yourselves treasures on earth" (Matthew 6:19). After working on the taxes, I don't think I'll be guilty of that! "Lay up for yourselves treasures in heaven, where neither moth nor rust destroys and where thieves do not break in and steal. For where your treasure is, there your heart will be also" (Matthew 6:20-21).

Have you experienced, as I have, that when you take time off to be with the Lord, those piles of work seem more manageable?

For further reflection: Luke 12:13-21 – I bet he had his taxes done, but…

Hence, all earthly treasure! / Jesus is my pleasure, / Jesus is my choice.
Hence, all empty glory! / Naught to me Thy story / Told with tempting voice.
Pain or loss, / Or shame or cross / Shall not from my Savior move me
Since He deigns to love me.[2]

March 17

Saints, Sacrifices, and Servanthood

"I will most gladly spend and be spent for your souls," wrote St. Paul to the Corinthians (2 Corinthians 12:15). That's what St. Patrick did. Born in England in the fourth century, young Patrick was kidnapped by pirates and sold into slavery in Ireland. He escaped, studied theology, and returned to Ireland as a missionary. Tradition says Patrick established 300 churches and baptized 120,000 people.

No one spent and was spent like Jesus. "Though he was in the form of God, [Jesus] did not count equality with God a thing to be grasped, but emptied himself, by taking the form of a servant … He humbled himself by becoming obedient to the point of death, even death on a cross" (Philippians 2:6-8).

The cross! Another legend would have us believe that St. Patrick rid Ireland of its snakes. When Israel complained about their hard lot in the wilderness, God sent fiery serpents. The people repented and God had Moses raise a bronze serpent on a pole. Anyone who looked up to that bronze serpent was saved from death (see Numbers 21:4-9). "As Moses lifted up the serpent in the wilderness, so must the Son of Man be lifted up, that whoever believes in him may have eternal life" (John 3:14-15).

Whether the stories (outside of biblical revelation) told about the saints are fact or legend, their purpose is to point us to Jesus. "Since we are surrounded by so great a cloud of witnesses, let us also lay aside every weight, and sin which clings so closely, and let us run with endurance the race that is set before us, looking to Jesus" (Hebrews 12:1-2).

For further reflection: John 12:27-36 – "When I am lifted up…"

Ev'ry wound that pains or grieves me / By Your wounds, Lord, is made whole;
When I'm faint, Your cross revives me, / Granting new life to my soul.
Yes, Your comfort renders sweet / Ev'ry bitter cup I meet;
For Your all-atoning passion / Has procured my soul's salvation.[1]   *Amen.*

March 18

Hope for the Rejected

My daughter once asked how to encourage a friend who was rejected for a job. That set me to recalling all the times I've experienced rejection. I was surprised; quite a list! Rejections have clouded your life, too.

Jesus knew rejection. "He was despised and rejected by men" (Isaiah 53:3). Misery loves company but when your spirit has been crushed you want more. You want to know, as my mom often said, that the sun is indeed shining, even when you can't see it. Earthly rejections are hard reminders of a far greater problem. We fallible sinners aren't acceptable to the holy and just God without someone stepping forward on our behalf. Jesus knew rejection, but you want more than someone to commiserate with you; you want a deliverer who breaks in with hope.

The Gospel is that Jesus Christ, rejected by men and crucified but raised on the third day, breaks into our dreary, beclouded souls with hope for eternity and hope for today. Since God raised a corpse, I told my daughter, He certainly is able to resurrect shattered dreams in new, unanticipated ways. The key for us is to gather up those broken pieces and give them to our caring Father. What He will do with the pieces, time will tell, but since you love Him, the promise is that all things will work together for your good (cf. Romans 8:28). As children we learned that Humpty Dumpty couldn't be put back together by all the king's horses and all the king's men. But now you're grown, you've been given His Spirit to lead you to trust that the Father will put you together again in a new way, a more mature way, an even better way than you can now imagine. "Born again to a living hope through the resurrection of Jesus Christ" (1 Peter 1:3)!

For further reflection: Hebrews 4:14-16 – Jesus knows - draw near

Oh, all-embracing Mercy, / O ever open Door,
What shall I do without You / When heart and eye run o'er?
When all things seem against us, / To drive us to despair,
We know one gate is open, / One ear will hear our prayer.[1]   *Amen.*

March 19

A Model of Fatherhood

"Is not this Joseph's son?" (Luke 4:22) people puzzled about Jesus, and the Bible answers: *No, Jesus was miraculously conceived by the Holy Spirit* (see Matthew 1:20). If your mind balks at the possibility of a virgin birth, ask yourself if your God is bound by the laws of nature. So, no, Joseph wasn't the physical father but rather the "guardian" of God's Son.

Joseph modeled what fatherhood should be all about. First, he knew Jesus wasn't his child, and today we fathers need to remember that the children we beget are really God's children, entrusted to us to be raised in the ways of their true Father. Second, Joseph sacrificed for Mary and Jesus, taking them to Egypt to avoid murderous King Herod and then to Galilee to avoid murderous Archelaus. How much time do modern fathers set aside to be with wife and children – quantity time, not just quality time? Third and most important, Joseph was a pious man whose greatest devotion was not to family but to God. Out of that devotion to God came his exemplary fatherhood.

Today is the day of "St. Joseph, Guardian of Jesus" in the calendar of the church. Concordia Seminary professor Rick Marrs said in one of his chapel sermons, "God still gives out good works for us to do" (see Ephesians 2:10). Most modern fathers have an abundance of good works awaiting them!

For further reflection: Matthew 2:13-23 – His life became all about Jesus

Almighty God, from the house of Your servant David You raised up Joseph to be the guardian of Your incarnate Son and the husband of His mother, Mary. Grant us grace to follow the example of this faithful workman in heeding Your counsel and obeying Your commands; through Jesus Christ, our Lord, who lives and reigns with You and the Holy Spirit, one God, now and forever.[1] Amen.

March 20

TGIF! Friday Brings Freedom!

The days of the week have their – what shall I say – their personalities. Monday is the stern day, back to work, but who doesn't like Friday? Whether yours was a hard week or routine, when Friday comes it promises freedom. The weekend has its chores but most of us enjoy a bit slower pace of life when the weekend finally comes. TGIF!

Really, thank God it's Friday! Friday is the day Jesus Christ died and that offers great freedom. Freedom from eternal punishment for our sins: "Christ died for our sins" (1 Corinthians 15:3). Freedom from living in fear of death: "If we have died with Christ, we believe that we will also live with him" (Romans 6:8). Freedom from preoccupation with ourselves for humble service to others: "He humbled himself by becoming obedient to the point of death, even death on a cross. Therefore God has highly exalted him." "Have this mind among yourselves" (Philippians 2:8-9, 5). Freedom to sacrifice totally for others: "Greater love has no one than this, that someone lay down his life for his friends" (John 15:13).

The personality of Friday in Bible times was busy. Friday was the Day of Preparation when Jews would get necessary things done so they could enjoy the rest of Saturday, of their Sabbath. When we welcome Friday, we too should be mindful of preparation. "There remains a Sabbath rest for the people of God, for whoever has entered God's rest has also rested from his works" (Hebrews 4:9-10). Thank God when Friday comes. It's time to get ready for rest. Freedom!

For further reflection: Colossians 2:16 - 3:4 – Free to live every day to the Lord

O Lord, our heavenly Father, almighty and everlasting God, You have safely brought us to the beginning of this day. Defend us in the same with Your mighty power and grant that this day we fall into no sin, neither run into any kind of danger, but that all our doings, being ordered by Your governance, may be righteous in Your sight; through Jesus Christ, Your Son, our Lord, who lives and reigns with You and the Holy Spirit, one God, now and forever.[1] Amen.

March 21

Spring Affirms God's Goodness

The crocuses are blooming in our front yard, tulips and forsythias too. Years ago, the newspaper ran an article about scientists trying to discover how a plant knows when it's time to bloom.[1] That's way beyond me, but I do know Who sets the bloom in motion.

Spring reaffirms God's goodness. Wrote Maltbie Babcock:

This is my Father's world; / Oh, let me not forget

That though the wrong seems oft so strong, / God is the ruler yet.

This is my Father's world; / Why should my heart be sad?

The Lord is king; let heavens ring! / God reigns; let the earth be glad![2]

The earth does indeed bloom with gladness. Here before us God is keeping one of His promises. "While the earth remains, seedtime and harvest, cold and heat, summer and winter, day and night, shall not cease" (Genesis 8:22).

Does the gladness touch your spirit as well as delight your eyes? "You have been born again, not of perishable seed but of imperishable, through the living and abiding word of God … This word is the good news that was preached to you" (1 Peter 1:23, 25). This gives followers of Jesus a special joy in spring. Christians and non-Christians join together in welcoming the rebirth of spring but we Christians can share something more. He who sets the bloom in motion offers an inheritance that will never fade away (see 1 Peter 1:4). "Though the wrong seems oft so strong, God is the ruler yet."

"Our Savior Christ Jesus … abolished death and brought life and immortality to light through the gospel" (2 Timothy 1:10).

For further reflection: Song of Solomon 2:10-17 – The spring of His love

O God, I believe that You are the Father Almighty, maker of heaven and earth. I believe that You have made all creatures, I among them. You have planted my life in this beautiful world. You sustain the life you have given to me and all creatures. In spring You surround us with the blooms of Your splendor and in autumn the fading beauty moves us to You as the giver of eternal life. By Your Spirit, help me be a creature who forever thanks and praises You. Amen.

March 22

Not to Be Served, but to Serve

Failure… and follow-up.

"Jesus, would You do us a favor?" James and John asked just before Holy Week. "And what might that be?" "Let one of us sit at Your right and the other at Your left in Your glory." In other words, "Oh, we love You, Lord! Put us in La-Z-Boy®s, one on each side of Your throne. We just want to bask in Your glory." Jesus tried to tell them: "Fundamental failure, boys. That's not what I'm about" (cf. Mark 10:35-45).

Who was the last smelly person you befriended? When was the last time you passed on something so you could write a check to charity? When was the last time you spoke up for someone getting crucified by gossip? God's commandments to you about other people are not merely "Thou shalt not" but every commandment implies a "Thou shalt." "If you do good to those who do good to you, what benefit is that to you? For even sinners do the same. … But love your enemies, and do good, … expecting nothing in return, and your reward will be great" (Luke 6:33, 35). Getting out of your comfort zone is the way to follow up on our failure when we fall into the temptation of easy-chair religion.

That's our Jesus! "Whoever would be great among you must be your servant, and whoever would be first among you must be slave of all. For even the Son of Man came not to be served but to serve, and to give his life as a ransom for many" (Mark 10:43-45).

For further reflection: Psalm 119:65-72 – Faith without works is dead

Teach us the lesson Thou hast taught:
To feel for those Thy blood hath bought,
That ev'ry word and deed and thought
May work a work for Thee.[1]   *Amen.*

March 23

Start at the Cross – End at the Cross

Many Sundays when I was a parish pastor, just before the service was to begin, the acolytes would ask, "Pastor, which candles do we light first?" Our church had a gazillion candles near the altar. I answered with the direction someone had once given me: Start at the cross, and when the service is over put out the candles so that you end at the cross.

That's not a bad allegory for a Monday morning or any morning. What are you facing today? Take a moment to identify what's weighing you down. Start the day by identifying your crosses and then focus on Jesus' cross. If you ever scan the titles at a Christian book store, you start to think that Christians are always joyous, happy, and fulfilled. That doesn't fit your experience, does it? Four authors who wrote more realistically were Matthew, Mark, Luke, and John. You can open their books on almost any page and learn about Jesus and the cross, Jesus and suffering, and how Jesus who Himself experienced suffering is present now and close to you when your light flickers, ready to go out. "A faintly burning wick he will not quench" (Isaiah 42:3). Think of yourself as an acolyte, trying to keep the flame alive. Your directions: Start at the cross and end at the cross.

> From the cross Thy wisdom shining / Breaketh forth in conqu'ring might;
> From the cross forever beameth / All Thy bright redeeming light.[1]

For further reflection: Isaiah 58:5-10 – In the challenges, light breaks forth

Drawn to the Cross, which Thou hast blessed
With healing gifts for souls distressed,
To find in Thee my life, my rest,
Christ crucified, I come.[2]   Amen.

March 24

The Crying Stairs

"Hi, Christian here. Opa did bad.

"Opa came and visited Connor and me. He came to get us from preschool. Then he went with us to the park. I rode my new bike and Connor played in the sand. After the park, we went home. That's when Opa did a bad thing. He took his seat belt off before the car stopped. My teacher tells us to keep our seat belt on until the car is stopped. When Opa took it off too soon, I said, 'Oh, no.' Mommy said, 'OK, Christian, what does Opa have to do now?' I said he has to sit on the 'crying stairs.' The crying stairs are where I go when I have done something bad. Opa went and sat on the crying stairs. I told him what he had done wrong. Opa promised not to do it again.

"Do big people do things that land them on their own 'crying stairs?' When I get sent to the crying stairs, I tell Jesus what I did wrong. He still loves me. I hope all big people talk to Jesus when they're on the crying stairs."

For further reflection: Seat belts are one thing. Martin Luther suggests a way to know your serious sins:

> Consider your place in life according to the Ten Commandments: Are you a father, mother, son, daughter, husband, wife, or worker? Have you been disobedient, unfaithful, or lazy? Have you been hot-tempered, rude, or quarrelsome? Have you hurt someone by your words or deeds? Have you stolen, been negligent, wasted anything, or done any harm?[1]

For You have promised, Lord, to heed
Your children's cries in time of need
Through Him whose name alone is great,
Our Savior and our Advocate.
So we with all our hearts each day
To You our glad thanksgiving pay,
Then walk obedient to Your Word
And now and ever praise You, Lord.[2]   Amen.

March 25

Follow Up with the Resurrection!

Failure… and follow-up.

Without doubt, the greatest failure of Holy Week was Jesus of Nazareth. When I say "failure," I'm thinking of the conventional wisdom of that day. Many of His contemporaries saw Jesus as a rising star, not just religious but also political. Combining populist religious fervor with anti-Roman nationalism, Jesus could have had a great earthly future but it went awry. After a triumphant entry into Jerusalem on Palm Sunday, pundits would say He made a terrible political miscalculation. The old religious and political order trapped Him, they were unforgiving, and by Friday night He was dead. The world's judgment: Jesus was a failure.

> O darkest woe!
> Ye tears, forth flow!
> Has earth so sad a wonder,
> That the Father's only Son
> Now is buried yonder![1]

But Jesus knew all along how the drama would play out. Earlier "he began to teach them that the Son of Man must suffer many things and be rejected by the elders and the chief priests and the scribes and be killed, and after three days rise again" (Mark 8:31-32). He did rise, Easter. He lives right now, this moment. "Fear not, I am the first and the last, and the living one. I died, and behold I am alive forevermore, and I have the keys of Death and Hades" (Revelation 1:17-18). Jesus followed up the world's judgment of failure with resurrection. That's our hope.

Ponder His death but don't get stuck in Good Friday; follow up with Easter!

For further reflection: Hebrews 4:14-16; 5:7-9 – Not dead now - alive for you

Now no more can death appall, / Now no more the grave enthrall;
You have opened paradise, / And Your saints in You shall rise.
Alleluia![2]   Amen.

March 26

Were You There?

It's common in art history, people gathered around the cross. Often the people gazing on the sufferings of Jesus are those we would expect to see. So the Blessed Virgin Mary and St. John were painted by Lucas Cranach the Elder in his 1503 *Crucifixion*. Sometimes artists departed from a strict representation of the biblical account and included their own contemporaries before the cross. An example is *Adoration of the Trinity* by Albrecht Durer in 1511. By doing so, Durer and other artists show that Jesus' death is for all people.

Our imaginations paint pictures. Does your imagination place you at the cross?

Were you there when they crucified my Lord? …

Were you there when they nailed Him to the tree?

Oh… Sometimes it causes me to tremble, tremble, tremble. …

Were you there when they crucified my Lord?[1]

In *The Small Crucifixion*, Matthias Grünewald painted mother Mary and the disciple John standing at the cross, but Grünewald also painted Mary Magdalene kneeling before her Savior. "In three days' time she will again kneel at His feet, but then it will be in a garden outside His tomb, and she will be radiant with joy."[2] Our Lenten devotions before the suffering Savior become most meaningful when we remember that His Easter victory over sin and death is going to be celebrated… and we'll be there!

For further reflection: Mark 16:1-8 – "You will see him, just as he told you"

Almighty God the Father, through Your only-begotten Son, Jesus Christ, You have overcome death and opened the gate of everlasting life to us. Grant that we, who celebrate with joy the day of our Lord's resurrection, may be raised from the death of sin by Your life-giving Spirit; through Jesus Christ, our Lord, who lives and reigns with You and the Holy Spirit, one God, now and forever.[3]   Amen.

March 27

Resurrection – Future and a Hope

Lent is no time to leave the resurrection of Jesus Christ in the shadows. Especially this Lent, when the news in the world is about war and rumors of war, when you face problems in your life that seem hopeless, when life is simply wearing you down… this Lent is no time to put Easter off.

"I have set the LORD always before me" (Psalm 16:8). Put Him before you, this One who conquered death. Too much happened in world history 2,000 years ago to think His resurrection is merely wishful thinking. Followers of the living Lord, "turned the world upside down" (Acts 17:6); His resurrection changed history.

Alive, before you, He testifies that the power of sin and evil has been broken. "It is finished" (John 19:30). Whatever bad is happening in your world is but the death rattle of that doomed enemy. As Paul writes, "He [Jesus] must reign until he has put all enemies under his feet. The last enemy to be destroyed is death" (1 Corinthians 15:25-26).

Christ is the first to rise; then His faithful. With resurrection, He brings a future. "I know the plans I have for you, declares the LORD, plans … to give you a future and a hope" (Jeremiah 29:11).

"I am with you always" (Matthew 28:20). Take Him out of your peripheral vision and set Him before your face. "In the world you will have tribulation. But take heart; I have overcome the world" (John 16:33). And all God's people say, *Amen!* "I have set the LORD always before me."

For further reflection: Martin Luther says that Jesus was born, suffered, and died, so "that I may be His own and live under Him in His kingdom and serve Him in everlasting righteousness, innocence, and blessedness, just as He is risen from the dead, lives and reigns to all eternity. This is most certainly true."[1]

Christ, the Life of all the living, / Christ, the death of death, our foe,
Who, Thyself for me once giving / To the darkest depths of woe:
Through thy suff'rings, death, and merit / I eternal life inherit.
Thousand, thousand thanks shall be, / Dearest Jesus, unto Thee.[2]   *Amen.*

March 28

Plan to Pause and Ponder

P-L-E-A-S-E. Take a little time today – now would be very good – to open the calendar in your phone or tablet, put a note on the fridge, whatever works for you… Take time now to plan spiritually for Holy Week, the most special week in the Christian year.

Without Holy Week, your sins would not be forgiven, you wouldn't have the fellowship of the Eucharist and the Church, and heaven would be pie-in-the-sky folly. Without Holy Week, you'd forget how terrible evil is, that we are forgiven sinners, and that Jesus' death opens heaven to us. Without Holy Week, your feelings would be untouched by grace – your guilt, anger, and fears would not be sanctified. Without Holy Week, you are irredeemably far from your heavenly Father.

So, P-L-E-A-S-E! Set aside times during the coming week when you can be by yourself to ponder how much the Son of God endured because of His love for *you*. Use some somber Lenten music to get into the mood. Reflect on your sins. Ponder passages about the passion. Isaiah 53 is classic. Psalm 22 is prophetic. Of course, read the passion accounts themselves in Matthew, Mark, Luke, and John. "Be still, and know that I am God" (Psalm 46:10).

> Do we pass that cross unheeding, / Breathing no repentant vow,
> Though we see You wounded, bleeding, / See Your thorn-encircled brow?
> Yet Your sinless death has brought us / Life eternal, peace, and rest;
> Only what Your grace has taught us / Calms the sinner's deep distress.[1]
> Amen.

So what's your plan?

For further reflection: Psalm 27 – One thing to seek after

Dear Jesus, don't let me speed by Your cross. In the days of Holy Week, help me pause and ponder. For right now, help me plan. Amen.

March 29

Struggling to Understand? Wait on the Lord

Failure... and follow-up.

When Jesus rode into Jerusalem on a donkey, St. John reports that the disciples didn't get it. "His disciples did not understand these things at first" (John 12:16a). Failing to understand, that's a daily part of my life, and probably yours as well. Back then the disciples actually saw Jesus. We don't; He's mysteriously present but unseen. What's going on, Jesus? We believe, but there's so much we don't understand... unless we're Pharisees. They have all the answers.

Back to humble know-nothings: Perhaps the most practical spiritual insight I've learned over the years is that we understand more about God when we look back. In hindsight we can better see what He was doing. When Moses asked to see God's glory, the LORD answered, "you cannot see my face, for man shall not see me and live." But He did put Moses in the cleft of a rock and said, "while my glory passes by ... I will cover you with my hand until I have passed by. ... You shall see my back, but my face shall not be seen." We seldom understand what God is doing now. So the follow-up to our failure to understand now is... wait. God will make His ways clearer in due time. Then we'll see, "I will be gracious to whom I will be gracious, and will show mercy on whom I will show mercy" (Exodus 33:18-23).

It took time for the disciples to understand the real reason Palm Sunday was a triumphant entry. "When Jesus was glorified, then they remembered that these things had been written about him and had been done to him" (John 12:16b). Let go of your need to know now; wait on the Lord.

We understand precious little. The little we understand is precious.

For further reflection: Psalm 118:19-29 – Failure... the stone the builders rejected - Following-up... we see in hindsight

Almighty and everlasting God, You sent Your Son, our Savior Jesus Christ, to take upon Himself our flesh and to suffer death upon the cross. Mercifully grant that we may follow the example of His great humility and patience...[1] *Amen.*

March 30

Righteous Anger – Unlimited Love

Dear Jesus, You asked Your disciples to watch with You (Matthew 26:38). I want to do that, knowing that my life depends upon all that You endured this week. On Palm Sunday in church I'm not distracted; I watch with You. However, the next day work begins anew and I cannot multitask everything expected of me. It's tempting to let You slip out of my mind until later this week, until Maundy Thursday and Good Friday when I'll pay attention again. But between Palm Sunday and Maundy Thursday, I ask Your Spirit to keep bringing my thoughts back to what You did on Monday of Holy Week.

Sunday You entered Jerusalem meekly on a donkey, but on Monday You showed Yourself in a different way. You "entered the temple and began to drive out those who sold and those who bought in the temple," and You "over-turned the tables of the money-changers and the seats of those who sold pigeons" (Mark 11:15). Jesus! What brought this on? The acts of religious people did, at least outwardly religious people. That they sold sacrificial animals and exchanged currency for offerings wasn't wrong. That they did this in the temple, in the Court of the Gentiles, that's what angered You. They crowded out people who needed to come to the temple and to Your Father. *It's our church*, the religious must have thought. *It's not for those people*. So you became angry, righteously so, and quoted Scripture, "Is it not written, 'My house shall be called a house of prayer for all the nations?'" (Mark 11:17; Isaiah 56:7).

Jesus, when we keep people away from You today, recall us to Your unlimited love for all people. When our business crowds out our witness to the welcoming Father, remind us to love You with all our being at all times. When the Church is so preoccupied with its ways of offering sacrifices of worship and praise that others feel unwelcome, remind us that You are not only the mild Jesus of Palm Sunday but also the righteously angered Son of God. And then, forgive us. Make us holy this week. Amen.

For further reflection: Luke 2:22-38 – Jesus' first visit to the temple

All are redeemed, both far and wide, / Since Thou, O Lord, for all hast died. Grant us the will and grace provide / To love them all in Thee![1]   *Amen.*

March 31

"Jesus, I Will Ponder Now"

"Jesus, I will ponder now."[1] Poet Sigismund von Birken invites us to do more than think about Jesus these next days. Talk to Jesus!

"Jesus, I will ponder now on Your holy passion."[1] Jesus, the world about me will slow down somewhat these next days. This slight slowdown is not simply my chance to catch up. This will be time with You.

"With Your Spirit me endow for such meditation."[1] Jesus, the day is coming when I will come before You in eternity. I will see You. Dear Jesus, give me Your Holy Spirit now so that my meditation upon Your passion will prepare my anxious heart.

"Grant that I in love and faith…"[1] Jesus, don't let me simply know about You. Increase my love for You. "I believe; help my unbelief!" (Mark 9:24).

"Grant that I in love and faith may the image cherish of Your suff'ring, pain, and death that I may not perish."[1] Jesus, You have not called me to die for You but to live for You. On my heart impress Your image so it is no longer I who live but You who live in me. Jesus, save me! Amen.

For further reflection: Psalm 71:1-14 – "I … will praise you yet more and more"

Almighty and everlasting God, grant us by Your grace so to pass through this holy time of our Lord's passion that we may obtain the forgiveness of our sins; through Jesus Christ, Your Son, our Lord, who lives and reigns with You and the Holy Spirit, one God, now and forever.[2]   Amen.

April 1

"In Quietness and in Trust"

The Bible records no activities of Jesus on Wednesday of Holy Week. Perhaps He was busy and we just don't know what He did. On the other hand, we can make an educated guess that Jesus chose to spend the day in rest and quiet at the place where He was lodging, the home of Mary, Martha, and Lazarus in Bethany.

That He should spend this day in quiet contemplation was His way of facing challenges. He had arrived at Bethany the Friday before, and at sunset began the daylong observance of Sabbath. No work was done on Sabbath, only contemplation of the Torah and communion with His heavenly Father. So Wednesday would have been a similar day of preparation for Thursday, for the Passover, for His agony in Gethsemane, preparation for facing His enemies who were closing in for the kill. Anticipating those hardships put Jesus in quiet meditation and prayer to His Father. Don't just do something; sit there. "Wait for the LORD" (Psalm 27:14).

When we find ourselves between Palm Sunday and Maundy Thursday, we do well to pause and ponder as Jesus often did. Am I focused upon the important events of Holy Week, focused on what Jesus did that changes my life now and for eternity?

"In returning and rest you shall be saved; in quietness and in trust shall be your strength" (Isaiah 30:15).

For further reflection: Psalm 56 – A prayer Jesus prayed - pray it as you watch with Him

Amen, that is, so shall it be.
Make strong our faith in You, that we
May doubt not but with trust believe
That what we ask we shall receive.
Thus in Your name and at Your Word
We say, "Amen, O hear us, Lord!"[1]

April 2

Out with the Old Yeast!

One preparation for keeping Passover is to rid the house of leaven. A candle is lit, a blessing spoken, and the house is searched in silence for any leaven. When it's found – as it will be, for some was hidden ahead of time – the leaven is put in a bag to be burned the next morning. The search, writes George Robinson, "underlies the importance of a break with the past, with the ties to Egypt and slavery."[1]

"A break with the past." Jesus, an observant Jew, kept the Passover on the Thursday of Holy Week. Yes, He anticipated a break, a break with the age-old tyranny of sin and evil by His sacrifice on the cross, and in giving us the Sacrament of His Supper He forgives our past sins and gives grace to amend our lives.

"Cleanse out the old leaven," wrote St. Paul, "that you may be a new lump, as you really are unleavened. For Christ, our Passover lamb, has been sacrificed. Let us therefore celebrate the festival, not with the old leaven, the leaven of malice and evil, but with the unleavened bread of sincerity and truth" (1 Corinthians 5:7-8).

The Great Litany[2], often used in Holy Week, addresses God – Father, Son, and Spirit – and then begins a long list of troubles that threaten each of us, including "from all sin, from all error, from all evil." "From all," not from some. "From the crafts and assaults of the devil," the Litany prays, "and from everlasting death, Good Lord, deliver us."

What in your past needs to be left behind? Can you identify two or three sins in the present that are not consistent with repentant living? Out with that old yeast! "Good Lord, deliver us"!

For further reflection: Mark 14:12-72 – What Jesus did on Thursday

O Lord, in this wondrous Sacrament [of the Lord's Supper] You have left us a remembrance of Your passion. Grant that we may so receive the sacred mystery of Your body and blood that the fruits of Your redemption may continually be manifest in us; for You live and reign with the Father and the Holy Spirit, one God, now and forever.[3]   Amen.

April 3

Seven Words from the Cross

Jesus' seven words from the cross…

"Father, forgive them, for they know not what they do" (Luke 23:34). But how often do we taste bitterness because we don't forgive those who have wronged us?

"Today you will be with me in paradise," Jesus said to the thief who confessed his sin (Luke 23:43). But do we expect heaven without personal repentance?

"Woman, behold, your son," He said to mother Mary. "Behold, your mother," He said to John (John 19:26-27). But do we let personal busy-ness stop our love for family?

"My God, my God, why have you forsaken me?" (Mark 15:34). God abandoned Jesus for a short time so that the full judgment against our sin would be felt. But do we trivialize sin?

"I thirst" (John 19:28). He said this to fulfill the Scripture, fulfilling all righteousness, but do we make Bible reading optional?

"It is finished" (John 19:30). No qualifications. Yes, we're sinners but the price of your sins was paid in full. *In full*. You can't work your way into heaven; you can only believe the One who opened the way through forgiveness.

"Father, into your hands I commit my spirit!" (Luke 23:46). Do you?

For further reflection: Ponder the seven words

May Your life and death supply
Grace to live and grace to die,
Grace to reach the home on high:
Hear us, holy Jesus.[1]   *Amen.*

April 4

Holy Week – the Defining Story of Our Lives

If you were to wrap your life up in one story, just one story, what would it be? Our lives are filled with countless little stories. We go to work in the morning and come home at night, or we don't go to work – laid off – wondering what we've accomplished. Everyone is looking to put their little stories into the context of the big, defining story of their lives.

Two thieves were crucified with Jesus. "One of the criminals who were hanged railed at him, saying, 'Are you not the Christ? Save yourself and us!'" (Luke 23:39). That thief's defining story is cynicism, death, and eternal death. But the big, overarching story for the other thief reads this way. "'Do you not fear God, since you are under the same sentence of condemnation? And we indeed justly, for we are receiving the due reward of our deeds; but this man has done nothing wrong.' And he said, 'Jesus, remember me when you come into your kingdom.'" Jesus answered him, "Truly, I say to you, today you will be with me in Paradise" (Luke 23:40-43). This thief's story? Confession of sin, forgiveness from Jesus, and the promise of Paradise.

Holy Saturday is a quiet day for observant Christians. Remembering that the Savior lay dead in a tomb puts us, or should put us, in a mood of quiet and contemplation. Do you try to fit God and Jesus into the story of your life? Better to put yourself into the Bible's story, into the big story that can bring all our little stories together. This is it, the Holy Week, the story that defines you and me eternally. Death to sin, buried with Christ, resurrection to new and everlasting life.

For further reflection: Romans 6:1-14 – Buried with Christ

Baptized into Your name most holy,
O Father, Son, and Holy Ghost,
I claim a place, though weak and lowly,
Among Your saints, Your chosen host.
Buried with Christ and dead to sin,
Your Spirit now shall live within.[1]   Amen.

April 5

Run to the Tomb!

The women returned from the tomb and told the disciples that Jesus had been raised from the dead. "But these words seemed to them an idle tale, and they did not believe them. But Peter rose and ran to the tomb…" (Luke 24:11-12).

Again and again the Spirit urges, *Run to the tomb!* When the circumstances of your life suggest that you're in a dead end… when friends and family disappoint you… when your prayers seem to go up and evaporate unanswered… when your heart and hope hit the ground with a thud… when words of faith seem an idle tale… then the Spirit of God invites, *Run to the tomb!*

Jesus just doesn't do things our way. He was born in a stable, not the palace of a king, rode into Jerusalem on a donkey, not a regal horse, died that we might live… He just doesn't conform to our reasoned expectations. He's always going before us. Our joy is to follow.

Peter ran to the tomb because he remembered what Jesus had said. So too the women – "they remembered his words" (Luke 24:8). In all you do today, remember God's promises to you and let the empty tomb resurrect your hope.

For further reflection: Think back to all the times the Lord brought you through in an unexpected way. "Who from our mother's arms / Has blessed on our way / With countless gifts of love / And still is ours today."[1] *Run to the tomb!*

Now I will cling forever / To Christ, my Savior true;
My Lord will leave me never, / Whate'er He passes through.
He rends death's iron chain; / He breaks through sin and pain;
He shatters hell's dark thrall; / I follow Him through all.[2]

April 6

Thanks, God, I Needed That

Thanks, God, I needed that. I mean Easter and Easter church. Nice job of gently reminding me of my place.

Look at all those people who only show up at Christmas and Easter! Some of us think that, but Jesus was always glad when crowds came to Him (Matthew 5:1). He still is (Matthew 11:28).

Look at that guy with earrings – and the young woman with a tattoo! Those people in our church? But don't You have a word in the Bible about looking at the heart, not the outward appearance (1 Samuel 16:7)?

People sure do dress differently for church these days. That's your Easter finest? But who am I to impose my expression of piety upon others (James 2:2-4)?

Yup, Lord, nice job of shifting the center of the universe from me to You. For some people, this year's Easter worship is their last Easter on this side of eternity. *Their* last worship? Maybe it's *my* last worship. That possibility lies well with my soul. "Because I live, you also will live" (John 14:19). But I'm definitely not waiting to die! "It is no longer I who live, but Christ who lives in me. And the life I now live in the flesh I live by faith in the Son of God, who loved me and gave himself for me" (Galatians 2:20).

My biggest takeaway from Easter church? Tears. Easter makes my eyes mist up. I know my faith will falter in the months ahead; always does between the great festivals of faith. I'm kind of Christmas and Easter myself! Times of discouragement and tears. But those tears will glisten because of Easter. You promise to one day wipe away all tears from our eyes (Isaiah 25:8; Revelation 7:17). Thanks, God, I needed that.

For further reflection: Luke 18:9-14 – The Pharisee would notice the C & E Christians too!

He lives to silence all my fears; / He lives to wipe away my tears;
He lives to calm my troubled heart; / He lives all blessings to impart.[1]

April 7

Still on the Job

If Jesus were your typical American, what might He have done in the days right after Easter? My guess is that He would have slept late. After all, the last week had been brutal. Staying, I presume, with His friends Mary, Martha, and Lazarus, Jesus would surely have talked with Lazarus about resurrection. They had both experienced it, though in different ways. I imagine that one of these days after Easter, Jesus would go out to buy some retirement clothes – His working days behind Him. Perhaps He might even go up to Jerusalem Motors where He'd purchase an RV. In that RV, He and the disciples could see the Holy Land in a more leisurely way than when they had been busy preaching, teaching, and ministering to the needs of people. If Jesus were your typical American…

I know all that is silly, but there is a point. Jesus didn't retire. Easter is essential, of course. "If Christ has not been raised, your faith is futile and you are still in your sins" (1 Corinthians 15:17). But Easter wasn't the end for Jesus. He kept working: appearances through 40 days, Ascension, His Spirit poured out on Pentecost. He's still working today, active in His Church through Word and Sacrament. Retire? No. He who came for us, comes now to us, and will come again to take us home. Come, Lord Jesus! (Revelation 22:20).

For further reflection: 1 Peter 1:3-9 – Can't wait for Jesus to come!

Jesus Christ, be our lasting joy, / Our future great reward;
Our only glory, may it be / To glory in the Lord![1]   *Amen.*

April 8

Look Ahead!

"He is not here," announced the Easter angel. OK, so where is He?

How many times don't you and I seek Jesus where He's not to be found? The women sought Jesus in the grave but He wasn't there. Crises come into our lives – crises of health, of relationships, of work and finances, and finally death. It's common to wonder where God is when we're suffering so. We've predetermined where He should be and how He should be there, but when He doesn't show up according to our expectations, we become disillusioned.

"He is not here, for he has risen, as he said. … he is going before you to Galilee" (Matthew 28:6-7). Jesus is not only out of the tomb, but He's also out of our assumptions about God. He finds us where we're at, revealing His will through Spirit and Word, comforting and sustaining, inviting our trust, but never endorsing the status quo. "He is going before you." Now what else can you as a follower of Jesus do but look forward in faith to Him who says, "Come to me … and I will give you rest" (Matthew 11:28)?

Move on, move on! Total preoccupation with the present, our determining where and how God should act, makes it harder to anticipate the resurrection day that's coming. "Follow me," Jesus calls. He has risen and He is leading us home on a path strewn with His loving kindness.

For further reflection: Luke 24:13-35 – Jesus meets us where we're at, but doesn't leave us there

Jesus, lead Thou on / Till our rest is won.
Heav'nly leader, still direct us, / Still support, console, protect us,
Till we safely stand / In our fatherland.[1]   *Amen.*

April 9

Thanks, Mom!

I'm using this *Minute* to send greetings to my mother, whose birthday is today. Truth is, it's too late to get a card to her through the mail and I don't know how to do e-cards.

Mom, you sure did a lot for me, like the time my arm got caught in the ringer washing machine. Thanks for pulling it out! Is that why I have the biceps of Tweety Bird?

I don't remember, but you say toddler Dale threw a beer bottle out the window. Honestly, what kind of home life did we have?

Remember the times I said some bad words and you washed my mouth out with soap? Ivory® Soap: It floats!

You had three ways of telling us to obey. First way: "You kids are driving me batty." That always confused me. Earl Battey was a catcher for the White Sox and I couldn't figure out why you thought of him when we misbehaved. Second way: "I'm going to send you to the Glenwood School for Boys." Would she really do that? Third way, the best: "Remember the Fourth Commandment." It always worked. Faith, an appeal by the mercies of God (Romans 12:1).

Now, decades later, older women sometimes compliment my sermon at the church door. "Thanks," I say. "I'll tell my mother. She still worries about me." They smile at that because they understand. A mother's love never stops.

Happy Birthday, Mom!

For further reflection: 1 Samuel 2:18-21 – Do the children in your family know the code words, "Fourth Commandment?"

Thank You, O God, for all faithful mothers. Like Hannah, they have lovingly cared for our needs. You, Lord our God, be praised! From our mothers' arms You have blessed us on our way with countless gifts of love![1] Amen.

April 10

Our Fear, His Peace

"Peace be with you" (John 20:26). Although His sudden appearance startled them, His words reassured them. They hadn't been filled with peace but with fear, and for good reason. Jesus had been crucified a few days before. Why wouldn't the religious zealots who had gotten Jesus go after them next? "On the evening of that day, the first day of the week, the doors being locked where the disciples were for fear of the Jews…" (John 20:19).

What fears have you locked up, imprisoning your confidence, your hope, and your forgiveness to those who have wronged you? Someone has said that fear is simply "*f*alse *e*vidence *a*ppearing *r*eal." Sometimes that is true but not always. You know the doctor's diagnosis is true because you can feel it in your body. Continued unemployment or a job that still doesn't make ends meet – that's very real. Someone has hurt you so badly that you obsess about the wrong and go out of your way to avoid him or her. So much is real and it can lock you up, your emotions cowering in the corner.

"Peace be with you." Jesus' greeting doesn't remove the things that make us fearful. His offer of peace calms us as we face the trials and temptations all around us in a sinful world. A week later, the disciples met again behind locked doors, and again Jesus appeared, and again He said, "Peace be with you." They were learning that not seeing Jesus didn't mean He wasn't with them. You and I, disciples today, need to hear Jesus' words again and again, day after day. "These things are written so that you may believe" (John 20:31). What is false about fear is our assumption that the threat is stronger than our resurrected Lord. "Peace be with you."

For further reflection: Psalm 27 – Dear Lord, give me such confidence!

O God, our loving Father, if You are for us, who can be against us? When I become afraid, let Your Spirit give me the confidence that You will never fail me nor forsake me. For Jesus' sake! Amen. (cf. Romans 8:31; Hebrews 13:5)

April 11

Destination: Your True Home

Flying home from Washington, D.C., our plane entered its final approach into St. Louis, an approach I've been on hundreds of times. This time, however, the pilot turned the plane sharply to the left, descending faster than I was used to. He soon pulled up, began to circle the airport, and announced he would try the approach again, as soon as the tower would get him into a new "sequence."

That's a good word for the changes in our lives, "sequence." "For everything there is a season" (Ecclesiastes 3:1). Age puts us in new sequences, from birth through maturation and, sooner or later, the final approach to our true home. There are work sequences, from childhood jobs to adult work to retirement and, sooner or later, the final approach to our true home. Then there's the unexpected: accident, debilitating disease, financial collapse, legal problems, the death of your dearest, and you're sequenced into an unwelcome "new normal." Still, the ultimate goal is the same – to land safely in your true home.

"Change and decay in all around I see; / O Thou who changest not, abide with me."[1] We resist change, but it comes as we approach home, and sometimes the change is not welcome. Sometimes we're the victims; other times we ourselves cause the turbulence. In every time, we're strapped in for a ride of sin and grace, always yearning to get to our true home. It's especially in the turbulence, when we're white-knuckled, when we know "His grace has brought me safe thus far, / His grace will lead me home."[2] "He who began a good work in you will bring it to completion at the day of Jesus Christ" (Philippians 1:6).

I had another air experience that same week in 2007. Approaching Cedar Rapids, the pilot suddenly powered up and climbed rapidly. She said a plane ahead of us was too slow and we needed a new sequencing. *I've been through this before*, I thought. *Our pilots will land us safely.* Don't let God be your copilot. Trust God as pilot to sequence you through life's troubles toward your heavenly home.

For further reflection: Psalm 25 – Safety instructions

I need Thy presence ev'ry passing hour; / What but Thy grace can foil the tempter's pow'r? / Who like Thyself my guide and stay can be? / Through cloud and sunshine, O abide with me.[3]   Amen.

April 12

Unseen, He Is Present

The late E. Stanley Jones told the following story. "A Christian preacher was preaching in the bazaars in India, and a Mohammedan said, 'Padre Sahib, we have proof in our religion that you haven't got in yours. We can go to Mecca and find the tomb of Muhammad, but when you go to Palestine you can't be sure that you've got the tomb of Jesus.' 'Yes,' said the Christian preacher, 'you're right. We have no tomb in Christianity because we have no corpse.'"[1]

After Easter, Jesus popped in and out of the lives of His disciples. They're walking to Emmaus, He appears but then vanishes. They're together in a room in Jerusalem, He appears but then vanishes. That's the pattern until Ascension Day, when Jesus vanishes from sight for good … until, the angel promises, He reappears on Judgment Day. It's not that He's gone. "I am with you always" (Matthew 28:20). It's just that He's not visible to us, no body to be seen. Jesus popped in and out these 40 days after Easter to accustom His disciples to live by faith in His words … and not by seeing Him.

Even Jesus' enemies acknowledged that the tomb was empty (Matthew 28:11-15). If you agree, then God is more present than you see. Trust His promises now; see Him later. "Now we see in a mirror dimly, but then face to face" (1 Corinthians 13:13).

For further reflection: Mark 9:14-24 – "Help my unbelief!"

Lord, when our life of faith is done, / In realms of clearer light
We may behold You as You are / With full and endless sight.[2]   *Amen.*

April 13

The Bible Is Alive and Active[1]

Tsk, tsk, the Easter lilies fade away and so do the "C & Es," those people who only come to church on Christmas and Easter. Instead of complaining, why not stimulate those C & Es to more regular participation by sharing the excitement of our lively faith in the risen Christ?

A story from the American Bible Society:

> Ms. Shen Xiaoping … loves to read books of all kinds. One day her Christian neighbor gave her a copy of the Bible, saying, "This is the best book in the world. Choosing to ignore it would be the greatest loss of your life." It was years before Shen read the Bible. She remembered it only when she was due to go for an extended stay and medical checkup at the hospital. She took the "best book" with her and began to read. She read through every page of it in four days, unable to put it down.[2]

That Bible was one of 50 million Bibles printed in mainland China since 1987. Today Shen is a Christian.

On the first Sunday after the first Easter, doubting Thomas discovered that the resurrected Christ is real. The discovery of a living faith took time for Shen in China and may take some time for C & Es today. Wouldn't it stimulate their curiosity to know stories about the worldwide growth of faith in Jesus? Do you know that 900 people are being baptized every day in the Ethiopian Evangelical Church Mekane Yesus, a Lutheran church of seven million members? If regular churchgoers learn more about the growing number of people following Jesus, might the C & Es catch our excitement? Don't let the bloom fade!

For further reflection: John 20:24-31 – Blessed are those who believe

Lord Jesus, You promised that Your Gospel would be preached to the ends of the world. Today we rejoice that Your promise is being fulfilled in so many places, like China and Ethiopia. Blessed with the Gospel in America for so many years, let us not become complacent in faith. Keep our faith strong and guide us to winsome ways to invite more people to regular worship. Amen.

April 14

The Blessings of Disappointment

The Titanic hit an iceberg on this date in 1912. That ship, heralded as unsinkable, couldn't even complete one voyage. Do a quick memory check of other failures in the years since the Titanic sunk. In 1937, the great German airship Hindenburg went down in flames in New Jersey. In 1979, there was a nuclear disaster at Three Mile Island in Pennsylvania, and the world's worst nuclear disaster occurred in Chernobyl in 1986. Also in 1986, the space shuttle Challenger exploded shortly after takeoff, and in 2003 shuttle Columbia blew apart during its descent to earth. How many product recalls have there been over the years? How many lawsuits because of accidents from defective design or manufacturing? Did you ever own a Corvair? "Unsafe at any speed" was the way Ralph Nader dubbed it.[1]

The list could go on, but here's the point: The last century has taught us that science and technology are not infallible. We've become skeptical, and we've become skeptical about other things. The inevitable progress of humanity? How about two world wars, the Holocaust, and other genocides? The blessings of big central government? We're skeptical about that too. The institutional church? Our critics point to sexual scandals, accommodation to culture, fiscal misman-agement, hypocrisies, irrelevance... Here's what it comes to: We've seen too much to be trusting. We've had a century of putting our hopes in something or other, only to see our hopes dashed.

What a great blessing such disappointment can be! Our skepticism brings into clear focus what it means to trust Jesus Christ – to have, using the religious word, "faith." Can we prove to every skeptic that the promises of Jesus Christ are true? No, but that's what faith is, hanging on to Christ and to the words of His promises, sometimes in spite of what we see and experience. "We walk by faith, not by sight" (2 Corinthians 5:7).

For further reflection: Luke 13:1-5 – Tragedies, repentance, Jesus

O all-embracing Mercy, / O ever-open Door,
What shall I do without You / When heart and eye run o'er?
When all things seem against us, / To drive us to despair,
We know one gate is open, / One ear will hear our prayer.[2]

April 15

Rendering

Jesus says, "render to Caesar the things that are Caesar's, and to God the things that are God's" (Matthew 22:21). Today we're getting rendered!

Through most of western history, people have been wary of left-handers. The Greek word for the left is translated "well-named," a euphemism to ward off the evil that people thought was associated with the left hand. The Romans, in contrast, were blunt; the Latin word for the left hand is "sinister." Today we often regard government as sinister, especially when Uncle reaches deep into our pockets.

Interestingly, in theology the government is sometimes referred to as the "Kingdom of the Left." (The Church is God's "Kingdom of the Right.") That reference is not a slam. While no form of government or administration is perfect, the Bible makes clear that God intends government to bless our earthly life. Government "is God's servant for your good" (Romans 13:4).

So today we "render to Caesar," which means to give government their due (and maybe more!). We render to the Kingdom of the Left with prayer that it will fulfill its God-given purpose. And since the word "render" also means to melt down fat by heating, like rendering lard, it will be a mature reflection if today's 1040 burns down our expectations about all the government should be doing for us... burns it down to the lean truth about government in the Bible: "Rulers are not a terror to good conduct but to bad" (Romans 13:3).

For further reflection: 1 Samuel 8 – The weight of government on godly people

Continue, Lord Jesus, to teach Your people to know our left from our right. Give us delight and joy in our heavenly citizenship, the Kingdom of the Right. Help us do our duty to our fellow citizens, with whom we live in the Kingdom of the Left. May the faith that Your Spirit nurtures in us by Word and Sacrament make us good citizens and willing workers in our community and nation. Amen.

April 16

Out of Crumbling Circumstances, Resurrection!

Years ago I was in a field with a friend who is a farmer. He picked up a clod of dirt, played with it in his hand, and said, "Not yet." He explained that when dirt will crumble easily in his hand, then it's time to plow and plant. An illustration there: When you feel that your life is crumbling, it's the time when God will plant big spiritual growth into your outlook on life.

Martin Luther wrote about God's goodness, "The comfort is too great and the joy too glorious and the heart of man too small and narrow to have attained it."[1] How hard for us to know the comfort and the joy of God when our circumstances are crumbling!

That's the right time – when passages from God's Word can plant hope in our crumbled circumstances. "When the cares of my heart are many, your consolations cheer my soul" (Psalm 94:19). Then we learn that God really means *all* – not some, but *all*. "And we know that for those who love God all things work together for good, for those who are called according to his purpose" (Romans 8:28). So Luther concluded, "Through suffering, we may finally succeed and attain this heart and cheer, joy and consolation, from Christ's resurrection."[2] Out of crumbling circumstances, new life, resurrection!

For further reflection: John 6:60-69 – "Lord, to whom shall we go?"

In Thee, Lord, have I put my trust; / Leave me not helpless in the dust,
Let me not be confounded. / Let in Thy Word
My faith, O Lord, / Be always firmly grounded.[3]   Amen.

April 17

All Need Grace!

"Opa, I have a question."

"Connor, what is it?"

"When it's time to eat, my brother Christian says, 'It's time to say grace, guys; come on!' He learned prayers at preschool. He thinks it's his job to make sure we pray. So Christian makes us sit and pay attention. 'OK,' he says. 'I'm going to say grace. Sit down everybody. No spitting or talking while I say grace, OK, guys? If there's spitting or hitting, I'll stop the prayer, OK?' Then Christian prays."

"Opa, what do I do? I put my chin on my folded hands. *Just get on with it*, I think. The other day I looked at Mommy and rolled my eyes. When Christian paused to take a breath, I said, 'Amen. Eat!'"

"That's interesting, Connor. What's your question?"

"All that talking that Christian does – does that mean he's a better Christian than I am? Are the best Christians the ones who talk the most?"

"Connor, God made all kinds of people. Some people like to talk more than others. We shouldn't confuse a person's personality with a person's faith. Our Father in heaven says, *I judge people by what is in their hearts* (cf. 1 Samuel 16:7)."

For further reflection: Matthew 6:5-8 – Short or long, be sincere

To Thee our wants are known, / From Thee are all our pow'rs;
Accept what is Thine own / And pardon what is ours.
Our praises, Lord, and prayers receive / And to Thy Word a blessing give.[1]
Amen.

April 18

Now, but Not Yet

When bad things happen, you don't need a million Bible passages or confusing theologians to help you cope; you just need one or two basic truths. Over the centuries, the Church has drawn from Scripture some basic principles that can help you understand real life in a way that is faithful to God's promises. One such principle is "now, but not yet." Now we know the good things God has promised those who love Him, but do we have them? Sometimes not yet; sometimes the promises await fulfillment in heaven.

Every spring, tornadoes, floods, and extreme weather destroy homes, property, and lives across the country. "Now, but not yet" gives you a way to cope with the tragedy. Jesus stood up in a boat and told the wind and waves to be still; they quieted down (Matthew 8:26-27). He is the Lord of nature, but do we always see that? No, not yet. Maybe the winds haven't died down – not yet. Maybe the flood waters haven't begun to recede – not yet. Maybe your home hasn't been restored from the damage – not yet. So we have the promise of a perfect creation, but do we see it now? No, not yet (see Romans 8:18-25). Our trust in the heavenly Father yearns for the day when all the good things of God will be here and now.

> I waited patiently for the LORD; he inclined to me and heard my cry.
> He drew me up from the pit of destruction, out of the miry bog,
> and set my feet upon a rock, making my steps secure.
> He put a new song in mouth, a song of praise to our God. …
> Blessed is the man who makes the LORD his trust. (Psalm 40:1-4)

For further reflection: Mark 4:35-41 – Not trusting Jesus to calm the storm

In all the strife / Of mortal life / Our feet shall stand securely;
Temptation's hour / Will lose its pow'r, / For You will guard us surely.
O God, renew, / With heav'nly dew / Our body, soul, and spirit
Until we stand / At Your right hand / Through Jesus' saving merit.[1]   *Amen.*

April 19

Happily Ever After?

Some seminarians were telling me what they hope to do when they become ministers in congregations. Between the lines I heard them saying that they would arrive at their new churches, analyze what needed improvement, lead a change toward the better, and all would live happily ever after.

When I became the pastor of a congregation, I'd occasionally seek counsel from an older pastor, Rev. Henry Kuring. One time I was complaining that there always seemed to be some problem or other going on in the church. Henry laughed. "That's what the ministry is," he said, "one brushfire after another." So we won't live happily ever after?

Ministry reflects life, and in life bad things regularly happen. On this date, April 19, 1995, 168 people died in the bombing of the Alfred P. Murrah Federal Building in Oklahoma City. Since that day, evil has struck too many times, the bombing at the Boston Marathon one of the more recent terrible installments.

Jesus promises heaven to His followers, a promise that grows more meaningful with each experience of evil. "I saw a new heaven and a new earth … God himself will be with them as their God. He will wipe away every tear from their eyes and death shall be no more, neither shall there be mourning, nor crying, nor pain anymore, for the former things have passed away" (Revelation 21:1, 3-4).

Yes, ministry reflects life, and, dear seminarians, give your people life in all its abundance (John 10:10). Follow the example of Paul and Barnabas. They strengthened "the souls of the disciples, encouraging them to continue in the faith, and saying that through many tribulations we must enter the kingdom of God" (Acts 14:22). Hang your heart on Jesus' promise, "In the world you will have tribulation. But take heart; I have overcome the world" (John 16:33).

For further reflection: Genesis 45:1-15 – Joseph suffered evil but in the end, the sweet land of Goshen for his family

And, Lord, haste the day when the faith shall be sight,
The clouds be rolled back as a scroll,
The trumpet shall sound and the Lord shall descend;
Even so it is well with my soul.[1]   *Amen.*

April 20

Are You Dressed for Your Own Pity Party?

"Answer me when I call, O God of my righteousness!" (Psalm 4:1a). This psalm is a bedtime prayer, and an upset one at that. The psalmist is churning over some interpersonal strife. Whether you're a morning or an evening person, you probably have a time of day when you wear down, grouse because someone's bugging you, and dress for your own pity party.

The psalmist thinks it through. "You have given me relief when I was in distress" (Psalm 4:1b). He bases his prayer upon God's help in the past; just so, you, as a follower of Christ, reflect on past interpersonal conflicts that the Spirit of Christ has turned into reconciliation. "Be gracious to me and hear my prayer!" (Psalm 4:1c). "Help me as Thou hast helped me!"[1]

It's tough when you can't sleep because of interpersonal conflict. I know that personally! "Be angry, and do not sin; ponder in your own hearts on your beds, and be silent" (Psalm 4:4). Could it be that I'm a contributor to the interpersonal problem that has me so churned up? Should I stop tossing and turning now, give it to God in repentance, and resolve to work toward a solution tomorrow? When I'm on my bed, shouldn't I look up and be wrenchingly honest before God? "Offer right sacrifices, and put your trust in the LORD" (Psalm 4:5).

So when you take off your work clothes and get ready for bed, take off any self-righteousness that shows up as self-pity. "Jesus, Thy blood and righteousness / My beauty are, my glorious dress."[2] Then put your head on the pillow with this thought: "In peace I will both lie down and sleep; for you alone, O LORD, make me dwell in safety" (Psalm 4:8).

For further reflection: Proverbs 28:13; Matthew 18:15-20 – Three sides to every conflict: yours, the person's with whom you're upset, and God's

I thank You, my heavenly Father, through Jesus Christ, Your dear Son, that You have graciously kept me this day; and I pray that You would forgive me all my sins where I have done wrong, and graciously keep me this night. For into Your hands I commend myself, my body and soul, and all things. Let Your holy angel be with me, that the evil foe may have no power over me. Amen.[3]

April 21

"How Long, O Lord?"

"Hang in there!" You often hear that when you are suffering, but how do you do that? "Hang in there?" Hospitalization, loss of a loved one, natural disaster, financial ruin, family problems… what are you struggling with now? How do *you* hang in there when your strength and energy – when your will and hope – are almost gone? Almost? Maybe they *are* gone. How do you hang in there? Not easily. In my own experience, I've found that I barely hang on, only by the skin of my teeth. The ancient psalmist complained, "How long, O Lord? Will you forget me forever? How long will you hide your face from me?" (Psalm 13:1).

Complaining to the Lord means that you are going to your best source of help. God is your Creator, and God will prove Himself your Sustainer. "Oh! Had I not believed that I shall look upon the goodness of the Lord in the land of the living! / Wait for the Lord; be strong, and let your heart take courage; wait for the Lord!" (Psalm 27:13-14).

> O all-embracing Mercy, / O ever open Door,
>
> What should I do without You / When heart and eye run o'er?
>
> When all things seem against us, / To drive us to despair,
>
> We know one gate is open, / One ear will hear our prayer.[1]

So when you barely have the strength to hang in there, take it to the Lord, recite His promises, and trust His loving kindnesses to you. Jesus hung in there for you; He's alive, resurrected. Now is your time to hang on Him.

> We do not have a high priest who is unable to sympathize with our weaknesses, but one who in every respect has been tempted as we are, yet without sin. Let us then with confidence draw near to the throne of grace, that we may receive mercy and find grace to help in time of need. (Hebrews 4:15-16)

For further reflection: Psalm 25 – "Turn to me and be gracious to me, for I am lonely and afflicted"

Quiet in God! Whate'er of earthly bliss I am denied, dear Lord, deny not this, That calm, sweet peace that Jesus gives His own who cast their care on Him and Him alone – Quiet in God.[2] Amen.

April 22

The Cathedral of God's Creation

If you think of yourself in a place, where is it? Perhaps a factory? You mechanically crank out widgets – that's what you do – and live for the end of the day and long for retirement. Perhaps a store? You are about stuff – necessary stuff and nice stuff – getting the new in and the old, dated stuff out. Perhaps a country club? Relaxing with friends, playing – that's the essential you! Home? You are warm and welcoming, protective of your relatives. As good as your places may be, is any totally satisfying?

Do those places inspire you, ennoble you, give you a sense of awe that makes your day-to-day tedium and troubles bearable? Is there transcendence in your soul that makes you agree with poet Paul Gerhardt, "No trouble troubles me. / Misfortune now is play, / And night is bright as day"[1]?

On Earth Day, Christians remind ourselves that there is indeed such a place – a place that includes all the places of our lives. It's the cathedral of God's creation. Go outdoors. See the trees – pillars reaching up toward the vault of heaven. Lift up your eyes to the vault adorned with blue, with gray, with dark clouds and lightning. See the lights of the cathedral – the sun, the moon, the stars; windows that teach us. "The heavens declare the glory of God … Day to day pours out speech, and night to night reveals knowledge. / There is no speech, nor are there words, whose voice is not heard" (Psalm 19:1-3). Isn't this *the* place where you live?

And among the smaller places in the cathedral is your earthly church. It's the place where transcendence becomes personal. "God, who said, 'Let light shine out of darkness,' has shone in our hearts to give the light of the knowledge of the glory of God in the face of Jesus Christ" (2 Corinthians 4:6). Without Jesus, creation is capricious. With Jesus, awe. "What is man that you care for him?" (Psalm 8:4). Does your "architecture," like mine, need expansion?

For further reflection: Job 38-39 – Wow!

We praise You, O God, we acknowledge You to be the Lord.
All the earth now worships You, the Father everlasting.[2]   Amen.

April 23

No Waffling!

Many parents choose to let their children grow up without formal church, claiming: *We don't want to impose religion upon them.* "Children learn what they live," as they say, and parental indifference to the specific faith claims of the Church teaches children the same indifference. Oh, parents may say that they'll set an example of spirituality, but personal spirituality is usually unfocused and undisciplined when compared to the faith claims of the Church. Read these questions to confirmands in the Lutheran church.[1] Aren't they specific, permitting no waffling?

"Do you this day in the presence of God and of this congregation acknowledge the gifts that God gave you in your Baptism?" The confirmand answers, "Yes, I do."

"Do you renounce the devil? Do you renounce all his ways? Do you renounce all his works?" "Yes, I do renounce them."

"Do you believe in God, the Father Almighty?" "Do you believe in Jesus Christ, His only Son, our Lord?" "Do you believe in the Holy Spirit?" "Yes, I believe ..."

"Do you intend to hear the Word of God and receive the Lord's Supper faithfully?" "I do, by the grace of God."

"Do you intend to continue steadfast in this confession and Church and to suffer all, even death, rather than fall away from it?" "I do, by the grace of God."

That is not the laissez-faire attitude of popular culture to faith and church! In a 1938 sermon for confirmation, Dietrich Bonhoeffer said,

> Confirmands today are like young soldiers marching to war, the war of Jesus Christ against the gods of this world. It is a war that demands the commitment of one's whole life. Is not God, our Lord, worthy of this struggle? Idolatry and cowardice confront us on all sides, but the direst foe does not confront us, He is within us. "Lord, I believe; help Thou mine unbelief."[2]

For further reflection: "Receive the sign of the holy cross both upon your forehead and upon your heart to mark you as one redeemed by Christ the crucified."[3] Those words marked you and all the baptized for life!

Thine forever, God of Love! / Hear us from Thy throne above;
Thine forever may we be / Here and in eternity!
Thine forever! Shepherd, keep / These Thy frail and trembling sheep;
Safe alone beneath Thy care, / Let us all Thy goodness share.[4]　*Amen.*

April 24

In the Beginning… God

Are you looking forward to some spring yard work this coming weekend? Play some golf? Bike, hike, or jog? Maybe just sit outside after being cooped up inside all winter? Whatever you plan on doing, let me suggest a thought to take with you when you go outdoors.

Before the outdoors came into existence, before the universe came into existence, there was God. "In the beginning, God" (Genesis 1:1). Can you comprehend that? I can't. Before anything existed, there was only God. God… all alone… nothing else existing… only God. God… perfect in Himself… needing no one or anything else… only God. God… who simply is… the great "I AM" (Exodus 3:14). And now this amazing fact: God created something other than Himself. "In the beginning, God created the heavens and the earth" (Genesis 1:1).

Why would He do that? I'm speculating now, but only a bit. He created our world so He could delight in His creation and, getting personal, so He could be with you and me. Religious messages talk about seeking God, but the greater truth is that God seeks *you* and wants to be with *you*. After God had created the world, humans included, He looked at everything He had made and said repeatedly, "it was good" (Genesis 1). God showed it too. Delighting in His creation, He walked in the Garden of Eden in the cool of the day, seeking to be with Adam and Eve (Genesis 3:8).

Believe in godless evolution and you are ultimately an insignificant speck. Believe, on the other hand, that the Creator of the cosmos delights in you, comes to you personally in His Son, Jesus, who died, rose, and gives you His Spirit to guide and direct you – imagine that, you! – and you'll experience a *Wow, I matter*, awe of God! After winter, spring is so welcome. Outside to enjoy creation and life! Take this idea outdoors with you: "In the beginning, God."

For further reflection: Psalm 33 – "The eye of the LORD is on those who fear him"

Immortal, invisible, God only wise, / In light inaccessible hid from our eyes, Most blessèd, most glorious, the Ancient of Days, / Almighty, victorious, Thy great name we praise.[1]

April 25

The Living Voice of the Gospel

Let's start with free association. What do you think when I say, "Word of God?" You might very well think of the Bible, the book many of us greatly revere. Truth is, we severely limit the "Word of God" when we identify it only with printed words on pages in a book. An old Latin expression puts it more truly – *viva vox evangelii*, the living voice of the Gospel. "The word of God is living and active" (Hebrews 4:12). "The words that I have spoken to you are spirit and life" (John 6:63).

When Johannes Gutenberg invented movable type in the fifteenth century, the Word of God became increasingly identified with a printed book. The wide distribution of Bibles was a blessing, no doubt. But today we forget that the Word was originally shared orally, read and presented in public gatherings, passed from generation to generation through memory, truly a living voice.

For several years, I've been part of a special project at Concordia Seminary. Five of us memorized the entire Gospel of Mark and have presented all 16 chapters in St. Louis and beyond. The discipline of memorizing has been an eye-opener for us. In memorizing the Gospel, we have been forced to imagine what the events were like. In memorizing such long sections (I had 127 verses to memorize), we see themes and emphases that are hard to catch when simply reading the book. We better understand how people first received the Gospel: sitting, seeing, and hearing someone deliver it orally. So the point is this: Don't let the Word of God in your life be bound by a Gutenberg captivity. Those are thoughts for today, the "Day of St. Mark, Evangelist."

For further reflection: Psalm 119:9-16 – How many Bible passages are in your memory?

For Mark, O Lord, we praise You, / The weak by grace made strong,
Whose labors and whose Gospel / Enrich our triumph song.
May we, in all our weakness, / Reflect Your servant life
And follow in Your footsteps, / Enduring cross and strife.[1]   *Amen.*

April 26

"Either Way … I'll Be Home"

Lil was on her deathbed when I visited her. A lifelong, active member of our church, she knew her Savior. Lil didn't appear conscious, wasn't speaking, but I was taught always to pray because the patient might very well hear what you're saying. I prayed and then went into the Lord's Prayer in German. She did hear! Her lips started moving and she prayed in German with me. Hospital visits like that bolster a pastor's faith.

Visiting Roger is a dear memory as well. Roger also was well along in years and the prognosis was not good. He was alert, and so we talked about the Christian's confidence in heaven. I said it's OK to let go and let God bring you home. Those words brought a visible change to Roger's face, a visible peace. He simply needed to hear that Christian death is a transition to everlasting life; it's OK to let go. A day or so later he passed on.

Louise was another visit I remember, even now over 25 years later. When I walked into the hospital room, the family was present; they had been called in. I took Louise's hand and began to pray. While I was praying, I sensed by her hand that her heart had stopped. She had entered eternity with prayer. A sequel: A church member heard of her death during my prayer. He joked, "Pastor, if I'm in the hospital, please don't come and pray with me!"

He was joking because people of faith want their hand held, want to hear words of hope, need an undivided heart toward Jesus as they begin, as we begin, the journey "through the valley of the shadow of death" (Psalm 23:4). Don was much younger when he went in for serious heart surgery. Don said, "Pastor, either way when I wake up, I'll be home."

"'What no eye has seen, nor ear heard, nor the heart of man imagined, / what God has prepared for those who love him' – these things God has revealed to us through the Spirit" (1 Corinthians 2:9-10).

For further reflection: Psalm 23 – "Thou art with me" (KJV)

When at last I near the shore, / And the fearful breakers roar
'Twixt me and the peaceful rest, / Then, while leaning on Thy breast,
May I hear Thee say to me, / "Fear not, I will pilot thee."[1]   *Amen.*

April 27

God's Intermediaries Serve and Protect

This book was published several months after civil unrest and rioting in Ferguson, Missouri. When this book is old, there will surely be unrest in other cities and states. State police, National Guard, local and national media, they'll all be there, wherever "there" will be. But where's God?

Let's think this through. First, none of us sees God. John 1:18 – "No one has ever seen God." Why? "Man shall not see me and live" (Exodus 33:20). God's hiddenness is actually God's care for our lives.

Second, we still want to believe God is somehow present for good. Again the Bible is filled with promises, like Hebrews 13:5 – "I will never leave you nor forsake you."

Somehow then, God must be working behind the scenes, working through intermediaries. Government "is God's servant for your good. But if you do wrong, be afraid, for he does not bear the sword in vain" (Romans 13:4). Police, National Guard, elected authorities… God's behind them… and wants them to do justice. Notice, that's all external: coercion, force. Tear gas and handcuffs don't change the heart.

What changes the heart is the Spirit of God through the Word – what occupies us in church and in our devotion during the week. Paul says we should pray for authorities, "that we may lead a peaceful and quiet life, godly and dignified in every way. This is good, and it is pleasing in the sight of God our Savior, who desires all people to be saved to come to the knowledge of the truth" (1 Timothy 2:2-4).

Unseen, God is present. Things will get better when we all see that we are God's intermediaries for His will to be done in our troubled world.

For further reflection: James Madison: "What is government itself, but the greatest of all reflections on human nature? If men were angels, no government would be necessary. If angels were to govern men, neither external nor internal controls on government would be necessary. … You must first enable the government to control the governed; and in the next place oblige it to control itself."[1]

Martin Luther says "Daily bread includes … devout and faithful rulers, good government, good weather, peace…"[2] With government and governed in mind, pray to our Father who art in heaven.

April 28

"Forth in Thy Name, O Lord, I Go"

God said to Abraham, "Go from your country and your kindred and your father's house to the land that I will show you." Abraham didn't say, "Let me check it out and I'll get back to you." The Bible simply says, "So Abram went" (Genesis 12: 1, 4).

Spring days bring "Call Day" to the campus of Concordia Seminary, the day when our concluding students are told where God through the Church is sending them to serve as pastors and deaconesses. The students will line up in chapel, step forward one by one, and hear where in the country or the world they are being sent as they receive their first "calls" into ministry. Some have an inkling where they might be sent, those headed for team ministries, but no one knows for sure and most have no clue. It is a very real demonstration of putting oneself into the service of God – faith being put into action.

Jesus says to you and me, "If anyone would come after me, let him deny himself and take up his cross daily and follow me. For whoever would save his life will lose it, but whoever loses his life for my sake will save it" (Luke 9:23-24). You may not be called to move to an unknown land, but is your faith ready to venture into service today for Him? How will you respond if the Lord puts some person or some challenge before you that you had not included in your plan for today? "So Abram went."

For further reflection: Isaiah 6:1-8 – Forgiven, "Here I am! Send me."

Forth in Thy name, O Lord, I go, / My daily labor to pursue,
Thee, only Thee, resolved to know / In all I think or speak or do.[1]   *Amen.*

April 29

Last In, First Out

"Last in, first out." That's one of the perks of being Seminary president when "Call Day" comes and our students learn where the Church is sending them. The announcements happen in a festive service, joyous but anxious for students and their families, and the presidential perk is that I'm the last one to process in for the service but the first one to recess out. When I walk out, I head straight up to the balcony so that I can watch the students, calls in hand, walk out two-by-two.

They are going into a world they do not know and into experiences they cannot imagine. Some go with maturity; others have maturing ahead of them. Their average age is in the very early 30s. Some are A+ students but will need to learn better interpersonal skills. Others may not be good at parsing Greek or Hebrew but do have emotional intelligence, a characteristic of a good pastor. Some have seriously heavy student debts and are worried. Others have middling debts, and a few have none. I watch them walk out of the chapel and think of all the interactions I've had with them during their time here. But most of all I pray that they more and more consciously follow Jesus Christ. They know it already in their heads, that they can't put their faith in a seminary or in the institutional church or in their own abilities, good as they may be. They're walking out to experience sin and grace in the depth of their souls, and in that experience to be reminded that faith has no other resort than Jesus Christ. Looking down from the balcony, I admit that I get a bit teary-eyed. I also wish I were a young man again, walking out into life and ministry.

"Last in, first out" also happens to be the goal of people who go to church grudgingly. May these new pastors keep walking – walking in their communities, walking among their people – so that when Sunday comes more and more people will say, "I was glad when they said to me, 'Let us go to the house of the LORD!'" (Psalm 122:1).

For further reflection: Psalm 37 – An old man offers insights for a life of faith

Lord God, You have called Your servants to ventures of which we cannot see the ending, by paths as yet untrodden, through perils unknown. Give us faith to go out with good courage, not knowing where we go but only that Your hand is leading us and Your love supporting us; through Jesus Christ, our Lord.[1] *Amen.*

April 30

A Prompt to Prayer

Yesterday afternoon I worshipped at the shrine of the rain gauge.

My parents didn't teach me a reverence for the rain gauge. I don't remember if we even had one. The only thing I recall from my childhood about rain was wearing that heavy yellow slicker that made me sweat, and having to play indoors. Rain was just not an occasion of worship.

Years later I arrived at my first call in rural Southern Illinois, a dual parish in Venedy and New Memphis. Roy Martens asked, "How much rain did you get last night?" "I dunno." "Didn't you check your rain gauge?" "Don't have one." Stunned silence. *No rain gauge? How's he going to fit in here? He might have book learning but how can he appreciate God's creation if he doesn't have a rain gauge?* That was the beginning of my slow conversion to the rain gauge. Seminarians, if you're assigned to a rural church, don't arrive without your Bible and a rain gauge! "Pastor, how much rain did you get at your house?" When they know you've got one, you'll be more believable when you talk about faith.

That's written only partly tongue-in-cheek. Ask people in drought-stricken areas of the United States if they'd like to check the gauge to see how much rain the Lord gave them. The "shrine of the rain gauge" is your place to thank the Creator of all for the rain through which He sustains physical life. God "does great things and unsearchable, marvelous things without number: / he gives rain on the earth and sends waters on the fields" (Job 5:9-10).

Now in the city, Diane and I have a nice rain gauge from Northrup King near our patio, a gift from our friend Rev. Jeff Schanbacher. Yes, it's a shrine, a prompt to prayer. "Sing to the LORD with thanksgiving … / He covers the heavens with clouds; he prepares rain for the earth" (Psalm 147:7-8). What do you have in your yard to remind you to thank the Lord for sustaining your physical life?

For further reflection: Acts 14:15-17 – Rain is a witness to God

Are there any among the false gods of the nations that can bring rain? Or can the heavens give showers? / Are you not he, O LORD our God? We set our hope on you, for you do all these things. (Jeremiah 14:22)   Amen.

May 1

Limits of Love

"Hi, my name is Jacob. I am one year old, number four on the *Reflection* writing team. I am doing research. I have a question for you big people. Do you ever get stopped?

"I visited Oma and Opa's last weekend. I toddled all over the place. Toddled after balls. Throw a ball and go get it. But sometimes my toddling was stopped. Oma put a fence by the stairs to stop me. Where there's a will, there's a way. So I toddled another direction but still got swooped up. When we went to the store, Oma held my hand so I couldn't toddle wherever I wanted. Why can't I go wherever I want? Why can't I do whatever I want? When I get big like you, will I be able to do whatever I want?"

"Opa here. Good question, Jake. There are some places big people shouldn't go – things big people shouldn't do. When God came down on Mount Sinai, He told Moses to set limits so the people would not be hurt (Exodus 19:12). Then God said, 'Thou shalt' and 'Thou shalt not.' Big people call that God's Law. God gave the Law for the good of the people He loves. Jacob, you got stopped and swooped up because you're loved. God loves big people and doesn't want us to toddle into trouble. He tells us our limits because He loves us."

For further reflection: Psalm 119:9-16 – "In the way of your testimonies I delight"

Tender Shepherd, never leave them / From Thy fold to go astray;
By Thy warning love directed, / May they walk the narrow way!
Thus direct them, thus defend them, / Lest they fall an easy prey.[1]   *Amen.*

May 2

All in on a Long Shot

What are the odds? The odds for some horses in the Kentucky Derby will be good, but for other horses the odds will be so long that the horse's mother probably wouldn't bet on him.

The Bible has references aplenty to the power and the beauty of horses. Like Derby horses prancing to run, Job 39:21-22 says the horse "paws in the valley and exults in his strength … He laughs at fear and is not dismayed." Jeremiah 4:13 talks about "horses … swifter than eagles."

Such a surprise then that the prophet Zechariah says, "Rejoice greatly, O daughter of Zion! … your king is coming to you; righteous and having salvation is he, / humble and mounted on a donkey" (9:9). Is that why Jesus rode into Jerusalem on Palm Sunday on a donkey, to contrast His humility to a world that fawns over strength and beauty?

In Revelation 19:11 the heavenly Christ is pictured splendidly on a white horse … but He rides that horse *after* He rode the donkey. The crown comes after the cross. The Lord's "delight is not in the strength of the horse … but the LORD takes pleasure in those who fear him, in those who hope in his steadfast love" (Psalm 147:10-11).

Imagine betting on a jockey who rides a donkey? What really are the odds?

For further reflection: Philippians 2:5-11 – Cross before exaltation

Sooner or later, merciful Lord, You deliver our eyes from tears and our feet from stumbling. Help me use my weakness as an occasion to pray for Your enabling grace. Give me patient trust that You will bestow the crown after I've faithfully run the race. Give me a heart that rejoices in my weakness, not despite my weakness. For Your sake, dear Jesus! Amen.

May 3

"…Unless Someone Guides Me"

"Now an angel of the Lord said to Philip, 'Rise and go toward the south to the road that goes down from Jerusalem to Gaza.'" So Philip obediently went and came upon an Ethiopian government official who also was heading away from Jerusalem. "The Spirit said to Philip, 'Go over and join this chariot.'" He did, and took it from there – no further instructions needed. Seeing the Ethiopian reading a scroll of the prophet Isaiah, Philip asked, "Do you understand what you're reading?" "'How can I, unless someone guides me?' And he invited Philip to come up and sit with him." Philip began with the Isaiah text and told the Good News of Jesus. (Acts 8:26-40)

Imagine that story today. While "the Ethiopian" is being chauffeured or is making their own way on a busy sidewalk, they are absorbed in their cell phone or tablet, talking or answering e-mails. It's possible that they are scrolling through Isaiah or the Bible, but then again they might be into Islam or Hinduism or Facebook or CNBC checking stocks or whatever. There's no end of possibilities to keep all our faces focused on the screen. And what's our modern day "Philip" doing? By the way, that's you; that's me. You're close by, but absorbed in your own e-mail or Twitter or Facebook or listening to music with buds in your ear, whatever… and you never make contact with that person. Never make face-to-face contact! You know that's true because every day you and I meet people on the sidewalk with their faces in a screen and they never notice us, and maybe you're absorbed and never notice them. How can we share the hope that is in us if we don't *go* – a Great Commission word – and get out of our devices in public and make human con-tact?

For further reflection: Acts 20:17-38 – Face-to-face

Savior, shine in all Thy glory / On the nations near and far;
From the highways and the byways call them, / O Thou Morning Star.
Guide them whom Thy grace hath chosen / Out of Satan's dreadful thrall
To the mansions of Thy Father – / There is room for sinners all.[1]   *Amen.*

May 4

The Presumptuous Idolatry of Self

Deep, deep down I've got this feeling that I'm almost always right. For example, if my boss asks me to account for something I've done, I've got an answer. Sometimes survival instincts tell me to keep my mouth shut, but that's only a façade. True, there are a few minutes on Sunday morning when I set my self-justification aside, in the confession and absolution part of the church service. At that time, I put my head down and say what a miserable sinner I am. "You are forgiven" come the expected words from the ritual, my head pops up and my deep-seated instinct again takes control. Are all people like this?

I suspect so. The most basic question the Bible puts to us is whom do you love and trust above all else? Martin Luther wrote, "To have a god is nothing else than to trust and believe in that one with your whole heart … it is the trust and faith of the heart alone that make both God and an idol."[1] Who is your God?

The One who created you and me also judges us. "I the LORD search the heart and test the mind, / to give every man according to his ways, according to the fruit of his deeds" (Jeremiah 17:10). A person in recovery strives to get past self-justification. I do believe in the God who reveals Himself in the Bible, but I keep defaulting to myself as god. "Keep back your servant also from presumptuous sins; let them not have dominion over me!" (Psalm 19:13). How presumptuous, to put my faith and trust first and foremost in myself!

The true God is not only our creator and judge; He also rescues us from our presumptuous idolatry of self. "I have been crucified with Christ. It is no longer I who live, but Christ who lives in me. And the life I now live in the flesh I live by faith in the Son of God, who loved me and gave himself for me" (Galatians 2:20).

For further reflection: Deuteronomy 6:1-9 – God or an idol?

Grant that I only You may love / And seek those things which are above
Till I behold You face to face, / O Light eternal, through Your grace.[2]
Amen.

May 5

¡Buenas Noticias!

I'd pronounce it wrong, I'm sure. "*¡Cuidado! Piso Mojado.*" More and more we see signs in English and Spanish. This increasing bilingualism is new for me, just like *Cinco de Mayo* is something I didn't know existed until a few years ago. It's not a big deal in Mexico but this commemoration of a Mexican victory over the French on May 5, 1862 has taken on a life of its own in the United States.

It's easy to dismiss other languages, but language is the vehicle God has chosen to bring us His Good News in Jesus Christ. Vowels, consonants, subjects and objects, grammar, syntax … words … and words not originally in English.

People sometimes say we can't be sure what the Bible means because it's been translated so many times from ancient Hebrew and Greek. Nonsense! That sign, "*¡Cuidado! Piso Mojado.*" is translated: "Caution! Wet Floor." Just to be sure the truth is known, the sign also carries a drawing of a man slipping and falling. Truth can be known and it's coming to our world in many languages. Ignore God's words or take them for granted and the slip and fall will be terrible. Heed the translated truth and there will be an eternal festival coming your way! *¡Buenas Noticias!*

For further reflection: Hebrews 10:26-39 – "fearful … to fall into the hands of the living God"

Blessed Lord, You have caused all Holy Scriptures to be written for our learning. Grant that we may so hear them, read, mark, learn, and take them to heart that, by the patience and comfort of Your holy Word, we may embrace and ever hold fast the blessed hope of everlasting life; through Jesus Christ, Your Son, our Lord, who lives and reigns with You and the Holy Spirit, one God, now and forever. Amen.[1]

May 6

Coming in Fast and Filled with Hydrogen

The news regularly brings us the heartbreak of man-made disasters. On this date in 1937, the airship Hindenburg caught fire and crashed in Lakehurst, New Jersey. "Oh, the humanity!" cried out Herbert Morrison, reporting for WLS Radio, Chicago. Cars are recalled because design flaws result in deaths. A bridge collapses because of metal fatigue. Because of design flaws the explosion of the space shuttle is burned into our memories. Wherever man has built structures and machines, some fail and bring injury and death.

Luke 13 tells about the failure of a man-made structure. Jesus asked, "Or those eighteen on whom the tower in Siloam fell and killed them: do you think that they were worse offenders than all the others who lived in Jerusalem? No, I tell you; but unless you repent, you will all likewise perish" (Luke 13:4-5). We might imagine that we're good with God and therefore should be spared accident; that's what many religious people believed when Jesus walked among sinners, but it doesn't work that way. No matter how well I live, how truly I believe, and how careful I am, an accident may be just around the corner.

That should put a wholesome fear of God in us. Not a servile, cowering fear, dread that something terrible is about to happen, but reverent awe before God who "will command his angels concerning you to guard you in all your ways" (Psalm 91:11). When our kids go off on their own, pray God send His angels to protect them. When we step out in the morning, turn on the ignition to go to work, pray God that His angels commute with you. Accidents that result from design or human failure will still come because we are all fallible sinners – every one of us. Confidence in our technology notwithstanding, we will always be vulnerable creatures. Daily repentance points us to life eternal.

Through many dangers, toils and snares, / I have already come;

His grace has brought me safe thus far, / His grace will lead me home.[1]

For further reflection: John 9 ("All have sinned" - Romans 3:23) **– The self-righteous don't get it**

Not the labors of my hands / Can fulfill Thy Law's demands;
Could my zeal no respite know, / Could my tears forever flow,
All for sin could not atone; / Thou must save, and Thou alone.[2]   *Amen.*

May 7

Prayers for Our Nation

O eternal God, You sit mysteriously in the highest heavens but assure us of Your interest in our earthly lives. You have instituted governments for the good of all people. During these days when many Americans observe the National Day of Prayer, we must ask ourselves, where can we turn for help except to You, O Lord – You who are displeased with us because of our sins? Can entrenched interests turn America? Can political partisanship that seeks its own good more than the common welfare turn America? Is there hope if citizens dismiss reasoned discussion of the common good in favor of our own entitlements? The grave issues facing us will, we pray, make us humble in heart, cooperative in political conversation, and intent upon wise stewardship of this nation during our time for the sake of all who will come after us. If we must be further divided and broken in order that America become a repentant people in whom righteousness flourishes, then so be it. Should that be our prospect in the next years, then we beg that Your Spirit comfort us even as we learn the hard lesson that the chastening is for our good and only in You is our hope and continued life.

Give to all our leaders, especially to the President and Congress, wisdom beyond their own insights. Make their rooms large enough for partisan friends and foes alike. Unless You, O Lord, build the house, we labor in vain to build it. Unless You keep the nation, our leaders watch in vain (Psalm 127:1). We ask this for America, not according to our merits but according to Your mercy, through Jesus Christ. Amen.

For further reflection: Esther 4 – "For such a time as this"

He rules the world with truth and grace / And makes the nations prove
The glories of His righteousness / And wonders of His love[1]
Lord, so we sing at Christmas. Are we letting Your truth and grace have full sway, and are Your righteousness and love demonstrated together by our life? Lead us to true repentance and sincere amendment of life. For Jesus' sake. Amen.

May 8

Above the Chaos, a Higher Perspective

Every spring the snow melts in the Upper Midwest and people living downstream prepare for the Mississippi River to rise and maybe overflow its banks. Levees, sandbags, shelters… you see those pictures on the news. I suggest adding the picture of stilts.

When you think of floods in the Bible, the Great Flood of Noah comes immediately to mind (Genesis 6-9). If you start concentrating on whether it really happened or not – on finding the ark and the like – you easily get off track. Such inquiries and debates can be helpful, but they aren't the main thing on which to focus. More important is the chaos of a flood, the chaos that overwhelms the order we need to live. Biblical religion teaches that our Creator and Sustainer restrains the chaos. "The waters stood above the mountains. / At your rebuke they fled; at the sound of your thunder they took to flight. / The mountains rose, the valleys sank down to the place that you appointed for them. / You set a boundary that they may not pass" (Psalm 104:6-9). When the waters do pass their boundaries, one sure reason is that the world, nature included, continues to rebel against God's good order.

So levees, sandbags, boats… and stilts. Diane and I have lived all our married life in the St. Louis region – big time river country. The congregations we first served were divided by the Kaskaskia River, a tributary of the Mississippi. In the bottom lands near the river, it's common to see some homes and cabins built on stilts. When the floods come, as they must in our still fallen world, the house on stilts offers safety and a different perspective. So it can be with faith. "The LORD sits enthroned over the flood; the LORD sits enthroned as king forever" (Psalm 29:10). Like stilts, faith gives a higher perspective on our momentary problems. Should you be struggling now with chaos, we pray for you the hope that order will soon be restored.

For further reflection: Genesis 8:20-22 – After the flood

His oath, His covenant and blood / Support me in the whelming flood;
When ev'ry earthly prop gives way, / He then is all my hope and stay.
On Christ, the solid rock, I stand; / All other ground is sinking sand.[1]

May 9

Is Your Transmitter Turned On?

Years ago I preached for my friend, Pastor Jim Rogers, and found a telling typo in a song printed in the worship folder: "My Savior, my closet friend." Is Jesus your closet friend or your closest friend?

Another friend, Paul Clayton, used to begin the broadcast day for Christian radio station KFUO (850 AM, St. Louis, Missouri). Paul told me he once signed on early in the morning, still dark outside, and began the broadcast day by playing Christian songs, giving weather and news, and talking about the Christian faith. Sometime later, a regular listener called the studio: "Paul, have you turned on the transmitter?" Whoops! Transmitter off; no Christian message going out.

Is Jesus your closet friend or your closest friend? And if He's your closest friend, is your transmitter turned on, ready to share the hope that is in you?

After Pentecost, Peter and John were "broadcasting" the Good News about Jesus throughout Jerusalem. That upset the religious establishment, who hauled them into headquarters and told them to stop. To that, Peter and John said, "Whether it is right in the sight of God to listen to you rather than to God, you must judge, for we cannot but speak of what we have seen and heard" (Acts 4:19-20). Where did they get the courage to say that? From Jesus, their closest friend. "No longer do I call you servants … but I have called you friends, for all that I have heard from my Father I have made known to you" (John 15:15).

You may well be a quieter person than Peter and John, but in your own way you can tell people about your closest friend. That starts every morning by turning on the "transmitter," holy living that will make people want to hear what you have to share. "In your hearts revere Christ as Lord. Always be prepared to give an answer to everyone who asks you to give the reason for the hope that you have. But do this with gentleness and respect" (1 Peter 3:15 NIV).

For further reflection: Acts 4; 5:12-29 – The whole story of their boldness

Ashamed of Jesus, that dear Friend, / On whom my hopes of heav'n depend?
No; when I blush, be this my shame, / That I no more revere His name.[1]

May 10

A Mother's Love

Years ago, over 25, a March day I think, I set out to drive to my mom's house in Chicago. When it started to snow, Interstate 57 quickly became packed with snow and slick, really slick. Bitter cold winds were blowing across the open farm fields, blowing so hard that some semis were swept into the ditch. Traffic crept along at five miles an hour. Exit ramps were treacherous, so I couldn't turn around. I couldn't call anyone – no cell phones then. I was scared, white knuckles on the steering wheel… and I got angry. My mother's a stickler for being on time. I was angry about the tongue-lashing I was sure to get.

What should have been a four-hour trip turned into a ten-hour ordeal. All that time I sharpened my tongue to answer every conceivable criticism for being late. I convinced myself that I could answer anything, answer whatever she might throw at me with a sharp, edgy comeback. So when I finally pulled into her driveway, I was ready for her, or so I thought. She came running at me, tears pouring down her cheeks, gave me a big hug, and sobbing, gasping for air, she said, "I thought something had happened to you." I wasn't ready for a mother's love.

Scared, angry, defensive… Because we easily forget that we are loved, we observe Mother's Day to thank God for His love through our mothers.

> Now thank we all our God / With hearts and hands and voices,
> Who wondrous things has done, / In whom His world rejoices;
> Who from our mother's arms / Has blest us on our way
> With countless gifts of love / And still is ours today.[1]

For further reflection: Isaiah 66:7-14 – A mother's love reflects God's love for His Church

Such care for us, dear Father, when You instituted the family and created motherhood! Through faithful mothers You give us Your loving kindnesses. Make us thankful beyond words so that our lives and devotion will tell our mothers how much we love them and thank You for them. Amen.

May 11

A Place of Honor

"You can't judge a book by its cover." That's especially true about your parents.

"Honor your father and your mother," God says (Exodus 20:12). Honor. Not "love" or "obey," though the Bible teaches that we should also give our parents love and obedience. "Honor."

Martin Luther wrote about honoring parents.

> To fatherhood and motherhood God has given the special distinction … that He commands us not simply to love our parents but also to honor them. With respect to brothers, sisters, and neighbors in general, He commands nothing higher than that we love them. Thus, He distinguishes father and mother above all other persons on earth, and places them next to Himself. For it is a much greater thing to honor than to love. Honor includes not only love but also deference, humility, and modesty, directed (so to speak) toward a majesty hidden within them. It requires us not only to address them affectionately and reverently, but above all to show by our actions, both of heart and of body, that we respect them very highly and that next to God we give them the very highest place. Young people must therefore be taught to revere their parents as God's representatives.[1]

God gave the Ten Commandments on two tablets (Exodus 32:15). The first group of commandments tells us our duties toward God, leading with "You shall have no other gods before me" (Exodus 20:3). The second group deals with our duties toward our fellow human beings. At the head of that group God put, "Honor your father and your mother." "Next to God we give them the very highest place." You can't judge a book by its cover, but *the book*, God's book, tells us to revere the majesty within our parents.

Of course, this implies that parents understand that they are God's representatives. Of course?

For further reflection: Proverbs 30:17 – A verse we memorized in parochial grade school - it's scary but it helps instill honor toward parents

Help us Your holy Law to learn, / To mourn our sin and from it turn
In faith to You and to Your Son / And Holy Spirit, Three in One.[2]   Amen.

May 12

"Go" Can Be Local

Mani and Aaiti were apprehensive. About to land in St. Louis, eager to be reunited with family members who had already immigrated, they were especially motivated by hope that their three children would have more opportunities in America than in their native Nepal. Still, they were fearful about living in a new country where they didn't know the language. Who will meet them? Who will help them get acclimated? They were met by relatives, by a worker from the International Institute, and by the love of Christ through an organization called Christian Friends of New Americans. CFNA aided them with health and wellness screening, enrolled the children in their after-school tutoring program, and connected Mani and Aaiti to Ascension Lutheran Church. At Ascension, they and their relatives participate in bilingual Bible study, worship, and fellowship. In January 2014, 21 Nepalese were baptized and one adult, a member of their extended family, was confirmed.

The Great Commission tells us, "Go therefore and make disciples of all nations" (Matthew 28:19). "Nations" means people groups. "Go" in the past meant long journeys to far-off countries. That's still needed, but now as never before, "go" can be local – to volunteer with a church or organization that welcomes immigrants to America with the love and care of Jesus. The volunteers of Christian Friends of New Americans were the open arms of Jesus and His Body to Mani and Aaiti and their children, Santosh, Sandip, and Tika.

In the spring of 1922, an architect named Charles Klauder was engaged to design a new campus for Concordia Seminary. Visit the campus or the website and see the monumental Gothic buildings Klauder designed. Are the people in our monumental Gothic churches ready to welcome new people? If the people in your church aren't ready, maybe a field trip to a place like Christian Friends of New Americans would be a good start.

For further reflection: Leviticus 19:33-34; Deuteronomy 10:19-22 – Read these passages in light of the Good Samaritan (Luke 10:25-37)

Dear Lord Jesus, You have broken down the dividing walls of hostility between different peoples by reconciling us all to God through Your cross. Enlarge the welcome of Your Church so that there will be no stranger and alien but together all will be fellow citizens with the saints and members of the household of God. Amen. (Ephesians 2:11-22)

May 13

Empty Nests, Fulfilled Lives

A few years ago my coworker Fred told me that he was going to the graduation of his grandchild from eighth grade. "Do they wear gowns?" I wondered. "Yes," Fred said and then spoke proudly about his grandchild's ability.

While Fred was watching those gowns at his grandchild's graduation, I sat in the yard and watched high school graduates in their gowns process into the Seminary chapel for their baccalaureate service. I started to think about the grief of their parents. Grief comes when you experience a loss… and it's not only on the death of a loved one. When your child graduates from high school, you're beginning to lose a special part of your life. Grief grows by degrees. Diane and I stood silently and watched our oldest daughter, freshly out of law school, leave home to drive, car-loaded, to Washington, D.C. to begin her career. Our house had an emptiness, a grief. "Weeping may remain for a night, but rejoicing comes in the morning" (Psalm 30:5). Both of our daughters have done very well in their careers but what gives us the deepest satisfaction is that they and their families know their Lord and His Church.

"For everything there is a season" (Ecclesiastes 3:1). Like Fred, we can be proud of our graduates, however small or large their gowns. Each time they put on a gown, it's another milestone inviting us to reflect on our passing of God's gifts to the next generation and on our greatest duty in our shortening time of grace. "One generation shall commend your works to another, and shall declare your mighty acts" (Psalm 145:4).

For further reflection: Luke 2:41-52 – Treasuring the Child

Our Father and Father of our Lord Jesus, when we feel loss because our children grow and leave us, give us Your Spirit to pray for them as they venture into their adult lives. By Your Spirit, fill the empty place in our heart with hope for their future because they are, after all, not our children but Yours. Help them trust that You, their Father, will not fail them nor forsake them. Amen.

May 14

Is Your Congregation Stuck in the Past?

You go to Europe and you visit big old cathedrals that are little more than tourist destinations. Some have even been converted into museums. I'm afraid many American Christians have a museum mentality about church. A curious place, focused on the past, the keeper of ancient stories, if you're "into" such things. For them, the truth is that Jesus is "out of sight, out of mind."

Out of sight, yes, but only for a while. On Ascension Day Jesus withdrew His visible presence from human sight, but He isn't gone. It's not like "Elvis has left the building." "I am with you always," He promised (Matthew 28:20). The challenge of Ascension is that "out of sight" does not lure you into "out of mind." Jesus promises to come again. "I will come again and take you to myself" (John 14:3). "Men of Galilee, why do you stand looking into heaven?" the angels asked the disciples. (They must have looked like tourists gawking at an amazing old cathedral!) "This Jesus, who was taken up from you into heaven, will come in the same way as you saw him go into heaven" (Acts 1:10-11). If you and I don't hold that promise close to our hearts, our home churches are indeed likely to become museums of past times, of ancient days when Jesus walked the earth. Without a heart-held trust in Jesus' return, churches are only remnants of those days when people really did take God at His Word. And if you don't go about today with an expectation of Jesus' return, why would you be surprised that you feel faith and church is irrelevant? But go about today knowing that Jesus is coming back, and you'll be filled with a lively hope for today and the future.

This is not to minimize the past. Forgiveness for sin and the hope of resurrection come from past events, but like the eyes in your head, faith looks forward. Are you? "Though you do not now see Him, you believe in Him and rejoice with joy that is inexpressible and filled with glory, obtaining the outcome of your faith, the salvation of your souls" (1 Peter 1:8-9).

For further reflection: Acts 1:6-11 – Gawkers get a promise

You are the way, the truth, the life; / Grant us that way to know,
That truth to keep, that life to win, / Whose joys eternal flow.[1]   *Amen.*

May 15

Heading toward Extinction?

Daughter Elizabeth was talking with three-year-old Christian about what he wants to be when he grows up. Several days later they drove by a church. Here's how the conversation went.

Christian: "Opa pastor at that church?"

Elizabeth: "No, Christian, Opa is at another church. Christian, do you want to be a pastor when you grow up?"

Christian: "No, I want to be a dinosaur."

If the men and women who graduate this month from Concordia Seminary go out only to talk about the past, they'll only be curators of a church museum. True, they'll point out interesting things about long-ago Jesus, but they'll be dinosaurs leading their congregations closer to extinction.

"I the LORD search the heart and test the mind, / to give every man according to his ways, according to the fruit of his deeds" (Jeremiah 17:10). Though spoken long ago, that's present tense; our graduates must present the Word of that searching God so that it is "living and active" to your life today (Hebrews 4:12). The first president of our Seminary, C.F.W. Walther, told seminarians not to "stand in your pulpit with a sad face (as if you were asking people to come to a funeral), but like men who are wooing a bride or who are announcing a wedding."[1] That requires preaching and listening that knows and assents to what happened in Bible times, but that's not saving faith without confidence and trust in God's Gospel work in our lives today. "In Thee, Lord, have I put my trust."[2] Walther: "Write your sermons in such a way that you can say, 'If anyone hears this sermon and is not converted, it is his own fault if he goes home from my church unconverted and hardened.'"[1]

"The church is prepared to face every crisis that arises," my friend told me, and then added, "that arises in 1953." Graduates, woo the people to the heavenly Bridegroom! Grandson Christian will not be a dinosaur when he grows up. Pray that our future church workers won't be either!

For further reflection: 2 Timothy 4:1-5; Titus 2:1-15 – Paul's charge to pastors

The servants Thou hast called / And to Thy Church art giving / Preserve in doctrine pure / And holiness of living. / Thy Spirit fill their hearts, / Endue their tongues with power; / What they should boldly speak, / Oh, give them in that hour![3]   Amen.

May 16

A Prayer for Our Military

Today let us offer prayers to God for the men and women of our armed forces. What oppression, what chaos would be ours were it not for all who served and died on our behalf! Their resolute character, their sacrifice and courage shame so many of our petty pursuits. Dear God, continue to equip every man and woman in uniform with the qualities that preserve peace in our dangerous and hate-filled world.

Let us pray for the families of our military personnel. How worrisome to know that the child you bore and raised, the wife or husband you have embraced, is now far away and in grave danger. Dear God, send Your angels to keep them in all their ways.

Let us pray for those whose homes have been visited with the sad news of the death of their loved one. Dear God, give the comfort we would but cannot give.

Let us pray for our wounded veterans. Their lives have been defined by the wounds they received while defending us. Dear God, help us to care for "him who has borne the battle, and his widow and his orphan" (Abraham Lincoln).[1]

Let us pray for our culture – too self-indulgent, too impatient – so that we learn that heaven cannot be had on earth and begin to imitate the One who "came not to be served but to serve, and to give His life as a ransom for many" (Mark 10:45).

Let us pray to the Lord. Lord, have mercy!

For further reflection: Psalm 147 – God, the ultimate source of healing, care, peace

"O you who hear prayer, to you shall all flesh come" (Psalm 65:2). We come, great God, in the name of our Savior Jesus, and ask that You give Your mercies to our military personnel, their families, and to our wounded veterans. May we who have received mercy, show mercy. Amen.

May 17

Trusting the Promises of God

Jesus rises from the ground, ascends, and when a cloud covers Him, He is no longer seen. Still today, no longer seen. We live by faith, not by sight, and that's not easy (cf. 2 Corinthians 5:7).

As people of faith, we wrestle with experiences that don't fit our notion of how things should work. Just as people don't rise from the ground unaided, many of our natural experiences in life don't seem to fit with the idea of a close, personal God who cares for us. When we find ourselves not seeing the goodness of God in our lives, we have only faith, only God's promises of His goodness to us. We don't see God. We don't see Jesus. "No one has ever seen God" (John 1:18). "You cannot see my face, for man shall not see me and live" (Exodus 33:20). Since a hidden God, like rising from the ground unaided, goes against our natural desire to see and hear, to touch and experience, some people build idols and we Americans worship worldly power, consumerism, and celebrity. Living amidst worshippers of what is seen, we followers of Christ can only trust the promise. "This same Jesus, who has been taken from you into heaven, will come back in the same way you have seen Him go into heaven" (Acts 1:11).

When you have gone through tough times, I mean really tough, and had nothing to hang onto except the promises of God, then in hindsight you see that God, though hidden, truly is personal, close, and caring. Faith does sustain us. Hymns say it; the Bible teaches it.

> When all things seem against us, / To drive us to despair,
> We know one gate is open, / One ear will hear our prayer.[1]
> Faith shall cry, as fails each sense, / Jesus is my confidence![2]

"We look not to the things that are seen but to the things that are unseen. For the things that are seen are transient, but the things that are unseen are eternal" (2 Corinthians 4:18).

For further reflection: Psalm 42 – "Why are you cast down, O my soul?"

I am trusting Thee, Lord Jesus; / Never let me fall.
I am trusting Thee forever / And for all.[3]

May 18

Don't Pitch Your Hope!

The writers of the Bible never tire of telling how God's Word impacts lives. That's why we read and see ourselves in the stories from so long ago. The adventures of Moses or David, the faithfulness of Samuel or Isaiah, the cross-carrying of Paul or Peter, and all the others… In their stories we look for parts of our stories, so that "through endurance and through the encouragement of the Scriptures we might have hope" (Romans 15:4).

One Saturday in spring I needed some compost for the garden, so I went to the Seminary's massive compost piles. My eyes fell upon an Easter lily that someone had thrown away. How symbolic, I thought. We celebrate the resurrection of Jesus Christ when Easter rolls around but when the lilies have faded, we often toss out the lively hope that comes from the resurrection. Why throw the lily away?

Gardeners know that a lily that has bloomed can be planted in the yard and it will bloom again and again and again. So I scooped up that tossed lily and planted it where I'll see and enjoy the blooms to come. Sure enough, come to campus and I'll show you that exact lily. Such symbolism! Instead of tossing hope on a pile of dying stuff, Christians immersed in the stories of The Story have a hope planted by the Spirit that blooms again and again and again. That was my experience. Do you see reminders of God in things that other people just pass by?

> This is a sight that gladdens – / What peace it doth impart!
> Now nothing ever saddens / The joy within my heart.
> No gloom shall ever shake, / No foe shall ever take
> The hope which God's own Son / In love for me hath won.[1]

For further reflection: 1 Peter 1:3-9 – Lively hope!

Dear Jesus, help me see my life in the stories of the Bible. Let me see myself as a member of Your body. If You had not been raised, our faith would be in vain. But You are raised, the firstfruits of those who sleep (cf. 1 Corinthians 15:12-20). Wherever I look, may I look out from a heart filled with resurrection optimism! Amen.

May 19

Learning Church

"Daaa… Here I come. Here comes Jacob. I'm fourth in *Cinco de Meyer*. I love throwing. I was at Oma and Opa's last weekend. I found balls. I threw balls. I toddled after them and threw them again and again. Fun! Sunday they took me to church. Mommy carried me up at Communion. I had my baby LEGO®s with me – big LEGOs. I threw them. I threw them from the Communion rail to right in front of the altar. Big people chuckled. Opa, you laughed big laughs."

"Sure did, Jacob, but you probably won't do it again, not if your parents keep bringing you to church… and I know they will. That's because church habits are learned. After we get baptized, we learn more about Jesus. We learn church habits, hopefully good church habits. Sooner or later you learn that you can't throw LEGOs and eat Cheerios® in church forever.

"Jacob, you make me think. Older church people sometimes assume everybody knows church habits. Maybe everybody did once upon a time but not anymore, especially when more and more people haven't grown up in church. Big church people don't always take time to teach newer people – like liturgy…"

"Opa, what's 'liturgy?'"

"There you go."

For further reflection: Ephesians 6:1-4 – Children learn what they live

Taught to lisp Thy holy praises / Which on earth Thy children sing,
Both with lips and hearts, unfeigned, / Glad thank-offerings may they bring;
Then with all the saints in glory / Join to praise their Lord and King.[1]

May 20

Dying to Self

In 2011 a tornado struck Joplin, Missouri and took 158 lives. Two years later 24 people, including 7 children in an elementary school, were killed when a tornado hit Moore, Oklahoma. No use listing more tragedies. Nature can take life.

Adversity may come suddenly and tragically, like the tornadoes, or we're ground down slowly. One way or another, the end will come, and that's depressing. Who hasn't retreated into feeling sorry for themselves? When I ask seminarians if they hope that their preaching will take unpleasant feelings away from their people, they nod, "Yes." To that I say, "No, you don't want to do that." In a strange way, unwelcome to us, the Spirit of God can use the sadness and weariness of our lives to lead us into deeper trust that our true life is with the resurrected Christ, and that's invigorating.

This is dying to ourselves. It best happens before the tornado or accident or disease takes our physical life. Think of the Great Flood when only Noah and his family survived (Genesis 6-9). How unexpected that disaster was to the people who died! And yet, they had their time of grace, their daily grinds that should have led them to think about their end, to repent and turn their lives from self to God. "For as in those days before the flood they were eating and drinking, marrying and giving in marriage, until the day when Noah entered the ark, and they were unaware until the flood came and swept them all away, so will be the coming of the Son of Man" (Matthew 24:38-39).

Dying to self can be a blessing of our daily, sometimes wearisome grind. They didn't do it in Noah's time; you are different! "Set your mind on things that are above, not on things that are on earth. For you have died, and your life is hidden with Christ in God. When Christ who is your life appears, then you also will appear with Him in glory" (Colossians 3:2-4).

For further reflection: James 4:13-17 – "If the Lord wills…"

My end to ponder teach me ever / And, ere the hour of death appears,
To cast my soul on Christ, my Savior, / Nor spare repentant sighs and tears.
My God, for Jesus' sake I pray / Thy peace may bless my dying day.[1]
Amen.

May 21

"How Was School?"

This time of year a tent goes up at Concordia Seminary – a large tent that is put up in the garden setting next to the President's House. It's there that a reception is held for graduates and their families the evening before commencement ceremonies.

You see people every day who place no value upon an education; that's sad, but often it's because that's the way they were raised. Under the tent we say "Thank you" to all those parents who kept asking their little children, "What did you learn at school today?" and kept hearing, "Nuttin." "Then why are we sending you to school?" "I dunno." Slowly it dawns on the child that he or she has learned something, and by college or graduate school has learned a lot.

Years ago I sat in a crowded corner in a hot gymnasium and watched my daughter Elizabeth graduate from Valparaiso University. The feeling was overwhelming. My parents grew up in the Depression when so many people had to go without so many things that today we take for granted, including higher education. Watching my daughter graduate, I understood like never before why my parents always and earnestly asked, "How was school today?"

"He who increases knowledge increases sorrow" (Ecclesiastes 1:18). Perhaps so, but the education parents provide can orient their children to heaven so that they truly value their blessings on earth. "The fear of the LORD is the beginning of knowledge; fools despise wisdom and instruction" (Proverbs 1:7).

For further reflection: Proverbs 3:1-12 – Blessings from godly learning

Wisdom's highest, noblest treasure, / Jesus, is revealed in You.
Let me find in You my pleasure, / And my wayward will subdue.[1]   *Amen.*

May 22

Blessing and Equipping the Saints

The academic year winds down at Concordia Seminary and students receive their degrees and certificates for ministry. Following this, they will be using their hard-earned knowledge in the service of the Church and its congregations.

"When he ascended on high ... he gave gifts to men. ... he gave the apostles, the prophets, the evangelists, the shepherds and teachers ..." (Ephesians 4:8, 11). On the day Jesus ascended, there was no Paul the great apostle, just Saul the persecutor. On the day Jesus ascended, there was no Peter who knew that the Gospel was for Gentiles as well as Jews, no Peter who could stand up and preach boldly in defiance of hostile authorities. On the day Jesus ascended, there was no Book of Acts, not yet the amazing spread of the Good News. On the day Jesus ascended, there were no Church fathers, no reformers, and none of the people who shaped our Christian faith traditions. On Ascension Day so much was in the future. The Great Commission had been given and God's Spirit began to fulfill the promise at Pentecost: "This gospel of the kingdom will be proclaimed throughout the whole world" (Matthew 24:14).

We see the work of God in retrospect. In the 2,000 years since His ascension, our Lord Jesus has indeed given gifts and given pastors and teachers. As seminaries hold their commencement exercises, God is still giving gifts to His Church. For over 175 years, Concordia Seminary has provided over 12,000 pastors to the Church, who have equipped "the saints for the work of ministry, for building up the body of Christ" (Ephesians 4:12). Our prayer and our labor is that, generations from now, people will look back to these days and the years still to come and say, "The ascended Lord gave shepherds and teachers."

For further reflection: 2 Timothy 1:1-14 – The Gospel entrusted to the next generation

God of the prophets, bless the prophets' sons;
Elijah's mantle o'er Elisha cast.
Each age its solemn task may claim but once;
Make each one nobler, stronger than the last.[1]   *Amen.*

May 23

Marriage as a Reflection of Christ's Love

When a retired pastor said he regretted never preaching on Luke 23:34 for a wedding, I decided to do it. On a Saturday back in 2002, I preached on Jesus' words, "Father, forgive them, for they know not what they do" (Luke 23:34).

OK, chuckle, but then think about it. No human relationship is like marriage. What preparation could completely ready us for all we experience in marriage? No one fully knows what they're getting into when they get married, even in a second marriage. For Christians, there's an additional lack of knowing. We understand marriage as a reflection of Christ's love for His followers, the Church. The husband is to love his wife with the sacrificial love Jesus showed the Church, and when he does, the wife willingly responds with her love, modeling the Church's response of total love for Jesus. What couple standing before the altar can possibly anticipate how richly their Christ-inspired love will grow?

Forgiveness is at the heart of Christian marriage. Jesus spoke those words when He was on the cross paying the price for our sins. Those who crucified Him didn't know what they were doing, that they were putting to death the Son of God. More than that – the high priest Caiaphas had unwittingly said "it would be expedient that one man should die for the people" (John 18:14). Jesus did die for the people, for the forgiveness of all people, including forgiveness for husbands and wives. Marriage requires many things; the best preparation is a spirit of mutual forgiveness. With forgiveness, there's no limit to the richness of love, love between husband and wife, love from God.

No, we don't know… how wonderfully our forgiving Father, for Jesus' sake, can bless our marriages.

For further reflection: Ephesians 5:20-33 – Selfless, mutual love

Jesus, Savior, wash away / All that has been wrong today.
Help me ev'ry day to be / Good and gentle, more like Thee.
Let my near and dear ones be / Always near and dear to Thee.
O bring me and all I love / To Thy happy home above.[1]   *Amen.*

May 24

"Do You Understand What You Are Reading?"

What's your favorite Bible translation, and why?

Pentecost celebrates God's Holy Spirit coming upon the first followers of Jesus. The disciples were able to speak to visitors to Jerusalem in their native language – a Rosetta Stone experience! "We hear them telling in our own tongues the mighty works of God" (Acts 2:11).

In 2011, we celebrated the 400th anniversary of the King James Version. Albert Cook of Yale University wrote, "No other book has so penetrated and permeated the hearts and speech of the English race as has the Bible."[1] True enough, but after four centuries the King James Bible is not easy to understand. For example, Psalm 88:13 says, "in the morning shall my prayer prevent thee." Huh? Praying to God in the morning will stop Him from doing things? No, "prevent" used to mean "come before." "In the morning my prayer *comes before* you." The King James Bible has over 500 words that have changed their meaning or are no longer used.

That the people at Pentecost heard about God's works in their own languages teaches us that God wants people to understand His Word in their own daily language, the way they really speak. Is the King James your favorite for sentimental reasons? If so, might it be dusty? Like a flower that was beautiful in its time but is now dried out, closed for years in the pages of a book? What translation best helps you understand the "mighty works of God?" What translations – plural – do you use to compare and learn? Jesus says His words are "spirit and life" (John 6:63). The Word of God won't work in your life if it's not understood!

For further reflection: Acts 8:26-40 – Trying to understand God's Word

Almighty God, send Your Holy Spirit into our hearts that He may rule and direct us according to Your will ... and lead us into all truth that we, being steadfast in faith, may increase in all good works and in the end obtain everlasting life; through Jesus Christ, our Lord.[2]   *Amen.*

May 25

Sacred Ground

Years ago, I visited the Vietnam Memorial. The memorial was still new at the time of my visit. In addition to the famous wall, there's a statuary of combat soldiers, life-size statues that your imagination easily makes lifelike. An elderly woman, well-meaning, told her husband to stand by the statues so she could take a picture. He quickly said "no," his hushed words and humble body language clearly indicating the place was too sacred for such tourist stuff.

In my teaching, I sometimes have students watch the D-Day landing from *Saving Private Ryan*. Standing in the back of the room, I watch their silent attention. The scene over, I ask how they feel. They start to intellectualize, but I hold them to their feelings. No abstract thoughts, now their responses are profoundly human and subdued. Have the years of relative peace at home led us to intellectualize, to forget the horror of war and the cost so many paid for us?

Not far from the Vietnam Memorial there are other memorials. The World War II Memorial impresses upon silent visitors the global scope of war's horrors. The Korean War Memorial also has statues, and if you see them at night, you imagine being in Korea. The darkness of our sinful world is deep, and the sacrifices we remember on Memorial Day are sacred. With hand over heart, let us show due gratitude and devotion… and let us teach it to the next generation.

For further reflection: Amos 5:12-15 – Silence in evil times

Almighty God, You alone can establish lasting peace. Forgive our sins, we implore You, and deliver us from the hands of our enemies that we, being strengthened by Your defense, may be preserved from all danger and glorify You for the restoration of tranquility in our land; through the merits of Your Son, Jesus Christ, our Lord.[1]   Amen.

May 26

The Postures of Prayer

Years ago I happened to watch Charles Stanley on TV. Rev. Stanley is a good teacher and spoke about the value of getting down on your knees to pray. Not just figuratively but actually, physically getting down on your knees to pray. He said that posture is a reminder to be humble before God.

"Pray without ceasing" (1 Thessalonians 5:17). Christians have often puzzled over that command. Certainly you can't always have your hands folded, your head bowed, and maybe even your knees bent all day long. I'll admit that when it comes to the formal postures of prayer, I'm not very good. As I get older, I think I'm starting to understand better. To "pray without ceasing" is not about the posture of your body but the posture of your mind. Is your every waking thought, word, and action before others done in dialogue with God? Are you constantly thinking vertically as well as horizontally? And yes, some of those times you also put your body in a special posture.

When our daughter Elizabeth, mother of Christian, Connor, and Nick, had to enter the hospital, I went off by myself and bent my knees in prayer. It often takes something serious to get us down in total humility. C.S. Lewis called pain "God's megaphone."

> It removes the veil; it plants the flag of truth within the fortress of a rebel soul. If the first and lowest operation of pain shatters the illusion that all is well, the second shatters the illusion that what we have, whether good or bad in itself, is our own and enough for us. Everyone has noticed how hard it is to turn our thoughts to God when everything is going well with us.[1]

So we strive under the Spirit to think constantly of God, and we especially thank Him when events lead us to bend the knee – especially then!

For further reflection: Luke 22:39-46 – Always in communion with His Father, sometimes kneeling

O let Your mighty love prevail / To purge us of our pride
That we may stand before Your throne / By mercy purified.[2]   *Amen.*

May 27

When You're Deeply Hurt

Sometimes a verse puts your troubles into a few short words. Psalm 34:19 begins, "Many are the afflictions of the righteous." You're on the short end. Someone is spreading lies about you, cheating you in some deal, using you, not following the Golden Rule… Such are the afflictions that trouble sincere and godly people.

The psalmist continues with this promise, "but the LORD delivers him out of them all." Many times the wrong does not seem righted; you think you're not being delivered. Maybe you read this now with a hurt because someone has treated you unjustly. One way forward is to get even. The other way is to trust the promise, "the Lord delivers him out of them all." Trusting those words is the way to go.

"The eyes of the LORD are toward the righteous and his ears toward their cry" (Psalm 34:15). The psalmist depicts God in human terms. His eyes are focused on you; His ears are open to your cry. "Jesus, looking at him, loved him" (Mark 10:21). God does look at you with a face – the face of His Son made flesh. "For God, who said, 'Let light shine out of darkness,' has shone in our hearts to give the light of the knowledge of the glory of God in the face of Jesus Christ" (2 Corinthians 4:6). The glory that lightens your heart in the darkness of unjust suffering is your God and Savior. He's been there Himself and so "he cares for you" (1 Peter 5:7).

So if people are doing you wrong, if you can't get them to stop, and if, this is a big if, you're not retaliating but trusting God to set things right, this verse, Psalm 34:19, is for you. It's affirmation as you go today with Christ.

For further reflection: 1 Peter 4:12-19 – Entrust your cause to God - do good

When we seek relief / From a long-felt grief, / When temptations come alluring, / Make us patient and enduring. / Show us that bright shore / Where we weep no more. / Jesus, lead Thou on / Till our rest is won. / Heav'nly leader, still direct us, / Still support, console, protect us, / Till we safely stand / In our fatherland.[1]   Amen.

May 28

Make Time for the Compassionate Route

Does your chest ever tighten when workplace pressures keep you from giving time and attention to people who need your help? You want to be a Good Samaritan but the boss, the next meeting, the bottom line, pressure you to pass by on the other side?

Life doesn't fit into nice, tidy organizational and personal schedules. It probably never did. Jesus made up the story of the Good Samaritan, but it reflects real-life situations. The Samaritan is traveling, probably on business. He happens upon the victim of robbers, has compassion, tends his wounds, and takes him to an inn. "He took out two denarii and gave them to the innkeeper, saying, 'Take care of him, and whatever more you spend, I will repay you when I come back'" (Luke 10:35). In other words, *On my way back home from this business trip, I'll settle up with you*. Compassion slowed him down a little bit, but it was the way he went about his business duties.

Jesus knows real life when He speaks to us. "The people sought him and came to him, and would have kept him from leaving them, but he said to them, 'I must preach the good news of the kingdom of God to the other towns as well; for I was sent for this purpose'" (Luke 4:42-43). Jesus pursued His "business" but He went about it with compassion. Read the sequel: His "business trip" was constantly interrupted by opportunities to show mercy, and He did.

The priest and the Levite passed by uncaring because life was all about them. If you compartmentalize your life, divide your heart between God and other things, you'll feel squeezed between production and compassion. But when you love God with all your heart, soul, strength, and mind, compassion and productivity are not antithetical. The love of God poured into you makes compassion the way you go about today's business. It may leave you a bit ragged at times but Jesus commends it. "You go, and do likewise" (Luke 10:37).

For further reflection: Luke 4-6 – Skim these chapters and see how often Jesus responds to interruptions by people

Spirit of God, help me love You with all my heart, soul, strength, and mind, and then reflect it in my love for every person I meet today. In Jesus' name. Amen.

May 29

The Cycle of True Rest and Hard Work

You've probably had this conversation with a coworker. "Did you have a good weekend?" Back comes the answer, "Worked around the house the whole time." Translation: *I'm coming back to work tired, not happy to be here.* I recall a conversation with Diane about an upcoming weekend. There was plenty of work to be done – in the house, in the yard, catching up at the office – but we decided to take it easy.

God's wise guidance invites us to sometimes leave things undone. "Six days you shall labor, and do all your work, but the seventh day is a Sabbath to the LORD your God. On it you shall not do any work" (Exodus 20:9-10). The divine pattern for people is to alternate, not intermingle, rest and work. Jesus followed the pattern rigorously, not just observing Saturday as Sabbath but taking time away from His ministry every day to be alone with His Father. Or did He take His cell phone and briefcase with Him when the "office" was closed? Jesus isn't stupid. He knows the blessings of alternating true rest and hard work. Rest centers body, mind, and spirit on God, the first great commandment. Going back to work with renewed energies takes to others the love of God we ourselves have experienced in rest, the second great commandment (Matthew 22:34-40).

As much as we dislike the aggravations that come with work and sometimes the people that cause them, aggravations are blessings reminding us we're not above our Master. "If I then, your Lord and Teacher, have washed your feet, you also ought to wash one another's feet. ... a servant is not greater than his master" (John 13:14, 16). To get into a mind-set that isn't flustered by the nuisances and annoyances that come with work, we have to take time for reflection, weekly and daily. What work will you leave undone this weekend?

For further reflection: Isaiah 40:28-31 – Renew your energy

Almighty God, merciful Father, who created and completed all things, on this day when the work of our calling begins anew, we implore You to create its beginning, direct its continuance, and bless its end, that our doings may be preserved from sin, our life sanctified, and our work this day be well pleasing to You; through Jesus Christ, our Lord.[1] *Amen.*

May 30

God Is Already There

When Diane and I arrived at our first church, someone, probably the previous pastor, had put this on the church sign: "Don't be afraid of the future. God is already there." That's always true – true for graduates going into an unknown future, and true for you and me whatever tomorrow may bring.

The LORD said to Jacob, "I am with you and will keep you wherever you go … I will not leave you until I have done what I have promised you" (Genesis 28:15).

The LORD replied to Moses, "My presence will go with you, and I will give you rest" (Exodus 33:14).

"When you go out to war against your enemies, and see horses and chariots and an army larger than your own, you shall not be afraid of them, for the LORD your God is with you, who brought you up out of the land of Egypt" (Deuteronomy 20:1).

"Fear not, for I have redeemed you … When you pass through the waters, I will be with you; and through the rivers, they shall not overwhelm you; / when you walk through fire, you shall not be burned" (Isaiah 43:1-2).

"Don't be afraid of the future. God is already there." Jesus is the "Yes" to God's promises to us (cf. 2 Corinthians 1:20). "Behold, I am with you always, to the end of the age" (Matthew 28:20).

For further reflection: 2 Kings 6:8-17 – "Those who are with us are more than those who are with them"

"I know the plans I have for you … plans for welfare and not for evil, to give you a future and a hope" (Jeremiah 29:11). Lord, that's what You promised Your people when they were in exile. There are times when I feel alone and scared about the future. Remind me now of Your promise, "I will never leave you nor forsake you" (Hebrews 13:5). I ask this for Jesus' sake. Amen.

May 31

Diary of a Bible

I came across the following *Diary of a Bible* in a church newsletter. The author is unknown.

January: A busy time for me. Most of the family decided to read me through this year. They kept me busy for the first two weeks, but they have forgotten me now.

February: Clean-up time. I was dusted yesterday and put in my place. My owner did use me for a few minutes last week. He had been in an argument and was looking for some references to prove he was right.

March: Had a busy first day of the month. My owner was elected president of the PTA and used me to prepare a speech.

April: Grandpa visited this month. He kept me on his lap for an hour reading from 1 Peter 5:5-7. He seems to think more of me than do some people in my own household.

May: I have a few green stains on my pages. Some spring flowers were pressed in my pages.

How does the diary of your Bible read this far into the year?

For further reflection: Jeremiah 6:16; Romans 15:1-7 – Where do you look for daily guidance?

Blessed Lord, You have caused all Holy Scriptures to be written for our learning. Grant that we may so hear them, read, mark, learn, and inwardly digest them that, by patience and comfort of Your holy Word, we may embrace and ever hold fast the blessed hope of everlasting life; through Jesus Christ our Lord.[1]   Amen.

June 1

In Awe of Creation, Seek the Creator

I teased a friend yesterday, "Didn't see you in church Sunday." "Went fishing," he said. "I worshiped in the cathedral of creation."

Indeed, creation is God's great cathedral and often reminds me of the hymn, "O forest leaves, so green and tender, / That dance for joy in summer air, / O meadow grasses, bright and slender, / O flow'rs, so wondrous sweet and fair, / You live to show His praise alone; / With me now make His glory known."[1]

But tornadoes, hurricanes, floods, and earthquakes can turn the cathedral of creation into a house of horrors. What conclusion can we draw? That God is capricious? That He teases us with nature's beauty, lures us into complacency about His being, and then slams us with unstoppable destruction? We may be adults, but like cowering children we know the cathedral can be a big, scary place. We need a revelation, something more than nature, to teach us the being of God, to assure us that His thoughts toward us are good and loving. When Jesus says, "Heaven and earth will pass away, but my words will not pass away" (Matthew 24:35), He's reminding us that the cathedral of creation isn't enough.

"Then the LORD rained on Sodom and Gomorrah sulfur and fire" (Genesis 19:24). Abraham "looked down toward Sodom and Gomorrah and toward all the land of the valley, and he looked and, behold, the smoke of the land went up like the smoke of a furnace" (Genesis 19:28). Jesus used that house of horrors to warn people that there's more than worldly living. "But I tell you that it will be more tolerable on the day of judgment for the land of Sodom than for you" (Matthew 11:24).

Nature's beauty and brutality point us to a mysterious God we cannot know by ourselves. Only the revelation of Jesus in the Bible shows sinners a loving heavenly Father. "No one knows the Father except the Son and anyone to whom the Son chooses to reveal him" (Matthew 11:27).

For further reflection: Romans 8:5-11 – You need the Spirit of Christ!

Heavenly Father, You did not send Your "Son into the world to condemn the world, but in order that the world might be saved through him" (John 3:17). Send Your Holy Spirit through Word and Sacrament to reveal to us Your dependable goodness and love. For Jesus' sake. Amen.

June 2

"Pay Attention to What You Hear"

"Pay attention to what you hear," says Jesus in Mark 4:24. I've been thinking about that a lot lately, and my reflections tell me that one reason many people find Christianity irrelevant is because they're not discriminating about what they hear. Think about it. All day long our ears are assaulted with words. Studies show that we spend an excessive amount of time in front of TVs and monitors. We walk or jog with buds in our ears. We talk with people. And then there are the e-mails, blogs, Facebook, Twitter, all the words that we let into our unguarded souls. Some of the words in you are, I hope, God's words but the majority of words assaulting you are not. No wonder many of us are strangers to solitude and silence, thinking there's something unnatural about it.

Exposing ourselves to so many words tempts us into a position of judgment. *I will decide what's good and what's not, what to do and what not to do.* That, friend, is idolatry. Lee Kwan Yew wasn't writing about religion but wrote truly, "We can ill afford to let others experiment with our lives."[1] A Christianity that is relevant to daily life starts with a faith assumption: The Word of God in Jesus Christ is the story of my personal life. If you take that as your starting point, then you're going to filter what you hear. You break the habit of watching this or hearing that. You use media with discernment. You pick your peers carefully. You decrease the barrage of words and visual images, and increase your time in silence with the Bible. In short, you "pay attention to *what* you hear." "If anyone has ears to hear, let him hear" (Mark 4:23).

So when the precious seed is sown, / Life-giving grace bestow

That all whose souls the truth receive / Its saving pow'r may know.[2]

For further reflection: Jude 17-22 – Keep yourself special

O Spirit of God, words, words, words! Jesus promises that You will bring to remembrance all that He says to His disciples (cf. John 14:26). Living in a world of words, help me be discerning about what words I take into my soul. Bring me peace as You bring me words of my Savior. Amen.

June 3

Hang onto God's Promises!

"It's hard to have patience with people who say 'There is no death,' or 'Death doesn't matter,'" wrote C.S. Lewis. "Cancer, and cancer, and cancer. My mother, my father, my wife. I wonder who is next in the queue."[1]

"O LORD, how long shall I cry for help, and you will not hear? / Or cry to you 'Violence!' and you will not save? / Why do you make me see iniquity, and why do you idly look at wrong?" (Habakkuk 1:2-3). Straight to God, no pious masking of how he truly felt, the prophet Habakkuk complained about the collapse of justice in society.

God's answer is also straightforward and simple: *Trust Me!* Be your trouble cancer, injustice, or any other problem in our sinful, broken world, God's answer fits. "The righteous shall live by his faith" (Habakkuk 2:4). That is, hang onto God's promises. Live by them now; live by them forever. Now: "we walk by faith, not by sight" (2 Corinthians 5:7). Forever: "I am the resurrection and the life" (John 11:25). "When Christ who is your life appears, then you also will appear with him in glory" (Colossians 3:4).

Hanging onto God's promises – sometimes against the evidence – produces hope, not just hope that cancer and other vexations will be cured and one day eliminated, but hope that is optimistic and confident in resurrection to unending life. "The last enemy to be destroyed is death" (1 Corinthians 15:26). "Hope does not put us to shame, because God's love has been poured into our hearts through the Holy Spirit who has been given to us" (Romans 5:5).

Are you or a friend standing in that queue? God stands in line with you. "Hope in God; for I shall again praise him, my salvation and my God" (Psalm 43:5).

For further reflection: 2 Corinthians 4:16 - 5:10 – "We walk by faith, not by sight"

We walk by faith and not by sight, / No gracious words we hear
From Him who spoke as none e'er spoke, / But we believe Him near.
Help then, O Lord, our unbelief; / And may our faith abound;
To call on You when You are near / And seek where You are found.[2]
Amen.

June 4

Recipients of Selfless Love

It started June 4th and concluded on June 7th, 1942. Today we commemorate the Battle of Midway.

Midway is located 1,200 miles northwest of Hawaii. The United States Navy had learned that Japan intended to capture Midway to serve as an outpost in the war. As a large contingent of the Japanese Navy steamed toward Midway, it was ambushed by forces under the command of Admiral Chester Nimitz. American losses were heavy: one aircraft carrier and 150 planes. Torpedo Squadron 8, flying outdated planes, lost all but one of its 30 pilots and gunners. But their sacrifice allowed higher-flying Dauntless dive bombers to attack. Japan's navy was crippled for the rest of the war, losing four of its nine aircraft carriers. The Battle of Midway turned the tide of the war.

The generation of our parents, grandparents, and great-grandparents was willing to face the horrors of war so you and I could live as we do today, in freedom and in hope. Were they afraid? Certainly. Would they have preferred to stay home? No doubt. But the cause was clear, the effort just. They lived and many died for us, their fellow citizens. Sacrifice for others, that's selfless love. Remembering that you and I are recipients of selfless love, may we prove ourselves worthy of the trust given to us by those who fought and died these days so long ago at Midway.

For further reflection: John 15:12-13 – The model of selfless love

O Trinity of love and pow'r / Our people shield in danger's hour;
From rock and tempest, fire and foe, / Protect them wheresoe'er they go;
Thus evermore shall rise to Thee / Glad praise from air and land and sea.[1]
Amen.

June 5

Every Heartbeat a Gift

One of the great benefits of Concordia Seminary is the opportunity to learn from renowned scholars and speakers. In 2011, Dr. Thomas Troeger of Yale Divinity School lectured on campus and shared the following true story.

Dr. Troeger was a patient in the intensive care unit of the hospital. It was his first morning after major heart surgery and, as he slowly began to wake up, he heard banging. Bang. Bang. Bang. Bang. Regular and irritating – Bang. Bang. Bang. Bang. He thought it must be construction workers driving piles for some new hospital addition. *Dear God. I'm in the hospital. Please stop that banging!*

What sometimes happens when you pray for something? Sure enough – Bang. Bang. Bang. Bang. It didn't stop. As I said, Dr. Troeger was just beginning to wake up. As he became more alert, he remembered that his surgeon had told him that the new valve in his heart would make a regular pounding noise but also promised that it would quiet down in time. *Dear God, cancel that last prayer! Forget what I said!*

Then Dr. Troeger drew his captivated audience to the moral of his story. Bang. Bang. Bang. Bang. Each sound is another heartbeat of life from God. Your heart beats about 100,000 times a day. Multiply that by the days and years of your life. Dr. Troeger remarked that he's never gotten a bill from God for any of his heartbeats. Has God billed you? Every heartbeat is a gift to you from your loving Creator. Every heartbeat is a grace enabling you to give thanks to God and gratefully serve others.

> Rejoice, my heart, be glad and sing, / A cheerful trust maintain;
> For God, the source of ev'rything, / Your portion shall remain.
> He is your treasure, He your joy, / Your life and light and Lord,
> Your Counselor when doubts annoy, / Your shield and great reward.[1]

For further reflection: Psalm 30 – "Joy comes with the morning"

O let the people praise Thy worth, / In all good works increasing;
The land shall plenteous fruit bring forth, / Thy Word is rich in blessing.
May God the Father, God the Son, / And God the Spirit bless us!
Let all the world praise Him alone; / Let solemn awe possess us.
Now let our hearts say "Amen!"[2]

June 6

"A Time for War ... a Time for Peace"

Evil exists, murderously aggressive evil, and sometimes it can only be countered by sacrifice. On this date in 1944, D-Day, President Franklin Roosevelt addressed the nation and offered this prayer.

> Almighty God, our sons, pride of our nation, this day have set upon a mighty endeavor, a struggle to preserve our Republic, our religion, and our civilization, and to set free a suffering humanity. Lead them straight and true; give strength to their arms, stoutness to their hearts, steadfastness in their faith. ... They will be sore tried, by night and by day, without rest – until victory is won. The darkness will be rent by noise and by flame. Men's souls will be shaken with the violences of war. ... Some will never return. ... Give us faith in thee; faith in our sons; faith in each other; faith in our united crusade. Let not the keenness of our spirit ever be dulled. ... With thy blessing, we shall prevail over the unholy forces of our enemy. Help us to conquer the apostles of greed and racial arrogances. ... Thy will be done, Almighty God. Amen.[1]

The grief war brings is easily forgotten by generations who have lived in relative peace and not known war's horror. Visit the National Mall in Washington, D.C. and you are impressed by the monuments, but the sad truth is that almost every monument commemorates war. "For everything there is a season ... a time for war, and a time for peace" (Ecclesiastes 3:1, 8). "He who is prudent will keep silent in such a time, for it is an evil time. / Seek good, and not evil" (Amos 5:13-14). Remembering the photos of soldiers leaving landing crafts, sloshing through water, some to die, others to fight on... The call to us is sacrifice in our own time and place to advance God's justice against evil. "Let justice roll down like waters, and righteousness like an ever-flowing stream" (Amos 5:24).

For further reflection: Micah 4 – "Nation shall not lift up sword against nation"

Almighty God, You alone can establish lasting peace. Forgive our sins, we implore You, and deliver us from the hands of our enemies that we, being strengthened by Your defense, may be preserved from all danger and glorify You for the restoration of tranquility in our land; through the merits of Your Son, Jesus Christ, our Savior.[2]   Amen.

June 7

"Ta-da!"

"Hi, Christian here! Opa visited me and Connor last week. Opa held baby 'Nonnor' but I rocketed around the house. I threw balls in the living room. I colored on paper... and the wall. And I climbed up on the furniture and jumped down. When I jumped down, I threw my arms up and said, 'Ta-da!' I know no fear. Ta-da! Opa told Mommy to be sure to know the quickest way to the emergency room.

"Opa left. He went home to St. Louis. Then Opa drove to Chicago. He was on the highway. Where is Monee, Illinois? Opa got caught in a storm in Monee. He saw a tornado. It was coming right at him. Picture that: Opa and a tornado – two big winds on a collision course! Opa found a place to hide. He didn't say, 'Ta-da.' The tornado was stronger. Opa was afraid.

"Opa, you should practice what you preach. 'There is no fear in love, but perfect love casts out fear' (1 John 4:18). Even when bad things happen, knowing you're loved helps you weather the storm. When you big people get afraid, do you throw up your arms... and pray? Do you put away fear... and say, 'Ta-da?'"

For further reflection: Psalm 135 – When He sends the wind, praise the Lord. Ta-da!

With You, O Lord, I cast my lot; / O faithful God, forsake me not,
To You my soul commending.
Lord, be my stay, / And lead the way
Now and when life is ending.[1]   Amen.

June 8

Head to Heart – Heeding His Call

In the earlier years of our marriage, I often was out working in the yard in the late afternoon when Diane would call, "Time to eat." I heard her clearly but always kept working: planting a few more flowers, pulling a few more weeds, doing whatever. "I'll be there right away," meaning, "I'll come whenever it suits me."

I've been thinking about Ephesians 4:1, "I therefore, a prisoner for the Lord, urge you to walk in a manner worthy of the calling to which you have been called." That's God's guidance; follow Jesus in your daily life. It's been said that the longest 18 inches in the world is the distance between the head and the heart. When Diane called me in to eat, her message had trouble getting past my self-centeredness to sink down into my heart. Our ears hear the call of Christ, our eyes see it when we read the Bible or devotional literature, and our brain gets it. Blockage? Do the teachings and Sacraments of Sunday get carried into your life on Monday? When you awake, when you work, when you rest at the end of the day, are you asking the Spirit of God to take the Gospel's motivation the full 18 inches into a life worthy of your high calling?

Jesus says, "You did not choose me, but I chose you and appointed you that you should go and bear fruit and that your fruit should abide" (John 15:16). The fruit of a motivated heart is to live worthy of your calling, "with all humility and gentleness, with patience, bearing with one another in love, eager to maintain the unity of the Spirit in the bond of peace" (Ephesians 4:2-3). Diane calls; I now come immediately. Jesus calls, and you? What do you do?

For further reflection: 1 Corinthians 11:23-34 – Head and heart to His meal

Direct us, O Lord, in all our doings with Your most gracious favor, and further us with Your continual help, that in all our works begun, continued, and ended in You we may glorify Your holy name and finally, by Your mercy, obtain eternal salvation; through Jesus Christ, our Lord.[1]   *Amen.*

June 9

Swerving Ahead?

"After this many of his disciples turned back and no longer walked with him" (John 6:66). "Some have swerved from the faith" (1 Timothy 6:21). "Hymenaeus and Philetus ... have swerved from the truth" (2 Timothy 2:17-18). "Demas, in love with this present world, has deserted me" (2 Timothy 4:10). Do you imagine that you'll never "swerve from the faith?"

When Robert Robinson wrote the beautiful hymn, "Come, Thou Fount of Every Blessing," he penned these haunting lines, "Prone to wander, Lord, I feel it; / Prone to leave the God I love."[1] The story is told – whether true or not, God only knows – that a woman was humming the hymn and asked what he thought about it. He said, "Madam, I am the poor unhappy man who wrote that hymn many years ago, and I would give a thousand worlds, if I had them, to enjoy the feelings I had then." Robinson died on this date in 1790.

"Jesus said to the Twelve, 'Do you want to go away as well?' Simon Peter answered him, 'Lord, to whom shall we go? You have the words of eternal life, and we have believed, and have come to know, that you are the Holy One of God'" (John 6:67-69). Jesus confronts me in Sunday worship in a way that doesn't happen during the week. Bible readings, sermon, and prayers confront me with ideas I wouldn't have on my own. Receiving the Sacrament with others reminds me that true faith is not an individual choice. Personally, I'm afraid of flying solo into eternity and need the discipline of going to church.

You don't become an inactive church member unless you're first an active churchgoer. That means you could well be the inactive, the delinquent member of the future. "Therefore, my beloved, ... work out your own salvation with fear and trembling, for it is God who works in you, both to will and to work for his good pleasure" (Philippians 2:12-13).

For further reflection: Hebrews 10:19-38 – Serious words

Oh, to grace how great a debtor / Daily I'm constrained to be;
Let that grace now, like a fetter / Bind my wand'ring heart to Thee:
Prone to wander, Lord, I feel it; / Prone to leave the God I love.
Here's my heart, O take and seal it, / Seal it for Thy courts above.[1]   *Amen.*

June 10

Our Hope and Confidence "in the Dash"

It always happens. In early June I look through a list of names, paying special attention to the names with an asterisk. Seminary alumni return to campus and the Jubilarian Service commemorates those who graduated 50 years ago. The names with asterisks? Those in the class who have died.

As we get older, we know that an asterisk will be coming to our name. That makes getting together for reunions an indescribably rich human experience, and very real, very true to the facts of life. For those who are younger but old enough to know what life is like, seeing jubilarians get together should be encouraging, especially when those jubilarians gather and show their confidence in the resurrection of Jesus Christ and their own future resurrection from the dead. They say the dash between a person's birth date and death date is most important. Our Seminary reunion service includes this prayer for all of us still "living the dash:"

> By joys of life, by human love, by affection and fidelity of friends; by capacity for pleasure and sense of humor; by persistency in hope of things to come: Edify us and draw us ever nearer to You. By sorrows of life; by our falls and failures; by our disappointments and disasters; by stern discipline of loneliness; by realized dreams and by heartache of unsatisfied desires: Form us and draw us ever nearer to You. Amen!

For further reflection: "I believe in ... the resurrection of the body, and the life everlasting. Amen." (Apostles' Creed) – Do those words give you hope and confidence "in the dash?"

O Spirit of God, You have surrounded us with a great cloud of witnesses. When we see older people faithfully follow the Lord Jesus, inspire us to emulate their example. Strengthen us all through Your Word and Sacrament, those who are near the end of their pilgrim way and those who still have a long road before them. May the fellowship of the Church lead us to fix our eyes on Jesus. Amen. (cf. Hebrews 12:1-2)

June 11

A Profound Mystery

When my daughter was married back in 2004, I wrote the following words to the new couple.

Dear Elizabeth and Darren,

Welcome back from your honeymoon! For a long time I intended to write a *Minute* about your marriage, but thought it wisest to wait until "the deed was done" so I could sort out my thoughts and feelings.

A good story has a lead, and there's no doubt your marriage is a good story. The love both sets of parents have for you, our pride at your accomplishments, gratitude that you've both remained true to Christian devotion and worship... those are all possible leads. But here's the lead I've settled on – mystery. The simplicity of your marriage service in the magnificent setting of the Chapel of St. Timothy and St. Titus on the Concordia Seminary campus highlighted the great mystery of Christian marriage. When St. Paul wrote about the mutual love and service a Christian husband and wife should show one another, he grounded it in the love Jesus Christ shows His Church, the selfless giving of the heavenly Bridegroom in love for His bride. "This mystery is profound, and I am saying that it refers to Christ and the church" (Ephesians 5:32).

As I walked you down the aisle, your eyes were filled with tears of joy and you said, "This is surreal." Perhaps the best thing we can all do is keep marriage that way – surreal, dreamlike – marriage as a magnificent sanctuary in which we radiate the love of God in our small, daily ways. So looking back at your joyous day, I readily admit that I don't quite get it, and I hope none of us presume to understand marriage fully. That, I pray, is a beginning of wisdom.

Love,

Dad

For further reflection: Proverbs 9:1-12 – A home established by the Wisdom of God

O Spirit of the Father, / Breathe on them from above, / So searching in Your pureness, / So tender in Your love, / That, guarded by Your presence, / And kept from strife and sin, / Their hearts may heed Your guidance / And know You dwell within.[1]   *Amen.*

June 12

"It Is No Longer I Who Live"

I was asked what it takes to be a good model of the Christian faith. That's a theoretical question until you internalize it. We will be judged according to our works (2 Corinthians 5:10; 1 Peter 1:17). That fact makes the question very relevant.

Here's my answer: It's not something to think about. If you put your foot on the floor in the morning determined to be a model Christian for your family, you're starting off on the wrong foot. Go to work with the goal of being an exemplary Christian, same thing. You're focusing on the wrong person – yourself.

"I have been crucified with Christ. It is no longer I who live, but Christ who lives in me. And the life I now live in the flesh I live by faith in the Son of God, who loved me and gave himself for me" (Galatians 2:20). That doesn't leave any room to be something yourself. If Jesus Christ fills your heart and mind, and His teaching and example are your beliefs and guides for conduct, then the Spirit of God will present a reflection of the Savior through you. Don't try to justify yourself by being a good model of Christianity.

> What our Lord wants us to present to Him is not goodness, nor honesty, nor endeavor, but real solid sin; that is all He can take from us. And what does He give in exchange for our sin? Real solid righteousness. But we must relinquish all pretense of being anything…[1]

What kind of model you are is not something to think about when you get up in the morning, but it should be something to think about at the end of the day. "Jesus, Savior, wash away / All that has been wrong today. / Help me ev'ry day to be / Good and gentle, more like Thee."[2]

For further reflection: Romans 8:1-11 – The Spirit of Christ in you

I thank You, my heavenly Father, through Jesus Christ, Your dear Son, that You have graciously kept me this day; and I pray that You would forgive me all my sins where I have done wrong, and graciously keep me this night. For into Your hands I commend myself, my body and soul, and all things. Let Your holy angel be with me, that the evil foe may have no power over me. Amen.[3]

June 13

The Gift of Tears

The ancient rabbis said that God felt so sorry for Adam and Eve as He watched them trudge out of paradise that He gave them help to cope in their new, now sinful world. He gave them the gift of tears.

Times of tears call for the sweetest religion. So much religious talk focuses upon what God's people should be doing. Fine, the Bible is filled with many commands and exhortations. Tears, however, remind us that this world remains broken, despite all our Christian good works.

"Put my tears into your bottle" (Psalm 56:8). God has, always will. See how the Savior gently approached Mary (John 20:11-18): "Why are you weeping?" (verse 15). You have your reason for tears and Mary had hers. "They have taken away my Lord, and I do not know where they have laid him" (verse 13). She had lost a loved one; He died and she thought He was gone. When life brings tears to your eyes, do you imagine your Lord Jesus is dead?

"Jesus said to her, 'Mary'" (verse 16). He calls you by name in Baptism. Jesus didn't condemn Mary for her tears and when He calls us, "O ye of little faith" (Matthew 8:26 KJV), He is inviting us to trust more and more in His Gospel which brings life and immortality to light (cf. 2 Timothy 1:10).

"I have seen the Lord" (verse 18) Mary said to the others. When you weep from a broken heart, your Jesus puts a glisten into your tears, the glisten of hope in His resurrection. "The Lord of hosts … will swallow up death forever; / and the Lord God will wipe away tears from all faces" (Isaiah 25:6-8). (Also see Revelation 7:17.)

Until then, "Blessed be the God and Father of our Lord Jesus Christ, the Father of mercies and God of all comfort, who comforts us in all our affliction … with the comfort with which we ourselves are comforted by God" (2 Corinthians 1:3-4).

For further reflection: 1 Thessalonians 4:13-18 – "Encourage one another with these words"

He lives to silence all my fears; / He lives to wipe away my tears;
He lives to calm my troubled heart; / He lives all blessings to impart.
He lives, all glory to His name! / He lives, my Jesus, still the same;
Oh, the sweet joy this sentence gives: / I know that my Redeemer lives![1]

June 14

Under the Eternal Banner of Divine Love

"Does that star-spangled banner yet wave o'er the land of the free and the home of the brave?"[1]

It's just a piece of cloth, but today, Flag Day, we remember it's more than "just a piece of cloth." It's a symbol of our history, often glorious but not always so, a symbol calling us to continuing sacrifices for the common good and stirring our hopes for the future.

If your eyes look up to that flag, your heart is invited still higher to the banner of the Eternal God. "You have set up a banner for those who fear you, that they may flee to it from the bow. / That your beloved ones may be delivered, give salvation by your right hand" (Psalm 60:4-5). "His banner over me is love" (Song of Solomon 2:4 NASB).

Living and working on this earthly side of Jordan, it stirs us to look to the Stars and Stripes, to that symbol of this great nation. On both sides of Jordan, in this present life and on the other side, the heavenly side to which the Savior is leading us, we thrill to live under the eternal banner of divine love.

"May we shout for joy over your salvation, and in the name of our God set up our banners!" (Psalm 20:5).

For further reflection: Matthew 22:15-22 – Flag *and* Banner: When the First Amendment of our Constitution decrees, "Congress shall make no law respecting an establishment of religion, or prohibiting the free exercise thereof," it is acknowledging that we live under two sovereigns, the government and the deity whom our conscience serves.

And when in pow'r He comes, / Oh, may our native land
From all its rending tombs / Send forth a glorious band,
A countless throng, / With joy to sing
To heav'n's high King / Salvation's song![2]

June 15

Verbalize Your Fears

One night a horrific thunderstorm shook us out of bed. Our dog at the time was "Speaker," a wonderful family member who was about five years old – old enough to be afraid of thunder and loud noises. As Diane and I tried to reassure him, I thought about the dog's inability to reason and talk. Scared, he couldn't talk about his fear. Shuddering, he couldn't understand our words of reassurance.

> Is life to thee a mystery, are some things hard to bear?
> Does God reveal all clearly as heavenward thou dost stare?
> Or dost thou stop and wonder amid life's stormy days
> Why God in all His wisdom doth lead in such dark ways?[1]

Unlike animals, you and I have been gifted by God with rational minds and voices that can both analyze and verbalize our feelings. How often we fail to do that! Sometimes we tremble in silence, not analyzing our fears and not speaking about them to trusted friends or loving family.

And taking that higher, to the Most High, shouldn't our personal prayer times include self-analysis of our fears, describing those fears to God with words and then, unlike animals, use the gift to read and hear and apply God's words of reassurance?

"He who dwells in the shelter of the Most High will abide in the shadow of the Almighty. / You will not fear the terror of the night" (Psalm 91:1, 5).

"Blessed is the one who finds wisdom, and the one who gets understanding. / If you lie down, you will not be afraid; when you lie down, your sleep will be sweet. / Do not be afraid of sudden terror … for the LORD will be your confidence" (Proverbs 3:13, 24-26).

For further reflection: Mark 4:35-41 – Know God, know sleep

Thank You, Lord, for the gift of a mind that can think and for the gift of speech. Let my growing knowledge of Your Word calm my heart whenever it is troubled and may my words be an embrace of care for others who are scared. Amen.

June 16

Sweet Times

"Diane has been happily married for seven years," I'm fond of saying. "Five minutes here, ten there, it adds up pretty quickly." "Out of how many years?" people ask. Today's *Minute* is the answer. I was captivated the first time I met her. We married in 1973, and today is our anniversary.

We've raised the kids and become the best of friends. Two wonderful daughters, fine families, and now the joys of grandparenting. One ritual comes in the late afternoon – she gives our dog, Ferdie, Triscuits®, we have our drinks and talk. Early to bed, early to rise (we're not party people), we continue our visiting in the morning while watching national politics. But then it's time to work, and we love to work. Diane has been active in community, church, and now campus, truly a model of selfless civic service. When the grandkids come over, I say, "Camp Opa is about work" but then Oma shifts her work to indulging the boys.

There's a tinge of sadness as time marches on and our remaining time together grows less, but that makes these times so much sweeter. There have been bumps of course, but looking back we see it is true: "Unless the LORD builds the house, those who build it labor in vain" (Psalm 127:1). Diane, your number of happy years is going to increase dramatically! Love, Dale

For further reflection: Genesis 2:18-25 – God instituted marriage for our good

Heavenly Father, You established marriage and family for the good of all people. Help those of us who have been blessed with many years of marriage be examples to young people who are just starting out. Give them grace to fulfill their vows to one another and to You their whole life long. May Your mercies for all people also come through us to those who are not married as we enfold them in the love of Your Church. In Jesus' name. Amen.

June 17

Sunday Verses – Week-long Devotion

As the workweek wears on, what, if anything, do you retain from last Sunday's worship? And if you are still hanging onto one thought from worship, have you been curious enough to read more about it in the Bible?

Dietrich Bonhoeffer:

> Almost all of us have grown up with the idea that the Scripture reading is only a matter of hearing the Word of God for this particular day. That is why for many the Scripture reading consists only of a few, brief, selected verses which are to form the guiding thought of the day … There can … be little doubt that brief verses cannot and should not take the place of reading the Scripture as a whole.[1]

When I was growing up, my mother took her hymnal with her when she went to church. She slipped the church bulletin into her hymnal and when she returned home she put both book and bulletin on an end table. There they sat for the week, reminders of what we had heard in worship and an invitation to review Bible readings, hymns, and prayers. Because of that formative experience, it strikes me as very strange that many worshippers leave their service folders in the narthex as they head home. They may be motivated by ecological recycling but I take my bulletin home for spiritual recycling during the week. My week needs more than that one hour in church.

You'll find it very helpful to take a short verse or two from church into your workweek. Dietrich Bonhoeffer wrote: "they may find their place as texts for the week or as daily verses at the beginning of devotions …"[2] However, do that, he urges, in the context of reading much larger units of Scripture.

> The verse for the day is still not the Holy Scripture which will remain throughout all time until the Last Day. Holy Scripture is more than a watchword. It is more than "light for today." It is God's revealed Word for all men, for all times. Holy Scripture does not consist of individual passages; it is a unit and is intended to be used as such.[3]

For further reflection: Philippians 2:12-16 – Hold fast to the Word of life

Holy Spirit, motivate me to take small verses from church into my workweek. Discipline me to read larger sections of Scripture so that I better understand the shorter passages. I ask this for the sake of Jesus and all He has done for my salvation! Amen.

June 18

Living a Fulfilled Life – Single or Married

Be careful when you praise marriage and family…

Years ago, I gave the keynote address for the International Lutheran Singles Association. Attendees came from almost every kind of singles group you can imagine: young and old, widows and widowers, divorced and never married. These wonderful people taught me a lot. In addition to plenary sessions, workshops were offered on an array of topics: "Cooking for One," "Single Parenting Discussion Group," "Widows' Issues," "Basic Home Repair," "Sexuality and Singles," and "Sexual, Emotional, and Physical Abuse." Since I've been married for more years than I was single, the gathering was a reminder to me not to forget singles when speaking about marriage and family.

"Two are better than one" (Ecclesiastes 4:9). Married people, facing life together, easily forget how intimidating many situations can be when you face them alone. Illness, unemployment, finances, parenting, self-doubt, guilt, fear, loneliness… all that comes to every person, single or married, but those challenges are especially tough when you have no soul mate with you from sunup to sundown. Jesus is there, of course ("I am with you always," Matthew 28:20), but we like Jesus "with skin on." I wonder how often well-intentioned talk about marriage and family inadvertently turns a dagger in the heart of a single?

The very nature of the Church reminds us to be sensitive.

> There are varieties of gifts, but the same Spirit; and there are varieties of service, but the same Lord; and there are varieties of activities, but it is the same God who empowers them all in everyone. To each is given the manifestation of the Spirit for the common good. … For just as the body is one and has many members, and all the members of the body, though many, are one body, so it is with Christ. For in one Spirit we were all baptized into one body. (1 Corinthians 12:4-7, 12-13)

The people I met at that singles conference were great people – loving, welcoming, and in so many ways fulfilled. May we all be!

For further reflection: Psalm 16 – Never alone, always fulfilled

O Spirit of God, You have gathered a wonderful diversity of believers into the Body of Christ. With Your abundant gifts, we all have fullness of life. Help all members of the Body be equally caring toward one another, considerate in speech, and uplifting one another in joy. Amen.

June 19

Wired and Tired?

I've put myself into a detoxification program. I've known for a long time I had this problem, but never got up the courage to deal with it. Several times I came close to hitting bottom, but a week ago I hit it. I finally realized this is no way to live. So I stopped cold turkey: no business e-mails outside of business hours. Business day, business week over? I'm disconnected. Need something from me? When I come back to work – that's my detox regimen.

The Labor Department studies how we Americans spend our time. "Reading, socializing in person, and taking a second to think, have edged down since 2003."[1] Do *you* need to detox? From e-mails? Messaging? Facebook? Twitter? In denial about driving with that device in your hand? Take a second to think.

Think of the God implications. When you come before God at the end of your life, you won't be able to Google the right answers. Preparation requires solitude with God, not your screen.

Think of family and friend implications, "socializing in person." More hearts closer together, quality and quantity time. And don't get me started on earbuds!

Think of the personal peace you're giving away by being constantly connected. Can you sit in a room without the TV on, or do you mindlessly always have it on, cluttering your thoughts?

We're lured into living 24/7/365. However, God didn't create us to be nonstop productive. That's why the Creator designed our bodies and minds to sleep. When God rested on the seventh day and later instituted the Sabbath, He was commanding us to have restful, nonproductive times.

A recovered addict to alcohol told me that he hit bottom when he said, "I'm sick and tired of being sick and tired." My version: "I'm sick and tired of being wired and tired." And in case you're wondering, people know how to reach me should a real emergency happen.

For further reflection: John 14:27; Matthew 11:28-30 – Promises of peace

Lord, we pray that You bless us in our work, but we also ask You give us the willpower to disconnect from work and spend time with loved ones and most especially quiet time with You. To everything there is a season, a time to be connected and a time to put devices in their place. Amen.

June 20

It's Confirmation, Not Graduation…

A country church was having problems with bats in its steeple. The trustees improvised some ways to get rid of them, but to no avail. They called in a professional exterminator, but even he couldn't get the job done. Finally, one of the trustees said, "Pastor, let's confirm them. Then they'll never come back."

That old joke evokes a sad smile. Confirmation is a reaffirmation of the miracle God works in Holy Baptism. "Baptism … saves you" (1 Peter 3:21). Martin Luther explained that Baptism "works forgiveness of sins, rescues from death and the devil, and gives eternal salvation to all who believe this, as the words and promises of God declare."[1] Sadly, many young people imagine that confirmation is graduation from church.

Asked why they left, 18- to 29-year-olds surveyed by the Barna Group said the church is overprotective, shallow, anti-science, repressive, exclusive, and tolerates no doubt.[2] You may not think your congregation is like that, and maybe it's not, but keep in mind that you probably reflect the mind-set of a different generation. Getting behind those reasons, I suspect there's one commanding thing that we haven't taught and modeled for them: the fear and love of God. The fear of God in the Bible is not a cowering fear of punishment but a deep and profound awe that God comes to save us, that God is for us, not against us (cf. Romans 8:31). That's why we love Him. "What does the LORD your God require of you, but to fear the LORD your God, to walk in all his ways, [and] to love him …" (Deuteronomy 10:12). If we manifested that fear and love of God with gentleness and respect, maybe more of our confirmands would keep coming because they would be curious to learn more about the hope that is in us (cf. 1 Peter 3:15).

"Come, O children, listen to me; I will teach you the fear of the LORD" (Psalm 34:11).

For further reflection: 2 Timothy 3:14-17 – "Continue in what you have learned"

If ever they should from Thee stray, / Let them not roam too far away;
Seek them, Good Shepherd, and restore / Them safely to Thy fold once more.
Lead them, O Lord, while life shall last, / And when through death's dark vale
they've passed,
Grant them in Thy great fold to dwell / In heaven above, where all is well.[3] *Amen.*

June 21

A Father's Legacy of Love

Betty was the church secretary when I served as pastor of Holy Cross in Collinsville, Illinois. A widow, she told me more than once, "Pastor, I know it's not right. I know the greatest thing about going to heaven is seeing Jesus, but I sure do want to see my husband Al."

I have the same feeling about my father, Art. He was born in 1920 and passed away in 1985, and in those years he and my mom influenced Dale, Bruce, and Pam more than anyone else. Through most of his working career, father was a milkman. One day I was riding with him on the truck (those days, insurance rules were not as strict as today), and I noticed that he waved to a milkman from another dairy. "You know him?" I asked. "No," he said. "Then why did you wave?" "Because he's trying to make a living just like we are." Lesson learned. Respect all people, even the competition.

Father and his three brothers had a great sense of humor. I worked my way through college and seminary delivering milk at the same dairy, Dixie Dairy. One day, a customer complained to me that his half-gallon of milk had a clothespin in it! I apologized. Later when I told my dad, he said, "You should have told him that we're like Cracker Jack®, putting giveaways in the bottle." He told me to do anything with my life I wanted, but urged me to get a job dealing with the public. The ministry has been just that, and the sense of humor he gave me has helped me through many a day.

Betty wasn't wrong. The greatest thing about heaven will be seeing our Savior Jesus, but the Bible does teach that we'll know one another. Mysterious, I know; just trust the Word. I'll want to tell my father all that happened to me in my life, but most of all I'll thank him for those years between 1920 and 1985, years marked by a dash on his grave marker, years he lived so well and was a godly father. Of all he bequeathed to me, his quiet faith, devotion to family and church, and love of people are gifts from God. How are you and I living "the dash" in the times of our lives? What's our bequest to the future?

For further reflection: Exodus 20:12; 1 Samuel 2:12-26 – A man who was not a good father

Oh, blest that house; it prospers well. / In peace and joy the parents dwell,
And in their children's lives is shown / How richly God can bless His own.[1]

June 22

"The Lord Make His Face to Shine upon You"[1]

As the world turns, yesterday was the longest day of the year – the most hours of sunlight, so the meteorologists tell us. In the real lives we lead, we all have long days when the opposite is true – long, hard days, when the sun doesn't seem to be shining on our souls. In my own circle of acquaintances: a new widow, parents with a two-year-old in the hospital, a man diagnosed with cancer, underemployment, unhappy employment, unpaid bills... What might it be for you and your friends? Long, sunless days!

The earthly situation that stresses you is also a spiritual opportunity to be strengthened by the Spirit in the life of faith, of trusting God's promises. None of us seeks out adversity but it comes. You have to believe that God has protected us from more troubles than we can know, but He doesn't ward off all our problems. Like a loving parent, His hand reaches to lead us through the long days we have to endure. "Now for a little while, if necessary, you have been grieved by various trials, so that the tested genuineness of your faith – more precious than gold that perishes though it is tested by fire – may be found to result in praise and glory and honor at the revelation of Jesus Christ" (1 Peter 1:6-7). Some days, life is as unpleasant as a soap opera. Those are the long days that God especially blesses, as the world turns.

For further reflection: Psalm 25 – "Turn to me and be gracious to me"!

Lord, teach me "to count it all joy" when various trials come my way. You are strengthening my trust in Your promise that "suffering produces endurance, and endurance produces character, and character produces hope, and hope does not put us to shame, because God's love has been poured into our hearts through the Holy Spirit who has been given to us." Lord, "I believe; help my unbelief!" Amen. (James 1:2; Romans 5:3-5; Mark 9:24)

June 23

Learning to Forgive

In Luke 17:3-4 Jesus says, "If your brother sins, rebuke him, and if he repents, forgive him, and if he sins against you seven times in the day, and turns to you seven times, saying, 'I repent,' you must forgive him." We want more specifics. Does Jesus mean big Ten Commandment sins against you: murder, adultery, slander, things like that? Or does He mean little sins: resentment against you, little untruths about you, innocent flirting with your spouse, things like that? Or maybe there was no sin at all – we just don't like whatever he or she did. What's more, how is that person going to improve if I keep forgiving? We push back for more information; the devil's in the details.

Right before that command to forgive, Jesus laid down a general truth: "Temptations to sin are sure to come, but woe to the one through whom they come!" (Luke 17:1). Have I, have you ever done anything that somehow led another person to sin against God? Of course we have. Now that He has us looking in the mirror, not at the other person, Jesus warns, "Pay attention to yourselves!" (Luke 17:3). Are we – we who have sinned and led others to sin – are we the ones to define the conditions of forgiveness? And when we talk to that person who has sinned against us, are we speaking words that reflect the One who forgives us or do our words only unleash our raw hurt? Am I getting in the way of God showing His forgiveness and His patience through me? Who is the Holy One? The devil is indeed in the details!

Is your life totally Jesus-centered? If it is, you forgive. "Pay attention to yourselves!"

For further reflection: Matthew 21:28-32 – Changing your mind about forgiving the one who sins against you

O God, by the patient endurance of Your only-begotten Son You beat down the pride of the old enemy. Help us to treasure rightly in our hearts what our Lord has borne for our sakes that, after His example, we may bear with patience those things that are adverse to us; through Jesus Christ, our Lord.[1]   Amen.

June 24

A Weedy Problem

Glechoma hederacea, the botanists call it, is a member of the mint family. Diane and I know it as "Creeping Charlie," a weed that sends out runners, countless runners. Try as we do, we can't get rid of ol' Creeping Charlie.

Go to a garden store and you might see a little sign for sale: "The kiss of the sun for pardon, / The song of the birds for mirth, / One is nearer God's heart in a garden / Than anywhere else on earth."[1] That was written by Dorothy Frances Gurney and it's true in some ways. This year we've got more cardinals and finches than usual in our backyard. Momma and Poppa Rabbit were busy; more bunnies this year than ever before. The Creator has done so well, and you don't need church or a Bible to figure that much out.

But then there's ol' Creeping Charlie, and you know that something isn't quite right in God's garden. "Seek the LORD while he may be found" (Isaiah 55:6). You follow the runners but they only lead you from one trouble to the next. You try to pull out all that is wrong in life but, just like Creeping Charlie, you know your victory will be short-lived. Finally you come to see the value of a garden guide, not a book from the garden shop but a Bible, which explains the "weeds" of life and offers the promise of a time and place where evil will be uprooted forever.

> Blessed be the God and Father of our Lord Jesus Christ! According to his great mercy, he has caused us to be born again to a living hope through the resurrection of Jesus Christ from the dead, to an inheritance that is imperishable, undefiled, and unfading, kept in heaven for you. (1 Peter 1:3-4)

That's when we'll be nearer God's heart than anywhere on earth!

For further reflection: 1 Peter 5:6-11 – A guide for working in the earthly "garden"

O happy harbor of the saints, / O sweet and pleasant soil!
In thee no sorrow may be found, / No grief, no care, no toil.
O Christ, do Thou my soul prepare / For that bright home of love
That I may see Thee and adore / With all Thy saints above.[2]   *Amen.*

June 25

Are You an Apatheist?

Antonius Felix was the procurator of Judea from 52 to 60 A.D. As a financial and sometimes military official who answered to the emperor in Rome, Felix understandably had other things on his mind when Paul was on trial and wanted to share Jesus. Felix said, "Go away for the present. When I get an opportunity I will summon you" (Acts 24:25). You might call Felix an "apatheist." The word was coined by blogger Hemant Mehta to describe a growing fact of American life – spiritual apathy: 44% of us spend no time seeking "eternal wisdom," 46% don't think about whether they'll go to heaven or not, 28% say "It's not a major priority in my life to find my deeper purpose."[1]

"Apatheists" aren't new. "Christian Questions with Their Answers" were written in the sixteenth century for people preparing to take Holy Communion. *Question 20* and its answer:

> *But what should you do if you are not aware of this need and have no hunger and thirst for the Sacrament?*
>
> To such a person no better advice can be given that this: first, he should touch his body to see if he still has flesh and blood. Then he should believe what the Scriptures say of it in Galatians 5 and Romans 7. Second, he should look around to see whether he is still in the world, and remember that there will be no lack of sin and trouble, as the Scriptures say in John 15-16 and in 1 John 2 and 5. Third, he will certainly have the devil also around him, who with his lying and murdering day and night will let him have no peace, within or without, as the Scriptures picture him in John 8 and 16; 1 Peter 5; Ephesians 6; and 2 Timothy 2.[2]

Are you an apatheist like Felix? "Today, if you hear his voice, do not harden your hearts" (Hebrews 3:7-8). Also read Psalm 95:7-8.

For further reflection: Take a look at some of the passages listed above in the quotation from the Catechism

Delay not, delay not! Why longer abuse / The love and compassion of Jesus, thy God? / A fountain is opened; how canst thou refuse / To wash and be cleansed in His pardoning blood?[3]

June 26

God Bless the Next Generations of Pastors

This is the time of year when many Concordia Seminary graduates are getting ordained and beginning their pastoral ministries. How should church members and freshly-minted pastors interact?

With respect: "Let no one despise you for your youth," Paul told Timothy (1 Timothy 4:12). Age does not make an older person better than a younger person. God is the impartial judge of us all, and were it simply a question of who has sinned the most, old people would win (1 Peter 1:17). Young and old, we are equally forgiven by Jesus' death, and together have a heavenly future because of His resurrection. True, young people should respect their elders, the Fourth Commandment, but that's for orderly life this side of heaven. A young pastor should respect his elders. Paul told young Timothy to treat older men "as you would a father, [and treat] younger men as brothers, older women as mothers, younger women as sisters, in all purity" (1 Timothy 5:1-2).

And laity and clergy, please go at the Lord's work with clear mutual expectations. Paul Wilkes:

> If they are to succeed, this generation of seminarians must, of course, be educationally and spiritually sound, politically aware, as conversant with demography as they are with morality. They must be sensitive to race, ethnicity, gender, and sexuality, but they must not drive us up still another wall with their convictions. … When our future clerics speak, we want to hear powerful yet measured voices bringing out the moral dimension of life, and not only the politics of the left wing of the Democratic Party or the right wing of the Republican, masquerading as religious belief. We want them to be people who in some tiny way reflect the mercy and goodness of the God we want to know.[1]

God bless the next generations of pastors. May they lead us to grow in the faith, hope, and love that are in Christ Jesus. We who are older will especially need that from them as they prepare us for eternity.

For further reflection: Titus 1 – Commands to another young pastor

Lord of the Church, we humbly pray / For those who guide us in Thy way / And speak Thy holy Word. / With love divine their hearts inspire. / And touch their lips with hallowed fire / And needful strength afford.[2]   Amen.

June 27

A Blessed Union

Are you going to a wedding this weekend? Had you lived in Wittenberg, Germany in 1525, you might have attended Martin Luther's wedding.

Celibacy didn't spark the Reformation; the rediscovery of God's undeserved kindness in Christ did. Luther felt the Gospel frees us from groveling to human church rules, a freedom that could be expressed by clerical marriage. Still, the prospect of marriage didn't appeal to Luther personally. So when a former nun, Katharina von Bora, suggested Luther could marry her, he thought "no."

We men may be slow but sometimes we eventually get it. On June 10th Martin and Katie were betrothed, which in those days constituted a legal marriage. And at 10:00 A.M. on the 27th,

> Luther led Katharina to the sound of bells through the streets of Wittenberg to the parish church, where at the portal in the sight of all the people the religious ceremony was observed. Then came a banquet in the Augustinian cloister, and after dinner a dance at the town hall. In the evening there was another banquet.[1]

When Luther had sent out the invitations, he wrote to a friend, "You must come to my wedding. I have made the angels laugh and the devils weep."[2] May all our marriages do the same!

For further reflection: 1 Corinthians 7 – Some practical principles for marriage

Lord Jesus, who's laughing? In this day and age, Satan must be snickering every time he's able to break up a marriage. Thank You for every marriage that endures, for every husband and wife who live under Your Word and in their daily lives model the love You have for the Church. Those blessed marriages strengthen society, honor You, put smiles in our hearts, and make the angels laugh. Amen.

June 28

Communal Blessings

During Communion, there's some… hmm… what shall I call it? There's some idle time, time when you're sitting while other people are going forward to receive the Sacrament. Growing up I was taught to meditate during that time and not look at the people going up to Communion. "Ugly dress." "He doesn't look healthy." "Wonder how their marriage is doing."

An interesting report was published some years ago in *American Sociological Review*. The report shows a connection between having close friends in the congregation and being "extremely satisfied" with life in general. Sadly many of those who go to church every week but have no close friends in the congregation were no happier than those who never attend congregational services.[1] Shouldn't the people who go forward to Communion be your friends? After all, we share the same confession. Shouldn't some be your close friends? Church isn't just Jesus and me. Church is Jesus and His Body.

> God has so composed the body … that there may be no division in the body, but that the members may have the same care for one another. If one member suffers, all suffer together; if one member is honored, all rejoice together. Now you are the body of Christ and individually members of it." (1 Corinthians 12:24-27)

These days I watch more than sing. *There's Pauline at the Communion rail; I wonder how she's doing since Allen died. There's Vernon; he must be about 90 but he faithfully comes. Tim and Lynn – their son is a pastor – they must be rightfully proud. Oh, my, that is an ugly dress, but Dale, that's not what it's about.* "For the forgiveness of sins" (Matthew 26:28) – my sins, her sins, all our sins – "body of Christ." These are my friends, and they witness to me as we together sojourn toward heaven.

For further reflection: 2 Corinthians 1:3-7 – A caring church

One bread, one cup, one body, we, / Rejoicing in our unity,
Proclaim Your love until You come / To bring Your scattered loved ones home.
Lord Jesus Christ, we humbly pray: / O keep us steadfast till that day
When each may be Your welcomed guest / In heaven's high and holy feast.[2]
Amen.

June 29

"When in the Night I Sleepless Lie"

"Hi, Christian here! I do something new every day. Last week I made Mommy and Daddy very happy. I slept through the whole night. Tummy down, diaper end up, and I slept and slept and slept. I felt so good, and Mommy and Daddy were happy with wonderful little me!

"Opa says that sometimes he has trouble sleeping through the night. What do you big people do when you wake up at night? We babies toss and turn because we think something is wrong. Do you big people toss and turn like that? We babies cry because we're scared and alone. Do you big people feel like that? When we babies wake up and cry, Mommy comes and tells me, 'Christian, dear, it's all right.' Who do you big people listen to and hear say 'it's all right?'

"Opa likes hymn verses. Opa says,

> When in the night I sleepless lie, / My soul with heav'nly thoughts supply;
>
> Let no ill dreams disturb my rest, / No pow'rs of darkness me molest.
>
> Oh, may my soul in Thee repose, / And may sweet sleep mine eyelids close,
>
> Sleep that shall me more vig'rous make / To serve my God when I awake![1]

"Opa, maybe you should try sleeping in the baby position!"

For further reflection: Psalm 4 – "In peace I will both lie down and sleep"

Lord Jesus, who dost love me, / Oh, spread Thy wings above me
And shield me from alarm!
Though evil would assail me, / Thy mercy will not fail me:
I rest in Thy protecting arm.[2]   Amen.

June 30

Coming Apart? Come Apart!

The stresses and strains of life sometimes leave you feeling as if you're about to come apart. You know better than anyone else that your appearing to have it all together is a façade. You look together, but so did Humpty Dumpty sitting on the wall.

Jesus and His disciples were so busy that they couldn't even find time to eat. Time to get away for a group retreat! "Come ye yourselves apart into a desert place, and rest a while" (Mark 6:31 KJV). When people and work have you ready to "come apart," do just that – come apart with Jesus. "You will find rest for your souls" (Matthew 11:29).

Well, it sounded like a good idea. They set off but "many saw them going and recognized them, and they ran there on foot from all the towns and got there ahead of them" (Mark 6:33). *Good Lord, can't we get any time to ourselves?* Now watch Jesus. He still showed compassion, fed 5,000, and then "made his disciples get into the boat and go before him to the other side … while he dismissed the crowd. And after he had taken leave of them, he went up on the mountain to pray" (Mark 6:45-46). The plan for a group retreat hadn't worked out but Jesus remained determined that He would still "come apart" to be with His Father.

You too. When your family and coworkers can't get the R&R you all know you need, come apart by yourself. A few minutes to meditate upon a Bible verse, a short walk during break, prayer without ceasing… find your own personal way to come apart. You'll then return to the stress with a renewed peace to share. However, that won't be enough. You still need a group retreat, a coming apart with family and friends. We call that "church," and that retreat is always no more than a few days away.

"All the king's horses and all the king's men / Couldn't put Humpty together again."[1] Devotion and worship can. "You keep him in perfect peace whose mind is stayed on you" (Isaiah 26:3).

For further reflection: Zephaniah 3:14-20 – God promises to bring His people apart

Grant us Thy peace throughout our earthly life, / Our balm in sorrow and our stay in strife; / Then, when Thy voice shall bid our conflict cease, / Call us, O Lord, to Thine eternal peace.[2]   Amen.

July 1

"Our Citizenship Is in Heaven"

Should you visit Concordia Seminary around the Fourth of July, you'll see small American flags all over the campus. Diane and I plant them as a small patriotic gesture, and you probably display the flag as well.

That raises questions about church and state. Church and state had a cozy relationship through most of the twentieth century. "In God we trust" was made the national motto. Presidents spoke freely about Christian faith in public addresses. The commercial world shut down on Sunday because everyone knew you were supposed to go to church. Whether you did or not, well... Today, the twenty-first century, it's different and many Christians feel at odds with the prevailing culture and various government actions. Here's the question: God bless whose America, theirs or ours?

The constitutional distinction between church and state reflects the two great commandments, "Love the Lord your God … love your neighbor as yourself" (Matthew 22:37, 39). The "love" Jesus lays on us is selfless. Love "does not insist on its own way … [it] bears all things" (1 Corinthians 13:5, 7). In one profound sense, it makes no difference to a Christian where our culture goes or what our government does. Who proved to be the good neighbor in Jesus' parable about the Good Samaritan? "'The one who showed him mercy.' And Jesus said to him, 'You go, and do likewise'" (Luke 10:37) Ours is faith in the eternal that is shown in good works here and now. Let your display of the flag remind you that God wills us to do good works in our neighborhoods, communities, and nation (see Ephesians 2:10). If Christians bring a change in America's prevailing culture, thank God. Should that not happen, this culture is not our judge. "Our citizenship is in heaven, and from it we await a Savior, the Lord Jesus Christ" (Philippians 3:20).

For further reflection: Micah 6:8 – Founding father James Madison wrote, "Justice is the end [goal] of government. It ever has been and ever will be pursued until it be obtained, or until liberty be lost in the pursuit."[1]

May ev'ry mountain height, / Each vale and forest green,
Shine in Your Word's pure light, / And its rich fruits be seen!
May ev'ry tongue / Be tuned to praise
And join to raise / A grateful song.[2]   Amen.

July 2

Unspoken Prayers Answered

There will be times in your personal devotion when something jumps out at you, or better that I say, something gets into your head and down into your heart. When that happens, don't rush on! Pause and ponder. I was truly moved to meditation when I came across the following prayer in my devotional reading.

> I asked God for strength, that I might achieve; I was made weak that I might learn humbly to obey.
>
> I asked for health, that I might do great things; I was given infirmity, that I might do better things.
>
> I asked for riches, that I might be happy; I was given poverty, that I might be wise.
>
> I asked for power, that I might have the praise of men; I was given weakness, that I might feel the need of God.
>
> I asked for all things, that I might enjoy life; I was given life, that I might enjoy all things.
>
> I got nothing that I asked for but everything that I hoped for. Almost despite myself, my unspoken prayers were answered. I am, among all men, most richly blessed. Amen.[1]

Should you choose, you can spend more than a minute – more than a once-through – meditating on those words. Adding to its poignancy, this prayer was allegedly found in the pocket of a Confederate soldier killed at "Devil's Den" in the Battle of Gettysburg, on this day in 1863.

Jesus: "No one can serve two masters, for either he will hate the one and love the other, or he will be devoted to the one and despise the other. You cannot serve God and money" (Matthew 6:24).

For further reflection: 1 Kings 3:5-15 – Another wise prayer

Hence, all earthly treasure! / Jesus is my pleasure, / Jesus is my choice. Hence, all empty glory! / Naught to me the story / Told with tempting voice. Pain or loss, / Or shame or cross / Shall not from my Savior move me Since He deigns to love me.[2]

July 3

Liberty, with "Solemn Acts of Devotion"

John Adams addressed the Continental Congress on July 1st, 1776. Thomas Jefferson said Adams was "not graceful nor elegant, nor remarkably fluent," but spoke "with a power of thought and expression that moved us from our seats."[1] It was effective indeed. The next day, July 2nd, the delegates approved the Declaration of Independence.

Adams wrote to his wife Abigail:

> The second day of July 1776 will be the most memorable epoch in the history of America. I am apt to believe it will be celebrated by succeeding generations as the great anniversary festival. It ought to be commemorated as the Day of Deliverance by solemn acts of devotion to God Almighty. It ought to be solemnized with pomp and parade, with shows, games, sports, guns, bells, bonfires, and illuminations, from one end of this continent to the other, from this time forward forever more.[2]

On July 4th the delegates voted a second time for the Declaration of Independence. At noon on July 8th it was read to the public with the ringing of bells and officially signed on August 2nd. Today, well over two centuries later, we are entering an Independence Day observance that will be celebrated much as John Adams wished. May we also observe our freedom with "solemn acts of devotion to God Almighty."

For further reflection: Leviticus 25:10 – Words cast on a bell - inscribed in our hearts?

Almighty God, Maker of heaven and earth, fill us with awe that we are a free people. May we who confess Your Son observe our freedom "with solemn acts of devotion" to You and selfless service to others so that our fellow citizens will believe with us that "our help is in the name of the LORD" (Psalm 124:8). In Jesus' name. Amen.

July 4

Explaining Self-Evident Truths

"We hold these truths to be self-evident," says the Declaration of Independence, "that all men are created equal, that they are endowed by their Creator with certain unalienable Rights, that among these are Life, Liberty and the pursuit of Happiness…"

Not all people held those truths to be self-evident. One out of five Americans did not agree with the Revolution. Over 700 colonists signed a petition in Scott's Tavern in New York, stating that they were "steadily and uniformly opposed" to the Revolution, calling it was the "most unnatural, unprovoked Rebellion that ever disgraced the annals of Time."[1]

Many Americans today hold those truths to be self-evident, but not because they come from the Creator. They believe these individual rights are inherent in us, not gifts from God – or, if we want to give God a little lip service, these "self-evident truths" came from God, but like the god of the deists, he went away and left us on our own.

We're no longer in a time when the Church has a privileged place in American culture. Some Christians complain about America's cultural and moral decline, but don't forget, Christians continue to be by far the largest religious group in the United States. If great civic truths are not as self-evident today as in the past, shouldn't we teach how they come from the Creator of us all? What better way to teach fundamental truths than by involvement in lives of service to community and country?

"If my people who are called by my name humble themselves, and pray and seek my face and turn from their wicked ways, then I will hear from heaven and will forgive their sin and heal their land" (2 Chronicles 7:14). Let this be evident to our fellow citizens as they watch you and me follow Jesus Christ.

For further reflection: Deuteronomy 30 – Words of civic responsibility to believers

Save us from weak resignation / To the evils we deplore; / Let the gift of your salvation / Be our glory evermore. / Grant us wisdom, grant us courage, / Serving You whom we adore, / Serving You whom we adore.[2] *Amen.*

July 5

Make Hope Evident for All to See

Back in 1776, the day after Independence Day must have been a day of great hope for many Americans, at least the ones who knew what had happened. News traveled more slowly then. But hope is not easily realized. In August, the Continental Army was trapped on Long Island, New York. Although many Americans escaped, the next month, September, the Continental Army was completely driven out of New York. It would be seven years before independence would be fully realized. Seven years. Hope is not easily realized.

What is true in civic life is also true in your personal life. Hope is not easily realized, and unless you nurture your hopes, they will turn to despair. Every aspect of your life has a spiritual dimension. Every problem you face, every battle that leaves you wounded or bloodied, can easily replace hope with despair. It takes effort to nourish hope, and nothing is better than this picture of hope – the empty tomb of the resurrected Jesus Christ. He lives and offers the hope that will sustain you. With His perfect timing, God will keep His promises (2 Timothy 2:13).

George Washington wasn't the first leader who had the task of caring for hope. Ancient Egypt endured seven years of famine, but because God had given a leader whom He blessed with foresight, Joseph, the people got through until the earth again yielded food. Any nation needs leaders with foresight to anticipate the hard times. When they come, as they always do, leaders need to instill hope. You are a leader too. In your family, among coworkers and friends, sharing hope that comes from the promises of God sustains people tempted to despair. In our ASAP world, the good news of real hope travels slowly. Make hope a verb that is evident in your life. "Let us not grow weary of doing good, for in due season we will reap, if we do not give up" (Galatians 6:9).

For further reflection: Genesis 41 – Providence provides leaders for hope

O God, You are the answer to our questions. You have promised that one day You will wipe away every tear from our eyes. Then our questions will cease and our praise will be pure. Grant that we guard the image of hope in our souls. Amen.[1]

July 6

Forgiveness Brings the Greatest Freedom

What's the greatest freedom in your life?

We look to God for many things: for health, for family, for peace. That's fine, but God is more than Walmart where you pick and choose the goodies you want. God, as the Bible tells it, is holy and made us to be that way … but we're not. Unless you get together with God on His terms, other things are counter-productive and sooner or later you'll regret prioritizing them. Without the forgiveness of sins, all the other goodies are here today and gone tomorrow.

We're back to where we're supposed to be – at one with God, reconciled – when we trust that Christ paid the price for our sins. You might still feel guilty about some things, people might continue to throw your wrongs in your face, but God says, *The price has been paid. You and I are at peace.* "There is therefore now no condemnation for those who are in Christ Jesus" (Romans 8:1). Now that we've celebrated our national freedom, I hope you'll rank freedom from guilt and peace with God as the greatest gift of all, a gift that lasts, a gift from which countless blessings flow.

With any freedom comes responsibility. Gospel freedom brings the responsibility of taking recurring guilt to the cross, and not slipping back under the condemnation of the Law. "For freedom Christ has set us free; stand firm therefore, and do not submit again to a yoke of slavery" (Galatians 5:1).

Have you ever heard anyone say that justification by grace through faith alone is too easy? It's not; oh, it's not! Keeping the freedom of God's Gospel takes constant vigilance, lest we backslide into the guilt that the Law brings.

For further reflection: Galatians 3:10-29 – The purpose of the Law is to lead us to see our need for a Savior

My sin is very sore and great, / I mourn beneath its dreadful load;
O free me from this weight, / My Savior, through Thy precious blood;
And with Thy Father for me plead / That Thou has suffered in my stead;
From me the burden then is rolled. / Lord, I lay hold on Thy dear promises
*   of old. Amen.*[1]

July 7

Fret Not Yourself!

When I was a kid, my fingers used to break out. Some ointments helped a bit, but not much. It turned out to be from nerves, from worrying about things. I grew out of it, maybe matured out of it, until one night some years ago. I woke up in the middle of the night, furiously scratching a couple fingers. I was worrying about something at the Seminary, afraid that it wouldn't turn out right, and so my digital barometer, my fingers, registered the storm in my soul.

A day or two later my morning devotion took me to Psalm 37:8, "Fret not yourself; it tends only to evil." *Yeah*, I thought, *but...*

Diane and I had been away from campus. Those were days before I had a smartphone and tablet, and couldn't keep up with work away from the office computer. When we finally came back, I opened my e-mails and found that my coworkers had already tackled the task that had me worried. "Fret not yourself; it tends only to evil." "Repetition is the mother of learning."[1]

What is the evil? Oswald Chambers:

> Have you been bolstering up that stupid soul of yours with the idea that your circumstances are too much for God? Put all your "supposing" on one side and dwell in the shadow of the Almighty. Deliberately tell God that you will not fret about that thing. All our fret and worry is caused by calculating without God.[2]

> His wisdom never plans in vain,
> Nor falters nor mistakes.
> All that His counsels may ordain
> A blessed ending makes.[3]

For further reflection: Psalm 37 – Let the Word work on your worries

I thank You, my heavenly Father, through Jesus Christ, Your dear Son, that You have kept me this night from all harm and danger; and I pray that You would keep me this day also from sin and every evil, that all my doings and life may please You. For into Your hands I commend myself, my body and soul and all things. Let Your holy angel be with me, that the evil foe may have no power over me. Amen.[4]

July 8

Are You Planning for Eternity?

St. Louis summers usually include some 100 degree, muggy, oppressive days. That always prompts some minister to put this up on the church signboard: "You think this is hot?"

If you have doubts about hell, consider the possibility of hell in light of how you are using or misusing the time God is giving you now, the time of grace. In *The Saints Everlasting Rest*, written in 1650, Richard Baxter puts these words on the lips of a person who didn't think hell was a real possibility... until he found himself there.

> How many weeks and months and years did I lose, which if I had improved, I might now have been happy! Could I find no time to study the work for which I had all my time? No time, among all my labors, to labor for eternity? Had I time to eat and drink and sleep and none to save my soul? Could I take time to secure the world and none to try my title to heaven?[1]
>
> The day is surely drawing near / When Jesus, God's anointed,
> In all His power shall appear / As judge whom God appointed.
> Then fright shall banish idle mirth, / And flames on flames shall ravage earth / As Scripture long has warned us.[2]

Wrote another seventeenth century theologian, John Gerhard: "It is wiser to be concerned about escaping this eternal fire by true repentance than to engage in an unprofitable argument as to the nature of this fire."[3]

So the summation, from Baxter: "Study thoroughly this one word – eternity."[4]

For further reflection: 2 Corinthians 5:10; 1 Peter 1:17; Hebrews 9:27 – You can't take this final exam over!

May Christ our intercessor be / And through His blood and merit
Read from His book that we are free / With all who life inherit.
Then we shall see Him face to face, / With all His saints in that blest place
Which He has purchased for us.[5]

July 9

A Lesson in Patience

"Opa here. Thank you, Drew and Jacob, for helping me understand the word 'long-suffering.' For only three years old and eighteen months old, you are good teachers."

"What do you mean, Opa?"

"Drew, tell our friends about what you did yesterday."

"We sneaked upstairs and found a big white board."

"Drew, they call that Styrofoam™."

"Thanks, Opa. We crumbled it up and threw it all over the floor. When Styrofoam is crumbled, it even sticks to the wall."

"Drew, you call that static electricity. So, what did you do next?"

"Opa, we stood over the railing and threw the Styrofoam down the stairs. We made it snow. That was so much fun!"

"Uh, not exactly what Oma and I thought. It took us two hours to clean up the snowstorm."

"Really? We didn't notice. We went on to other things."

"So boys, staying here at our house, you are teaching us about 'long-suffering.' You remind me of the word in the Bible. 'The longsuffering of our Lord is salvation' (2 Peter 3:15 KJV). Our heavenly Father is patient, long-suffering with us, His children. We should be the same way too. Long-suffering is a part of the fruit of the Spirit (Galatians 5:22-23). You boys are giving us real spiritual growth!"

"Glad to help, Opa!"

For further reflection: Exodus 34:1-9 – "Slow to anger"

How can I thank You, Lord, / For all Your loving kindness,
That You have patiently / Borne with me in my blindness!
When dead in many sins / And trespasses I lay,
I kindled, holy God, / Your anger ev'ry day.[1]

July 10

Nuture Hope

What do you do when you've had your heart set on something… and you don't get it? How do you react when you've worked hard and long for something… and you don't get it? "Hope deferred makes the heart sick" (Proverbs 13:12).

Hope is a special plant in God's garden. It's seasonal – with its times to bloom and its times to fade and eventually come to an end. "So now faith, hope, and love abide, these three; but the greatest of these is love" (1 Corinthians 13:13). Why is love the greatest? Because love is eternal; "love never ends" (1 Corinthians 13:8). Love is the greatest because "God is love" (1 John 4:8). Hope, and faith as well, are temporary gifts from God to help us toward eternity. "Hope that is seen is not hope. For who hopes for what he sees? But if we hope for what we do not see, we wait for it with patience" (Romans 8:24-25). When God calls us to Himself, calls you to eternal love, you'll no longer need hope. Your hope will be realized.

Until then, hope needs nurture. It needs the remembrance of baptismal water, when the sign of Christ's cross was made over your forehead and heart "to mark you as one redeemed by Christ the crucified."[1] To bloom in this earthly life, hope needs nurture from the Body and Blood of Christ, in, with, and under the bread and wine in the Sacrament of the Altar. Hope blooms when it's tended every day with words that point us again and again to the fulfillment of all God's promises in Jesus Christ (2 Corinthians 1:20). "For if we have been planted together in the likeness of his death, we shall be also in the likeness of his resurrection" (Romans 6:5 KJV). So, tend hope, trusting the faithfulness of God that the time of eternal love will come!

For further reflection: Psalm 42 – "Set your hope fully on the grace that will be brought to you at the revelation of Jesus Christ" (1 Peter 1:13)

Only Jesus can impart / Balm to heal the wounded heart,
Peace that flows from sin forgiv'n, / Joy that lifts the soul to heav'n,
Faith and hope to walk with God / In the way that Enoch[2] trod.[3]

July 11

The Church Bell Rings for Thee

If you go to church this weekend, and I hope you will, be careful. Churches have ways of teaching us how to hide our impurities and sins. Not that they mean to – it just happens. "God, I thank you that I am not like other men … I fast twice a week; I give tithes of all that I get" and I sometimes sit in church and think I don't need a Savior quite as much as some other people I know (Luke 18:11-12).

Jesus once said, "No one sews a piece of unshrunk cloth on an old garment. If he does, the patch tears away from it, the new from the old, and a worse tear is made" (Mark 2:21). Look as good to others as you may, you can't put the patch of appearing religious on an impure and sinful heart. The devil uses the ways of churches to deceive us into thinking that our shows of being religious are compatible with our self-serving heart. It won't work, "the patch tears away from it, the new from the old, and a worse tear is made."

"But that is not the way you learned Christ! … put off your old self … and … put on the new self, created after the likeness of God in true righteousness and holiness" (Ephesians 4:20, 22, 24). So be careful in church lest the devil game the system and deceive you. Pray in church, pray always, that the Spirit make you new within, a person of one cloth, clothed in true righteousness and holiness.

How loudly does the church bell ring in your ears? Jesus says, "I came not to call the righteous, but sinners" (Mark 2:17). "God, be merciful to me, a sinner!" (Luke 18:13).

For further reflection: Matthew 6:1-16 – Warning against hypocrisy

I do not come because my soul / Is free from sin and pure and whole / And worthy of Thy grace;

I do not speak to Thee because / I've ever justly kept Thy laws / And dare to meet Thy face.

I know that, though in doing good / I spend my life, I never could / Atone for all I've done;

But though my sins are black as night, / I dare to come before Thy sight / Because I trust Thy Son.[1]   *Amen.*

July 12

Helping Your Pastor Prepare His – No, Your – Sermon

Let's hope your pastor is not like the old joke about the minister who used the hymn right before the sermon to prepare! Thorough preparation by your pastor is demanded because the sermon belongs to you, the parishioners, at least in part.

Thomas Long of Candler School of Theology writes, "The picture of the preacher sitting alone in the study, working with a biblical text in preparation for the sermon, is misleading. It is not the preacher who goes to the Scripture; it is the Church that goes to the Scripture by means of the preacher."[1]

We all have questions about life and about God. Many laypeople work for a living, with little time during the week to study the Bible. Those who are faithful in studying the Bible haven't had the privilege of a seminary education in the Scriptures. Thomas Long again: "The church prepares and trains its ministers, including sending them to seminaries, not because ministers are better or smarter than other Christians, but because the church needs workers equipped to help the church to know the truth and to live in its light."[2]

Because ordination did not bestow all knowledge upon your minister, you can help your pastor prepare the sermon by asking sincere questions about God's ways in the world. "Pastor, I've been wondering about…" "Pastor, I've been struggling with…" "Pastor, I know that God … but I don't see it happening." A pastor who truly cares about his people will constantly listen to their real questions and continually go into the study to keep on searching God's Word for helpful answers. That's why the sermon prepared by the pastor belongs to the parishioners, and all together listen to God's Word centered on Jesus Christ. Could it be that one reason some sermons aren't engaging is because we're not sharing with our pastors our real-life questions about God's ways in the world?

For further reflection: Luke 2:41-47 – Questions in church

Lord Jesus, You are "the way, and the truth, and the life." Nicodemus came to You with questions. Paul, after his conversion, consulted with Your apostles to make sure he was preaching correctly. Help us talk with our pastors about Your Word, mutually asking questions and mutually blessed by Your Spirit through our searching. Amen. (John 14:6; 3:1-2; Galatians 2:2)

July 13

Is Your Illness an Opportunity?

When you're sick, many things go on hold. You get a cold and don't get as much done as normal. However, when you go into the hospital for treatment of a serious illness, your inner thoughts and feelings don't go on hold. A serious diagnosis weighing on your mind, your body in the hospital for mystifying tests and procedures, you're anxious – *What's to become of me?* – fretting over so many things in life still left to do. Your thoughts and feelings kick into high gear.

Christians turn to God with prayers for successful treatment. I'm sure I will too, but I've come to hope my attitude will be something even better, that my prayers will ask for something I know God will grant because it is His will. Strange as it sounds, I'd hope to have an attitude of *What an opportunity! I'm being stripped of my reliance on anyone or anything except God. It's me and God; my Savior and me.* Unwelcome as it is, life-threatening illness is a time when you are forced to focus on what Jesus says – "one thing is necessary" – and that will not be taken away from you (Luke 10:42). Think of where you will be a hundred years from now; isn't this forced purifying of your affections the best outcome of all?

> I am continually with You; you hold my right hand.
>
> You guide me with your counsel, and afterward you will receive me to glory.
>
> Whom have I in heaven but you? And there is nothing on earth that I desire besides you.
>
> My flesh and my heart may fail, but God is the strength of my heart and my portion forever. (Psalm 73:23-26)

For further reflection: Psalm 23 – The Lord be with you

Lord, Thee I love with all my heart; / I pray Thee, ne'er from me depart,
With tender mercy cheer me. / Earth has no pleasure I would share,
Yea, heav'n itself were void and bare / If Thou, Lord, were not near me.
And should my heart for sorrow break, / My trust in Thee no one could shake.
Thou art the portion I have sought; / Thy precious blood my soul has bought.
Lord Jesus Christ, my God and Lord, my God and Lord,
Forsake me not! I trust Thy Word.[1]   *Amen.*

July 14

All Star Parenting

Ask a grade school child, "What do you want to be when you grow up?" and you'll often hear, "I want to be a baseball player" or a football player or tennis star or whatever. That might happen but most won't make any All Star Game. In fact, numerous studies have shown that many American parents believe that life will not be better for their children. Without throwing a bucket of cold water on their youthful dreams, we want to give them a soul-deep hope that can take the inevitable strikeouts.

Three words are scattered throughout the Bible: faith, hope, and love. Love is the unconditional love that God gives us in Christ, the kind of love that young people need to know will always be there for them. Love is the greatest because it is forever (see 1 Corinthians 13:8). Faith is not forever; it is provisional. Faith is trusting the promises of God until faith gives way to heavenly sight. A young person needs contentment, the contentment that comes from trusting God's promises in the Bible – faith, to cope with whatever life may bring. Faith and love put a smile on our face, and that smile reflects hope in God. Adults know that it's a learned skill to have soul-deep hope even while striking out. "Why are you cast down, O my soul, and why are you in turmoil within me? / Hope in God" (Psalm 42:11). Sharing such mature hope with children is All Star parenting!

For further reflection: 2 Timothy 4:1-8 – Sports metaphors to model perseverance

Father of all wisdom, I need some! My own youthful idealism has met reality and I see how things really are in life. Give me a wise skill to encourage young people in their aspirations. Help them see a friend in me that I can show them what a friend they have in Jesus. Amen.

July 15

"Lord, Teach Us to Pray"[1]

"Our Father who art in heaven … Forgive us our trespasses as we forgive those who trespass against us." Jesus teaches us sinners to beg the Father for forgiveness. Your outward conduct may be OK, but our thoughts and heart conceal sin. He perfectly kept the Ten Commandments that you and I daily break. He suffered and died to pay the punishment for our sins. It's quite simple; we ask the Father for forgiveness and, grateful to Him, we forgive others for Jesus' sake.

How would it read if Americans had authored this prayer? It wouldn't be directed to "Our Father who art in heaven" but instead to other people: "You, please forgive me my trespasses so I can go and do whatever it is I want to do." And the American prayer would continue, "I won't necessarily forgive those who trespass against me. I want to hang onto their guilt as a club that I can use against them whenever I want."

But Jesus teaches,

> *I earned forgiveness for you even though you don't deserve forgiveness. So I ask you to share My forgiveness with others. I'm not saying you should condone the wrong that was done to you. I'm not saying you should not pursue justice in proper ways. I am saying, don't let the person who wronged you keep emotional control over your life. Forgive as I have forgiven you. Forgiving the person who wronged you will bring you freedom; forgiveness breaks the emotional hold they have over you.*

"For freedom Christ has set us free; stand firm therefore, and do not submit again to a yoke of slavery" (Galatians 5:1).

That's what He teaches. Do you follow Him as your Lord?

For further reflection: Matthew 18:21-35 – The unforgiving servant

Grant me the strength to do / With ready heart and willing
Whatever You command, / My calling here fulfilling;
That I do what I should / While trusting You to bless
The outcome for my good, / For You must give success.[2]   Amen.

July 16

The Blessings of the Long Grind

The long grind, all the responsibilities, all the work, all the worries, day by day, year by year… why?

Lay part of it on God. "All our days pass away under your wrath; we bring our years to an end like a sigh. / The years of our life are seventy, or even by reason of strength eighty; / yet their span is but toil and trouble" (Psalm 90:9-10). God could whisk the burdens away, give us country club living without any care, but no.

"You have set our iniquities before you, our secret sins in the light of your presence" (Psalm 90:8). God is just; our offenses must be punished. God will vindicate Himself; who are we to blame Him? Lay the blame on us. Holy and most gracious God, have mercy and hear us!

On this date in 1861, 33,000 Union soldiers marched toward Manassas, 30 miles west of Washington, D.C., to fight 22,000 Confederates in the first major battle of the Civil War. "Many Washingtonians rode out to Manassas Junction in their carriages with their packed lunches in hope of watching the rebels surrender soon after the first shots were fired." ASAP? On July 21, it was the Union army that was defeated. Secretary of War Edwin Stanton wrote, "The rout, overthrow, and demoralization of the whole army were complete." Four years later, 620,000 had been killed, the equivalent of 5 million in today's population.[1]

ASAP just doesn't fit life the way we have to live it. "Return, O LORD! How long? Have pity on your servants!" (Psalm 90:13). Jesus is God's answer to that prayer. The sinless Son of God took the anger of the Father against our sins. That being so, why still the long grind? Blessings in disguise. It reminds us not to trivialize the long-suffering of God, to cling to Jesus' righteousness, and to look to that day when we're free of sinning.

> Alleluia cannot always / Be our song while here below;
>
> Alleluia, our transgressions / Make us for a while forgo;
>
> For the solemn time is coming / When our tears for sin must flow.[2]

For further reflection: James 5:7-11 – Endurance

Therefore in our hymns we pray Thee, / Grant us, blessed Trinity, / At the last to keep Thine Easter / With Thy faithful saints on high; / There to Thee forever singing / Alleluia joyfully.[3]

July 17

Slow Down Your Summer!

This is a summer advisory. Please be alert to the possibility that your summer is speeding by. In only a month, schools will start reopening! Have you taken some significant downtime yet?

Remember when kids chased after the milkman to get some ice, or after the Good Humor® truck for ice cream?

Remember when you played ball or dolls or rode your bike or climbed a tree? You actually wanted to go outside and play! Stay inside with the computer? Are you crazy?

Remember when cutting the lawn wasn't hired out to a company but to a kid? Sometimes he used a push mower; he was the power!

Remember when it got so hot you slept on the floor near the front door because that was the best place to catch a bit of breeze?

Remember when you got bored? Your parents didn't go into a panic and come up with things for you to do. You got bored – they wisely let you be bored – and you got better acquainted with the second most important person in your life: yourself. And remember when summer's downtime gave you time with the most important person: your God, your Creator, your Savior?

This has been an alert. Slow down your summer!

For further reflection: Psalm 90 – It takes unhurried time to "get a heart of wisdom"

O measureless Might, ineffable Love,
While angels delight to hymn Thee above,
Thy humbler creation, though feeble their lays,
With true adoration shall sing to Thy praise.[1]

July 18

Everyone Loses in the Blame Game

"For better or for worse?" I was at our home in Collinsville, Illinois. That's where we raised our kids, made our mortgage payments for 30 years, where we often retreat, and most likely will retire. Diane called and said, "When you come back to campus, please bring that gallon of paint." Lest I forget, I immediately got it, opened the car hatch, and put it right in. Some hours later, I was driving back to St. Louis on a city street – I was daydreaming, yes, I admit it – when all of a sudden I snapped back to attention and hit the brakes to avoid a rear-ender. Seconds later, I wondered, *What's that smell?* Yup, my sudden stop had tipped the gallon of paint – white paint flowing all over the black interior of the back of the car. *How am I going to explain this to Diane? Diane, why didn't you put that lid on more securely the last time you used it?* She'll say, *Dale, why didn't you set it on the floor? Why were you tailgating?*

So what happened? Each of us made a feeble attempt to lay blame on the other but we instinctively knew it wasn't worth an argument. After decades of marriage, you learn that everyone loses in the blame game. When the Pharisees asked Jesus why Moses permitted divorce, He said, "Because of your hardness of heart" (Mark 10:5). A husband and wife can legitimately blame each other for many things, but without daily patience and forgiveness it will lead to hardness of heart in a marriage. Paint dries slowly, and hardness of heart doesn't happen overnight. "This at last is bone of my bones and flesh of my flesh. … they shall become one flesh" (Genesis 2:23-24). Diane and I put the lid on blame and worked together to clean up my mess.

For further reflection: Galatians 5:16-24 – Fits of anger - patience

Our heavenly Father, when the door of our home is closed and no one can see, we often show ourselves more self-centered than selfless. Yet You patiently bear with us, forgiving our sins and hardness of heart for Jesus' sake. By Your word and Spirit, give us love that "is patient and kind," love that "bears all things" and "endures all things." Amen. (1 Corinthians 13:4, 7)

July 19

Voluntary Exile

Why go to church? Because I need my own Patmos.

> I, John, your brother and partner in the tribulation and the kingdom and the patient endurance that are in Jesus, was on the island called Patmos on account of the word of God and the testimony of Jesus. I was in the Spirit on the Lord's day, and I heard… (Revelation 1:9-10)

Because John didn't hide the Gospel light, he was exiled to Patmos, an island in the Aegean Sea. On Sunday, "the Lord's day," God's Word came to him. Don't you need escape, a voluntary exile from the tussles and temptations of sinful life so that God might speak to you? The workaday world is unrelenting in its demands upon you. Where shall you find "the patient endurance that [is] in Jesus"? "Come away by yourselves to a desolate place and rest a while" (Mark 6:31).

The old-fashioned way of keeping "the Lord's day" – businesses closed, socially expected to go to church – was different than today. The old ways acknowledged publicly and with some compulsion that church worship is unique. Today the compelling uniqueness of church must be personal. "I was in the Spirit on the Lord's day, and I heard…" The mystery given to John in Revelation was mystery centered on Jesus Christ. "Fear not, I am the first and the last, and the living one. I died, and behold I am alive forevermore, and I have the keys of Death and Hades. Write therefore the things that you have seen…" (Revelation 1:17-19). "Come to me" (Matthew 11:28). Surrounded by death, He promises His life. Beset by our fears, He promises His presence. Bewildered by life, He gives us His Word. "How long, O LORD?" we sigh (Psalm 13:1; Revelation 6:10), and He gives us patient endurance (Revelation 1:9). It's all heard on our own Patmos on the Lord's day.

> Joy of the desolate, light of the straying, / Hope of the penitent, fadeless and pure; / Here speaks the Comforter, tenderly saying, / Earth has no sorrow that heav'n cannot cure.[1]

For further reflection: Ecclesiastes 5:1-7 – Fear God in church

Speak, O God, and I will hear Thee, / Let Thy will be done indeed. / May I undisturbed draw near Thee / While Thou dost Thy people feed. / Here of life the fountain flows; / Here is balm for all our woes.[2]

July 20

"The Heavens Declare the Glory of God"[1]

And God said, "Let there be lights in the expanse of the heavens to separate the day from the night. And let them be for signs and for seasons, and for days and years, and let them be lights in the expanse of the heavens to give light upon the earth." And it was so. And God made the two great lights – the greater light to rule the day and the lesser light to rule the night – and the stars. (Genesis 1:14-16)

On July 20, 1969, we creatures of God were blessed with a new view of the magnificence of His creation. "The *Eagle* has landed," and for the first time man stood on another heavenly body, that "lesser light" that rules the night.

Over the centuries, religious zealotry has taken many forms. Physical atrocities committed in the name of "God," doctrinaire believers contemptuous of those who disagree, and now many contemporary Americans fashion their personal faith according to their own desires. People! "Lift up your eyes on high and see: who created these?" (Isaiah 40:26). "Know that the LORD, he is God! It is he who made us, and we are his" (Psalm 100:3).

Washington University in St. Louis has an exact replica of the Mars rovers *Spirit* and *Opportunity*, launched in June and July, 2003. When I walk through the campus, I often visit that replica and gaze awestruck at the photos from Mars. It lifts my soul higher than any church steeple. How vast Your creation, O God! Apollo 11 landed at "Tranquility Base." The world today is far from tranquil, but we could take "one small step" in that direction by paying attention to pictures sent to us from light years away, by marveling at the creation closer to home, outside your door, and with eyes opened, experience anew what modern man has largely forgotten – the fear of God.

"And God saw everything that he had made, and behold, it was very good" (Genesis 1:31).

For further reflection: Psalm 8 – In the vastness of creation, He cares for us

Praise to the Lord! O let all that is in us adore Him!
All that has life and breath, come now with praises before Him!
Let the Amen / Sound from His people again; / Gladly forever adore Him![2]

July 21

Life Isn't Fair!

"Life isn't fair." That's what St. Louis Cardinals outfielder Randal Grichuk tweeted when he learned of the death of teammate Oscar Taveras. Taveras, 22 years old, and his 18-year-old girlfriend were killed in October, 2014 when Taveras apparently lost control of his car on a rain-slick street in his native Dominican Republic. Taveras had a bright future in major league baseball as a power-hitting outfielder, but the St. Louis Post-Dispatch headlined, "Forever Left Untold."[1]

"Life isn't fair" is often said and it's true. Life isn't fair because the Law can't deliver what it promises. Background: The Law, whether it's rules of the road or God's great "Thou shalt's" and "Thou shalt not's," promises that proper conduct will be rewarded and improper conduct punished. That's fair. Oscar Taveras was developing his baseball talent and, as a result, should have become a major league superstar. Not to be. Why do we say, "No good deed goes unpunished?"[2] Because you can't depend upon the principle of Law to deliver what it promises. Good works don't always result in a person getting their due. The reason is sin. Try as we might, no one can keep God's commandments or meet human expectations. Insidious sin mucks everything up.

Jesus kept the Law, obeyed every "Thou shalt" and "Thou shalt not." You might think that His death was unfair – He had done no wrong – but in the eternal scheme of things Jesus' death was fair. Sin deserves punishment and God exacted it. "The wages of sin is death" (Romans 6:23a). The Good News is that Jesus substituted for us by suffering the consequence of our failure to live up to the Law. His death was sacrifice for you and me; that's selfless love. "The free gift of God is eternal life in Christ Jesus our Lord" (Romans 6:23b).

Our sympathies to all who grieve because life really is unfair. Jesus Christ promises the restoration of life as it should be. "Within the kingdom of His might / All things are just and good and right: / To God all praise and glory!"[3]

For further reflection: Galatians 3:21-29 – Law and sin - promise and Christ

Our works cannot salvation gain; / They merit only endless pain,
Forgive us, Lord! To Christ, we flee, / Who pleads for us endlessly.
Have mercy, Lord![4]

July 22

That Day, That Joyous Day

Let's do a little Bible study. Zephaniah – most of us would have to use the Bible's table of contents to find where it is!

Chapter One: *The day of the Lord is near* and oh, that day will be a doozy. "A day of wrath is that day, a day of distress and anguish, / a day of ruin and devastation, a day of darkness and gloom, / a day of clouds and thick darkness" (1:15). *God will definitively punish sin.* "Depart from me, you cursed, into the eternal fire prepared for the devil and his angels" (Matthew 25:41).

Chapter Two: *Is there any hope?* "Seek the LORD, all you humble of the land, who do his just commands; / seek righteousness; seek humility; perhaps you may be hidden" (Zephaniah 2:3). *Hide yourself in faith in Jesus.* "Now the righteousness of God has been manifested apart from the law, although the Law and the Prophets bear witness to it – the righteousness of God through faith in Jesus Christ for all who believe" (Romans 3:21-22).

Chapter Three: *Anticipating that day:* "The LORD your God is in your midst, a mighty one who will save; / he will rejoice over you with gladness; he will quiet you by his love; / he will exult over you with loud singing" (Zephaniah 3:17). *Trusting Jesus is the way to that joyous day.* "You have died, and your life is hidden with Christ in God. When Christ who is your life appears, then you also will appear with him in glory" (Colossians 3:3-4).

Let's review our quick study. The words "that day" appear often and refer to God's terrible judgment on sin. Only the righteous will come safely through that day. We sinners don't have it; God gives it to us through faith in Jesus. Look forward: You will appear with Jesus in glory!

That from a little Bible book you may have never read. Explore the Bible and you'll find the greatest of treasures. Congratulations!

For further reflection: Now that you have the overview, read Zephaniah

Jesus, Thy blood and righteousness / My beauty are, my glorious dress;
Midst flaming worlds, in these arrayed, / With joy shall I lift up my head.
Bold shall I stand in that great day, / Cleansed and redeemed, no debt to
  pay;
Fully absolved through these I am / From sin and fear, from guilt and
  shame.[1]

July 23

Fear Drives Us to the Father

"Fear not." The Bible says it Lord knows how many times. Preachers pontificate about it. But I'm here to tell you, I'm afraid… of many things.

Since we live near something called the "New Madrid Fault Line," the Midwest has an earthquake every now and then. Scientists tell us New Madrid is one big bad fault, and sooner or later a horrendous earthquake is sure to come. Am I afraid? No, not if I'll be standing in the middle of an Illinois cornfield. But you know where I'll be when the big one hits? I'll be stuck in traffic on a bridge over the Mississippi River. Plop. How long can I tread water?

Oh, let's not forget asteroids! And what else?

Personally, I'm weary of religious people mouthing that there's nothing to be afraid of. When you and I deny fear, we dumb down our appreciation of the care of the Creator for His creatures. Creation is in bondage to decay; read about it in Romans 8:18-25. Rumbles of the ground and terrors from the sky are powerful motivators to seek present help and eternal deliverance from the Redeemer of life and Sustainer of all things. See Hebrews 1:3. And when Christians brush off another's fear, or don't even ask if something is troubling you, then we eviscerate the loving care that should characterize the Body of Christ. How much more you and I can help each other if we'll acknowledge our fears, hold onto each other, and then hear and share His "Fear not!"

> The soul that on Jesus hath leaned for repose,
> I will not, I will not desert to his foes;
> That soul, though all hell should endeavor to shake,
> I'll never, no never, no never forsake![1]

"Fear not, for I have redeemed you; I have called you by name, you are mine" (Isaiah 43:1).

For further reflection: 2 Corinthians 1:3-7 – The God of all comfort

I am trusting Thee to guide me; / Thou alone shalt lead,
Ev'ry day and hour supplying / All my need.
I am trusting Thee, Lord Jesus; / Never let me fall.
I am trusting Thee forever / And for all.[2]   Amen.

July 24

Intercessor Training

A colleague was sharing with me his prayer routine, how he prays for his family, then intercedes for his larger family, and finally prays for his coworkers. I admitted that I'm not the best intercessor, for which I can make all kinds of excuses – but they're still excuses. "I urge that supplications, prayers, intercessions, and thanksgivings be made for all people" (1 Timothy 2:1).

Darren and Elizabeth are very good about saying bedtime prayers with Christian, Connor, and Nick. Years ago Darren shared with us what Christian, about four years old at the time, prayed for one night. "God bless Mommy and Daddy. God bless Oma and Opa. God bless Mahma and Pahpaw (Darren's parents)." Then Christian asked God to bless other people in his life, and finally closed with this: "And God bless the vacuum cleaner."

No one has a clue what that meant or why it was said. Maybe it was the Spirit's working in Christian's little heart in a way to get his Opa into the discipline of intercession. *After all, Opa, if I pray for a vacuum cleaner, you certainly should pray for people!*

> These holy conversations begin in childlike ways; we bring our supplications and words of thanks and praise. With care our Father listens to every thought expressed. Then answers our petitions in ways He knows are best.[1]

For further reflection: Matthew 15:21-28 – A mother's intercession comes from faith

Now the light has gone away; / Father, listen while I pray,
Asking Thee to watch and keep / And to send me quiet sleep.
Jesus, Savior, wash away / All that has been wrong today.
Help me ev'ry day to be / Good and gentle, more like Thee.
Let my near and dear ones be / Always near and dear to Thee.
O bring me and all I love / To Thy happy home above.[2] *Amen.*

July 25

Bringing Personality to the Life of Faith

Is that "fruit of the Spirit" (Galatians 5:22-23), or just your natural personality?

Today the Church commemorates James, called "James the Greater" or "James the Elder" because several disciples were named James. Probably the older brother of John, the two were in the family fishing business with their father Zebedee. This James was one of the first disciples Jesus called (Mark 1:19-20). He was selected to be an apostle (Mark 3:17), and with Peter and brother John was in Jesus' inmost circle (Mark 5:37; 9:2). No question about his sincerity.

Like you and me, James brought his unique personality to the life of faith. Jesus called James and John, "Sons of Thunder" (Mark 3:17), maybe because they blustered, like asking Jesus if they should call down fire from heaven upon hostile Samaritans (Luke 9:51-56). James was slow to learn self-denial. Aren't we all? When he and John asked Jesus if they could sit next to Him in glory, Jesus dismissed their request, "You do not know what you are asking" (Mark 10:37-38). Jesus' glory was to be raised up on the cross for our forgiveness; see John 12:32-33. James matured as he followed Jesus, becoming more Christ-like, all the way to martyrdom, the first of the apostles so to die (Acts 12:2).

James's spiritual growth leads us to wonder if our own individual personality traits have come to Christ-like maturity. C.F.W. Walther:

> We must not think that only people who make a display of their godliness are true Christians… Read the Gospels! Notice how the disciples spoke with the Lord and how they acted in His presence. They spoke their minds plainly – even John, the beloved disciple. Christ did not denounce them as being unconverted because of this. Rather, He treated them as converted people who, nevertheless, still carried a sizable portion of the old Adam with them.[1]

You have good traits. Are they the work of the Holy Spirit in you or are they just your natural personality? Sanctification means that more and more of our natural personalities are replaced with the mind of Christ.

For further reflection: Ephesians 4:1-16 – Maturing personalities

O Lord, for James we praise You, / Who fell to Herod's sword; / He drank the cup of suff'ring / And thus fulfilled Your word. / Lord, curb our vain impatience / For glory and for fame, / Equip us for such suff'rings / As glorify Your name.[2]   Amen.

July 26

More Than Meets the Eye

Ancient Syria was sending raiding parties into Israel. One morning Elisha's servant awoke, stepped outside, and to his horror saw their city surrounded by enemy Syrians. Do you ever feel besieged by your problems? Trying to follow Jesus, do you ever feel under attack? "Alas, my master! What shall we do?" (2 Kings 6:15).

Elisha said, "Do not be afraid, for those who are with us are more than those who are with them" (2 Kings 6:16). He then prayed for God to open the servant's eyes. "So the LORD opened the eyes of the young man, and he saw, and behold, the mountain was full of horses and chariots of fire all around Elisha" (2 Kings 6:17). When you live by faith, there is more than meets the eye! "Have we trials and temptations? / Is there trouble anywhere? / We should never be discouraged – / Take it to the Lord in prayer."[1]

"Since we are surrounded by so great a cloud of witnesses, let us also lay aside every weight, and sin which clings so closely, and let us run with endurance the race that is set before us, looking to Jesus" (Hebrews 12:1-2). "Those who are with us are more than those who are with them"!

> Glorious things of you are spoken, / Zion, city of our God;
> He whose word cannot be broken / Formed you for His own abode.
> On the Rock of Ages founded, / What can shake your sure repose?
> With salvation's walls surrounded, / You may smile at all your foes.[2]

For further reflection: Ephesians 3:20 – "Far more abundantly than all that we ask or think"

O God, we have heard with our ears, our fathers have told us, / what deeds you performed in their days, in the days of old: ... for not by their own sword did they win the land, nor did their own arm save them, / but your right hand and your arm, and the light of your face, for you delighted in them. / You are my King, O God; ordain salvation for Jacob! ... For not in my bow do I trust, nor can my sword save me. / But you have saved us from our foes and have put to shame those who hate us. / In God we have boasted continually, and we will give thanks to your name forever. (Psalm 44:1, 3-4, 6-8)   Amen.

July 27

It's Morning Time!

Dear God, thank You for giving us another morning! We should thank You every morning but how does it usually go? We wake up, mental gears slowly begin to grind, and work and worry push down on our chest. Self-obsessed, but "I awake, and I am still with you" (Psalm 139:18).

You protected us through the night from harm and danger. How few the times we think about what could happen while we sleep! Yet, while I slept, You alone, O LORD, made me dwell in safety (cf. Psalm 4:8).

You awaken us to the wonderful creation all around. "The heavens declare the glory of God, and the sky above proclaims his handiwork" (Psalm 19:1). How few the morning times when we look outside and think: *Wow, what an amazing world!*

We awake with the cross marked on us in Baptism, but how long does it take for us to turn in thanks to You our Savior? "Were not ten cleansed? Where are the nine? Was no one found to return and give praise to God except this foreigner?" (Luke 17:17-18).

We awake to the good works You have prepared for us to do (Ephesians 2:10). What a privilege that our hands and feet should go on errands for You! Let Your favor be upon us and "establish the work of our hands!" (Psalm 90:17).

When our daughter Katie was a toddler, she'd wake up at the first light of morning, come into our bedroom, and happily announce, "It's morning time!" Why can't God's adult children wake with that same joy and anticipation? No good reason that I know.

> Awake, my soul, and with the sun / Thy daily stage of duty run;
> Shake off dull sloth and joyful rise / To pay thy morning sacrifice.
> All praise to Thee, who safe hast kept / And hast refreshed me while I slept;
> Grant, Lord, when I from death shall wake, / I may of endless light partake.[1]

For further reflection: Psalm 145 – "Every day I will bless you"

Father, Son, and Holy Spirit, help us live the gift of today with greater awe toward You. Help us strive to please You in everything. Let us see the duties and challenges of this day through the love and patience You have shown us. The past is forgiven; tomorrow is up to You; today is Your gift to us. Thank You! Amen.

July 28

Anger Calls for Reflection

Does anger ever serve a good purpose?

Some years ago, I walked to the cleaners to pick up some laundry. When I walked out of the cleaners with the clean clothes slung over my back, I stepped onto the main sidewalk without looking. A man walked up beside me and chided me for stepping right in front of him. He was very polite; I was very wrong. So what did I do? Outwardly I apologized, but inside I fumed. For the next block of my walk I was angry that someone had criticized me, wonderful me! Finally my conscience spoke: *Get a grip, Dale! You're not perfect; you're a sinner. Just admit it, get off your pedestal, and tell God your anger is wrong.*

Anger is a natural emotion, but not neutral, ever since the fall into sin. "The heart of the children of man is fully set to do evil" (Ecclesiastes 8:11). Anger calls for reflection. Do I think I'm above reproach? God is above reproach but I'm certainly not. Get off your pedestal and repent!

But Jesus showed anger, didn't He? He certainly did. "He looked around at them with anger, grieved at their hardness of heart" (Mark 3:5). Jesus showed anger when people obstructed the good purposes of God, when people did not hallow God's name or let His kingdom come. That's what filled Him when he cleansed the temple; "Zeal for your house will consume me" (John 2:17; Psalm 69:9).

Sometimes followers of Jesus feel justifiable anger, as at the murder of unborn children or the flaunting of immorality or the persecution of Christians. Sanctified impulses show the work of the Holy Spirit in us, but caution: Being suspicious of yourself is wisest even when you think your anger is justified. "Everyone who is angry with his brother will be liable to judgment" (Matthew 5:22). "Be angry and do not sin; do not let the sun go down on your anger, and give no opportunity to the devil" (Ephesians 4:26-27).

For further reflection: Genesis 4:1-16 – "A man of quick temper acts foolishly" (Proverbs 14:17)

Lord, let me win my foes / With kindly words and actions,
And let me find good friends / For counsel and correction.
Help me, as You have taught, / To love both great and small
And by Your Spirit's might / To live in peace with all.[1] *Amen.*

July 29

"The Everlasting Arms"

Got the blues? Sink one of my favorite Bible passages, Deuteronomy 33:27, into your heart. "The eternal God is your dwelling place, and underneath are the everlasting arms."

"The eternal God," it says. Eternal – God has no beginning and no end. "Lord, you have been our dwelling place in all generations" (Psalm 90:1). Through the centuries, God has seen it all. Why not ask Him for help with your problems?

"The eternal God is your dwelling place." Why not flee to a safe place? Why not take your heart and thoughts to Him? He's "Our shelter from the stormy blast, / And our eternal home."[1] He's just waiting to welcome you so that you feel finally at home. In His house you know that all will turn out well.

"Underneath are the everlasting arms." Does God have arms? No, not until He decided to help us and send His Son into our flesh. Jesus stretched out His arms on the cross to pay for your sins. Today those arms of Jesus are open to you. "Come to me, all who labor and are heavy laden, and I will give you rest" (Matthew 11:28).

His arms are everlasting – again, your eternal God. "Jesus Christ is the same yesterday and today and forever" (Hebrews 13:8). "Fear not, I am the first and the last, and the living one. I died, and behold I am alive forevermore, and I have the keys of Death and Hades" (Revelation 1:17-18).

Those arms are underneath. Feel the lift! "I was pushed hard, so that I was falling, but the LORD helped me. / The LORD is my strength and my song" (Psalm 118:13-14). Like the toddler you swoop up to hold before your smiling face, the Savior's everlasting arms uplift you to the countenance of your loving Father.

"The eternal God is your dwelling place, and underneath are the everlasting arms."
Faint not nor fear, His arms are near; / He changes not, who holds you dear;
Only believe, and you will see / That Christ is all eternally.[2]

For further reflection: Psalm 91 – "My refuge and my fortress"

O Lord, our God, we acknowledge Your great goodness toward us. Keep us this day under Your protective care and preserve us, securely trusting in Your everlasting goodness and love, for the sake of Your Son, Jesus Christ, our Lord.[3]   *Amen.*

July 30

What's on Your Agenda?

"Behold, how good and pleasant it is when brothers dwell in unity!" (Psalm 133:1).

Not always, but sometimes you see Christians discuss church business in the forbearing love of Christ. I recall attending a meeting that lasted several days and had an agenda chock-full of weighty issues. All in attendance were Bible believing Christians and, surprise, showed it. Dependable smiles and good will kept disagreements and divisiveness at bay. Earnest thought and talk were matched by earnest prayer. All went home at peace with one another. Well, maybe not all but almost all. Wherever the Word of Christ dominates a meeting, the Spirit is present with patience and restraint that makes for true unity.

"A healthy tree cannot bear bad fruit, nor can a diseased tree bear good fruit. ... you will recognize them by their fruits," Jesus said (Matthew 7:18, 20). Peter Steinke has consulted with hundreds of congregations and says that in every church, "How emotional processes are understood and handled plays a major role in outcomes."[1] "The fruit of the Spirit is love, joy, peace, patience, kindness, goodness, faithfulness, gentleness, self-control; against such things there is no law [bylaw!]. And those who belong to Christ Jesus have crucified the flesh with its passions and desires" (Galatians 5:22-24).

On the other hand, gridlock has dominated Washington, D.C. to the dismay and disgust of most Americans. "Bipartisanship" means "my party's way or the highway." James Davison Hunter: "The language of partisan politics has come to shape how we understand others."[2] This is because America has lost its center, the traditional culture that united us. Sometimes church meetings forget our Center. "'I follow Paul,' or 'I follow Apollos,' or 'I follow Cephas' ... Is Christ divided?" (1 Corinthians 1:12-13). How good it is then when the Body of Christ discusses weighty issues in unity. "It is like the dew of Hermon, which falls on the mountains of Zion! / For there the LORD has commanded the blessing, life forevermore" (Psalm 133:3).

"So then let us pursue what makes for peace and for mutual upbuilding" (Romans 14:19).

For further reflection: Acts 15:1-29 – Unity in an important meeting

Holy Spirit, ever living / As the Church's very life; / Holy Spirit, ever striving / Through us in a ceaseless strife; / Holy Spirit, ever forming / In the Church the mind of Christ: / You we praise with endless worship / For Your fruits and gifts unpriced.[3]

July 31

Security in Stuff?

It's good when business inventories are down because products are being sold. On the other hand, high inventories indicate a sluggish economy and possible layoffs. In a similar way, a large inventory in your personal fiscal life can be spiritually dangerous.

Jesus told a parable about a farmer who had such a good year that he decided to tear down his barns and build bigger ones to handle his bulging inventory (Luke 12:13-21). "There I will store all my grain and my goods" (verse 18). Nothing wrong with that. Good and well-maintained facilities, reserves for the proverbial "rainy day," diversified income… these are indicators of a well-run business and on a smaller scale a healthy household economy. Should you arrive at such a sweet situation, what's your next thought? "And I will say to my soul, 'Soul, you have ample goods laid up for many years; relax, eat, drink, be merry'" (verse 19). He died that night. His big inventory and sweet financial position did him no good. "One's life does not consist in the abundance of his possessions" (verse 15).

Remember that classic scene from *I Love Lucy* when Lucy and Ethel are working in a candy store? Their job is to process the candy coming off the conveyor belt. Faster and faster the candy comes. Can't keep up! They stuff it in their pockets, stuff it in their blouses, stuff it in their mouths… Too much stuff! That scene made us laugh. Does God smile, sadly smile at us for basing our future well-being on stuffing away investments, properties, diversified income, our own personal "inventories?" Your effort to provide for the future is not the problem but basing your security on stuff can be fatal.

"So is the one who lays up treasure for himself and is not rich toward God" (verse 21). "Take care, and be on your guard against all covetousness, for one's life does not consist in the abundance of his possessions" (verse 15).

For further reflection: Deuteronomy 26:12-19 – Financial planning dominated by an awareness of God

Take my life and let it be / Consecrated, Lord, to Thee; / Take my moments and my days, / Let them flow in ceaseless praise, / Let them flow in ceaseless praise.
Take my silver and my gold, not a mite would I withhold; / Take my intellect and use / Ev'ry pow'r as Thou shalt choose, / Ev'ry pow'r as Thou shalt choose.[1]   *Amen.*

August 1

Love Your Neighbor

Our front porch has two rockers and faces the street. As the day winds down, Diane and I often sit there, talk about whatever, and enjoy each other's company. Oh yes, our dog Ferdie is there too, getting his own "happy hour" snacks. "God settles the solitary in a home" (Psalm 68:6).

We wave at neighbors who drive by, say "hi" to those who walk by, and generally see what's happening on the block. On the porch we come out from our private home and, by the same token, the street catches a glimpse of the people "who live there." Who knows whom we might greet? "Some have entertained angels unawares" (Hebrews 13:2).

"The worst thing that happened to the U.S.," says Rick Massie of Jackson Hole, Wyoming, "was the invention of the electric garage-door opener: It shuts down behind you and people don't come out."[1] Maybe not the worst thing, but it is a symptom of a profound change in America. Marc Dunkelman writes in *The Vanishing Neighbor*, "The sorts of relationships my grandparents had taken for granted while raising the children – between neighbors and colleagues, often across generations – had withered."[2] Americans are still tight with family and these days we have our social media contacts, but what's now missing is the middle, the casual interactions with people in the neighborhood. The rockers on our porches are largely empty.

Decades ago, Diane or I would ask, "Where are the girls?" "Oh, they're down the street at Angie's" or "at Dorothy's" or "at Ruth's." The neighborhood has changed and we don't all know one another on our block. My duty to God is not just to go to church but also to obey this great command: "You shall love your neighbor as yourself" (Matthew 22:39). A good start is to sit on the front porch, greet people as they go by, and while away your time thinking about the blessings of neighbors.

For further reflection: Genesis 18:1-15 – Whiling away the time, surprise!

O God, our great Creator, You bless us with neighbors. Traditional homes on streets, apartments and condominiums in high rises, rooms in care facilities... Wherever I live, You want me to love my neighbor as myself. As Your Son modeled love for all people, may Your Spirit teach me never to meet a stranger. For Jesus' sake. Amen.

August 2

Putting It All on the Line

A surprising amount of my work time is spent signing documents for the Seminary. I sign contracts, check requests, form letters, personal letters, memos... Every day there's a file folder waiting on the desk for my "John Hancock." Your signature is sought for many things as well: sign checks, redo your home loan, take ownership of a car, sign in to enter a secured building, end a letter... You write your John Hancock.

On this date, August 2nd, back in 1776 John Hancock did sign his name along with many other colonial leaders on the Declaration of Independence. It could have turned out differently; they could have been signing their own death sentence, but thank God that we look back on that day as a shining moment for our lives and our country. Sometimes when you sign your name you're putting it all on the line.

Martin Luther wrote:

> Faith is a living, daring confidence in God's grace, so sure and certain that the believer would stake his life on it a thousand times. This knowledge of and confidence in God's grace makes men glad and bold and happy in dealing with God and with all creatures. And this is the work which the Holy Spirit performs in faith.[1]

Could you sign your name to that declaration?

For further reflection: Romans 16:22 – Tertius signs the letter of faith

All that I am and love most dearly – / Receive it all, O Lord, from me.
Let me confess my faith sincerely; / Help me Your faithful child to be!
Let nothing that I am or own / Serve any will but Yours alone.[2]   Amen.

August 3

Even Forgiven Sin Has Consequences

Raised in Chicagoland, Diane and I are fans of the Chicago White Sox. Back in 1919, the Sox won the pennant and were favored to beat the Cincinnati Reds in the World Series, but some Sox took bribes and threw the series. On August 2, 1921, eight "Black Sox" were acquitted in court but the very next day the new commissioner of baseball, Judge Kenesaw Mountain Landis, banned them from baseball. Even forgiven sin has consequences.

A young boy had frequent anger tantrums. So his father told him, "Each time you feel yourself getting angry, take out your anger by pounding a nail into the backyard fence." The boy did and over time picked up the hammer and nails less and less. The father complimented his son's improved behavior but then led him to the backyard fence, put the hammer in the boy's hand, and asked him to start removing the nails. When the boy had taken the last nail out, the father asked, "What do you see?"

"The holes left by the nails," was the answer.

"So it is with us," said the father. "Our anger goes away but the damage we can do when we're angry remains."

It's also that way with our sins that hurt others. Heaven acquits us, but here on earth the consequences of what we've done continue. That's why weekly worship is so important. Because the consequences of forgiven sins continue on earth, and because the devil uses those unpleasant consequences to accuse us and make us doubt God's forgiveness, we need to hear again and again these words of worship: "In the mercy of almighty God, Jesus Christ was given to die for us, and for His sake God forgives us all our sins."[1] God nailed Jesus to the cross; you are forgiven. In heaven the consequences, the holes, will be no more.

For further reflection: 2 Samuel 12:1-25 – Consequences: "the sword shall never depart from your house"

O God, forsake me not! / Take not Your Spirit from me;
Do not permit the might / Of sin to overcome me.
Increase my feeble faith, / Which You alone have wrought.
O be my strength and pow'r – / O God, forsake me not![2]   *Amen.*

August 4

Mercies at Home

Columnist Elinor Markgraf wrote about her bout with pneumonia. Confined to her home, she turned to books. "I can't think for a minute why I planned to read the letters from Harry Truman to his wife, Bess. Initially, Harry seemed like a fine guy, concerned and doting toward his wife and child. But after a couple hundred letters, I started feeling downright sorry for Bess."[1]

Ha! When I discovered Diane had kept all the letters I wrote to her when we were dating, I was surprised and, like Ms. Markgraf feeling sorry for Bess, I felt sorry for Diane. I was a student in St. Louis and she was teaching in Chicagoland. My letters were essentially pre-computer form letters: I miss you, here's what I did today, and I love you. No one's ever described me as a romantic. We still laugh about it – that bundle of boring letters.

How do you define "intimacy?" In my experience, women define it as emotional closeness; men think of it as the closest of physical relations. When I meet with a couple preparing for marriage, I share my wish that the years ahead will see them become the best of friends and that they'll come to a time when the children have been raised, their bills have been paid, and they can sit and enjoy each other's presence. That, I've come to believe, is true intimacy. Wrote Ms. Markgraf, "Why she saved the darn things is beyond me."[1] I think the answer is love, and most men are slow understanding it.

The Bible often speaks of "mercy" in the plural – "mercies" – because the Creator's acts of loving kindness to His creatures are many. His many mercies make a home a safe place, an intimate place, where husbands and wives can drop any masks they might show the world, sit together, and enjoy the goodness of God and each other.

For further reflection: Ruth 1:15-18 – Safe at home

O God of mercy, God of might, / In love and pity infinite,
Teach us, as ever in Thy sight, / To live our lives in Thee.
In sickness, sorrow, want, or care, / May we each other's burdens share;
May we, where help is needed, there / Give help as unto Thee![2]   *Amen.*

August 5

"But Let Him Ask in Faith…"

Years ago I was sitting on the couch – I still remember it so clearly – and I was caught up in my habitual mix of fretting and praying. It's like spaghetti, *What am I going to do?* and *God, please help* all mixed up in one bowl, worries and hopes all jumbled in one prayer time.

Then came one of those *Dale, the problem is you* moments.

> If any of you lacks wisdom, let him ask God, who gives generously to all without reproach, and it will be given him. But let him ask in faith, with no doubting, for the one who doubts is like a wave of the sea that is driven and tossed by the wind. For that person must not suppose that he will receive anything from the Lord; he is a double-minded man, unstable in all his ways. (James 1:5-8)

I remember it clearly. I felt like Goliath, struck down right in the middle of my big thick head. *Oh, I'm such a giant at solving my problems!* Whoosh, the stone comes from the slingshot. *No you're not, Dale. You're a double-minded doubter. If you don't trust Me on this problem, how are you the rest of the time?* My spaghetti mix of fretting and wishy-washy praying was all wrong. It's not only counterproductive (you won't get your wimpy wish), but it's an out-and-out offense to God: *God, I don't have enough confidence in You to stop my worrying.*

If we leave our prayer times a spaghetti bowl of worries and petitions, the meal will prove unsatisfying. Every prayer time needs to come to this surrender: Our petitions to God are based on confidence that in Christ He is our loving and involved Father. Can you relate to my experience?

For further reflection: Luke 24:13-27 – Jesus comes to doubting disciples

Give ear, O LORD, to my prayer; listen to my plea for grace. / In the day of my trouble I call upon you, for you answer me. / Teach me your way, O LORD, that I may walk in your truth; unite my heart to fear your name. / I give thanks to you, O Lord my God, with my whole heart, and I will glorify your name forever. / For great is your steadfast love toward me. (Psalm 86:6-7, 11-13)   Amen.

August 6

Gracious Communication, Old-School Style

Picture some caveman drawing on the wall of his cave, or a biblical writer bent over parchment or papyrus. How old, how slow! Now picture me handwriting thank-you letters. I love writing with a fountain pen to paper, my hands away from the quick keyboard and instant Internet. Am I a dinosaur?

Penmanship obviously is not one of the commandments, but the pen can help pierce through the superficiality of modern relationships. Our little lives are dominated by decisions made by giant corporations and faraway government. Their automated systems and bureaucratic regulations are not only impersonal, they also provide a convenient curtain for uncaring people to hide behind. Years ago, a donor came up to me and thanked me for the handwritten note I had sent him. "I know it came from a computer," he said, "but thank you." "Harold, no! I actually wrote that!" Our communication technologies, as wonderful as they are, contribute cynicism to interpersonal relationships. Your pen can pierce through.

God's love has been spoken into our hearts through His Word. "You shall have no other gods before me," says the God of redemption (Exodus 20:3). His redeeming love in us will show itself in the words that we put forth. First, in our words to God: "You shall not take the name of the LORD your God in vain" (Exodus 20:7). Then in our words before God to others: Jesus says, "Let what you say be simply 'Yes' or 'No'; anything more than this comes from evil" (Matthew 5:37). "Let your speech always be gracious, seasoned with salt, so that you may know how you ought to answer each person" (Colossians 4:6). Of course, you can do that with a keyboard, but handwriting better helps you "do to others what you would have them do to you" (Matthew 7:12 NIV).

Obviously my letters go out by snail mail. It's all so slow, so time consuming! The time is consumed caring about the person to whom you write – time consumed putting the best construction on everything.

For further reflection: Galatians 6:11 – I mean what I've written!

Lord, help me to understand that however I communicate, my words should come from an undivided heart that is sincere in its love for You and for other people. Let the people who receive my words know that I truly care. For Jesus' sake. Amen.

August 7

Where Is Your Treasure?

God speaks, but do we obediently hear?

Some of the most soothing words Jesus says to us are these:

> Do not be anxious about your life ... life is more than food, and the body more than clothing ... which of you by being anxious can add a single hour to his span of life? ... Consider the ravens ... God feeds them ... Consider the lilies ... Solomon in all his glory was not arrayed like one of these ... your Father knows ... seek his kingdom, and these things will be added to you. (excerpts from Luke 12:22-34)

Jesus wraps up those promises with something we easily skim over. "For where your treasure is, there will your heart be also" (verse 34). He doesn't say, *Where your heart is, your treasure will be also.* It's our nature to put our feelings, our thoughts, our heart first, but the heart can be deceitful (Genesis 6:5). In fact, Jesus teaches that the heart is the source of all evil; see Mark 7:21-22. Instead of going from the inside out, from heart to treasure, Jesus says examine what it is outside of you that you value. Whatever your external treasure, Jesus promises your heart will follow.

When I hosted the television show *On Main Street* for Lutheran Hour Ministries, I interviewed a couple that was struggling with financial problems. A financial adviser counseled the couple to cut up their credit cards and, to make his point, he pulled out a pair of scissors. They did cut up their cards but you could see on their faces that they didn't want to. They were caught between the ingrained habits of their heart and the goal of living debt-free. Whether it's money or time or some other worry, are you caught between the dominating habits of your heart and true treasure? If you are, thank God and pray for more Spirit-led struggle! Jesus is your treasure. Your Father will provide the rest.

For further reflection: Malachi 3:6-12 – When it rains, it pours

One thing's needful; Lord, this treasure / Teach me highly to regard.
All else, though it first give pleasure, / Is a yoke that presses hard!
Beneath it the heart is still fretting and striving, / No true, lasting happiness
ever deriving.
This one thing is needful; all others are vain – / I count all but loss that I
Christ may obtain![1]   Amen.

August 8

In or Out!

Years ago our dog "Speaker" (What a great dog he was!) was at the door, looking like he wanted to come in. So Diane opened the door. All our dogs get the kindest treatment from Diane! She opened the door but Speaker wouldn't come in; he just looked at her. "In or out!" she demanded.

That brought back memories of my childhood. "In or out," Mom used to say, and she would often add: "Stop slamming the screen door!" I wonder how many kids today know what a "screen door" is. Anyway, "In or out! Stop slamming the screen door!" was part of the liturgy of summer. And it's part of the liturgy of faith. In Proverbs 9 the Bible says, "Wisdom has built her house" and calls, "Whoever is simple, let him turn in here!" (verses 1 and 4) And what is Wisdom? Says the New Testament, it's "Christ the power of God and the wisdom of God" (1 Corinthians 1:24). We Christians are prone to confess Jesus on Sundays and then go out and act contrary to what we've professed. How kind that Jesus, the Wisdom of God, doesn't demand "In or out!" when we sin, but keeps inviting "Come to me" (Matthew 11:28). "Whoever comes to me I will never cast out" (John 6:37).

So, sinner, keep slamming that screen door! Just make sure you do it as you keep going back in to Him.

> Today Your gate is open, / And all who enter in
> Shall find a Father's welcome / And pardon for their sin.
> The past shall be forgotten, / A present joy be giv'n,
> A future grace be promised, / A glorious crown in heav'n.[1]

For further reflection: Matthew 18:21-22 – Read these verses as the one who keeps sinning

You are the way, the truth, the life; / Grant us that way to know,
That truth to keep, that life to win, / Whose joys eternal flow.[2]   Amen.

August 9

"Whoever Comes to Me I Will Never Cast Out"

Over the years, John 6:37 has given me great encouragement and specific direction in many times of uncertainty. Jesus promises, "whoever comes to me I will never cast out."

When you're fretting over your future… when someone you trusted lets you down… when your resources are exhausted… when the diagnosis puts you in a panic… when you've suffered an immense loss… "whoever comes to me I will never cast out."

"Come unto Me, ye fainting, / And I will give you life."

O cheering voice of Jesus, / Which comes to aid our strife!

The foe is stern and eager, / The fight is fierce and long;

But Thou hast made us mighty / And stronger than the strong.[1]

When you're too embarrassed to admit your sin… when you've damaged a relationship beyond repair… when you think there is no forgiveness for what you've done… when church professionals leave you feeling that your faith is inferior… when worship seems irrelevant… when you're losing trust in God's promises…

"And whosoever cometh, / I will not cast him out."

O patient love of Jesus, / Which drives away our doubt,

Which, though we be unworthy / Of love so great and free,

Invites us very sinners / To come, dear Lord, to Thee![2]

And when the end is near… "whoever comes to me I will never cast out." Jesus tells you why:

For I have come down from heaven, not to do my own will but the will of him who sent me. And this is the will of him who sent me, that I should lose nothing of all that he has given me, but raise it up on the last day. For this is the will of my Father, that everyone who looks on the Son and believes in him should have eternal life, and I will raise him up on the last day. (John 6:38-40)

For further reflection: Mark 2:13-17 – They welcomed His call

O bringer of salvation, / Who wondrously have wrought, / Thyself the revelation / Of love beyond our thought; / We worship Thee, we bless Thee, / To Thee, O Christ, we sing; / We praise Thee, and confess Thee / Our gracious Lord and King.[3]   Amen.

August 10

"Put on the Lord Jesus Christ"

One Sunday afternoon, exhausted from the morning's preaching, I settled into a window seat near the back of the plane. Now come two women, thirtyish, assigned the two seats to my left. The moment they see my clerical collar they start in. "Oh, good, a priest. Now we know we'll be safe."

Clerical garb produces different reactions. In Boston I'm sure to get a sincere, "Hello, Father" from someone. Other times people see it and try to goad me – maybe a few cuss words. I don't think these two women were putting me on; they thought I was their good luck charm. Imagine that, reduced to a rabbit's foot!

I wasn't in the mood. "Jesus," I said, "loves me and is going to take me to heaven. He might use this flight to do it."

That shut 'em up. *We're sitting next to a nutcase!*

At the end of the flight I got nice, which I should have been at the start. Turned out they were backup performers for the pop singer Engelbert Humperdinck and wow, they had interesting stories to tell.

Another time I got "collared" waiting for a flight out of St. Louis. A young woman comes up and says – I'm not making this up – "What kind are you?" "I'm Lutheran." "I'm going to Detroit because my father just committed suicide. Is he in heaven?" I learned he was a Vietnam vet who had dealt with post-traumatic stress for years. I couldn't answer her ultimate question, but gave what comfort I could.

What do we clergy think when we put on our special garb? Are we consciously putting on an invitation to talk about God and Jesus? Or are we advertising *I'm holier than thou*? What do you think when you see the collar? Respect for the cloth as reverence for God? Or someone hiding from the real world? Clothes don't make the man, or the woman either. God's grace can, unless our rebellious sinful nature stubbornly refuses. Grace, Baptism, faith going public in sanctified, obedient living. Whatever we wear, every person we encounter is someone God loves. "Put on the Lord Jesus Christ" (Romans 13:14).

For further reflection: Ephesians 4:17-32 – Daily repentance!

Oh, may Thy love possess me whole, / My joy, my treasure, and my crown!
All coldness from my heart remove; / My ev'ry act, word, thought be love.[1]   *Amen.*

August 11

The Gracious Hours of the Night

Ah, the blessings of sleep! Then again, maybe you sometimes have trouble sleeping through the night and don't wake up feeling refreshed. It's a rare night when we don't fall asleep with some problem on our mind. Either way – sleeping straight through the night or unwelcome tossing and turning – I've come to believe that God really brings blessings and guidance during the nighttime hours. "He who keeps you will not slumber" (Psalm 121:3).

Lying in bed, you're postured for grace. Grace means God gives, quite opposite from what we achieve by our working. Worrying in bed is work, and gets you what? Handing your problems over to the Lord is the way through – your help from His grace. "Ponder in your own hearts on your beds, and be silent. / Offer right sacrifices, and put your trust in the LORD" (Psalm 4:4-5). "I cried aloud to the LORD, and he answered me from his holy hill. / I lay down and slept; I woke again, for the LORD sustained me. / I will not be afraid of many thousands of people who have set themselves against me all around" (Psalm 3:4-6).

When we live our waking hours conscious of His words and ways, He'll use the gracious hours of the night to show us how to face the problems of the day. "It is in vain that you rise up early and go late to rest, / eating the bread of anxious toil; for he gives to his beloved sleep" (Psalm 127:2). That's why Jesus – the Son of God come into our flesh – was able to sleep through a storm. He was in perfect communion with His heavenly Father. Jesus asks His disciples, "Where is your faith?" (Luke 8:22-25).

For further reflection: Genesis 28:10-22 – A rocky night's sleep

Forgive me, Lord, for Thy dear Son, / The ill that I this day have done,
That with the world, myself, and Thee, / I, ere I sleep, at peace may be.
Oh, may my soul in Thee repose, / And may sweet sleep mine eyelids close,
Sleep that shall me more vig'rous make / To serve my God when I awake!
When in the night I sleepless lie, / My soul with heav'nly thoughts supply;
Let no ill dreams disturb my rest, / No pow'rs of darkness me molest.[1]
Amen.

August 12

Those People? In My Heaven?

Child abusers, rapists, and murderers… in heaven?

Jesus told a parable (Matthew 20:1-16) about a boss who paid his workers for the full day they had put in. At the same time he paid a full day's wage to some workers he had engaged for only one hour. *Whoa!* crabbed the first workers. *Not fair!* Jesus' point wasn't about earthly wages but rather that eternal salvation is a gift from God, not the result of our works. "For by grace you have been saved through faith. And this is not your own doing; it is the gift of God" (Ephesians 2:8).

Only the Lord knows if child abusers, rapists, and murderers truly repent, but if they do, biblical teaching tells us they'll be received by Jesus into heaven. Can we forget the thief on the cross (Luke 23:39-43)? "'Jesus, remember me, when you come into your kingdom.' And he said to him, 'Truly, I say to you, today you will be with me in Paradise'" (Luke 23:42-43). Can we forget that Jesus died in the place of the murderer Barabbas (Mark 15:6-15)?

It still strikes me as grossly unfair. Our natural reaction is just like those who grumbled when Jesus went into the home of Zacchaeus. "They all grumbled, 'He has gone in to be the guest of a man who is a sinner'" (Luke 19:7). Our natural reaction shows how radical, how scandalous Jesus' message is to our instinctive belief that we should be rewarded for our decent life. The deepest spiritual use of the commandments is not to justify how we've tried to live but to see ourselves in need of God's gift of salvation. See Galatians 3:24.

"I came not to call the righteous, but sinners" (Mark 2:17). Abusers, rapists, murderers… in heaven? Your reaction reveals a lot about where you are spiritually.

For further reflection: "Most merciful God, we confess that we are by nature sinful and unclean. We have sinned against You in thought, word, and deed, by what we have done and by what we have left undone. We have not loved You with our whole heart; we have not loved our neighbors as ourselves. We justly deserve Your present and eternal punishment."[1] Do you truly believe this?

If you, O LORD, should mark iniquities, O Lord, who could stand? / But with you there is forgiveness, that you may be feared. (Psalm 130:3-4)

August 13

The Church in the City

Over the decades, my denomination pretty much abandoned the major metropolitan areas of the United States. We weren't alone; other denominations moved out too, and for understandable reasons. So this isn't about blame. People seek good and safe places to live. We want good schools for our children and would rather not shop in stores with bars on the windows.

The real city is a strange place. Oh, I can handle myself quite well walking on Broadway in New York or Michigan Avenue in Chicago, and so can you, but what about living in Harlem or Chicago's South Side? Living in the city can be stimulation on steroids, but you can't let your guard down. Fear in the city is definitely not "*f*alse *e*vidence *a*ppearing *r*eal." To those who have moved out, the real city is strange – a foreign, foreboding place.

"How shall we sing the LORD's song in a foreign land?" asked the psalmist when he and his people were exiled in Babylon (Psalm 137:4). Do small-town and suburban Christians wonder what it's like to be faithful to Jesus deep in the city? People who didn't move out watch their churches decline or close. The church competes against countless entertainments. Support networks are less natural; you have to develop your own "Seinfeld and Friends." If we who have been out of the big city for a generation or more really care, would we know how to sing the Lord's song among the millions?

Early Christianity spread mainly through the great urban centers of the Mediterranean region. Today there are stirrings among church people to get back into the city because God wants His Church where the masses are. Jesus "saw a great crowd, and he had compassion on them" (Mark 6:34). Doesn't the Great Commission send a truly mission-minded church back into the city? "Seek the welfare of the city where I have sent you into exile, and pray to the LORD on its behalf, for in its welfare you will find your welfare" (Jeremiah 29:7). I don't know about you, but this makes me uncomfortable sitting in my cushy suburban church pew.

For further reflection: Jonah 1-4 – Out of his comfort zone

All are redeemed, both far and wide, / Since Thou, O Lord, for all hast died. Grant us the will and grace provide / To love them all in Thee![1]   *Amen.*

August 14

Are You Dressed for Battle?

On this date in 1945, Japan accepted the Allied terms of surrender. I can't imagine the feelings Americans had at the surrender and such a costly victory.

Christians have spiritual enemies who have not yet surrendered, enemies who want to rob you of the confidence and goodness that Jesus Christ gives. "For we do not wrestle against flesh and blood, but against the rulers, against the authorities, against the cosmic powers over this present darkness, against the spiritual forces of evil in the heavenly places" (Ephesians 6:12).

My friend Mark, a former military chaplain, keeps a little piece of paper on the mirror with this question: "Are you dressed for battle?" Put on the faith and hope that are in Jesus Christ and go to the tasks of this day, go to your battle station watchful. "Take up the whole armor of God, that you may be able to withstand in the evil day, and having done all, to stand firm" (Ephesians 6:13).

And dress assured that the ultimate victory will be yours because Christ rose, He conquered our enemies, and He gives you His Spirit. "Every tongue (will) confess that Jesus Christ is Lord, to the glory of God the Father" (Philippians 2:11).

> I bind unto myself today / The pow'r of God to hold and lead,
>
> His eye to watch, His might to stay, / His ear to hearken to my need,
>
> Against the demon snares of sin, / The vice that gives temptation force,
>
> The natural lusts that war within, / The hostile foes that mar my course;
>
> I bind unto myself the name, / The strong name of the Trinity,
>
> By invocation of the same, / The Three in One and One in Three.[1]

For further reflection: Ephesians 6:10-20 – The parts of your battle uniform

Almighty God, send Your Holy Spirit into our hearts that He may rule and direct us according to Your will, comfort us in all our temptations and affliction, defend us from all error, and lead us into all truth that we, being steadfast in faith, may increase in all good works and in the end obtain everlasting life; through Jesus Christ our Lord.[2]   Amen.

August 15

More Like Him

Have you noticed how some couples look alike as the years go by? They show it's not "me," but "we." Would you describe your relationship with God the same way? "It is no longer I who live, but Christ who lives in me" (Galatians 2:20). Is it your intent today to:

> … be found in him, not having a righteousness of my own that comes from the law, but that which comes through faith in Christ, the righteousness from God that depends on faith – that I may know him and the power of his resurrection, and may share his sufferings, becoming like him in his death, that by any means possible I may attain the resurrection from the dead. (Philippians 3:9-11) ?

Are you giving ample room to the Spirit to grow you more and more into His likeness? Ponder that in your heart.

Today the church calendar honors "Mary, Mother of Our Lord." Talk about an inseparable relationship between a person and God! The hymn, "Crown Him with Many Crowns"[1] describes Mary's life completely intertwined with her son and Savior: "Fruit of the mystic rose (the "fruit" is Jesus; the "rose" is Mary), / Yet of that rose the Stem, / The Root whence mercy ever flows, / The Babe of Bethlehem." That's sublime poetry and, if you think about it, you can only conclude that the relationship between the believer and the Savior goes beyond rational explanation. It is a mystery of faith, that we love Him with all our heart, soul, mind, and strength.

When Jesus told His disciples that faith as small as a mustard seed can move a mountain (Matthew 17:20), He could well have pointed to His mother, a simple girl who became mother of the world's Savior. "I am the servant of the Lord; let it be to me according to your word" (Luke 1:38). So inseparable the believer and the Savior! Are you letting Him become who you are?

For further reflection: Luke 1:39-55 – The Gospel reading for St. Mary, Mother of Our Lord

We sing with joy of Mary, / Whose heart with awe was stirred
When, youthful and astonished, / She heard the angel's word.
Yet she her voice upraises / To magnify God's name,
As once for our salvation / Your mother she became.[2]   *Amen.*

August 16

The Blessings of Downtime

August is half over. If you haven't already, please take significant time off!

Your time off benefits your family. One of my pleasant memories from childhood was August, the month when my dad took his two-week vacation. No doubt he did home projects, I can't remember. Here's what I do remember: he was home; we were home. To this day, decades later, I'm blessed by the memory of his time off with us.

The Old Testament Sabbath was "*to* the LORD your God" (Exodus 20:9-10, italics mine). There's proof aplenty that downtime can bless your relationship with God. Jesus' disciples were sent out to do the Lord's work, but their spiritual growth came when they weren't working, when they were with the Lord. "He appointed twelve (whom he also named apostles) so that they might be with him and he might send them out" (Mark 3:14). Jesus kept before His disciples the need to stop work and be with Him. "'Come away by yourselves to a desolate place and rest a while.' For many were coming and going, and they had no leisure even to eat" (Mark 6:31-32). "*To* the LORD your God." But wasn't "the Sabbath … made for man, not man for the Sabbath" (Mark 2:27)? Exactly! What better way to treasure life and family than time off with them in God's quiet peace? Spend time with Jesus and people will notice. "They recognized that they had been with Jesus" (Acts 4:13).

And so it comes full circle. I think the popular word is "holistic." Downtime with Jesus is appreciated by others, most immediately by your family. Don't waste August with all work!

For further reflection: Colossians 2:16-17 – The Old Testament Sabbath fulfilled in Christ / Genesis 2:1-3 – Why did God rest? To admire His creation - "Let us therefore strive to enter that rest" (Hebrews 4:11)

Can the soul be sad or lonely / In Thy company, O Christ,
Looking to Thee, and Thee only, / Keeping with Thee constant tryst[1]?
Life amid serenest quiet / Like a brooklet flows along,
Undisturbed by tempest riot, / Singing hope's expectant song.
Blessed are the green oases / Here and there for pilgrims stored,
As they follow in the traces / Of the footprints of the Lord![2]

August 17

Think and Do

When I was in grade school, we had a series of workbooks called *Think and Do*. I don't remember what the workbooks were about, but the title stuck with me. Think and do is a good reminder as you plunge into every day. Think about God's promises and trust that He won't renege on them as you go about your daily doings.

A rich young man once came to Jesus and asked, "What must I do to inherit eternal life?" (Luke 18:18). Jesus replied that he should keep the commandments. When the young man said he did, Jesus stunned him. "'Sell all that you have and distribute to the poor, and you will have treasure in heaven; and come, follow me.' But when he heard these things, he became very sad" (Luke 18:22-23). Oswald Chambers wrote about that encounter, "Jesus did not go after him, He let him go. Our Lord knows perfectly that when once His word is heard, it will bear fruit sooner or later."[1]

Visiting a church in Torgau, Germany, I was taken by a Latin inscription near the pulpit. No worshipper can see this inscription; only the preacher sees it, and then only when he leaves the pulpit. "In quietness and in trust shall be your strength" (Isaiah 30:15). That is to say – Preacher, think about it. If you've properly spoken the promises of God, be still now and let God work on their hearts through His promises. For us who hear sermons and have our daily times with the Word, think about this promise: "It is God who works in you, both to will and to work for his good pleasure" (Philippians 2:13). "When once His word is heard, it will bear fruit sooner or later."

"If you love me, you will keep my commandments" (John 14:15). Think and do.

For further reflection: Mark 4:26-29 – "Every healthy tree bears good fruit" (Matthew 7:17)

Direct us, O Lord, in all our doings with Your most gracious favor, and further us with Your continual help, that in all our works begun, continued, and ended in You we may glorify Your holy name and finally, by Your mercy, obtain eternal salvation; through Jesus Christ, our Lord.[2]   *Amen.*

August 18

Is Our Hypocrisy Turning Off Young People?

Hypocrisy on Wall Street and in Washington?

How about hypocrisy in the Church? "Young outsiders have lost much of their respect for the Christian faith."[1] That's one of the conclusions from a 2007 survey of 18- to 29-year-olds by the Barna Group and published in the book *unChurched*. 2007 was some years ago, so if you think there's no longer any hypocrisy among us, have a nice day and I hope we'll get together tomorrow.

But if you're still reading… why the loss of many young adults? For one thing, "They are skeptical of our morally superior attitudes. They say Christians pretend to be something unreal, conveying a polished attitude that is not accurate."[2] 30-year-old Erin was abused by her husband, "even though he taught Bible studies about how husbands should love their wives." Jake, 32, said, "My former pastor used to teach Baptism by immersion, then he got a better job with the Presbyterians and now teaches Baptism can be done by sprinkling. What you believe depends on where the paycheck is coming from, I guess."[3]

unChurched also quotes Philip Yancey: "Having spent time around 'sinners' and also around purported saints, I have a hunch why Jesus spent so much time with the former group: I think he preferred their company. The sinners were honest about themselves and had no pretense … In contrast, the saints put on airs."[4]

Hypocrites aren't always conscious of their hypocrisy. The scribes and Pharisees whom Jesus blistered for hypocrisy in Matthew 23 probably were sincere in what they believed and did. You and I are too. Jesus saw through them, and the "sinners" – the dregs of society – probably saw through them as well. Today the least, the last, and the lost often see the inconsistencies between our own profession and practice. Would more conversation with people outside the Church help us see ourselves more accurately? Doesn't it break your heart that we seem to be losing our young people?

For further reflection: Mark 2:15-17 – Shocking, He eats with sinners!

Lord, let me win my foes / With kindly words and actions, / And let me find good friends / For counsel and correction. / Help me, as You have taught, / To love both great and small / And by Your Spirit's might / To live in peace with all.[5]   *Amen.*

August 19

Zoom In on the Psalms

The image on your phone or tablet isn't large enough? Want the picture bigger? Do the magic thing with your fingers and presto, the print is larger and you can see it clearly.

When a follower of Jesus zooms in on the Psalms, the picture of the ages gets clearer. At first blush, each psalm is about something in someone's life long ago. For example, the writer of Psalm 118 had survived a battle and so he exults: "Glad songs of salvation are in the tents of the righteous … I shall not die, but I shall live" (Psalm 118:15-17). OK, good for him. You read further and come across this: "The stone that the builders rejected has become the cornerstone" (verse 22). Whoa! As a Jesus follower you know that the New Testament uses that passage for Jesus. You reread and see the psalm also describes Jesus. "I shall not die, but I shall live" came to fulfillment in Jesus, who did die but arose and lives forever. Zoom even closer. Since Jesus promises, "Whoever believes in me, though he die, yet shall he live" (John 11:25), you also see your future in the psalm. You shall not die, but live! "Glad songs of salvation are in the tents of the righteous."

The Psalms are the prayer book of the Bible. There's probably no emotion of your life that isn't talked about and prayed about in the Psalms. More than that, the Psalms were Jesus' personal prayer book. He prayed these very words you are reading and praying. The psalmist long ago, you, Jesus… people of the kingdom, members of the Body of Christ, all united in praying the psalm. "This is the LORD's doing; it is marvelous in our eyes. / This is the day that the LORD has made; let us rejoice and be glad in it" (Psalm 118:23-24). Zoom in; the picture of the ages gets very clear!

For further reflection: Matthew 21:33-44; 1 Peter 2:4-10 – See how the New Testament uses Psalm 118

Almighty God, You exalted Your Son to the place of all honor and authority. Enlighten our minds by Your Holy Spirit that, confessing Jesus as Lord, we may be led into all truth; through the same Jesus Christ, our Lord, who lives and reigns with You and the Holy Spirit, one God, now and forever.[1] *Amen.*

August 20

How Do You Respond to What You Get?

Sometimes you pray for relief and get it. One Sunday our pastor prayed for much needed rain and, thank You, Lord, the next night it came. But what do we do after we get relief from weather or from other things for which we pray? "Jesus answered, 'Were not ten cleansed? Where are the nine? Was no one found to return and give praise to God except this foreigner?' And he said to him, 'Rise and go your way; your faith has made you well'" (Luke 17:17-19).

Other times you pray but relief comes too late. During one summer of record heat, I saw several trailers hauling hay. Cattle should be in pastures, not eating the hay that's been stored up for winter. Some places it did rain, but it came too late and the temperatures remained too hot for corn to mature. "There came from the ruler's house some who said, 'Your daughter is dead. Why trouble the Teacher any further?' But overhearing what they said, Jesus said to the ruler of the synagogue, 'Do not fear, only believe'" (Mark 5:35-36).

Most disappointing: You pray for relief and it doesn't come, not even late. Maybe you pray for rain, maybe for your battle with cancer, maybe for improvement in a rocky marriage… God seems to be saying, "No." How do we react then?

> Though the fig tree should not blossom, nor fruit be on the vines, / the produce of the olive fail and the fields yield no food, / the flock be cut off from the fold and there be no herd in the stalls, / yet I will rejoice in the LORD; I will take joy in the God of my salvation. (Habakkuk 3:17-18)

It's not simply getting what you pray for; it's how faith responds whatever you get. Trusting God sees the silver lining of His mercy in whatever cloud is heavy on your soul. "Though he slay me, I will hope in him" (Job 13:15). Why?

> The Lord has promised good to me, / His Word my hope secures;
> He will my shield and portion be / As long as life endures.[1]

For further reflection: Lamentations 3:19-23 – "His mercies never come to an end"

When peace, like a river, attendeth my way, / When sorrows, like sea billows, roll; / Whatever my lot, Thou hast taught me to say, / It is well, it is well with soul.[2] Amen.

August 21

In Every Season of Life, Look to Jesus

A friend asked about perseverance. He happens to be an athlete, but we all need perseverance in our lives.

Jogglers need it. I don't run too much anymore – my knees can't take it – but when I was running my wife coined the word "joggler" to describe my style: jogging and waddling. Years ago, daughter Katie encouraged me to enter a 10K with her. She was a Big 12 Conference runner – has the medals to prove it – so she zipped through the race, but this old joggler was struggling. I found the will to keep going when I imagined Katie waiting for me at the finish line, her approving smile welcoming me.

Faces help me persevere. Family members, friends, anyone who smiles approvingly helps keep me going. The dearest face of all is the face we anticipate seeing at the end of life's race. "Now we see in a mirror dimly, but then face to face" (1 Corinthians 13:12). Press on! "You have said, 'Seek my face.' / My heart says to you, 'Your face, LORD, do I seek'" (Psalm 27:8).

Do you have a personal mission statement? Some Christians do. For example, "I want to share Jesus in everything I do" is fine but not specific to a season of life. My daughters are married and raising young children. Their mission statement would be different than their parents who are closer to the end of the race. To increase your perseverance through immediate problems, know the distinctive features of your present stage in the long haul toward "the end result of your faith, the salvation of your souls" (1 Peter 1:9 NIV). If you're young and the climb is uphill, does the promise of blessing pull you on? If you're weary, do moments of devotional rest give you your second wind? Older and nearing the finish line? Let the thrill of seeing Jesus invigorate your steps toward home. Joggle on! "I can do all things through him who strengthens me" (Philippians 4:13).

For further reflection: Hebrews 12:1-14 – "Looking to Jesus"

Run the straight race through God's good grace; / Lift up your eyes, and seek His face.
Life with its way before us lies; / Christ is the path, and Christ the prize.
Faint not nor fear, His arms are near; / He changes not, who holds you dear;
Only believe, and you will see / That Christ is all eternally.[1]

August 22

Aha! Now I Get It!

Philip was led to a man reading Isaiah. "Do you understand what you are reading?" Philip asked, and the man answered, "How can I, unless someone guides me?" (Acts 8:30-31).

Suppose you're on your deathbed and know absolutely nothing about God or Jesus. Time to learn! You ask for a minister; one comes and tells you about the Savior, but speaks in a foreign language that you don't understand. Words must be understood to work.

Professor Thomas Long reminds us that the sermon belongs to the people, not to the preacher.[1] It belongs to people who don't have and probably don't want theological degrees, who are struggling with whatever in their daily lives, but who are led to church to get a good word from God. Mercy, grace, redemption, law, gospel, and other words are rich in meaning but mean nothing unless understood. For example, take that last word, "Gospel." Many people assume they've heard the Gospel if they heard the words Jesus and Christ often. Not necessarily true. If Jesus is presented as the giver of new Christian laws, then it's not Gospel but Law – Law that cannot save. True Gospel "teaches that we have a gracious God, not through our merit but through Christ's merit, when we so believe."[2]

The good preachers I know are restless. They're consumed with curiosity to know more about God's ways in today's world, and they're not satisfied with secondhand depictions about how people are. They're constantly going to real people to hear from them. By going to people facing real-life situations, they're firing themselves up for that moment in preaching when they see on someone's face, *Aha! Now I get it!* Do you ask your pastor real-life questions, not to stump him but so he can help you better understand?

For further reflection: "Human beings cannot be justified before God by their own powers, merits, or works. But they are justified as a gift on account of Christ through faith when they believe that they are received into grace and that their sins are forgiven on account of Christ, who by his death made satisfaction for our sins. God reckons this faith as righteousness."[3]

Teach us to know the Father, Son, / And You, from both, as Three in One
That we Your name may ever bless / And in our lives the truth confess.[4]   *Amen.*

August 23

Wedding Vows Become Present Tense

For my wife Diane, I put my dishes in the dishwasher. For her, I emptied the dishwasher. For her, I didn't yank the sheets in the middle of the night, but let her have more than half. For her, I made the bed in the morning. For her, I surrendered the remote. For her, I endured HGTV® and the Food Network. For her, I have tagged along to the store. For her, I didn't say anything about my money worries. For her, I didn't ask, "Why in the world did you do it that way?" For her and to her, I apologized – even though I knew I was right. Let's face it. The woman is blessed! For Diane, I've done all those things and many others I can't think of... I've done all those things at least once, some several times, over more than 40 years of marriage. Past tense. History.

As they say, you're only as good as your last show. "Husbands, love your wives." That's present tense. That's now. The motivation is Jesus Christ. He didn't think it was all about Him when He offered Himself for our salvation. He made it about us, the heavenly Bridegroom giving Himself up for His bride the Church. "Husbands, love your wives, as Christ loved the church and gave himself up for her" (Ephesians 5:25). "Christ loved ... gave himself up." Past tenses. Past tenses so that we might show loving service to our brides here and now in the present.

"Will you have this woman to be your wedded wife, to live together in the holy estate of matrimony as God ordained it? Will you nourish and cherish her as Christ loved His body, the Church, giving Himself up for her?"[1] Those questions from the wedding service are in the future tense. The future has come. "Let us consider how to stir up one another to love and good works" (Hebrews 10:24).

For further reflection: Matthew 2:13-23 – A model husband, for Jesus' sake

Lord Jesus, because of Your sacrifice for us all, inspire husbands to loving good works in marriage. By the same inspiration, help wives encourage their husbands and respond to good works with respect and love. Amen.

August 24

"Unless the LORD Watches Over the City…"

This is a day to remember that America is not invincible, that enemies can defeat us. On this date, August 24th, in 1812, the British army marched on Washington, D.C. At Bladensburg, Maryland, the British had defeated American militiamen, even though the British were outnumbered. With nothing between the British and the Capitol, President James Madison and the government fled the city.

Stop and picture that – the President of the United States and government officials fleeing the Capitol.

When snipers in Washington killed four British soldiers, orders were given to destroy the White House and Capitol. Writes Robert Rimini: "The burning of the House (of Representatives) chamber was especially severe. All the mahogany furniture was piled high in the room and ignited with rocket fuel. The blaze consumed everything but the outer walls."[1]

Stop and picture that – the Capitol burning.

Was it just luck or was it divine Providence when a violent rainstorm came and put out the fires? One Washingtonian called it a "hurricane." Was it luck or an answer to prayer that the whole city didn't burn?

"I urge that supplications, prayers, intercessions, and thanksgivings be made for all people, for kings and all who are in high positions, that we may lead a peaceful and quiet life, godly and dignified in every way" (1 Timothy 2:1-2).

Stop and picture that – citizens praying because we know, "Unless the LORD watches over the city, the watchman stays awake in vain" (Psalm 127:1).

For further reflection: Psalm 146 – Trust not in…

God of the nations, You instituted government for our welfare. We do ask You graciously to lead us to choose wise leaders who fear You. Should You grant that to us, help us nevertheless to place our trust for the nation's well-being with You. We, Your people, ask this for Jesus' sake. Amen.

August 25

Bye, Jesus!

"Hi, Christian here! I went to church Sunday. Mommy took me up front for the children's sermon. Pastor talked and I listened, part of the time. The rest of the time I watched the girl next to me. Do big people do that too? Do you only pay attention part of the time? After the children's sermon was over, Mommy took me by the hand and walked me back to our pew. While we were walking back, I turned and waved. I said, 'Bye, Jesus!' Big people laughed. Why did big people laugh? Weren't we leaving Jesus?

"Please, big people, help me understand. Isn't that His house? We go to visit Him and then we say, 'Bye' and leave. When we leave, doesn't Jesus stay behind in church? He doesn't go home with me, does He? He doesn't go with me to day care, does He? He doesn't go with you big people to work, does He? He's not there when you are worrying or arguing or alone or crying, is He? Don't you leave Jesus in church?

"I am *not* asking Opa about this. I will think it through myself. Don't we say 'Bye, Jesus' when we leave church?"

For further reflection: Psalm 139 – "The word is near you" (Romans 10:8)

Day by day, at home, away, / Jesus is my staff and stay.
When I hunger, Jesus feeds me, / Into pleasant pastures leads me;
When I thirst, He bids me go / Where the quiet waters flow.[1]

August 26

Grouse On?

I took a bike ride the other day on one of the trails in our county. What a beautiful, late summer day to be outside!

I rode along and noticed countless grasshoppers. Those little guys can do a lot of damage. Some trees have already started to lose their leaves. That's a pain – raking leaves. If you're content to let them fall, your neighbor is upset with you.

Some woolly worms cross the path. I wonder if they really do predict how severe the coming winter will be. Man, I hate driving in snow.

Pedal on; grouse on!

Under an overpass I see that some girl has spray-painted, "Brian, you are my everything!" Or was it a boy? Look out Brian. You're getting a real winner, not to mention a vandal.

Grouse on!

I better get used to this pedaling. Our car has 130,000 miles on it and the last thing I want to do is take on car payments.

I could tell you more but my *Minute* is almost up. Have you ever noticed how human nature, sinful human nature, can ruin a perfectly nice time?

For further reflection: Psalm 148 – "Praise the LORD!"

Immortal, invisible, God only wise,
In light inaccessible hid from our eyes,
Most blessèd, most glorious, the Ancient of Days,
Almighty, victorious, Thy great name we raise.
Great Father of glory, pure Father of light,
Thine angels adore Thee, all veiling their sight;
All laud we would render: O help us to see
'Tis only the splendor of light that hides Thee.[1]

August 27

A Mother's Faithful Prayers

"Mom!" Once in a while kids call out "Dad," but we all know it's Mom who wins the calling contest.

Besieged mothers should call out too… for their children… to God. Today, August 27th, the church remembers Monica, a great pray-er for her child. Like many young people, her son gave up the Christian faith to sow his wild oats. It happens, these newly independent young adults going their own way, and it tears up a faithful mother more than most of us know.

Monica went to a priest for counsel. He told her, "Let him alone for a while; only pray to God for him." She pestered the priest more. "Go your way," he finally said, "and God bless you, for it is not possible that the son of these tears should be lost." And her son wasn't lost. Her son Augustine became one of the greatest leaders in the history of the Christian church.

Looking back, Augustine finally realized God was trying to get to him through his mother. He told God:

> Did you really then hold your peace? Then whose words were they but yours which by my mother, your faithful handmaid, you poured into my ears? None of them, however, sank into my heart to make me do anything. I thought that you were silent and that it was only she who spoke. Yet it was through her that you did not keep silence toward me.[1]

Remember, Mom, how your kids call to you? "Have we trials? Take it to the Lord in prayer."[2] Mothers, besieged by your children's needs, worried about their lives, call to the heavenly Father for them. "In the Lord your labor is not in vain" (1 Corinthians 15:58).

For further reflection: John 17:6-19 – Jesus' care for His disciples - our example to persevere in care for our children

"Suffering produces endurance, and endurance produces character, and character produces hope, and hope does not put us to shame, because God's love has been poured into our hearts through the Holy Spirit who has been given to us" (Romans 5:3-5). O Holy Spirit, may those words give mothers and fathers perseverance in raising godly children. For Jesus' sake! Amen.

August 28

Meet Them Where They're At

Carlyle Marney recounts a story told by David Reid, chaplain at the University of Edinburgh. It seems a young minister spent his whole time studying theology, never leaving his books to associate with his people.

"When asked how he liked his new parson, an old Scot said that he supposed he was all right, in the main, but six days he was invisible and the seventh day he was incomprehensible."[1]

Today's the anniversary of Martin Luther King, Jr.'s famous speech in 1963, *I Have a Dream*. Commentators praise the oratorical power of that speech, deservedly so. It is one of the greatest American speeches of all time. One reason it succeeded is because it tapped into some of the deepest feelings we Americans have, whatever our color. Dr. King knew the heartstrings of his audience. He identified with them, rather than pontificating to them. That's a requisite for successful communication.

The young minister that David Reid described may have known the truth, but he was incomprehensible because he didn't rub shoulders with people, didn't listen to their stories, didn't meet them where they were at. Sometimes we religious people have trouble with that.

> And the scribes of the Pharisees, when they saw that [Jesus] was eating with sinners and tax collectors, said to his disciples, "Why does he eat with tax collectors and sinners?" And when Jesus heard it, he said to them, "Those who are well have no need of a physician, but those who are sick. I came not to call the righteous, but sinners." (Mark 2:16-17)

For further reflection: John 4:1-10 – Meet them where they're at, but don't leave them there. Jesus crosses an ethnic line.

All are redeemed, both far and wide, / Since Thou, O Lord for all hast died. Grant us the will and grace provide / To love them all in Thee![2]   *Amen.*

August 29

Servants for Jesus' Sake

"For what we proclaim is not ourselves, but Jesus Christ as Lord, with ourselves as your servants for Jesus' sake" (2 Corinthians 4:5).

That's not how we often interact with one another, is it? We are all in authority structures: some higher, others lower. We understand the Roman official when he described himself as "a man set under authority, with soldiers under me: and I say to one, 'Go,' and he goes; and to another, 'Come,' and he comes; and to my servant, 'Do this,' and he does it" (Luke 7:8). Authority structures bless our life together. They give order instead of anarchy, guide us in our working relationships, win wars, land on the moon, and generally help get necessary things done. But esteem yourself on the basis of your place in the pecking order? Then you sin, because you set aside the servant attitude of Christ.

Dear God, I am the president of Concordia Seminary; I am the Grand Pooh-Bah around this place. I have authority. A voice came from heaven saying, *You have squat authority. Don't ever forget that I have redeemed you, a lost and condemned creature, purchased and won you from all sins, from death and from the power of the devil. And I didn't do it with gold or silver but with my Son's holy, precious blood and with His innocent suffering and death. And why? So that you might be My own, live under Me, and serve Me. Get it? Serve Me!*[1]

After washing His disciples' feet, Jesus said, "I have given you an example, that you also should do just as I have done to you. Truly, truly, I say to you, a servant is not greater than his master, nor is a messenger greater than the one who sent him. If you know these things, blessed are you if you do them" (John 13:15-17). Whatever your position, it's about service. Who's lord of your life?

For further reflection: Mark 10:35-45 – Gentiles and full-of-themselves disciples

Dear Jesus, You told Pontius Pilate, "You would have no authority over me at all unless it had been given you from above" (John 19:11). Help me not value myself because of any authority I have, nor let us be found striving after authority. With You living in my heart, I will be Your servant to all people. Amen.

August 30

Are You Stuck Between "Ah!" and "Huh?"

"In the world you will have tribulation. But take heart; I have overcome the world" (John 16:33).

Hide that promise in the inner chamber of your heart and you'll get through every day. Jesus' first disciples often found His sayings hard to understand, and so do serious disciples today. So when Jesus promised to speak openly about the Father, it was a high religious moment for the disciples. "Ah, now you are speaking plainly and not using figurative speech!" (John 16:29). We do have those great "ah!" moments – times when Christian faith seems so clear, so applicable, so relevant.

Jesus didn't deny the moment, but He did tell them why His promise would prove to be precious. "Do you now believe? Behold, the hour is coming, indeed it has come, when you will be scattered, each to his own home, and will leave me alone. Yet I am not alone, for the Father is with me" (John 16:31-32). At that moment they couldn't truly appreciate what He was saying, so much was still to come: His suffering, their scattering and shuddering in fear. Offsetting our high religious moments, we have troubled times when it seems Jesus has left us on our own. The thrill of religious insight gives way to doubt about His intimate presence in our lives. Name your fearful moment when you feel alone and Jesus seems far away. The "Ah, now you are speaking plainly" becomes "Huh? Jesus, where are You?". It's in those times when Jesus seems distant but the world so oppressively near that His Spirit can form in you more mature faith. Those are the times to call up the promise you've hidden in your heart. "In the world you will have tribulation. But take heart; I have overcome the world." Jesus' promise is His presence with you.

> This is a sight that gladdens – / What peace it doth impart!
> Now nothing ever saddens / The joy within my heart.
> No gloom shall ever shake, / No foe shall ever take
> The hope which God's own Son / In love for me hath won.[1]

For further reflection: John 20:19-23 – Jesus proves His promise is true

God gives me my days of gladness, / And I will / Trust Him still
When He sends me sadness. / God is good; / His love attends me
Day by day, / Come what may, / Guides me and defends me.[2]

August 31

"Open Thou My Heart to Hear"

Sometimes and some places, Bible words stream through my mind. In church, in Seminary, in reading, in conversation with Christians, in those niche places, Bible words rush through your minds too. Honestly, how many of those words stick? Once in a while, though, a Bible word does stick, does slow our whirring minds. "You have given me an open ear" (Psalm 40:6).

Sure, Lord, most times I've got an open ear, two of them in fact. In one ear and out the other! When the Bible is read in church, the lector says, "This is the Word of the Lord." "Thanks be to God" is the ritual answer, but would you be ready to take a test on what you just heard? It took someone, Eli, to get young Samuel to say, "Speak, for your servant hears" (1 Samuel 3:10). Truth is, my ear is often not open.

Someone has to open it. "Lord, open Thou my heart to hear," we sing, but God works through intermediaries. The preacher needs to use his training in rhetoric and his skill with words to get your attention, to open your ear so the Spirit can open your heart to the truth. Difficult life circumstances get your attention so the Spirit can apply the healing balm to where the hurt is. Someone or something pries open your closed ear and then the Word of the Lord opens your heart. Thank You, God, for the people and circumstances You use to give me an open ear!

> Lord, open Thou my heart to hear,
> And through Your Word to me draw near;
> Let me Your Word e'er pure retain;
> Let me Your child and heir remain.[1]

For further reflection: Just before you enter the Seminary chapel, there's a small granite inlay in the sidewalk that says, "Ecclesiastes 5:1." Look it up. Directions for worship!

Blessed Lord, You have caused all Holy Scriptures to be written for our learning. Grant that we may so hear them, read, mark, learn, and take them to heart that, by the patience and comfort of Your holy Word, we may embrace and ever hold fast the blessed hope of everlasting life; through Jesus Christ, Your Son, our Lord, who lives and reigns with You and the Holy Spirit, one God, now and forever.[2]   Amen.

September 1

Golden-Rule Communication

"What we need is more communication!" How many times have you heard that – in marriage, at work, at church, and in community? In this digital age, we don't need *more* communication but *better* communication. Some signs that could have been worded better:

On the door of a restroom: "Toilet out of order. Please use floor below."

At the entrance of a public building: "For anyone who has children and doesn't know it, there is a day-care center on the first floor."

In the kitchen area at a workplace: "After tea break, staff should empty the teapot and stand upside down on the draining board."

On the front door of a shop: "We can repair anything." And then this additional note was scribbled, "Please knock hard on the door – the bell doesn't work."

Humor aside, we've all known hurt feelings because time and care weren't taken to communicate kindly and well. "So whatever you wish that others would do to you, do also to them, for this is the Law and the Prophets" (Matthew 7:12). That's the Golden Rule, not simply sage advice but our Lord's command to us. Ask questions in conversation. Review what you've written to see if you're being clear and making sense. Learn how other people prefer to communicate. Women tend to communicate differently than men, and younger people use different means to communicate than older people. Just because you've said it doesn't mean it's truly been heard! Jesus begins the Golden Rule with the little word "so." Having just taught how good the heavenly Father is to those who pray to Him, Jesus draws a conclusion: So treat others as you want to be treated. Better communication!

And here's my favorite. A resell-it shop advertised this: "We exchange anything – bicycles, washing machines, etc. Why not bring your husband along and get a wonderful bargain?"

For further reflection: 2 Peter 3:14-18 – Even St. Paul could be hard to understand!

Lord, am I sometimes like those computer voices I get when I call companies, a virtual voice coming from a computer that doesn't really care? As the Father's ear is always open to my prayer, open my heart to communicate with others as I would have them communicate to me. For Your love's sake! Amen.

September 2

He Sees Your Struggles

Since His eye is on the sparrow (Matthew 10:29), God sees you, sees you as a father sees his beloved child. "As a father shows compassion to his children, so the LORD shows compassion to those who fear him" (Psalm 103:13).

Unemployed? It hasn't been easy, but He's brought you this far and will guide the rest of the way. God kept His promise to a very poor widow (1 Kings 17:7-16); He will see you through. "The jar of flour was not spent, neither did the jug of oil become empty, according to the word of the LORD" (verse 16).

Family in disarray? David was a man after God's heart, but his son Absalom rebelled against him. In a troubled home, one thing is needful (Luke 10:41-42). "Call upon me in the day of trouble" (Psalm 50:15).

Have you been lied to, slandered? "Everyone utters lies to his neighbor; with flattering lips and a double heart they speak" (Psalm 12:2). "Let those who suffer according to God's will entrust their souls to a faithful Creator while doing good" (1 Peter 4:19).

Did you get yourself into this pickle? Will you admit it? "Father, I have sinned against heaven" (Luke 15:18). God is sovereign, but the sweetest theme of the Bible is His presence, His compassion, His loving look to you in His Son, the Man of sorrows. "There is joy before the angels of God over one sinner who repents" (Luke 15:10).

Whatever it is in your life, your Father sees. Sometimes He sees sin, and so He looks sadly, as Jesus looked at Peter after his denials (Luke 22:61). Other times He sees your good intentions, but, again like Peter, "The spirit indeed is willing, but the flesh is weak" (Mark 14:38). Your comfort and courage is that He sees you with heart. "He knows our frame; he remembers that we are dust" (Psalm 103:14).

"Who is like the LORD our God, who is seated on high, / who looks far down on the heavens and the earth? / He raises the poor from the dust and lifts the needy from the ash heap" (Psalm 113:5-7).

For further reflection: Psalm 16 – Why you can be glad

Now with the humble voice of prayer / Thy mercy we implore;
Then with a grateful voice of praise / Thy goodness we'll adore.[1]

September 3

Your Heavenly Father Knows What You Need!

"Do not be anxious, saying, 'What shall we eat?' or 'What shall we drink?' or 'What shall we wear?' For the Gentiles seek after all these things, and your heavenly Father knows that you need them all" (Matthew 6:31-32).

What do you need today? Something better at work? Just need work? Something better in a relationship? Just need a relationship? Something better in your finances? Just need more money? It's not really things outside yourself that you need. You are the object of need. You need someone to know you for who you are, the good and the bad, and who will still say, *I'm with you unconditionally.* Jesus says the Gentiles are preoccupied with externals, but your occupation is Him who knows you through and through. Desiring externals is a distraction.

"Your heavenly Father knows."

I had a stress test a few years ago. Got on the treadmill and all that. The official report was OK. I saw the images of my heart. There it was, doing its God-given thing: beating. Those heart images were a new look for me but something God has seen for all my years – and for all your years. "O LORD, you have searched me and known me! … You hem me in, behind and before, and lay your hand upon me. … you formed my inward parts; you knitted me together in my mother's womb" (Psalm 139:1, 5, 13).

"Your heavenly Father knows."

He knows you and He knows what you need. "But seek first the kingdom of God and his righteousness, and all these things will be added to you" (Matthew 6:33). If your first devotion is to the Creator, will He not see that you have the things you truly need? If your first devotion is to God's rule in your life, to His kingdom, will He not give you all the benefits of citizenship? If you prioritize the spiritual and eternal over the material and temporal, will He not bless you abundantly?

> Why spend the day in blank despair, / In restless thought the night?
> On your Creator cast your care; / He makes your burdens light.[1]

For further reflection: Psalm 37 – Take it from someone who knows

Many spend their lives in fretting / Over trifles and in getting / Things that have no solid ground. / I shall strive to win a treasure / That will bring me lasting pleasure / And that now is seldom found.[2]

September 4

Spiritual Growth "down on the Plain"

Francis Rossow is one of Concordia Seminary's revered professors and a memorable preacher. Years ago he called our attention to the words on a coffee mug someone had given him: *Expect a miracle.* "You have to wonder," he mused, "about what's in that coffee."

Same way with ads for churches. *Church of miracles* is how one local church promotes itself. *Transforming societies* promises another. *Celebratory music.* A new congregation in town advertises: *Enjoy church.* You have to wonder about truth in church advertising.

In *The Divine Conspiracy*, Dallas Willard shows how instantaneous religious experiences have replaced the slow process of spiritual growth on the American scene. The slow process of spiritual growth has "been replaced by either some ritual at a point in time – Baptism, confirmation – or a type of decision like Billy Graham's meetings."[1] Patrick Kampert comments, "One of the problems with current contemporary Christianity is that every Sunday, churches are offering 'life-transforming experiences.'"[2]

How about this for an advertising campaign? *"Work out your own salvation with fear and trembling."* That's in the Bible, Philippians 2:12, but it obviously doesn't cater to our desire for a quick fix to whatever spiritual malaise we're in. Instantaneous experiences can happen. "Today salvation has come to this house," Jesus announced to the crowd, but then He went on to Jerusalem and the family of Zacchaeus was left to pursue the life of sanctification in the light of their life-changing forgiveness (Luke 19:9). The Emmaus disciples lived in the afterglow of Jesus' resurrected presence: "Did not our hearts burn within us … ?" (Luke 24:32). "Your sins are forgiven" is your mountaintop experience (Mark 2:5; Luke 9:31). Coming off that, everything else is down on the plain, the life of sanctification, growing "up in every way into him who is the head, into Christ" (Ephesians 4:15). Another memorable line from Professor Rossow: "We know precious little about God, but the little we know is precious."

For further reflection: Romans 11:33-36 – "What wondrous love is this"![3]

O Spirit of God, when churches make unbelievable promises to bring people in, remind us that You began the good work in us and "will bring it to completion at the day of Jesus Christ" (Philippians 1:6). Amen.

September 5

The Blessings of Labor

Some biblical teachings about labor:

It's what God wants us to be about. "Go to the ant, O sluggard; consider her ways and be wise. / Without having any chief, officer, or ruler, / she prepares her bread in summer and gathers her food in harvest. / How long will you lie there, O sluggard?" (Proverbs 6:6-9). Jesus saw His life as work. "We must work the works of him who sent me while it is day; night is coming, when no one can work" (John 9:4). Therefore the people of Christ do good works. "For we are his workmanship, created in Christ Jesus for good works, which God prepared beforehand, that we should walk in them" (Ephesians 2:10).

Works show who really lives in your heart. "For it is God who works in you, both to will and to work for his good pleasure" (Philippians 2:13). On the other hand, some people "profess to know God, but they deny him by their works" (Titus 1:16).

The time will come when you will rest from your labors, not just for a weekend or vacation, but rest for eternity. "Blessed are the dead who die in the Lord … that they may rest from their labors, for their deeds follow them!" (Revelation 14:13).

Until that day, enjoy the rest you are able to take each day and each weekend, and may your labors be blessed. "Let the favor of the Lord our God be upon us, and establish the work of our hands upon us; yes, establish the work of our hands!" (Psalm 90:17).

For further reflection: Genesis 2:15; 3:14-19 – A good thing messed up

God, who made the earth and heaven, / Darkness and light:
You the day for work have given, / For rest the night.
May Your angel guards defend us, / Slumber sweet Your mercy send us,
Holy dreams and hope attend us / All through the night.[1]   *Amen.*

September 6

Temporal Thrones, Eternal Rest

I'm thinking how hard it can be to give up work. I know, some of you retired people will say that you don't know when you ever found time to go work; you're so busy now. You repositioned – became an active retiree. Good for you! That's fine for the time being, but even the works of an active retirement must one day be given up. How do you prepare yourself to face that day with calm?

In Genesis 1:26, God gave Adam dominion over the earth. We exercise that dominion through our labor. Whether pre- or post-retirement, the work you do is fulfilling the command to subdue the earth. It's like sitting on a throne, being lord over your little corner of the workaday world. But sooner or later, *the* Lord is going to come and claim all our little thrones. Be it by retirement, layoff, disability, or finally death, God reminds us that the dominion is His and we are only creatures of a day[1], dependent upon His grace. When you practice quiet Bible reading and meditation before your Creator and Redeemer, and daily rest from labor, you are preparing yourself for the day when you must give it up.

"In repentance and rest you shall be saved; in quietness and in trust shall be your strength" (Isaiah 30:15).

> I heard the voice of Jesus say, / "Come unto Me and rest;
> Lay down, thou weary one, lay down / Thy head upon My breast."
> I came to Jesus as I was, / So weary, worn, and sad;
> I found in Him a resting place, / And He has made me glad.[2]

For further reflection: Psalm 94 – Resting for a productive old age

Swift to its close ebbs out life's little day;
Earth's joys grow dim, its glories pass away;
Change and decay in all around I see;
O Thou who changest not, abide with me.[3]   *Amen.*

September 7

The Spirit Keeps Inviting Us

"Come to me, all who labor and are heavy laden, and I will give you rest" (Matthew 11:28).

"Come," Jesus says. He's always inviting us, His Spirit always wooing us. For some reason unknown to me, God has given us the terrible ability to resist His call – to say, "No." Still, He keeps inviting us to come.

"Come to me." I'm afraid this is where many churches go wrong. Churches can't save you. Only Jesus can. That's not to say you shouldn't bother with church. It's just to say that church should be about Jesus, not about itself.

"Come to me, all who labor and are heavy laden." That's me; isn't it you? Why are we this way, burdened and weary? Do we get so busy, do we carry so much because we want to prove that we're worthy of love and respect? That's a crushing load.

"Come to me … and I will give you rest." Lay your load down at His feet. Rest in His love for you. Rest in His strength… and, by the way, you'll be renewed to carry your burdens.

Don't just do something – sit there! "O Lamb of God, I come, I come."[1]

For further reflection: Matthew 17:1-8 – When you come down from the mountaintop to the workaday world, see Jesus only

O Jesus Christ, my Lord, / So meek in deed and word,
You suffered death to save us / Because Your love would have us
Be heirs of heav'nly gladness / When ends this life of sadness.
"So be it," then, I say / With all my heart each day.
Dear Lord, we all adore You, / We sing for joy before You.
Guide us while here we wander / Until we praise You yonder.[2]   *Amen.*

September 8

Are You Too Secluded?

On 72 secluded acres in metropolitan St. Louis, we faculty, staff, and students of Concordia Seminary begin a new academic year of preparing pastors and deaconesses for The Lutheran Church—Missouri Synod. The Seminary has been doing this for going on 200 years.

"Secluded" can present a problem. In 1884, Woodrow Wilson, then 28 years old, wrote to his future wife, Ellen Axson: "I am afraid of being a mere student. I want to be part of the nature around me, not an outside observer of it. … You'll never find in a cloister a fulcrum for any lever which can budge the world."[1]

Wilson wasn't opposed to academia. He was president of Princeton University from 1902 to 1910. What Wilson feared was isolation from the pressing issues of the day. Academic seclusion easily becomes seduction into self rather than service. When that happens, no fulcrum will be found to budge the world.

But seek seclusion in order to engage societal issues wisely and you'll find fulcrums. One stands out in world history. "When they saw the boldness of Peter and John, and perceived that they were uneducated, common men, they were astonished. And they recognized that they had been with Jesus" (Acts 4:13). What came from that seclusion with Jesus and their engagement with society? They "turned the world upside down" (Acts 17:6).

For further reflection: Galatians 1:15-18 – Before Paul became the great apostle we celebrate, he went into seclusion

O God, the source of all abiding knowledge, through Word and Sacrament You both enlighten the minds and sanctify the lives of those whom You draw to Your service. Look with favor on the seminaries and colleges of the Church, blessing those who teach and those who learn, that all the baptized may apply themselves with ready diligence to their tasks and faithfully fulfill their service according to Your will; through Jesus Christ, our Lord.[2] Amen.

September 9

What Bell Summons You Today?

Here's what daily life was like at Concordia Seminary in 1853.

> The day's work is regulated by a new clock in the new wing and a bell in the court, which resounds a great distance. It rings at five o'clock in the morning to signify to those not yet at work that it is time to get up. Fifteen minutes later joint morning devotion is held in the large lecture room under the direction of an instructor. Breakfast is served at 5:30 and then work begins. At 8:45 the bell rings as a warning to get ready for the morning lessons, which last from 9:00 to 12:00. After 12:00 dinner is eaten and the students are free until 2:00. Five minutes before that the bell rings, and afternoon lessons, which last until 5:00, begin. Then there is free time until 7:30 with supper at 6:30. At 7:30 the bell summons to work again, and at 8:45 the bell summons to vespers.[1]

What bell summons us to work and worship today? "For the love of Christ controls us, because we have concluded this: that one has died for all, therefore all have died; and he died for all, that those who live might no longer live for themselves but for him who for their sake died and was raised" (2 Corinthians 5:14-15).

> When morning gilds the skies, / My heart, awaking, cries,
> "May Jesus Christ be praised!"
> When evening shadows fall, / This rings my curfew call:
> "May Jesus Christ be praised!"[2]

For further reflection: Psalm 139:1-18 – You sleep, you awake - He is still with you

Lord, I my vows to Thee renew; / Disperse my sins as morning dew;
Guard my first springs of thought and will / And with Thyself my spirit fill.
Direct, control, suggest this day / All I design or do or say
That all my pow'rs with all their might, / In Thy sole glory may unite.[3]
Amen.

September 10

Protect Us from Stan

"Hi, Christian here. Guess what, Opa? Mommy and Daddy had me say bedtime prayers. They asked me, 'Christian, what are you thankful for?' I said that Jesus died on the cross. 'Why did Jesus die on the cross?' they asked. I gave them the answer: 'To forgive our sins and to protect us from Stan.'"

"That's good Christian. We do things and think things that God doesn't like. Even though we go to church, we need forgiveness, all of us. But, Christian, who is 'Stan?'"

"Opa, Stan is bad. Stan tries to get us to disobey God. Jesus died on the cross so that we could say, 'Stan, no! I'm not going to do that because that is not what God wants me to do.'"

"OK, Christian, now I understand who Stan is. He's real smart and real sneaky. The Bible says he's like a roaring lion who wants to devour us (cf. 1 Peter 5:8). He wants to take us away from God. Christian, do you want to know something else about Stan?"

"What, Opa?"

"A lot of big people don't take Stan seriously. They don't ask God to show them the tricky ways Stan tries to take us away from God's love. Christian, as you get older, keep learning about… Stan."

For further reflection: Matthew 4:1-11 – "But for us fights the Valiant One, / Whom God Himself elected. / Ask ye, Who is this?"[1]

Though Satan's wrath / Beset our path, / And worldly scorn assail us,
While You are near / We shall not fear; / Your strength shall never fail us.
Your rod and staff / Will keep us safe, / And guide our steps forever;
Nor shades of death / Nor hell beneath, / Our lives from You will sever.[2]

September 11

The Meyer Minute from September 11, 2001

I don't know what the situation will be as you read this. As I compose my thoughts, the news reports are still breaking from across the East Coast of the United States. One thing echoes in my mind: "The LORD saw that the wickedness of man was great in the earth, and that every intention of the thoughts of his heart was only evil continually" (Genesis 6:5).

As citizens of the United States, most of us calling ourselves Christians, we dare not be naïve about the world in which we live or the role our trust in God requires us to take. When a congressman asked me how to reconcile Christian love with his service on the House Anti-Terrorism Committee, I answered that it is also sacrificial love when our government and military personnel put themselves into danger and even combat to protect us. God has given the government the right to use force to protect its citizens (Romans 13). The memory of that conversation is strongly in my mind today.

As individuals we dare not be naïve, either. There are evil forces that want to attack the goodness of God in your life, to make you doubt, to shake you from your place of stability and peace. Peter (the one Jesus called "Rocky" but whose own behavior was anything but steady) reminds us, "Be sober-minded; be watchful. Your adversary the devil prowls around like a roaring lion, seeking someone to devour." Therefore, always, but especially today, God help us in our personal individual lives to stand firmly in His love and not to be tossed to-and-fro by the uncertainty of these early moments of terror. And, then, let us pray for wisdom as Christian citizens, that we might "Resist him (the devil), firm in your faith" (1 Peter 5:8-9).

For further reflection: Psalm 7 – Save us!

Lord, our final refuge and strength, deliver us from every evil of body and soul, and give comfort and peace to those who face the pain of loss or the uncertainty of a loved one's safety. Amen.

September 12

The Meyer Minute *from September 17, 2001*

Where is God in all this? Once again I have been reminded – I trust we all have – how precious little we know about the eternal God.

Last December, some friends took me to dinner near the top of the World Trade Center. You can imagine how spectacular the view of the New York skyline was, but I was most amazed by how small, how insignificant everything looked below. Even the Statue of Liberty appeared only an inch tall from high up on the 106th floor. After dinner, back down on the street, I knew I was back in real life: impatient motorists blowing their horns, business execs on cell phones, the homeless. A woman passes me. She's crying and I wonder why. Down on the street, not up on the 106th floor, was real life. I remember thinking that God sits high but looks low. Nothing down on the street is insignificant to God.

Oh, how we need the God who sits high to look low now! To look into the rubble caused by evil, to touch devastated families, to heal us, and to use us to make Liberty stand taller than she ever has stood before. With an expression of my respect to other world faiths, I believe that's what the cross of Jesus Christ is about. The most-high Son of God came down to suffer with us, and not only to suffer with us but also to suffer redemptively for us. The Spirit of God is in our land. He bends His ear to our sighs. He touches our tears with His mercies. He is ready to fill our hearts with new hope. God sits high but looks low.

Yes, there are so many questions about God that are unanswered, but He has shown us what He wants us to do down here. That is to follow Him, to do justice, to love mercy, and to walk humbly with our God (Micah 6:8). We know so precious little about God, but what we know is so precious.

For further reflection: Psalm 113 – Even in this, we praise God

O God of love, O King of peace, / Make wars throughout the world to cease;
The rage of nations now restrain: / Give peace, O God, give peace again![1]
Amen.

September 13

From Generation to Generation

Two blocks west or five blocks south. When I grew up, both sets of grandparents were close to home and we visited them all the time. I don't remember when it happened, but sometime this little kid figured out that Grandpa and Grandma were actually the parents of *my* parents. Those authority figures who kept telling me how to live my life? They were kids once too. Dad and Mom reprimand me? Hey, they were reprimanded by their parents. "Don't slam the door when you go out!" I bet they got yelled at for that too. Wow, was that great when it dawned on me that my parents were just grown up kids.

In these September days, we remember our grandparents. We even have a "Grandparents Day," although decades ago we didn't need an artificial day. We were at Grandma's and Grandpa's all the time, and we truly did show them the greatest of respect. After all, they deserved it. They had to raise our parents! Moral of the story: Young moms and dads, with all your parenting books and parenting videos and parenting websites, don't be obsessive about perfect parenting. If they haven't already, your kids will soon figure out that you were a kid too. When they do, when they bring up your foibles, as you probably did to your parents, an admitting smile will strengthen family love... from generation to generation.

It's easy to forget that we are all equal in the sight of God: grandparents, parents, children... We're equally children of the heavenly Father, forgiven by the blood of Jesus, and brought into, or for some, hopefully to be brought into, God's kingdom by the work of the Holy Spirit. True, we have different roles and places in the earthly scheme of things. God set it up that way for our good and for the good of society. Before God, however, we are all equal. What can be so great about grandparents is where they're living – farther down the road on their journey to heaven. With hindsight and freedom from parenting duties, they can share their story and God's story... from generation to generation.

For further reflection: Luke 2:25-38 – Intergenerational wisdom and blessing

So even to old age and gray hairs, O God, do not forsake me, / until I proclaim your might to another generation, your power to all those to come. (Psalm 71:18)   Amen.

September 14

Days of Awe

"Come, O children, listen to me; I will teach you the fear of the LORD" (Psalm 34:11).

The Bible talks about fear in several ways. One way is the feeling that you and I have when something bigger than we can handle comes right at us: something like 9/11 or a terrible medical diagnosis or realizing that you're on the verge of financial disaster. Such things are bigger than we are and threaten to do us in.

But the Bible also talks about the feelings we have when something overwhelming comes at us – not to do us in, but to help us. God for us, not against us (Romans 8:31). That evokes a feeling of "Wow!," of awe, of reverence… and that is what the Bible calls the "fear of God."

Our Jewish friends have a movable festival, just as we Christians have movable festivals like Easter. Sometime in these weeks, they observe Rosh Hashanah, which begins ten days called the "Days of Repentance" or "Days of Awe." For us Christians, the fulfillment and focus of our daily repentance and daily awe is our Savior Jesus Christ. "Great indeed, we confess, is the mystery of godliness: He was manifested in the flesh, vindicated by the Spirit, seen by angels, / proclaimed among the nations, believed on in the world, taken up in glory" (1 Timothy 3:16).

Do you get the "wow factor" of God? "The LORD is the stronghold of my life; of whom shall I be afraid?" (Psalm 27:1).

For further reflection: Psalm 111 – The fear of the Lord is…

Great God, You come to help us in Your Son Jesus Christ. Mary sang that Your mercy is for those who fear You from generation to generation. By Your Holy Spirit, instill in me such reverence and awe that You give me help and hope in Jesus that I may contend with all my other fears. Amen. (Luke 1:50)

September 15

Stepping Between

The Great Recession of 2008-2009 was not without some benefits, and one positive for me was praying much more for other people. "Intercessory prayer" they call it, coming from two Latin words that mean stepping in between. Pray for another person, intercede, and you're stepping between them and God to plead for them. This kind of selfless prayer is urged on us by the Bible. "Pray for one another" (James 5:16). "Pray for the peace of Jerusalem!" (Psalm 122:6). Jesus says, "pray for those who abuse you" (Luke 6:28). The prophet Samuel said, "far be it from me that I should sin against the LORD by ceasing to pray for you" (1 Samuel 12:23).

Proper intercessory prayer proceeds from selfless love for another person. Does yours? In praying for others, you can learn much about your own relationship with God. When you are having a disagreement with someone, do you pray that they will come around to your way of thinking? When you pray for someone out of work and soon out of money, do you pray merely for a job and money? Are you praying according to your will, or God's? "Not what I will, but what you will" (Mark 14:36). Are your intercessions bounded by your limited knowledge – or do you place the person into the unlimited care of God "who is able to do far more abundantly than all that we ask or think" (Ephesians 3:20)?

Oswald Chambers wrote, "Preaching the Gospel has a snare; intercessory prayer has none."[1] Done properly, intercession is the work of a heart tired of itself and aligned with God. No self-serving in it, only submission.

For further reflection: Genesis 18:22-33 – One of the most famous intercessory prayers of the Bible

The Lord's Prayer is not an individual's prayer; it is the prayer of the Church, God's family. "Our Father," not "my Father." Identify someone who needs your intercession and pray the Lord's Prayer with him/her in mind. Pray it on their behalf.

September 16

"In God Is Our Trust"

It was wartime. The British had already burned Washington, D.C. and now unleashed a horrific bombardment against Fort McHenry, the fort guarding the approach to Baltimore. Watching that 25-hour bombardment, a young Washington lawyer, Francis Scott Key, began a poem that he finished the evening of September 16, 1814. We call it "The Star-Spangled Banner."

It's so easy for us to forget that the poem was written in a time of great anxiety, "a perilous fight." Can you see? Is our flag still there? Those were no rhetorical questions then. That terrible assault could have taken the flag, the fort, and even the nation.

Key later wrote, "Through the clouds of the war the stars of that banner still shone in my view, and I saw the discomfited host of its assailants driven back in ignominy to their ships. Then, in the hour of deliverance, and joyful triumph, my heart spoke."[1]

For over two centuries, the price of our deliverance has been great. Truly, the flag would not wave today were it not for the kindness of heaven upon us. "No wisdom, no understanding, no counsel can avail against the LORD. / The horse is made ready for the day of battle, but the victory belongs to the LORD" (Proverbs 21:30-31). God, make us a nation of stronger character after Your righteousness!

For further reflection: Lamentations 3:1-33 – Hope amidst national defeat

The nation You have blest / May well Your love declare,
From foes and fears at rest, / Protected by Your care.
For this bright day,
For this fair land – / Gifts of Your hand –
Our thanks we pay.[2]   *Amen.*

September 17

"Create in Me a Clean Heart"

True or false: "When you get angry at someone but stifle your rage, you're not guilty before God."

When your doctor orders a cardiac catheterization, he knows you're not as healthy as you may appear. Just so God. "Man looks on the outward appearance, but the LORD looks on the heart" (1 Samuel 16:7). Your Great Physician has a sobering diagnosis about the condition of your heart. Jesus sees all sorts of evils that come from the sin-diseased heart (cf. Mark 7:21-23).

But what if you restrain the impulse of anger against someone else? After all, there's no civil law against sins of the heart as long as they stay concealed in your heart. Jesus is "not swayed by appearances" (Matthew 22:16). The angry impulse itself, even if restrained, is still sin against the holy God. It shows that we are "captive to the law of sin that dwells in my members" (Romans 7:23).

"The sacrifices of God are a broken spirit; a broken and contrite heart, O God, you will not despise" (Psalm 51:17). Your Savior is not only a Great Diagnostician; he is especially your Great Physician. He "forgives all your sins and heals all your diseases" (Psalm 103:3 NIV). His Spirit through Baptism covers the sin in your heart, but those deep-seated impulses remain a grave concern for the forgiven Christian. So the Spirit also works to create in you a heart of purer impulses (cf. Psalm 51:10). "It is God who works in you, both to will and to work for his good pleasure" (Philippians 2:13). Thus you strive to restrain the angry impulse against another person so that it doesn't become even worse, an outward sin. And if there is occasion for righteous anger, this is toward the *action* of another, not the person themselves. "In your anger do not sin" (Ephesians 4:26 NIV).

"You have died, and your life is hidden with Christ in God. Put to death, therefore, what is earthly in you … you must put them all away: anger, wrath…" (Colossians 3:3, 5, 8).

For further reflection: Romans 7:14-25 – A contrite heart You will not despise (cf. Psalm 51:17)

Lord, I my vows to Thee renew; / Disperse my sins as morning dew; / Guard my first springs of thought and will / And with Thyself my spirit fill.[1]   *Amen.*

September 18

"If God Is for Us…"

"He is not afraid of bad news" (Psalm 112:7a). Wow, did those words jump out at me! We've all gotten bad news in the past and dread the unexpected, devastating bad news yet to come. The middle of the night phone call, the policeman or minister showing up at your front door, the surgeon saying, "We did all we could, but it wasn't enough…" Simply writing those words makes me shudder. So why will you not fear bad news? "His heart is firm, trusting in the LORD" (Psalm 112:7b). Replace your preoccupation with yourself with trust in the Lord.

How do you get from preoccupation with self to trust in the Lord? Fear the Lord. "Blessed is the man who fears the LORD, who greatly delights in his commandments!" (Psalm 112:1). When we're apprehensive about bad news that is sure to come, we are obviously thinking about the future. When you fear God, you're also thinking about the future but with one decisive difference: hope. God will come to your help, to your support. "If God is for us, who can be against us?" (Romans 8:31).

When bad news takes away a dear part of your life, hope born from the fear of God makes your heart steadfast. That's why we not only fear God – that is, are in awe that He comes to help us – but we love Him and yearn for His words to hug us with hope. His hold of hope will put a glisten in your tears, because "weeping may tarry for the night, but joy comes with the morning" (Psalm 30:5). A part of us dies when bad news comes, oh, wrenchingly painful! We need not fear the bad news because our fear and love is directed to One who is greater, our Savior. "Peace I leave with you; my peace I give to you. Not as the world gives do I give to you. Let not your hearts be troubled, neither let them be afraid" (John 14:27).

For further reflection: Hebrews 6:13-20 – Anchored by hope

Hence, all fear and sadness! / For the Lord of gladness, / Jesus, enters in.
Those who love the Father, / Though the storms may gather, / Still have
*   peace within.*
Yea, whate'er / I here must bear, / Thou art still my purest pleasure,
Jesus, priceless treasure![1]

September 19

The Spiritual Blessing of Asking for Help

A young church couple invited me to talk with them about their troubled marriage. Good for them! Asking for help is a hard thing to do, in marriage and in many other areas of life. It's hard to ask for a loan. It's hard to admit failure in a job. It's hard to own up to an addiction and seek help. It's hard to get older and not be self-sufficient. Asking for help is hard because our natural pride tells us we can make it on our own. It's a First Commandment issue. Is God God, or are we? Who's the Creator? Who's the Redeemer who comes with help? Who's the Sanctifier who enables us to embrace heaven's unearned gifts?

Couples don't usually advertise their problems, and this young couple hasn't. For you to read and know that there are couples who seek help for their marriage should be encouraging. We all have the First Commandment struggle. We all experience how hard it is to face up to the fact that we're having trouble making it on our own in this life. Beyond the here-and-now problems where we seek help in temporal life, it's hard to admit that we'll never see heaven without help, total and complete help from our divine Helper. Some people give lip service to grace but really don't think they need help. How about you?

"Gracious is the LORD, and righteous; our God is merciful. / The LORD preserves the simple; when I was brought low, he saved me" (Psalm 116:5-6). Lord, help every couple who meet with a counselor and with a Christian pastor. Married or single, young or old, lead us all to acknowledge our need for Your grace in Jesus Christ. Amen!

For further reflection: Psalm 116:1-7 – May this be the outcome of all our problems!

Help, Helper, help in fear and need, / Have mercy, to my prayer give heed!
I know Thou lov'st me still as Thine, / Though 'gainst me world and hell combine.
My God and Lord, I trust in Thee; / What need I, if Thou art with me?
Help, Helper, help! Amen.[1]

September 20

What Does True Humility Look Like?

When the Dean of the Chapel assigned me to preach on Luke 14:7-11, verse 11 hit a raw nerve. "Everyone who exalts himself will be humbled, and he who humbles himself will be exalted." A few years ago, I heard that I had come across to a new acquaintance as arrogant. Ah, another blessed moment! Because Jesus "humbled himself by becoming obedient to the point of death, even death on a cross" (Philippians 2:8), the fruit of His Spirit should be manifest in us: "love, joy, peace, patience, kindness, goodness, faithfulness, gentleness, [and] self-control" (Galatians 5:22-23).

How to humble yourself? Put your head down and say "Aw, shucks?" Walk around church with some pious, unworldly look? We could, but still be full of ourselves. Some people are born with personalities that aren't pushy or prideful, but that doesn't equal humility before God. "Out of the heart of man, come evil thoughts, sexual immorality, theft, murder …" and on and on goes the list in Mark 7:21-22. Baptized, both saint and sinner, we can all block the fruit of the Spirit. When you do, you "go native" and the works of the flesh have their way, including pride and arrogance. Sanctification means letting the Word of Christ catheterize your heart so that your character traits and conducts become more and more like Jesus.

Early in our marriage, Diane said, "I can hear your mind slam shut." Given my German ancestry, I took that as a compliment but she meant it as a criticism. Lord, it's hard to be humble! Humility and the fruit of the Spirit are not "learned" as much as the Spirit through the Word wires them into our hearts. "We were buried therefore with him by baptism into death, in order that, just as Christ was raised from the dead by the glory of the Father, we too might walk in newness of life" (Romans 6:4).

"Make ye straight what long was crooked; / Make the rougher places plain. / Let your hearts be true and humble, / As befits His holy reign."[1]

For further reflection: Micah 6:8 – What to do

O God, You resist the proud and give grace to the humble. Grant us true humility after the likeness of Your only Son that we may never be arrogant and prideful and thus provoke Your wrath but in all lowliness be made partakers of the gifts of Your grace; through Jesus Christ, our Lord.[2]   *Amen.*

September 21

Are Your Ears Open?

Today is the Day of St. Matthew, Apostle and Evangelist.

Leroy Barber:

> I have spent my life living and working in the urban centers of Philadelphia and Atlanta. It is not out of the ordinary to watch drug deals on the church steps. The institution has made its own quiet and unspoken deal with the vendors who make their living there. People who most need the church are sitting outside, waiting to feel worthy enough to come. For the young who grew up on the streets, it's an age-old story: the drug-kingpin knows their name, and the pastor does not. The teachers at school don't think they can learn, but they conquer the "street classes" just fine. The street culture always pursues and welcomes them, but the doors of the church are open only on Sunday.[1]

Include Matthew in those rejects. He was a tax collector, and they were always on the take. In first century Israel, upright, religious people reserved the word "sinner" for the despised of society: adulterers, addicts, criminals, tax collectors, and the like – the people to whom Leroy Barber ministers. "God, I thank you that I am not like other men, extortioners, unjust, adulterers, or even like this tax collector" (Luke 18:11).

Oh, how Jesus scandalizes their church snobbery! Not only does He call Matthew but He even goes to relax at his home. "And as Jesus reclined at table in the house, behold, many tax collectors and sinners came and were reclining with Jesus and his disciples. And when the Pharisees saw this, they said to his disciples, 'Why does your teacher eat with tax collectors and sinners?'" Self-satisfied, self-righteous religious people speak their smothering sanctimony.

"When he heard it, he said, 'Those who are well have no need of a physician, but those who are sick. Go and learn what this means, 'I desire mercy [acts of loving kindness], and not sacrifice [ritual worship].' For I came not to call the righteous, but sinners'" (Matthew 9:10-13). Can we hear echoes of Jesus' sarcasm today?

For further reflection: Psalm 119:65-72 – "Lord give us such a faith as this"![2]

Praise, Lord, for him whose Gospel / Your human life declared, / Who, worldly gain forsaking, / Your path of suff'ring shared. / From all unrighteous mammon, / O raise our eyes anew / That we in our vocation / May rise and follow You.[3]   Amen.

September 22

Start with Grace

One of these evenings our Jewish friends begin, perhaps already began, their celebration of Yom Kippur, a movable holy day. Yom Kippur is the Day of Atonement, the day when sacrifices were made for the forgiveness of Israel (see Leviticus 16). Christians believe this practice foreshadowed the sacrifice of Jesus on the cross for our sins.

It begins in the evening. The Genesis account of the creation of the world says that "there was evening and there was morning, the first day" (Genesis 1:5). That's typical Hebraic thought – the day begins at sundown, not sunup.

There's something spiritually rich in this. We are conditioned to think that the day begins with work and ends with rest. You get up in the morning, do your work, and earn the rest of the evening and the sleep of night. The Hebrew view is totally opposite. The day begins with the rest and sleep of the evening … understand God's grace … and then waking and work follow as our response to the graces received. This reflects the essence of the Christian faith, that our salvation, our reconciliation with God, our at-one-ment with Him, is purely a gift – grace. In response, we gratefully go to work.

"For by grace you have been saved through faith. And this is not your own doing; it is the gift of God, not a result of works, so that no one may boast. For we are his workmanship, created in Christ Jesus for good works, which God prepared beforehand, that we should walk in them" (Ephesians 2:8-10).

Our friends begin the Day of Atonement at sundown. We believers in Jesus can take a clue from that. Think of your day beginning at sundown, beginning with rest in God's grace in Christ. Then in the morning, joyfully rise and go to work to show your thankfulness to God. You are forgiven!

For further reflection: Mark 4:26-29 – Jesus lists sleep and night ahead of getting up for the work of day

Oh, may my sleep in Thee repose, / And may sweet sleep mine eyelids close, Sleep that shall me more vig'rous make / To serve my God when I awake![1] Amen.

September 23

Forgiveness: Once for All

Guilt is persistent, keeps coming at you. Even in the middle of the night, guilt can wake you and get you tossing and turning – useless, fretful tossing and turning.

Forgiveness is more flighty. It comes and goes, often going as soon as it has come. You hear words of forgiveness, maybe from a friend, maybe in church on Sunday, and feel better but before those words have settled in your heart they're evicted by that squatter, guilt.

Leviticus 16 spells out the ancient ceremony of Yom Kippur, the High Priest offering sacrifices for his personal sins and for the sins of the people. This had to be done every year; one year's sacrifice was not good for the next – guilt keeps on coming. In contrast, the New Testament presents the sacrifice of Jesus for our sins as an offering once and for all time, no need to repeat it.

> Every priest stands daily at his service, offering repeatedly the same sacrifices, which can never take away sins. But when Christ had offered for all time a single sacrifice for sins, he sat down at the right hand of God, waiting from that time until his enemies should be made a footstool for his feet. For by a single offering he has perfected for all time those who are being sanctified. And the Holy Spirit also bears witness to us … he adds, "I will remember their sins and their lawless deeds no more." Where there is forgiveness of these, there is no longer any offering for sin. (Hebrews 10:11-18)

Guilt can be a good thing. It goads us to the Priest who sacrificed Himself once and for all for our sins. The art of Christian spiritual living is to keep invoking that once-for-all forgiveness from God through Christ so that you keep evicting that squatter, guilt. "There is now no condemnation for those who are in Christ Jesus" (Romans 8:1).

For further reflection: Zechariah 3:1-5 – "Remove the filthy garments"

Lord, I believe Thy precious blood, / Which at the mercy seat of God
Pleads for the captives' liberty, / Was also shed in love for me.[1]   *Amen.*

September 24

Scripture in Our Daily Speech

Barry Koltnow of *The Orange County Register* once wrote about famous lines from movies that are part of our everyday speech.[1] Do you know which movies these expressions come from?

1. "We're not in Kansas anymore"
2. "Go ahead, make my day"
3. "If you build it, they[2] will come"
4. "Houston, we have a problem"
5. "Keep your friends close, but your enemies closer"

Answers: 1. *The Wizard of Oz*; 2. *Sudden Impact*; 3. *Field of Dreams*; 4. *Apollo 13*; 5. *The Godfather: Part II*

In a similar way, our daily speech includes expressions that people may not realize come from the Bible. Where do we find the origin of...

1. "To everything a season"
2. "Do unto others as you would have them do unto you"
3. "A house divided against itself will fall"
4. "An eye for an eye and a tooth for a tooth"
5. "Love your enemies"

Answers: 1. Ecclesiastes 3:1; 2. Matthew 7:12; 3. Luke 11:17; 4. Exodus 21:24; 5. Matthew 5:44

These are but a few examples of the Bible's impact upon our common speech. Since the Bible has had such a quiet but significant impact upon how people speak, just think about the enrichment that awaits you from taking more and more of the diction of the ages into your daily speech. Not only will your speech help edify others, it will keep the Spirit working in your own heart and life.

And where does this one come from? "God helps those who help themselves?" I don't know, but it's not in the Bible!

For further reflection: 2 Timothy 3:15-17 – We pass on the diction of the ages

God's Word is our great heritage / And shall be ours forever; / To spread its light from age to age / Shall be our chief endeavor. / Through life it guides our way, / In death it is our stay. / Lord, grant, while worlds endure, / We keep its teachings pure / Throughout all generations.[3] Amen.

September 25

Is Your Baptismal Life Out of Order?

The generation that designed and built the Chapel of St. Timothy and St. Titus on the campus of Concordia Seminary did well. It is a large space, large enough to remind us of our smallness in the great scheme of things eternal, and it's high enough to draw our eyes upward to the Source of our help. To enter the chapel you pass by the baptismal font, placed in the vestibule to symbolize that Baptism is the Sacrament of entrance into the Church. A feature of this font is its constantly circulating water. That too is a symbol, the newness of baptized life in Christ. "We were buried … with him by baptism into death, in order that, just as Christ was raised from the dead by the glory of the Father, we too might walk in newness of life" (Romans 6:4).

Some years ago a malfunction stopped the water from circulating. A maintenance man was summoned, couldn't get the water moving again, and so he attached a sign to the font – "Out of Order." Sometimes our faith stops functioning the way God intends. Maybe you haven't been to church for a long time. Maybe you're holding a grudge against someone and it's damaging your relationship with that person and with God. When "Out of Order" describes your faith life, no need to be re-baptized. When you get lost on a trip, do you return home and start over? No, you just find out where you got off course and get back on the right way. Baptism is a command of God, and the blessings of Baptism are as sure as His Word is sure. When your baptismal life gets "Out of Order," just get it fixed: Repent, welcome the forgiveness that will come down from on high, and then go on with your life's journey.

People say, "I was baptized." Yes, you were on some date in the past, but better to say, "I am baptized." What happened long ago is still as true today as God's Word is true for all eternity. "Newness of life," waters ever flowing!

For further reflection: 1 Peter 3:18-22 – Onboard Noah's Ark

With one accord, O God, we pray: / Grant us Your Holy Spirit.
Help us in our infirmity / Through Jesus' blood and merit.
Grant us to grow in grace each day / That by this sacrament we may
Eternal life inherit.[1]   *Amen.*

September 26

Why Did *You Doubt?*

"Why did you doubt?" (Matthew 14:31).

Why did you waver in your trust that God would bring you through? When you were seriously short of money... when the diagnosis shook your being... when people and relationships failed you... when the promise of your career tanked... why did you doubt?

Crossing a stormy Sea of Galilee late at night, the disciples are afraid. Jesus comes to them, walking on the water. First they think it's a ghost but realize it's Jesus! Peter asks to walk out to Jesus. He starts out but begins to sink from fear of wind and waves. "Lord, save me!" and Jesus pulls Peter out (Matthew 14:22-31).Then Jesus asks today's question, "Why did you doubt?"

Please notice the tense. "Did" is past tense. "Why *did* you doubt?" (italics mine). Jesus didn't crow over floundering Peter's lack of faith, "Why *do* you doubt?" present tense. No, first Jesus began to save him. "'Lord, save me.' Jesus immediately reached out his hand and took hold of him" (Matthew 14:30-31). It was only when Peter had confidence that he was being saved, only then did Jesus say in effect, *Peter, now that you know you'll be safe, let's analyze what happened.* "Why did you doubt?"

"Before they call I will answer; while they are yet speaking I will hear" (Isaiah 65:24). You who are redeemed for heaven, God knows your circumstances. He knows when you think you're going down, whatever the cause may be. He is already working your deliverance and already knows the day of your eternal deliverance. Like Peter, disciples come sooner or later to see the hints that God was indeed reaching down to save us. It's then, when we start to get it, that He invites the introspective look back, "Why did you doubt?" We see God from behind, and the more we look back at the times He's delivered us, the more we'll trust that He will save, even if we don't yet see it happening.

For further reflection: James 1:2-8 – Flailing faith

Heavenly Father, we pray that You would rescue us from every evil of body and soul, possessions and reputation, and finally, when our last hour comes, give us a blessed end, and graciously take us from the valley of sorrow to Yourself in heaven.[1] *Amen.*

September 27

Jesus Will See You Shortly

We all know the experience of going to a doctor's office and being told, "The doctor will see you shortly." Maybe you've gone to a lawyer or banker and been told, "Mr. or Ms. So-and-so will see you shortly." James 5:9 tells us, "behold, the Judge is standing at the door." It's not the doctor, lawyer, banker, or whoever – it's the Judge who will see you shortly. How do you feel about that?

It may happen through your death or the sudden coming of the Last Day, but judgment is promised to come. "And just as it is appointed for man to die once, and after that comes judgment, so Christ, having been offered once to bear the sins of many, will appear a second time, not to deal with sin but to save those who are eagerly waiting for him" (Hebrews 9:27-28). Even if you've given up on the Judgment Day thing, a presumptuous thing to do, still eternity is only one heartbeat away. Only one heartbeat away! Jesus will see you shortly.

Years ago I came across this sermon illustration. A stern judge was about to pronounce a guilty verdict upon an accused person, when suddenly a young child broke into the courtroom. The child eluded security, ran straight up to the judge, and hopped into his lap. The judge was his father. When your heart has beaten for the last time, will you rejoice to see the Judge? Do you now await His words, "Come, you who are blessed by my Father, inherit the kingdom prepared for you from the foundation of the world" (Matthew 25:34)?

"He is the one appointed by God to be judge of the living and the dead" (Acts 10:42).

For further reflection: 2 Peter 3:1-13 – The promise of His coming

Lord, let at last Thine angels come, / To Abr'ham's bosom bear me home,
That I may die unfearing; / And in its narrow chamber keep
My body safe in peaceful sleep / Until Thy reappearing.
And then from death awaken me / That these mine eyes with joy may see,
O Son of God, Thy glorious face, / My Savior and my fount of grace.
Lord Jesus Christ, my prayer attend, my prayer attend,
And I will praise Thee without end.[1]   *Amen.*

September 28

Strange Gifts from Our Creator

A friend is fighting cancer and his grown children are angry and scared as they see him struggle. Those emotions are natural. Anger comes when someone we love is threatened – this happens to make righteous anger a help in wartime combat. But cancer angers us because it threatens life and sometimes fighting back doesn't succeed. Fear is natural too. The cancer threatens our loving family circle; what's to become of me?

It's hard to realize that emotions, including unwelcome emotions like fear and anger, are strange gifts from our Creator. Many Christians don't think that way because we were raised to believe that faith is simply agreeing with certain doctrinal propositions, like you're a sinner and Jesus died for your sins. That's true, oh that's true! But faith is head and especially heart. Our raw feelings are powerful indicators of how it is with us and God. When we learn how to interpret and use them, God helps us in our need. "You keep him in perfect peace whose mind is stayed on you, because he trusts in you" (Isaiah 26:3).

We get afraid when something threatens us that we can't handle alone. Cancer fits that description. Our anger at cancer is anger because this fallen and sinful world threatens us. Sanctifying the anger by word and prayer makes anger a powerful and positive spiritual force. Our fear of the future is also a strange gift because it's incentive to go to Someone greater who is for us, Someone who is for us, not against us.

Thou art coming to a King, / Large petitions with thee bring;

For His grace and pow'r are such / None can ever ask too much.[1]

For further reflection: Isaiah 38 – Illness, "that the Son of God may be glorified through it" (John 11:4)

O Father of mercies and God of all comfort, our only help in time of need, look with favor upon Your servant who is ill. Assure him/her of Your mercy, deliver from the temptations of the evil one, and give patience and comfort in this illness. If it please You, restore him/her to health, or give grace to accept this tribulation with courage and hope; through Jesus Christ, our Lord.[2] Amen.

September 29

Angels on Duty!

No reason for you to know this as you plunge into your day of work, no reason to know this as you navigate dangerous traffic, no reason to know this as you walk in the crowds, not all kindly people, no reason to know… but in the calendar of the Christian church, today, September 29th, is the day of "St. Michael and All Angels." The archangel Michael shows up in the biblical books of Daniel (10:13-21, 12:1), Jude (9), and in Revelation 12:7-9…

> Now war arose in heaven, Michael and his angels fighting against the dragon. And the dragon and his angels fought back, but he was defeated, and there was no longer any place for them in heaven. And the great dragon was thrown down, that ancient serpent, who is called the devil and Satan, the deceiver of the whole world – he was thrown down to the earth, and his angels were thrown down with him.

Michael is our protector. Indeed, that's the task God has given to all the good angels. "He will command his angels concerning you to guard you in all your ways" (Psalm 91:11).

Commuting, working, contending with the crowds on the street, at the store or stadium… think of all the close calls you've had. Close calls? God commanded, called His angels concerning you. Angels aren't objects of worship but servants of God. Good thing God has them on duty more than one day a year for you and me! You're in good hands.

For further reflection: Genesis 28:10-17 – "Angels from the realms of glory"[1] and "I did not know it"

Still let them aid us and still let them fight,
Lord of angelic hosts, battling for right,
Till, where their anthems they ceaselessly pour,
We with the angels may bow and adore.[2]   Amen.

September 30

Heavenly Protection

"Hi, Drew here, or as Opa calls me, A. Dale. That stands for Andrew Dale, my real name. What an adventure I had on Sunday! I was exploring before we went to church. I was on the second floor and found a little door. I opened the little door... and then it all happened very, very fast. I hurtled down to the first floor, screaming all the way. I came out feet first in the laundry room on the first floor. I went down the laundry chute! Uncle Bruce said it was good Mommy and Daddy don't do laundry several times a day. I had a soft landing.

"When Opa heard I was OK, he laughed and then remembered. One Sunday morning in 1950... Opa was three years old... he was ready for church, playing outside waiting for his Mommy and Daddy... he fell on a step and had to go to the emergency room. Dr. Kampe sewed 15 stitches over his eye.

"Then Opa told me about an old painting. A child is leaning over the side of a bridge but an angel is there to protect the child. Opa says you big people might remember that painting. Opa said big people pray our heavenly Father send angels to watch over all God's children. They do! I am proof that there are angels even at the bottom of a laundry chute."

For further reflection: Matthew 18:10-14 – Angels watching over children of the Father

Father-like He tends and spares us; / Well our feeble frame He knows;
In His hands He gently bears us, / Rescues us from all our foes.
Alleluia, alleluia! / Widely yet His mercy flows.[1]

October 1

Good Grief

Grief – you experience it when someone you love has died, and you find yourself forced to go through grief's painful stages. There are other times when you grieve. You experience grief when your son or daughter has gone off to college. The house seems so empty; their absence saddens you. When you lose a job, you are plunged into grief as well. Your income and routine have been taken away from you. When a natural disaster comes (tornado, hurricane, flood, fire – things they call "acts of God") you are plunged into loss. Your home and possessions may be gone; your routines are upended. Grief is not limited to the loss of a loved one. It comes with any significant loss in life.

You can open your grief for healing acts of God, for God to make grief good. When Jesus told a rich young man to sell his possessions and follow Him, the young man "became very sad, for he was extremely rich" (Luke 18:23). Jesus brought him grief so that he might inherit eternal life. That you should suffer the loss of something very dear is unwelcome, of course, but it comes and hollows out your heart. Now what? "Disheartened by the saying, he went away sorrowful" (Mark 10:22), and that's where you can leave it, walking away from Jesus just as the rich young man walked away. Or you can comfort your soul with Jesus, who Himself knew grief. "Jesus wept" at the tomb of Lazarus but then raised His friend (John 11:35, 38-44). "Follow Me," He says, and I will give you life, life in all its fullness (cf. John 10:10).

> The security we crave would teach us to rest our hearts in this world and oppose an obstacle to our return to God … Our Father refreshes us on the journey with some pleasant inns, but will not encourage us to mistake them for home.[1]

For further reflection: Isaiah 53 – "A man of sorrows, and acquainted with grief"

Why should cross and trial grieve me?
Christ is near / With His cheer; / Never will He leave me.
Who can rob me of the heaven
That God's Son / For me won / When His life was given?[2]

October 2

Look to Jesus and Carry On

Do you know this kind of disappointment? Things work against your deepest wants and desires. It wasn't that you wanted to get something wrong or intended something sinful; no, you wanted something truly good, for yourself or for another – something godly, but it didn't come to pass. Holy hopes not realized – you feel disappointed, discouraged.

Encouragement at such times is welcome but it doesn't enable us. *You tell me to keep going, but I can't.* If Jesus is only an encouragement for you to keep slogging on, then you're still the one bearing your burden. But if Jesus dwells in you... Remember, "I have been crucified with Christ. It is no longer I who live, but Christ who lives in me" (Galatians 2:20). Verbally and sacramentally, Jesus has come into you and keeps coming. With Jesus in you, His ability to bear the cross becomes your ability to get on, get on joyfully. "Consider him who endured from sinners such hostility against himself, so that you may not grow weary or fainthearted" (Hebrews 12:3).

Disappointment? Of course! Don't be surprised. Circumstances and people are guaranteed to disappoint because people are fallible and our circumstances will always reflect a fallen creation. Your effort that started with good and godly intentions wasn't your mission in the first place; it's God's through you. You think it's failed? Has God told you that, or are you the judge of how His will is being accomplished? Look to Jesus and carry on.

"It is not the sharpness of the thorns that we should dwell on, but the sweetness of the rose."[1] "I can do all things through him who strengthens me" (Philippians 4:13).

For further reflection: Habakkuk 3:17-19 – "yet I will rejoice"

God's will is done when He breaks and hinders every evil plan and purpose of the devil, the world, and our sinful nature, which do not want us to hallow God's name or let His kingdom come; and when He strengthens and keeps us firm in His Word and faith until we die. This is His good and gracious will.[2]

Heavenly Father, may Your will be done through us! Amen.

October 3

Ordinary, Worshipful Moments in Marriage

I sat down and asked, "How long will this take?" The man with a New Jersey accent said, "In my case, it could be a couple of hours." The other men mumbled assent, not upset or angry, actually at peace with waiting. They were sitting on the benches outside a women's clothing store, and I had joined them.

The store had big glass windows so the men could see in. "Look, she's going up to the rack. You're in trouble. OK, she's backing away, she's sitting down; you're safe." Meanwhile, people walked by on the sidewalk. The women passing by didn't see us, intent on the displays, but if a man walked by, he commiserated. Out came Diane, "Dale, I found something." Like a puppy, I went in, did the trick of pulling out the plastic, and out we came. "Hey, guys – she said she saved me some money!" "She only bought one instead of two?" "Yeah, but we're going to another store down the street."

These are worshipful moments in marriage. "When they rise from the dead," Jesus says, "they neither marry nor are given in marriage" (Mark 12:25). God instituted marriage to help us through this life, to preserve us in all the demands and challenges, all the joys and sorrows of life on this side of eternity. Explaining creation, Martin Luther wrote that God "gives me clothing and shoes, food and drink, house and home, wife and children, land, animals, and all I have. He richly and daily provides me with all that I need to support this body and life."[1] These ordinary moments of life become worshipful when the Spirit of Jesus Christ leads us to understand them as part of the Father's all-encompassing provision to bring us safely to our eternal home. "So, whether you eat or drink, or whatever you do, do all to the glory of God" (1 Corinthians 10:31).

Have you seen the benches that have a life-sized bronze figure sitting on them? I bet he was an actual guy who really, really aged while he was waiting for his wife to finish shopping.

For further reflection: Proverbs 31:10-31 – Her husband praises her

Bless our going out, we pray, / Bless our entrance in like measure;
Bless our bread, O Lord, each day, / Bless our toil, our rest, our pleasure;
Bless us when we reach death's portal, / Bless us then with life immortal.[2]
Amen.

October 4

Are You a Handler of God?

Right now high-profile executives, government officials, and celebrities are being advised what they should or should not do. You've got to believe that they bristle; *What am I, a puppet?* And there's more than that. They have people deliberately keeping them out of the loop, people who think, *I'll handle this myself.* And now that I think about it, it's not only high-profile people who have handlers. We all have people who think they know what's best for us.

Are you a handler of God? Our fretting and worrying about what we should do is classic God-handling. *No need to bother God with this. I'll take care of it myself.* Theologians and religious people can be classic God-handlers. Doctrinal pronouncements, even when true, can leave us imagining we know our God to a T. We're simply following the disciples who repeatedly tried to handle the Son of God. "They were bringing children to him that he might touch them, and the disciples rebuked them. But when Jesus saw it, he was indignant" (Mark 10:13-14). I'd like to meet the person who doesn't try to handle God.

When our youngest grandson Nick was a year and a half, he'd toddle up to Opa and put out his arms to be picked up. A little child is pleased to be carried by an adult, but when we adults handle things ourselves, keeping God out of every loop, we're breaking the First Commandment, acting too big for our britches. "Truly, I say to you, whoever does not receive the kingdom of God like a child shall not enter it. And he took them in his arms and blessed them, laying his hands on them" (Mark 10:15-16).

We all need trusted people to advise us, to help us take care of our business. Just don't become a handler of God; let God handle you. "In all your ways acknowledge him, and he will make straight your paths" (Proverbs 3:6).

For further reflection: Mark 8:27-33 – Peter tries to handle Jesus. How did that turn out?

Lord, 'tis not that I did choose Thee; / That, I know, could never be,
For this heart would still refuse Thee / Had Thy grace not chosen me.
Thou hast from the sin that stained me / Washed and cleansed and set me
    free
And unto this end ordained me, / That I ever live to Thee.[1]

October 5

Congregational Frustrations? Hope Keeps Us Focused

Church meetings? Most of them weary me. The usual drill is some Bible reading and prayer, and then on to "the real business." I've seen the joy of new members disappear when they began to attend church meetings. "Is this what we signed up for?" No, you signed up to be among people who radiate confidence and optimism because God keeps His promises.

Peter Steinke has worked with over 200 congregations struggling through change and conflict, congregations who yearn to be more effective. He roots his observations and practical suggestions in hope. "Hope provides a new angle of vision. When things look bleak or unmovable, hope sees more than what is there. Hope can carry a congregation over the threshold of 'can't.'"[1]

What we dislike in the institutional church does not absolve us from participating. "On this rock I will build my church" (Matthew 16:18). It's "My Church," Jesus says, and He has something more universal and eternal in mind than just a local institution, and yet He's present in your local church. "Where two or three are gathered in my name, there am I among them" (Matthew 18:20). Jesus is your congregation's "business," and the task assigned to you and me is to get down more and more into dependence upon His promises. When we do, His Spirit will manifest Jesus' mission of service through our participation in the congregation. To walk away, to not together reflect Christ in us, our hope of glory, lets the world take over the institutional church. But hope never surrenders to the world. I have been crucified to the world (cf. Galatians 6:14).

In Jesus Christ "it is always Yes. For all the promises of God find their Yes in him" (2 Corinthians 1:19-20). The Spirit of Christ wouldn't let Paul give up on the Corinthian congregation. "Not that we lord it over your faith, but we work with you for your joy, for you stand firm in your faith" (2 Corinthians 1:24). Are you a helper of joy in your church?

For further reflection: 2 Corinthians 13 – Paul's closing words to a troubled congregation

O Lord Jesus, You have called us into Your Church. When we meet and discuss practical matters of congregational life, give us hope through knowing You are with us. Give us wisdom that in all decisions, easy and difficult, Your Church may be built up and our dependence on You steadily increase. Amen.

October 6

The Blessings of Memory

Every now and then I have a day that is especially hard, filled with appointments and meetings one after another, and some of them are – what's the phrase? – "rapid fire," not easy, sometimes a bit tense. It's the kind of day when a spiritual person thinks, *Get me through this, Lord!*

My parents and Lutheran school teachers threatened we'd never see adulthood if we didn't learn our memory work. Five days a week all through grade school we had to stand up and recite. Every school night before bed we had to recite our memory assignment to Dad or Mom. It's a sweet picture to imagine, little Dale, Bruce, or Pam standing there in pajamas, reciting, and then the good-night kiss. Passages from the Bible and catechism predominated, but hymns were also part of the discipline. So on one particularly tough adult day, a line from a hymn became my prayer before each new appointment or meeting: *I need Thy presence ev'ry passing hour.*[1] Did God call up that memory for me? I think so, and it gave me calm throughout the day. "You keep him in perfect peace whose mind is stayed on you" (Isaiah 26:3).

The Roman statesman Cicero called memory "the treasury and guardian of all things."[2] Looking back on my life, it was memory that built the architecture of my piety. To this day, memory continues to do needed maintenance and further building of my soul. We're never too old to memorize some precious promise – never too old to get the cobwebs out of childhood memory work. "These words that I command you today shall be on your heart" (Deuteronomy 6:6).

For further reflection: Deuteronomy 6:1-9 – Maintenance on your soul

Father of mercies, in Thy Word / What endless glory shines!
Forever be Thy name adored / For these celestial lines.
Here springs of consolation rise / To cheer the fainting mind,
And thirsting souls receive supplies / And sweet refreshment find.
Oh, may these heavenly pages be / My ever dear delight;
And still new beauties may I see / And still increasing light!
Divine Instructor, gracious Lord, / Be Thou forever near;
Teach me to love Thy sacred Word / And view my Savior here.[3]   *Amen.*

October 7

Freedom in Forgiveness

What does it mean to forgive others?

Years ago, I spoke at a prayer breakfast for guards who work in the military prison in Leavenworth, Kansas. My topic was forgiveness, the heart of the Christian message. "Forgive us our trespasses," we pray in the Lord's Prayer, "as we forgive those who trespass against us." Forgiveness is something we all need. If you don't think you need it, ask your wife… or your husband… or a coworker. "Surely there is not a righteous man on earth who does good and never sins" (Ecclesiastes 7:20).

Our Lord not only teaches us to ask for forgiveness, but to "forgive those who trespass against us." As I was speaking to the prison guards, I sensed I wasn't getting through to them. Their faces told me they're not with me. Later, my friend, the military chaplain who had invited me to speak, explained it to me. The guards thought I meant "forgive the prisoners and turn them loose." Oh, no! That's not what I meant, but obviously I hadn't been clear enough.

Forgiveness does not mean condoning wrong. Forgiveness does not mean letting the wrong happen again. Forgiveness does not mean turning the criminal loose. Forgiveness does mean that God, for Jesus' sake, forgives every sincerely repentant sinner – but earthly justice may well keep that forgiven sinner in jail for a long, long time.

What forgiving others does is let *you* out of "jail." Forgiving others lets you out of the bondage that you find yourself in because of their sin. Forgiving others breaks the hold that person has over your thoughts and feelings. Forgiving others cleanses your soul of the poisons that come from being unforgiving. Forgiving others lets you out of the jail of hurt, resentment, and bitterness.

And if you think that person must first apologize to you, then you're letting them keep you in jail.

For further reflection: Luke 4:16-21 – "He has sent me to proclaim liberty to the captives"

Forgive our sins, Lord, we implore, / That they may trouble us no more;
We, too, will gladly those forgive / Who hurt us by the way they live.
Help us in our community / To serve each other willingly.[1]   Amen.

October 8

Directing Our Thoughts to God

Have you noticed how much we speak *about* God, rather than *to* God? Sermons, Bible studies, testimonies of believers... all about what God has done. To put it grammatically, we talk about God in the third person[1], the same impersonal way we talk about the weather, taxes, what have you.

So I found it refreshing decades ago when I began reading St. Augustine's *Confessions* for the very first time. "Great art Thou, O Lord, and greatly to be praised; great is Thy power, and Thy wisdom infinite. And man wants to praise You, man who is only a small portion of what You have created..."[2] and on and on Augustine goes, second person[3], talking directly to God.

In my own life, courtesy of St. Augustine, I often phrase my quiet, usually humdrum thoughts in the second person, directly to God. The result of that little grammatical recasting of my mundane thoughts has been a tremendous advance in my spiritual life. I'm more aware of His presence when I take my thoughts directly to him, second person, than when I put Him off into the third person.

Jesus did talk *about* God. "Gentiles seek after all these things, and your heavenly Father knows that you need them all" (Matthew 6:32). But Jesus also talked *to* God in the second person in prayer. "My Father, if it be possible, let this cup pass from me" (Matthew 26:39). Sometimes Jesus talked straight to God and let the people around Him hear what He was saying. "I thank you, Father, Lord of heaven and earth, that you have hidden these things from the wise and understanding and revealed them to little children" (Matthew 11:25).

We all talk *to* God in prayer. Letting others hear our spontaneous prayers to God is a witness of His presence. However, if you relegate God to the third person, aren't you grammatically fencing him out of much of life, yours and those around you?

For further reflection: Read anywhere in Psalm 119 – The psalmist talks *to* God; read it and talk *to* God yourself

Our Father in heaven, help us to believe that You are truly our Father and we are Your children, so that we may with all boldness and confidence come to You as children come to their Father. For Jesus' sake. Amen.[4]

October 9

No Two Alike, yet "None Is Righteous"

"My name is Connor. I am the second correspondent on the *Timely Reflections* team. I am different than my brother Christian. My big brother Christian charges in. He rockets around the house. He sees a puddle on the sidewalk and plops into the puddle. He breaks loose from Daddy and Mommy and runs all over. Charge in now and ask questions later. That's my brother Christian. He's going to do a lot of repenting in his life!

"I'm not a charge-in guy. I look around a lot. As a baby, I let anyone hold me. 'Easy baby!' they said. A different personality than the charging Christian! Big people say about me, 'What a nice, well-behaved boy!' I won't need to repent as much as Christian.

"Opa, our editor, says, 'Don't kid yourself, Connor. God made us all different and gave all His children different kinds of personalities. Sin made us all sinners, charge-in guys and quiet guys too. 'There is not a righteous man on earth who does good and never sins' (Ecclesiastes 7:20). 'The LORD sees not as man sees: man looks on the outward appearance, but the LORD looks on the heart' (1 Samuel 16:7).'

"Do you big people ever think you don't need to repent as much as some other people do?"

For further reflection: Luke 18:9-14 – "None is righteous, no, not one" (Romans 3:10; also see Psalm 14:1-3)

Lord Jesus, think on me / And purge away my sin;
From earth-born passions set me free / And make me pure within.[1]

October 10

"Come unto Me"

"Come unto me, all ye that labour and are heavy laden, and I will give you rest" (Matthew 11:28 KJV).

When you're tired – too much work and not enough hours in the day – give up the effort for a time and go rest with Jesus. Close your eyes, step away from the desk, or go to a peaceful place in creation. "'Come away by yourselves to a desolate place and rest a while.' For many were coming and going, and they had no leisure even to eat" (Mark 6:31).

When you're sad for whatever reason – in grief, in dejection, feeling sorry for yourself, and convinced nobody cares – you know what? Someone does care; that's what the Body of Christ is about. "If one member suffers, all suffer together" (1 Corinthians 12:26). Open up to another follower of Christ, and together "come unto Me."

When you're fearful, anxious, worried… when you share your worry, only to hear, "It's wrong to worry…" when you can't simply "be happy" and put on the smiley face, then go to Jesus and trust He sees a good outcome to your worrisome problem. "For those who love God all things work together for good" (Romans 8:28). "Come unto Me."

When you're feeling guilty about something you've done… when you wish you could turn the clock back and do it over again, but this time you would do it right… then know you can't go back and do it over, but you can apologize and know that Jesus forgives. "Though your sins are like scarlet, they shall be as white as snow" (Isaiah 1:18).

When things are going well – so well that you don't feel a pressing need to hide yourself in the Rock of Ages – when joy and bliss, when contentment and satisfaction, a sense of being accepted and loved are yours… then remember Who gave you this pleasant season and heed this truth: "Prone to wander, Lord, I feel it; / Prone to leave the God I love."[1]

"Whoever comes to me I will never cast out" (John 6:37).

For further reflection: Psalm 119:73-80 – "Comfort me according to your promise"

O all-embracing Mercy, / O ever-open Door, / What shall I do without You / When heart and eye run o'er? / When all things seem against us, / To drive us to despair, / We know one gate is open, / One ear will hear our prayer.[2]   Amen.

October 11

"We Give Thee but Thine Own"

Fall means stewardship emphases in many congregations. When talk about giving rolls around, do you ever have the cynical thought: *They want more money?*

A well-to-do young man asks Jesus, "What must I do to inherit eternal life?" (Mark 10:17). Jesus replies, "You know the commandments," and recites several (Mark 10:19). "Teacher," the young man shoots back, "all these I have kept from my youth" (Mark 10:20). You and I react: *No you haven't. Sin isn't just outwardly keeping the commandments; it's down in the heart too. Every heart is corrupted by sin. No, you haven't kept them.*

Then this intriguing verse: "Jesus, looking at him, loved him, and said to him, 'You lack one thing: go, sell all that you have and give to the poor, and you will have treasure in heaven; and come, follow me'" (Mark 10:21). We easily agree about keeping the commandments, but this? Is Jesus telling you to give it all away too?

"Give us this day our daily bread," we pray in the Lord's Prayer. Martin Luther says:

> Daily bread includes everything that has to do with the support and needs of the body, such as food, drink, clothing, shoes, house, home, land, animals, money, goods, a devout husband or wife, devout children, devout workers, devout and faithful rulers, good government, good weather, peace, health, self-control, good reputation, good friends, faithful neighbors, and the like.[1]

All those things are given to you by your Creator. And know what? Sooner or later all of those things are going to be taken away from you. Job said famously, "Naked I came from my mother's womb, and naked shall I return. The LORD gave, and the LORD has taken away; blessed be the name of the LORD" (Job 1:21).

Christian stewardship manifests the work of God's Spirit in us through His Word and Sacraments. Generosity in giving is a voluntary self-reminder that you and I ultimately have nothing except following Jesus. Over the years of your life, a follower of Jesus will in fact do what Jesus said to the young man. "Life narrows down ... and there, in the narrow place, stands Jesus."[2]

For further reflection: Proverbs 11:23-28 – Generosity

We give Thee but Thine own, / Whate'er the gift may be;
All that we have is Thine alone, / A trust, O Lord, from Thee.[3]   *Amen.*

October 12

Heading into the Unknown? Hold onto Jesus!

"You fool! You'll fall off the end of the earth!" Christopher Columbus must have heard that many times. He thought he knew where he was going, a new route to India, but he didn't have a clue.

What does the future hold for you? You know very well your clues about the future may not prove true. No wise person is cocksure about the future, and that leaves room for worry and fear. The dependable things and people of the past may be taken from you. Could Columbus fall off the earth? Have you ever had a nightmare that you were falling? What's to become of me?

Venturing into an unknown future is a recurrent theme throughout the Bible. In fact, it's God's way with us. "Follow Me," Jesus says. He's already in that future. As we grope in the dark, we pray ourselves into the future, "Do not forsake me, O LORD! O my God, be not far from me!" (Psalm 38:21).

> Lord God, You have called Your servants to ventures of which we cannot see the ending, by paths as yet untrodden, through perils unknown. Give us faith to go out with good courage, not knowing where we go but only that Your hand is leading us and Your love supporting us; through Jesus Christ, our Lord. Amen.[1]

For further reflection: Genesis 12:1-4 – No guarantees about the trip, only the promise

Spirit, come and help me think this through. I'm fearful about the unknowns that lie before me. Help me put them in perspective. Isn't death the biggest of all unknowns? Talk about falling off the end of the world! Spirit, You come from Jesus and He has made the journey through death to life. I can trust Jesus. Help me hold onto Him in faith through all that is to come. Amen.

October 13

"Casting All Your Anxieties on Him"

"What if?" That's the favorite question of worriers.

"What if something happens to my child?" It could happen, but the Bible encourages you to be "casting all your anxieties on him, because he cares for you" (1 Peter 5:7).

"What if I get laid off?" "What if I continue to be unemployed?" It can happen, also to faithful children of God, but you are "casting all your anxieties on him, because he cares for you."

"What if I make the wrong decision?" Perhaps you will, time will tell, but you're still "casting all your anxieties on him, because he cares for you."

"What if I get criticized?" No doubt you will, even if you do what is right. "No good deed goes unpunished." You're still "casting all your anxieties on him, because he cares for you."

What if… you fill in the blank. What is it that has you anxious? In her book *Tame Your Fears*, Carol Kent cites a 1987 study "which concluded that women are two to three times more prone to chronic worry than men are."[1] Some more than others, but we all are anxious and troubled about something. "You are anxious and troubled about many things, but one thing is necessary" (Luke 10:41-42).

Anxieties can be strangely good, and sincere trust in the promises of God knows why. "Humble yourselves, therefore, under the mighty hand of God so that at the proper time he may exalt you, casting all your anxieties on him, because he cares for you" (1 Peter 5:6-7).

For further reflection: Matthew 6:25-34 – Your Father knows

"Take it to the Lord in prayer."[2] *Lord, I'm worried about… (you fill in the blank). I ask You to help me see my anxiety in a different way. Lighten my anxiety with the promises of Your Word. For Jesus' sake. Amen.*

October 14

Downsides of Multitasking

I composed this *Minute* while sitting in a meeting. Most of you know how to pull this off, how to be in a meeting but have your mind on other things. You get yourself a seat in the back, take your papers out and turn to your own work, but every now and then do something to give the impression you're engaged in the meeting. Most of us are experienced at multitasking. We've all done the religious version during boring Sunday sermons, looking engaged but planning out the week, paying the bills, and the like.

Just a second…

OK, I'm back. The speaker was looking right at me and I had to look back – had to look like I'm really into it.

Multitasking may be a way to get a lot of work done but it's addictive and not always good. I find it especially hard to keep my mind focused during prayer. Prayer is like a meeting. You address God and open the meeting, you and your God, but soon your multitasking mind inevitably goes off to other things. When the "meeting" adjourns, "Amen," you haven't accomplished the purpose of that meeting: an intimate, renewing time with your Father and your Savior. Whose loss?

Dietrich Bonhoeffer:

> It is one of the particular difficulties of meditation that our thoughts are likely to wander and go their own way, toward other persons or to some events in our life. Much as this may distress and shame us again and again, we must not lose heart and become anxious, or even conclude that meditation is really not something for us. When this happens it is often a help not to snatch back our thoughts convulsively, but quite calmly to incorporate into our prayer the people and the events to which our thoughts keep straying and thus in all patience return to the starting point of meditation.[1]

He's looking your way!

For further reflection: Psalm 86:11-13 – An undivided heart

Oh, to grace how great a debtor / Daily I'm constrained to be;
Let that grace now, like a fetter / Bind my wand'ring heart to Thee:
Prone to wander, Lord, I feel it; / Prone to leave the God I love.
Here's my heart, O take and seal it, / Seal it for Thy courts above.[2]   *Amen.*

October 15

"Quick to Hear, Slow to Speak"

Think you know what someone else believes?

Ancient Romans misunderstood much about Jews. Because the Jews observed every seventh day as the Sabbath, Romans assumed they were lazy. Wrote the satirist Juvenal, "It's their fathers who are to blame, taking every seventh day as a day of laziness and separate from ordinary life."[1] That's a caricature. Scholar Erich Gruen: "Most Romans contented themselves with a half-baked idea, frequently repeated but never examined."[2]

Christianity started as a sect within Judaism, some Jews coming to believe in Jesus with Gentiles joining them in faith. When these Jews were getting heat because of misrepresentations about Christianity, Peter encouraged them to do two things. First, good works. "Keep your conduct among the Gentiles honorable, so that when they speak against you as evildoers, they may see your good deeds and glorify God on the day of visitation" (1 Peter 2:12). Second, cool conversation. "In your hearts honor Christ the Lord as holy, always being prepared to make a defense to anyone who asks you for a reason for the hope that is in you; yet do it with gentleness and respect" (1 Peter 3:15).

Peter's advice still makes great sense today. Half-truths continue to be bandied about – just look at so much on the Internet – but when it comes to something as eternally significant as religious belief, assumptions should be explored before being asserted. That cuts two ways. You and I need to let curious people know "with gentleness and respect" what we truly believe, but we also need to hear patiently what other people believe. When a student asked how to convince someone of the truth of biblical Christianity, I answered that he should put it on the back burner and first find out what that person believes and why. Real love means real listening. "Quick to hear, slow to speak" (James 1:19).

For further reflection: John 4:7-42 – Jesus witnesses by talking with a woman about *her* life

Almighty and everlasting God, You would have all to be saved and to come to the knowledge of the truth. Enlighten them with the knowledge of Your glory that they may know the riches of Your heavenly grace and, in peace and righteousness, serve You, the only true God; through Jesus Christ, our Lord.[3]

October 16

What Are You Leaving Behind?

A *Dennis the Menace* cartoon has stuck with me; the reason is obvious. The cartoon shows Dennis standing in the midst of one super messy bedroom, his exasperated mother glowering at him. Dennis looks up at her and says, "Now, what's the problem?"

If you ever visit Concordia Seminary, and I hope you will, you'll see that the president's office is neat and clean. That's because I want it to look good when we have the privilege of welcoming people to campus. There's another reason. It's probably not an accident that the names Dale and Dennis are close together in the alphabet. The official office is clean because I work from another office on campus, and that office is filled with piles: piles on the desk, piles on the floor, piles on the shelves. When I go to heaven, that office will be sealed with yellow disaster tape. That's the point: heaven is our true home, not here. Leaving piles of unsettled stuff for those who will survive us is a burden to our heirs that we could have lightened.

"The time of my departure has come" (2 Timothy 4:6). Paul didn't have an estate to square away, but his love for Jesus motivated him to care for the future of the Church when he would be gone. He told Timothy, "What you have heard from me in the presence of many witnesses entrust to faithful men who will be able to teach others also" (2 Timothy 2:2).

There are two great commandments: love God wholly, and then love your neighbor as yourself (Matthew 22:34-40). About the first, we look forward with anticipation to that day when we'll see our God and Savior face-to-face. Remembering your church in your will witnesses your love of God to the next generation. About the second great commandment, "love your neighbor as yourself" (verse 39), who is your neighbor? Doesn't it include those who survive you? We're going to our true home; look around. "Now, what's the problem?"

For further reflection: Proverbs 1:8; 2:1; 3:1; 4:1; 5:1, etc. – A father bequeaths wisdom to his son

Lord Jesus, in the hour of Your death, You provided for Your mother Mary (John 19:26-27). May our love for You motivate us to provide for those we love and for Your Gospel mission after You've brought us to see You face-to-face. Amen.

October 17

Is God's Word Captive on the Page?

Look around. Can you find the Word of God, pick it up and hold it? Years ago, I heard a former executive of CNN speak. I can't remember his name but he obviously understood the world of broadcasting and was a committed Christian. He spoke to us about the "Gutenberg captivity of the Word of God." He said we've let ourselves think that the living and active Word of God is confined, captive to the print and pages bound in the Bible.

Acts 8:26-40 tells about an Ethiopian struggling to understand Isaiah 53. Because the Ethiopian could not understand who the passage was talking about, the Good News was being held captive in the letters of the Isaiah scroll. An angel told Philip to take the road south from Jerusalem to Gaza. Philip obeyed and then the Spirit said, "Go over and join this chariot" (verse 29). In other words, meet them where they're at; so Philip met the Ethiopian where he was at and initiated a conversation. "Do you understand what you are reading?" (verse 30). When the Ethiopian showed a willingness to talk, Philip began with the Isaiah text and told the Good News of Jesus. End result: They came to an oasis, the Ethiopian asked to be baptized and Philip obliged him. The Word of God was no longer captive to print and pages. Is your Bible so well used that the Word is freed to be in your heart and life?

> For the word of God is living and active, sharper than any two-edged sword, piercing to the division of soul and of spirit, of joints and of marrow, and discerning the thoughts and intentions of the heart. And no creature is hidden from his sight, but all are naked and exposed to the eyes of him to whom we must give account. (Hebrews 4:12-13)

For further reflection: Revelation 1:12-18 – The sword of Jesus' Word

Almighty God, grant to Your Church Your Holy Spirit and the wisdom that comes down from above, that Your Word may not be bound but have free course and be preached to the joy and edifying of Christ's holy people, that in steadfast faith we may serve You and, in the confession of Your name, abide unto the end; through Jesus Christ, our Lord.[1]   *Amen.*

October 18

Suffering, an Outreach to God's Love

Some years ago, Dr. Stanley Hauerwas delivered the annual Carondelet Lecture at Fontbonne University in St. Louis and spoke about disability. Professor of theological ethics at the Divinity School of Duke University, he said the term itself is problematic – that we should label other people "disabled" all the while assuming that we are 100% able. The term "vulnerable" is no better.

Dr. Hauerwas said prevailing societal attitudes toward suffering are terribly flawed. "We now want to believe that whatever besets us is purposeless. And so we ask physicians to relieve us." "We must eliminate suffering," popular thinking goes, "to get on with being human." So we look at suffering as a medical problem to be eliminated, and thereby we open the door to a terrifying totalitarianism. "Today people believe an inadequately trained priest cannot harm you but an inadequately trained physician can." That's scary.

To imagine that suffering has no purpose leads us away from love, from giving of ourselves to others in community. "Suffering," he said, "is God-given as an outreach to God's love." So whether it's our attitudes toward the, quote, "disabled," or other trials of your day, "suffering," he said, "is God-given as an outreach to God's love."

The priest and Levite in Jesus' parable of the Good Samaritan had flawed attitudes toward suffering – but the Samaritan? He got it; he understood suffering as "an outreach to God's love." The famous parable is told in only one Gospel, the Gospel written by a physician (Luke 10:29-37). Today the Church observes "St. Luke, Evangelist." A physician for the body and an evangelist for the soul, his carefully researched writings, the Gospel of Luke and the Acts of the Apostles, continue to invite us in our needs and sufferings to reach out to God's love. No wonder St. Paul called him, "Luke the beloved physician" (Colossians 4:14).

For further reflection: Luke 1:1-4; Acts 1:1-3 – Writings researched for certainty

For that belov'd physician / All praise, whose Gospel shows / The Healer of the nations, / The One who shares our woes. / Your wine and oil, O Savior, / Upon our spirits pour, / And with true balm of Gilead / Anoint us evermore.[1]

October 19

Swinging the Club of Guilt

We don't know what had been done, but someone had grievously hurt fellow church members and they were swinging the club of guilt. It's a very useful thing, that club of guilt. Whenever you feel the need, you can clobber the sinner and send the strong message that you're in control of the relationship.

"For such a one, this punishment by the majority is enough," Paul wrote, "so that you should rather turn to forgive and comfort him, or he may be overwhelmed by excessive sorrow" (2 Corinthians 2:6-7). Paul's advice is profound. A person can only live with so much guilt. Judas Iscariot felt so guilty that he took his life (Matthew 27:5). Many people convinced of their guilt withdraw from the people they've hurt, feeling too ashamed to show up as if nothing had happened. Without forgiveness, that shame keeps the sinner away from the fellowship that claims to be welcoming and forgiving.

"So I beg you to reaffirm your love for him," Paul pleads (2 Corinthians 2:8). "Anyone whom you forgive, I also forgive" (2 Corinthians 2:10). If the pastor and church officers have dealt with that sinner and spoken God's word of forgiveness, are you going to act above the command to forgive?

"What I have forgiven … has been for your sake in the presence of Christ, so that we would not be outwitted by Satan; for we are not ignorant of his designs" (2 Corinthians 2:10-11). Forgiving one another keeps the devil at bay. The prophet Zechariah pictures Satan as the accuser of God's people (Zechariah 3:1). In Revelation he is called "the accuser of our brethren" (12:10 KJV). Why not? The devil knows plenty to accuse every person in your congregation, including you and me. Zechariah heard, "The LORD rebuke you, O Satan!" (Zechariah 3:2). And in Revelation the accuser is thrown down because the forgiven "have conquered him by the blood of the Lamb" (Revelation 12:11). When you and I forgive the brother or sister who has sinned, Satan is defeated here and now. So for Jesus' sake, put the club of guilt down!

For further reflection: "Forgive us our trespasses, as we forgive those who trespass against us"

Oh, how blest it is to know: / Were as scarlet my transgression, / It shall be as white as snow / By Thy blood and bitter passion; / For these words I now believe: / Jesus sinners doth receive.[1]   *Amen.*

October 20

All Work and No Play?

"My name is Drew. I am the third member of the *Reflection* writing team. When I was seven months old, I flew to St. Louis – brought Mommy with me. Why did I go to St. Louis? That's the subject of this *Timely Reflection*.

"I didn't go because of the World Series. Go, Cardinals, but go without me. I went to spend time with my Oma and Opa. It is interesting to watch how they spend time. Oma was waiting many weeks for me to come. She bought a little stroller. One day we walked around the campus. That is, when I wasn't crawling around the house. Watch me go! Oma bought me Cardinals clothes. I like the little red footie pajamas she got me, of course with the Cardinals logo. Oma is all about being with me.

"Opa? He's different. Opa loves me too but Opa has trouble sitting still and just being with people. He is driven to work. I can see when he is struggling. *This is family*, he thinks. *I should love this time while I can.* But Opa's so used to working that it's hard for him to sit still. Do any of you big people know that problem? Do you shortchange your family because of work?"

For further reflection: Deuteronomy 5:12-15 – Quantity family time

Except You build it, Father, / The house is built in vain;
Unless You, Savior, bless it, / The joy will turn to pain.
But nothing breaks the union / Of hearts in You made one;
The love Your Spirit hallows / Is endless love begun.[1]

October 21

Walking by Faith

I've long been suspicious about having a favorite Bible verse. As great as a favorite verse is, it tempts you not to get deeper into Scripture. It's like never changing the prescription on your eyeglasses. You get older and need a better view of life. Here's a passage that I'll bet no one has as a favorite, but yet is immeasurably profound.

Exodus 3:11-12 – "Moses said to God, 'Who am I that I should go to Pharaoh and bring the children of Israel out of Egypt?' He said, 'But I will be with you, and this shall be the sign for you, that I have sent you: when you have brought the people out of Egypt, you shall serve God on this mountain.'"

Read that again; think it through. Moses knows his limits, that he's not able to lead Israel out of Egypt by himself. He opens the door for God to give him some proof that this mission will be successful. That's common sense; who wants to go out on a limb and get cut off? But God says, *Just do what I say. When you lead the people back to this mountain, then you'll know in hindsight that My promise is true.* God gives Moses the impossible task of a lifetime and gives no immediate proof of His help! *Just do it. When it's done, then you'll know – not before.* "We walk by faith, not by sight" (2 Corinthians 5:7).

Oswald Chambers:

> Faith brings us into right relationship with God and gives God His opportunity. God has frequently to knock the bottom board out of your experience if you are a saint in order to get you into contact with Himself. God wants you to understand that it is a life of faith, not a life of sentimental enjoyment of His blessings.[1]

My favorite passage? My list continues to grow because the prescription changes with my maturation. "For now we see in a mirror dimly, but then face to face" (1 Corinthians 13:12). Keep expanding your verses of insight!

For further reflection: Hebrews 11:1, 23-29 – "By faith Moses…"

Sing, pray, and keep His ways unswerving, / Perform thy duties faithfully,
And trust His Word; though undeserving, / Thou yet shalt find it true for thee.
God never yet forsook in need / The soul that trusted Him indeed.[2]
Lord, let this be my trust! Amen.

October 22

Two Sides of Faith

You set out in life with high hopes but then reality runs over your ideals. If you were blessed to grow up in a Christian home, you learned about the love of God, but then you see so much suffering and wonder if "God is love" was Sunday School pabulum. You learned the Ten Commandments, but see Christians hypocritically break them. Result: Your feelings about Christian faith grow weaker.

Most Americans would probably define "faith" as a sincerely held opinion. There is indeed a subjective side to Christianity, but the Bible teaches another side to faith – an aspect of faith that precedes and should be the foundation for any feelings we have. That other side of faith is the objective truth revealed in the Bible, the Gospel, the promises of God. That's not born into us, not hard-wired into our feelings at birth, but comes from outside; it's a revelation.

Speaking at a retreat for older adults, I shared my conviction that those unwelcome things that weaken our feelings about the Christian faith are in fact occasions for God to draw us more and more to focus on His promises, on the Good News of Jesus Christ. "The Lord disciplines the one he loves, and chastises every son whom he receives" (Hebrews 12:6; see also Deuteronomy 8:5; Psalm 94:12; Revelation 3:19). The focusing gets painfully personal as the years progress. God slowly but surely takes away from us the good gifts He has given – family, health, and finally this life itself – all so you will trust more and more what He has revealed to us about the Savior Jesus. I could see by their eyes, they knew exactly what I meant.

"You guide me with your counsel, and afterward you will receive me to glory" (Psalm 73:24).

For further reflection: Isaiah 46:3-4 – "And then, when gray hairs will their temples adorn, / Like lambs they will still in My bosom be borne"[1]

And should my heart for sorrow break, / My trust in Thee no one could shake.
Thou art the portion I have sought; / Thy precious blood my soul has bought.
Lord Jesus Christ, my God and Lord, my God and Lord,
Forsake me not! I trust Thy Word.[2]   Amen.

October 23

Prayers Ascend for One Another

I once was talking with a childhood friend who has spent most of her adult years struggling with a serious illness. When I asked how she coped, she said it was most helpful to know that others were praying for her.

A doctor may believe in the supernatural; we've heard about believing physicians who pray as they go about their work. A doctor's diagnosis and suggested treatments are in the natural realm of cause and effect, but prayers add a supernatural dimension, asking the touch of heaven upon scientific medical procedures. God has demonstrated time and again that He can step into our closed system of natural cause and effect. The chief example is the coming of His Son. From the unseen world Christ comes into our world, and from His coming God's interventions continue to multiply outward. Your prayers for those in need demonstrate your belief that God truly is involved in day-to-day things. It's another demonstration that followers of Jesus really do live by faith, not just sight (cf. 2 Corinthians 5:7).

So to any of you who are sick, facing surgery, undergoing treatments, longing for health, we assure you of our prayers. Life is not just the horizontal dimension of cause and effect. Reality is also vertical, heavenward, and that dimension we invoke for you.

> Blessed be the tie that binds / Our hearts in Christian love;
> The fellowship of kindred minds / Is like to that above.
> Before our Father's throne / We pour our ardent prayers;
> Our fears, our hopes, our aims are one, / Our comforts and our cares.[1]

For further reflection: Mark 5:21-43 – Intercessions to Jesus for the sick

Our heavenly Father, You teach Your Church, "Confess your sins to one another and pray for one another, that you may be healed. The prayer of a righteous person has great power as it is working" (James 5:16). Help me in my personal prayers to intercede for those who are ill. When I worship in church, help me pay attention when congregational prayers are offered for the sick. Remind me to tell people that I pray for them. In Jesus' name. Amen.

October 24

Does God Sometimes Drop It?

"I love God," said five-year-old Eric Smith to his mother. "He takes good care of us. He's got the whole world in His hands. But sometimes He drops it." "What?" Mom asked. "You know," Eric answered, "like when they have those earthquakes in California."

Very insightful, Eric! Does God always – always – take care of us? Earthquakes and the like suggest that God sometimes does drop it. So do the diseases that afflict our bodies. But no, God doesn't drop it. "God saw everything that he had made, and behold, it was very good" (Genesis 1:31). What looks like God dropping it is really the effect sin has had on all things, not only on us but also on the world of nature in which we live. You might say that when Adam and Eve sinned and when we sin, we've jumped out of God's hand and taken nature with us. "Creation waits with eager longing for the revealing of the sons of God. For the creation was subjected to futility…" (Romans 8:19-20).

And thinking about dropping, I spent part of the weekend raking leaves, nature's reminders of decay and death. But when I looked up at the almost bare branches, I was reminded that there will be buds in spring. Good Friday gives way to Easter. Eric, our young theologian, has it essentially right. God does take good care of us. Amid falling leaves and quaking ground, God promises new life. "For the creation was subjected to futility, not willingly, but because of him who subjected it, in hope that the creation itself will be set free from its bondage to corruption and obtain the freedom of the glory of the children of God" (Romans 8:20-21). God's great hands are reaching down and picking us up! "Christ in you, the hope of glory" (Colossians 1:27).

For further reflection: Amos 1:1; Zechariah 14:1-9 – Like the earthquake when Uzziah was king, flee to God's promise

Lord, when I feel the effects of sin in my own life, when nature is unkind and even cruel, and when I'm tempted to think that You've dropped it, then take my thoughts to Good Friday when the earth quaked at Your suffering for this sinful world, and to Easter when the stone was moved and the way opened to that day when all again will be good. Amen.

October 25

Completely Dependent on God's Grace

Martin Luther struggled for years to get right with God but continued to be tormented by his guilt. Then he discovered – better that I say he was lead to discover – the Bible's teaching that the good things we do aren't enough to save us and never will be enough. That includes our religious works like going to church, doing devotions, contributing to church and charities, and so on. You just can't pile up enough merits to climb into heaven, can't work your way out of the hole of guilt. Only God's forgiveness and kindness in Jesus Christ saves us, only grace. Sounds good, but Dietrich Bonhoeffer cautioned about "cheap grace,"[1] and with so much at stake, literally heaven or hell, we have to wonder how we can appreciate the gift of grace more.

Many people resist asking for help when we need it. Reflecting on her victory over cancer, Dee Simmons wrote, "Never try to go it alone. You need the love of others fully as much as you need the medicines your doctor prescribes, and maybe even more. Other people's love and encouragement can rebuild our inner person at times when we believe that's impossible. Reach out to that love."[2]

Asking for help is one little way to appreciate God's grace more. Forgiveness is grace and salvation a gift, not the result of your work. Asking someone now and then for some needed help can be a little earthly reminder that ultimately we are dependent upon our loving God for His help. We all know people who refuse to take help, even if, as we say, their life depends on it. Our life does depend upon help. "By grace you have been saved through faith. And this is not your own doing; it is the gift of God, not a result of works" (Ephesians 2:8-9).

For further reflection: Luke 16:19-31 – Which one knew his life depended upon help?

My guilt, O Father, You have laid / On Christ, Your Son, my Savior.
Lord Jesus, You my debt have paid / And gained for me God's favor.
O Holy Spirit, Fount of grace, / The good in me to You I trace;
In faith and hope preserve me.[3]   *Amen.*

October 26

Do You Only Vote for Christians?

You can expect it. Every election season some minister will publicly support some candidate, giving the reason that the preferred candidate is Christian while the opponent is not. Does Christian faith compel us to vote only for Christians?

The Bible suggests the answer is no. When Paul encouraged us to pray for government officials (1 Timothy 2:1-2), when Paul was on trial (Acts 24-26), when both Peter and Paul wrote about the positive effects government can have on the life of the Church (1 Peter 2:13-17; Romans 13), they were referring to non-Christian government officials. Narrow down. Do you think you need Christians in office in order to advance Christian causes? Shouldn't the Church be doing that on its own? If you want to make the government an instrument of the Church, the day will come when the Church becomes an instrument of the government. "Render to Caesar the things that are Caesar's, and to God the things that are God's" (Mark 12:17).

Article VI of the Constitution says, "No religious test shall ever be required as a qualification to any office or public trust under the United States." Elections do have consequences for the moral life of the nation, but the personal faith of one candidate is less important than the community service and witness of Christian citizens and congregations.

> Keep your conduct among the Gentiles honorable … Live as people who are free, not using your freedom as a cover-up for evil, but living as servants of God. Honor everyone. Love the brotherhood. Fear God. Honor the emperor. … always being prepared to make a defense to anyone who asks you for a reason for the hope that is in you. (1 Peter 2:12, 16-17; 3:15)

For further reflection: Isaiah 45:1-7 – A ruler not from God's people is used by God for the good of God's people

Lord, keep this nation under Your care. Bless the leaders of our land that we may be a people at peace among ourselves and a blessing to the other nations of the earth. Grant that we may choose trustworthy leaders, contribute to wise decisions for the general welfare, and serve You faithfully in our generation; through Jesus Christ, our Lord.[1] *Amen.*

October 27

Come Down from Your Lofty Perch!

I've got the story of Zacchaeus on my mind, that "wee little man" who climbed up the sycamore tree to catch a glimpse of Jesus. "And when Jesus came to the place, he looked up and said to him, 'Zacchaeus, hurry and come down, for I must stay at your house today'" (Luke 19:5). These verses have captured my thoughts, Luke 19:6-7: "So he hurried and came down and received him joyfully. And when they saw it, they all grumbled, 'He has gone in to be the guest of a man who is a sinner.'"

What's the culture of your church: sinners who joyfully receive Jesus and let it show, or religious people who grumble about others? Every place has its own culture – its attitudes, assumptions, spoken and unspoken ways of acting. A place's culture is not spelled out in the bulletin or official words but is something you sense, you experience. I recall going to guest preach at a church in Illinois. Got there before the service – obviously! I stood in the narthex with my robe in hand and no one, no one came up to greet me. I felt like a leper with my white leper's robe in hand! *Good luck if you're not one of us.* What kind of culture does your church have?

At the root of this problem, too common in churches I'm afraid, is delusion that our outward religious life makes us better than others before God. I'm not, and neither are you. When you're eagerly hearing a Gospel-centered message, are you still a sinner? When you receive Jesus' body and blood in His Supper, are you still a sinner? Obviously yes! You're not sinning when you penitently receive His forgiveness in Word and Sacrament, but you're still a sinner. Do you ever have sinful thoughts in church, in the holiest of places in the holiest of times? Surely you do. Make haste and come down from your lofty perch! Like Zacchaeus, gladly receive Jesus and contribute to a culture of joy in your church.

For further reflection: Mark 3:1-6 – Hard hearts in church

O Hope of ev'ry contrite heart, / O Joy of all the meek!
To those who fall, how kind Thou art, / How good to those who seek!
Jesus, our only Joy be Thou / As Thou our Prize wilt be!
Jesus, be Thou our Glory now / And through eternity.[1]   *Amen.*

October 28

Faith, Hope, and Love

Its two legs were built simultaneously, each slowly rising at a slant until finally meeting 630 feet in the air. On this date in 1965, the top section of the Gateway Arch in St. Louis was put in place. Our nation's tallest monument, the arch symbolizes America's westward expansion into the Louisiana Purchase of 1803.

For me it offers an additional symbolism: faith, hope, and love. You find that triad often in the Bible, most famously in 1 Corinthians 13:13. "So now faith, hope, and love abide, these three; but the greatest of these is love." Like the legs of the arch, faith and hope are rising to something greater. Faith is the trust God works in us, trust that hangs onto His promises, even hanging on when everything we experience tells us to give up on God. Because God keeps His promises, we can have hope that the best is yet to come. Through faith and hope the Spirit of God lifts the soul to divine love, that is, to God Himself – "God is love" (1 John 4:8). That's why love is the greatest, topping out the spiritual life and lasting forever.

To me the most impressive view of the arch is standing beneath it. How about you? Do you look at the challenges of the day by letting faith and hope guide your eyes heavenward toward love?

For further reflection: Romans 5:1-5 – Find faith, hope, and love in these verses

Come down, O Love divine; / Seek Thou this soul of mine,
And visit it with Thine own ardor glowing;
O Comforter, draw near, / Within my heart appear,
And kindle it, Thy holy flame bestowing.[1]   *Amen.*

October 29

"He Who Is in You Is Greater"

Halloween's almost here, and jumping out to scare us is the annual debate among some Christians: Halloween, harmless holiday or demonically dangerous?

Some Christians talk like good and evil are two equal forces. Though evil can be strong, it's not equal to God. By definition, God alone is God and demonic forces are inferior. While evil wins some battles, God, being God, will win the war.

> Though devils all the world should fill, / All eager to devour us,
> We tremble not, we fear no ill, / They shall not overpow'r us.
> This world's prince may still / Scowl fierce as he will,
> He can harm us none, / He's judged; the deed is done;
> One little word can fell him.[1]

Don't, however, be unconcerned. Years ago my children went out trick-or-treating and somehow didn't fall into the occult. Our concern was to give our kids a full, Christ-centered spiritual life for the real world. Under God's blessing, that's the parenting I commend to you.

"There are two equal and opposite errors into which our race can fall about devils. One is to disbelieve in their existence. The other is to believe, and to feel an excessive and unhealthy interest in them."[2]

For further reflection: Matthew 4:1-11 – "O little flock, fear not the foe"![3]

Spirit of God, help parents live their lives in Christ and model that for their children. While "we do not wrestle against flesh and blood, but ... against the spiritual forces of evil," plant deeply in us the conviction that "He who is in you is greater than he who is in the world." Amen. (Ephesians 6:12; 1 John 4:4)

October 30

Who's Your Enemy?

Do you have an enemies list? Being the kind of person you are, you'll probably say, "No, but there are a few people…"

"We do not wrestle against flesh and blood, but against the rulers, against the authorities, against the cosmic powers over this present darkness, against the spiritual forces of evil in the heavenly places" (Ephesians 6:12). Years ago I heard Dr. John Kleinig use that passage to remind us that ultimately we do not have human enemies. Think about that. As a follower of Jesus, you ultimately have no human enemies. When you find yourself in disagreement, argument, or strife with another person, remind yourself that he, that she is not your real enemy. Your adversary may be used by the devil, our ultimate enemy, but God loves your opponent's immortal soul. "Father, forgive them, for they know not what they do" (Luke 23:34). Our task is to win that person – not to our point of view – but to God's truth in the Gospel of peace.

Martin Luther was a battler and some of the things he wrote against his "enemies" make polite people blush. Tomorrow is the anniversary of Luther posting his 95 theses on the door of the Castle Church in Wittenberg, Germany, the public beginning of the Reformation. Luther's most famous hymn is "A Mighty Fortress is Our God."[1] The first verse talks about the devil and ends on a depressing note: "on earth is not his equal." But in verse two Luther immediately sings about the victor over our ultimate enemy. "With might of ours can naught be done, / Soon were our loss effected; / But for us fights the valiant One, / Whom God Himself elected. / Ask ye, Who is this? / Jesus Christ it is. / Of Sabaoth Lord, / And there's none other God; / He holds the field forever."

I think it's OK to have an enemies list, just as long as you struggle to know that your list is a list of people God loves, every last one of them. Make that list your prayer list. Welcome every encounter with them. Seventy times seven! For Jesus' sake.

For further reflection: Romans 12:14-21 – God, help me do that!

Fill with the radiance of Your grace / The souls now lost in error's maze;
Enlighten those whose inmost minds / Some dark delusion haunts and blinds.[2]
Jesus, I'm especially thinking of…   Amen.

October 31

"I Believe That Jesus Christ … Has Redeemed Me"

Halloween… also the day when Professor Martin Luther in 1517 sparked the Reformation by posting 95 theses, 95 propositions for academic debate. Something Luther wrote in 1529 gives the deepest insight into what the Reformation is all about:

"I believe that Jesus Christ, true God, begotten of the Father from eternity, and also true man, born of the Virgin Mary, is my Lord, who has redeemed me, a lost and condemned [creature], …"[1]

Ouch! That hurts! I'm a lost and condemned creature? But doesn't the brokenness of our world suggest it's true? Who are we to exempt ourselves? Who am I to imagine I'm not lost and condemned?

"… purchased and won me from all sins, from death, and from the power of the devil; not with gold or silver, but with His holy, precious blood and with His innocent suffering and death, …"[1]

Not with gold or silver, and also not with a well-performing portfolio, not with an election result, not with health and happiness, but "with His innocent suffering and death."

"… that I may be His own and live under Him in His kingdom and serve Him in everlasting righteousness, innocence, and blessedness, just as He is risen from the dead, lives and reigns to all eternity."[1]

That means He's a present reality – present reality! "Where two or three are gathered in my name, there am I among them" (Matthew 18:20). Though we don't see Him, He's here. Don't you know it?

"This is most certainly true."[1]

Do you agree?

For further reflection: 1 Peter 1:17-21 – "Not with gold or silver"

Rock of Ages, cleft for me, / Let me hide myself in Thee;
Let the water and the blood / From Thy riven side which flowed,
Be of sin the double cure: / Cleanse me from its guilt and pow'r.
Not the labors of my hands / Can fulfill Thy Law's demands;
Could my zeal no respite know, / Could my tears forever flow,
All for sin could not atone; / Thou must save, and Thou alone.[2]   *Amen.*

November 1

The Saint in the Mirror

Today is All Saints' Day. The media and masses get excited when someone is declared a saint, like Pope John Paul, and someday maybe Mother Teresa. The lavish praise poured upon the work of these saints strikes me as strange in one way. Aren't we all supposed to be doing that? "Do not neglect to do good and to share what you have, for such sacrifices are pleasing to God" (Hebrews 13:16).

In New Testament usage, the word "saints" is applied to all who follow Christ (e.g., Romans 1:7; 2 Corinthians 1:1). No long process to sainthood here; you either are or you aren't. And if you are, you do. "You will recognize them by their fruits. Are grapes gathered from thornbushes, or figs from thistles? So, every healthy tree bears good fruit, but the diseased tree bears bad fruit. ... Thus you will recognize them by their fruits" (Matthew 7:16-17, 20).

Martin Luther: "Oh, it is a living, busy, active, mighty thing, this faith. It is impossible for it not to be doing good works incessantly. It does not ask whether good works are to be done, but before the question is asked, it has already done them, and is constantly doing them."[1] Of course, "saint" can also be applied to exemplary Christians. But why, I wonder, do we look to Calcutta or Rome or wherever? Why don't more of us see a saint in the mirror?

For further reflection: Romans 16:1-16 – All saints!

O almighty God, by Whom we are graciously knit together as one communion and fellowship in the mystical body of Jesus Christ, our Lord, grant us so to follow Your blessed saints in all virtuous and godly living that we may come to those unspeakable joys which You have prepared for those who unfeignedly love You; through our Lord Jesus Christ, Your Son, who lives and reigns with You and the Holy Spirit, one God, now and forever. Amen.[2]

November 2

Certainty in the Face of Death

I've heard this said, and from my own experience I know it is true. The minister visits a dying person and asks, "Are you ready for eternity?" "I hope so," comes the answer; "I've tried to lead a good life." Dear God, don't let me, don't let anyone reading this *Reflection*, approach that final journey with such waffling!

All Saints' Sunday is observed by many churches in early November. Some congregations have the custom of tolling the church bell as the name of each member who has died in the last year is read. Why the ceremony? Why the joyous hymns of All Saints' Sunday? Because of a flimsy "I hope so?" Because the deceased tried to lead a good life? St. Paul approached eternity with none of that. "I know whom I have believed, and am convinced that he is able to guard what I have entrusted to him until that Day" (2 Timothy 1:12 NIV).

Certainty in the face of death can't be found in yourself. "Pastor, I know I'm not perfect." What does Scripture say about not being perfect? "Whoever keeps the whole law but fails in one point has become accountable for all of it" (James 2:10). Therefore, this prayer: "Enter not into judgment with your servant, for no one living is righteous before you" (Psalm 143:2). Certainty has to come from Someone other than yourself and from someplace other than the good Christian life you may have tried to lead. Certainty must come from One who brings forgiveness for your sins, and Himself came through the valley of the shadow of death alive. He promises, "Because I live, you also will live" (John 14:19). Jesus' promise gives you hope that is sure and certain. "I will fear no evil, / for you are with me" (Psalm 23:4).

"If we have died with him, we will also live with him; / if we endure, we will also reign with him; / if we deny him, he also will deny us; / if we are faithless, he remains faithful – / for he cannot deny himself" (2 Timothy 2:11-13).

For further reflection: Hebrews 6:13-20 – "A sure and steadfast anchor of the soul"

Now no more can death appall, / Now no more the grave enthrall;
You have opened paradise, / And Your saints in You shall rise. Alleluia![1]

November 3

"The Almighty Has His Own Purposes"

In early November our nation votes. There have been other times when our country was deeply divided, not just recent years, and Christians were set against each other. President Abraham Lincoln was a student of the Bible and his second inaugural address shows how its divine wisdom shaped his leadership.

> Both [sides] read the same Bible and pray to the same God, and each invokes His aid against the other. It may seem strange than any men should dare to ask a just God's assistance in wringing their bread from the sweat of other men's faces [slavery], but let us judge not, that we be not judged. The prayers of both could not be answered. That of neither has been answered fully. The Almighty has His own purposes. "Woe unto the world because of offences! for it must needs be that offenses come; but woe to that man by whom the offence cometh!" [Matthew 18:7 KJV].[1]

Romans chapter 1 teaches that God lets people do what they want, at least for a time. Whoever wins at the end of a long election campaign when the polls close on Election Day, can thank God but should not presume that heaven is aligned with his or her platform. Election winners have been given an opportunity but time will tell. As President Lincoln said, "The Almighty has His own purposes."

> The will of God is always best / And shall be done forever;
> And they who trust in Him are blest, / He will forsake them never.
> He helps indeed / In time of need, / He chastens with forbearing;
> They who depend / On God, their friend, / Shall not be left despairing.[2]

For further reflection: 2 Chronicles 36:15-16 – The end result for a nation that did only what it wanted

Lord, keep this nation under Your care. Bless the leaders of our land that we may be a people at peace among ourselves and a blessing to the other nations of the earth. Grant that we may choose trustworthy leaders, contribute to wise decisions for the general welfare, and serve You faithfully in our generation; through Jesus Christ, our Lord.[3]   Amen.

November 4

And the Exit Poll Says… Time to Move On…

I'm an early riser, so I was up at 5:30 the morning after the election, when I bumped into an old friend. "Morning," I mumbled, and then added, "Wow, what a night!" "What do you mean?" my old friend asked. "Duh, the election! You voted, didn't you?"

My friend – I've known him for years and assumed I knew him well – said, "Well, no." "What? You didn't vote?! How come?" He said, "Hey, I've been around a long, long time. I've seen how it goes. Was the election important? Yeah, but it's not the biggest thing on my mind."

This is turning into a challenging conversation. "Well then," I pushed back, "what is on your mind?" "Look," he said, "elections come; elections go. Parties come; parties go. Aren't you supposed to get up every morning and do what is right? Aren't you supposed to live by some higher standard than political gain? Hanging your hope or your disappointment on some election, isn't that shallow?"

Hmm… He got me thinking. Should I see the elections in a different way, a higher way? Maybe politics isn't the beginning or the end of the world. Whoops! Forgetful me! I forgot to tell you who was challenging me: God. Call it morning devotion. Life goes on; God is. Win or lose, keep living His life.

For further reflection: Psalm 2 – God's seen it all. Eyes on His Son.

O God, our help in ages past, / Our hope for years to come,
Our shelter from the stormy blast, / And our eternal home:
Before the hills in order stood, / Or earth received her frame,
From everlasting Thou art God, / To endless years the same.
O God, our help in ages past, / Our hope for years to come,
Be Thou our guard while life shall last / And our eternal home![1]   *Amen.*

November 5

Are You Missing the Awe of Creation?

Euonymus alatus compactus, the botanists call it. For us commoners, it's the "burning bush," and here on the Seminary campus it's providing a spectacular display of fall color. True to its common name, its leaves have turned a brilliant red. The popular name comes from Exodus 3: "The angel of the LORD appeared to him [Moses] in a flame of fire out of the midst of a bush. He looked, and behold, the bush was burning, yet it was not consumed" (Exodus 3:2). God said, "take your sandals off your feet, for the place on which you are standing is holy ground" (Exodus 3:5).

How many people, I fear, are missing the awe of creation? How many are obsessed with the screen on their smartphone? "When through the woods and forest glades I wander,"[1] I have my attention focused on a screen? Duh! In this most beautiful time of the year, we're obsessed with our own problems? Could it be that autumn is God's billboard advertising that He is able to help you with your problems? "Earth's crammed with heaven / And every common bush afire with God: / But only he who sees, takes off his shoes, / The rest sit round it, and pluck blackberries."[2]

"And Moses said, 'I will turn aside to see this great sight, why the bush is not burned'" (Exodus 3:3). Be a child again, a child of God, and take a long look. Marvel. And when you turn aside and look at a burning bush, you'll see that old *Euonymus alatus compactus* has ridged branches, not round and smooth. I wonder why? Perhaps for no practical reason, save the Creator looking down with delight as you and I with childlike wonder marvel at nature. "And God saw everything that he had made, and behold, it was very good" (Genesis 1:31). So many opportunities to marvel at God's creation, but what do we do? Rush on to the next meeting, click the next link, pluck our BlackBerry®s (or iPhone®s or Android™s, or what have you).

For further reflection: Psalm 33 – Fear, awe, hope, and joy in the Creator

All Thy works with joy surround Thee, / Earth and heav'n reflect Thy rays,
Stars and angels sing around Thee, / Center of unbroken praise.
Field and forest, vale and mountain, / Flow'ry meadow, flashing sea,
Chanting bird, and flowing fountain / Call us to rejoice in Thee.[3]

November 6

Get Your Feelings Out to God

Every pastor has heard someone say, "I'm angry at God." A good response, in my opinion, is to say, "That's normal; don't be ashamed, but do tell God that you're angry with Him."

Late in 1941, sometime after the Nazi invasion of Norway, Bishop Eivind Berggrav said this in a sermon:

> Prayer in times of great need has its difficulties. It seems impossible to pray. At the most one can protest, and more easily accuse God. I dare, in the name of Jesus Christ, to say: Yes, do it! Accuse God face to face if it is impossible for you to approach Him in any other way. He will understand you... Speak out to God, break through all the false ideas of piety, and come to God Himself... Personal need, family need, national need – if it becomes a prayer, even though only a cry to begin with, even though only a momentary sigh – if only it is directed towards God, it will give deliverance. Need which becomes bitterness creates a canker. Need which becomes a prayer creates life.[1]

Get your feelings out to God, that's what the prophet Jeremiah told Israel after Jerusalem had been destroyed. "Let tears stream down like a torrent day and night! Give yourself no rest, your eyes no respite! ... Pour out your heart like water before the presence of the Lord! / Lift your hands to him for the lives of your children, / who faint for hunger at the head of every street" (Lamentations 2:18-19).

"Need which becomes bitterness creates a canker." So the scribes of the Pharisees complained, "Why does he eat with tax collectors and sinners?" (Mark 2:16). "Need which becomes a prayer creates life." Jesus said, "I came not to call the righteous, but sinners" (Mark 2:17).

For further reflection: Mark 7:24-30 – A woman argues with Jesus

Bow down Your gracious ear to me / And hear my cry, my prayer, my plea;
Make haste for my protection, / For woes and fear / Surround me here.
Help me in my affliction.
You are my strength, my shield, my rock, / My fortress that withstands each shock,
My help, my life, my tower. / My battle sword, / Almighty Lord –
Who can resist Your power?[2]   Amen.

November 7

What Do You Do?

We've all been there, talking with someone we don't know. A natural icebreaker is to ask, "What kind of work do you do?" I asked that often until I heard the "correctness police" announce that I should focus on the person separate from whatever work he or she does. It's plausible, that a person is quite separate from the work he or she does.

Plausible but not completely true, not if you remember that the Bible teaches that God judges our works daily and will judge us all on the Last Day (see 2 Corinthians 5:10; Romans 1:18; Zechariah 3). Where is it, then, that you and I do the works that God judges? Obviously at work, at home, in community, and in country. "What you do" is where you show who you are, your deeds showing how you the person fulfill your purpose in life. Life is all about relationships, starting with our relationship to God and flowing to others. Yes, Christ forgives our sins in relationships, but that doesn't render what you do in relationships irrelevant. "Without faith it is impossible to please him" (Hebrews 11:6).

> Here is a call for the endurance of the saints, those who keep the commandments of God and their faith in Jesus. And I heard a voice from heaven saying, "Write this: Blessed are the dead who die in the Lord from now on." "Blessed indeed," says the Spirit, "that they may rest from their labors, for their deeds follow them!" (Revelation 14:12-13)

But that will come for you and for me later, in God's time. For now the question remains, "What do you do?"

For further reflection: John 15:1-11 – Who you are, and Whose you are

Merciful Father, through Holy Baptism You called us to be Your own possession. Grant that our lives may evidence the working of Your Holy Spirit in love, joy, peace, patience, kindness, goodness, faithfulness, gentleness, and self-control, according to the image of Your only-begotten Son, Jesus Christ, our Savior.[1]   *Amen.*

November 8

Coheirs of the Grace of Life

In early November of 1842, Abraham Lincoln married Mary Todd. Six years later they had two sons, Robert and Edward, and were living in Washington, D.C. because Mr. Lincoln had been elected to the House of Representatives. That April, Mrs. Lincoln left Washington and took the boys to Lexington, Kentucky for a long visit with her family.

Alone in D.C., Abraham wrote,

> Dear Mary: In this troublesome world, we are never quite satisfied. When you were here, I thought you hindered me some in attending to business; but now, having nothing but business – no variety – it has grown exceedingly tasteless to me. I hate to sit down and direct documents, and I hate to stay in this old room by myself.[1]

Just like a man! "When you were here, I thought you hindered me some in attending to business." What makes some men so focused on work that we regard our wives as a hindrance … until they're gone? I'll venture a minister's musings. Many Americans imagine religion and love are the exclusive domain of women. Not so, says St. Peter, a man experienced with marriage. "Husbands, live with your wives in an understanding way, showing honor to the woman as the weaker vessel, since they are heirs with you of the grace of life, so that your prayers may not be hindered" (1 Peter 3:7). A husband's first "business" should be spiritual integrity dominated by grace and lived out gently with his beloved coheir of heaven. Maybe we husbands obsess about work because we imagine that we, not grace, are the source of good things in marriage.

For further reflection: Proverbs 31:10-31 – The resume of a coheir of the grace of life

O God, our Creator, You have instructed us that "a man shall leave his father and his mother and hold fast to his wife" (Genesis 2:24). Forgive husbands when we don't live with our wives as coheirs of the grace of life. Give wives Your gracious Spirit to winsomely lead husbands into their spiritual roles in marriage and family. Bless the business work that wives and husbands do as grateful thanks for Your grace in Christ Jesus their Savior. Amen.

November 9

Tear Down These Walls!

In 1961, communist leader Erich Honecker ordered a wall built around the city of East Berlin. That infamous Berlin Wall separated families, prompted East Berliners to risk their lives for freedom, and became a hated symbol of the Cold War. "Mr. Gorbachev, tear down this wall!" said President Ronald Reagan in a speech near the Brandenburg Gate. The wall did fall, on this date, November 9, 1989. Today you have to look hard to find anything left of that wall of separation but, if you're old enough, the joy at its unbelievable fall is still remembered.

St. Paul used the image of a broken-down wall to describe the unity that Jesus Christ brings to Jews and Gentiles. The Good News of Jesus can reconcile people who have dealt with one another only on the basis of the Law and its demands and threats.

> For he himself is our peace, who has made us both one and has broken down in his flesh the dividing wall of hostility by abolishing the law of commandments expressed in ordinances, that he might create in himself one new man in place of the two, so making peace, and might reconcile us both to God in one body through the cross, thereby killing the hostility. (Ephesians 2:14-16)

The world still has its dividing walls of hostility – real and virtual. So also does our nation. And the Church's sad divisions don't model the better way, the way of unity that Jesus Christ brings between people. "There is one body and one Spirit – just as you were called to the one hope that belongs to your call – one Lord, one faith, one baptism, one God and Father of all, who is over all and through all and in all" (Ephesians 4:4-6). What if the world saw that in us? Spirit of God, tear down these walls!

For further reflection: Matthew 5:43-48 – Jesus talks about your enemy

O come, Desire of nations, bind / In one the hearts of all mankind;
Bid Thou our sad divisions cease, / And be Thyself our King of Peace.
Rejoice! Rejoice! / Emmanuel / Shall come to thee, / O Israel![1]   Amen.

November 10

Strength through Repentance

"Nick, my man! What happened to you?"

"Opa, Mommy took me for my first haircut. What's the big deal?"

"Oma was starting to call you 'Nicole' because your hair was so long. We were wondering if you were going to be a modern Samson."

"Huh?"

"Oh, Samson was a baby born long ago. God had a mission for him, to save Israel from its enemies. The sign of God's mission was that Samson would never get a haircut. Things were going fine until Samson's girlfriend, one of the enemy, flirted with him. 'Please tell me where your great strength lies' (Judges 16:6). He forgot his mission for the Lord and told her. 'If my head is shaved, then my strength will leave me, and I shall become weak and be like any other man' (Judges 16:17). So she gave him his first haircut and, sure enough, Samson's strength left him."

"You mean I won't be strong because I got a haircut?"

"No, no, no. Long hair was the sign on Samson's head. The sign on your head is the water and Word of your Baptism. That set you on God's mission. Live in His strength and you'll help many people."

"Did Samson ever get strong again?"

"Just once. He repented, God restored his strength, and Samson pulled down a big building. He died and so did the enemy, but God's people were saved. So when you forget you're on God's mission, repent – He'll forgive and give you new strength for His mission."

For further reflection: Judges 16:18-31 – Blinded by treacherous love, repentance, new strength

My faithful God, You fail me never; / Your promise surely will endure.
O cast me not away forever / If words and deeds become impure.
Have mercy when I come defiled; / Forgive, lift up, restore Your child.[1]

November 11

Love's Selfless Service

Today is Veterans Day. With our military personnel deployed around the world, this day of respect comes at an opportune time. Originally it was called Armistice Day, so proclaimed by President Wilson in 1919. It was made a federal holiday in 1938 and in 1954 Congress named it Veterans Day.

Our veterans and active military personnel demonstrate love. We don't associate the word military with the word love. Quite the opposite! What the military does seems to be the direct antithesis of love. But imagine yourself being shot at in an airplane. Imagine your ship being torpedoed. Imagine knowing that your Humvee could be bombed. Whether you were drafted or enlisted, you're putting your life on the line for others. We're not just talking about being a good citizen and going to vote, which, of course, is a wonderful privilege. We're talking about facing death to save others. Our veterans did that and did it for us.

"Greater love has no one than this, that someone lay down his life for his friends" (John 15:13). Love was at work, admittedly a strange manifestation of love, when our veterans put their lives on the line. Oh, how confused is our society's self-serving understanding of love! Love is more than romance; it is selfless service. And it shows why we thank a vet today.

For further reflection: Psalm 121 – Going out, coming in… from battle

O God of the nations, we thank You for the sacrifice of our veterans. They served so that we might have the blessings of freedom. We pray for those who serve around the world today. Keep them ever vigilant. Protect them in battle. Make their service noble by the knowledge that they are serving in selfless love. Lord, in your mercy, bring them home safely. Amen.

November 12

Does God Forgive?

I have found Oswald Chambers to be a welcome antidote to brain-dead Christianity. So my mind started whirling when he wrote, "The revelation of God is that He cannot forgive."[1]

Those of us who have spent much of our lives in the Church have heard countless times that God forgives. You don't deserve it. You can't earn it. Free gift. Sweet deal. Those outside the Church often hear this as a monstrous evasion of human responsibility. They hear us saying, *Do whatever turns you on; God's business is to forgive.*

The critics have a valid point, and Chambers calls us to think carefully about forgiveness. Since God is a perfectly just being, our self-willed ways are affronts that He cannot tolerate. Somebody has to pay. It should be you. That's why His Son's suffering on the cross is at the heart of the biblical message. His substitutionary suffering satisfied God's demand for justice. Forgiveness follows, not as our entitlement but as a gift that we trust with all our being. Yes, God forgives, but not by sweeping sin under the rug. "The soul who sins shall die" (Ezekiel 18:4). God kept that promise when He punished His Son to the point of death so that you and I can be forgiven. So when we Christians smugly lead lives that are less than holy, aren't we misrepresenting forgiveness and thumbing our nose at the Holy One?

> If you call on him as Father who judges impartially according to each one's deeds, conduct yourselves with fear throughout the time of your exile, knowing that you were ransomed from the futile ways inherited from your forefathers, not with perishable things such as silver or gold, but with the precious blood of Christ, like that of a lamb without blemish or spot. (1 Peter 1:17-19)

For further reflection: Matthew 27:45-54 – God punishes sin

My song is love unknown, / My Savior's love to me,
Love to the loveless shown / That they might lovely be.
O who am I / That for my sake / My Lord should take / Frail flesh, and die?
Here might I stay and sing, / No story so divine!
Never was love, dear King, / Never was grief like Thine.
This is my Friend, / In whose sweet praise / I all my days / Could gladly spend![2]

November 13

The Hand That Guides and Leads

"Humble yourselves, therefore, under the mighty hand of God" (1 Peter 5:6).

Do you ever feel that invisible, heavy hand of God upon you? We attribute our hard times to many things, to other people, and to unwelcome circumstances, but in some mysterious way God is involved. You can't escape God. "You hem me in, behind and before, and lay your hand upon me" (Psalm 139:5). Whatever earthly thing I may blame, God's hand is somehow in it, weighing down on me, reminding me to be humble.

We reach down our own hands to a small child. Perhaps you hold the child's hand as you walk, if the child lets you. When you see need to strengthen your hold, to pull the child back, to change direction, to guide the child in the way it should go, your hand gets heavier than the child may like. Is God only our Father when His hand is light upon us? "For we know, as children should, / That the cross is for our good."[1]

Father's hand is always on us in love. "Gently He leads us / With a true father's care ... Daily His blessing, His love, attends us."[2] You are secure in the hand of the Father; Jesus promises it. "My Father, who has given them to me, is greater than all, and no one is able to snatch them out of the Father's hand" (John 10:29). His promise helps us bear the present. "Humble yourselves, therefore, under the mighty hand of God so that at the proper time he may exalt you, casting all your anxieties on him, because he cares for you" (1 Peter 5:6-7).

For further reflection: Isaiah 41:13-14 – "Lord, take my hand and lead me"[3]

"I have set the LORD always before me; because he is at my right hand, I shall not be shaken. / Therefore my heart is glad, and my whole being rejoices" (Psalm 16:8-9). Help me, Lord, to know that You're right here, leading and guiding me. In Jesus' name. Amen.

November 14

Do You Hear the Church Bell Ringing?

About church bells…

My home church rang its bell every Saturday evening. That wasn't for the Saturday service – they didn't have that – but to remind the community that the next day was Sunday and worship. I didn't think much about that Saturday bell; I was a kid and just knew that it would ring to remind me about tomorrow. Reflecting back with the benefit of years, that Saturday evening bell was teaching me that there's an order to life, that my life is situated in a specific place and time, and that those around me in our place and time, our community, were being invited to hear God's Word.

The Swiss theologian Karl Barth wrote,

> On Sunday morning when the bells ring to call the congregation and minister to church, there is in the air an expectancy that something great, crucial, and even momentous is to happen. … God is present! God is present. The whole situation witnesses, cries, simply shouts of it, even when in minister or people there arises questioning, wretchedness, or despair. Then perhaps it is witnessed to best of all…[1]

God is present!

And during that momentous presence, many churches toll the bell during the Lord's Prayer, the Our Father. That old custom made it possible for those who were physically unable to go to church to pray along with the assembled congregation. Again, a sense of order, a sense of community, life ordered around the presence of God.

"If I speak in the tongues of men and of angels, but have not love, I am a noisy gong or a clanging cymbal" (1 Corinthians 13:1). Let the church bell ring strong and solid in your life. It's an invitation to affirm again your time and place in the presence of the Eternal.

> Bells still are chiming and calling, / Calling the young and old to rest,
> But above all the souls distressed, / Longing for rest everlasting.[2]

For further reflection: Mark 4:21-25 – "If anyone has ears to hear, let him hear"

Grant then, O God, Your will be done, / That, when the church bells are ringing, / Many in saving faith may come / Where Christ His message is bringing: / "I know My own, My own know Me. / You, not the world, My face shall see. / My peace I leave with you. Amen."[3]

November 15

"May This Strengthen and Preserve You…"

My friends give me more spiritual help than they'll ever know. After a long struggle against dread cancer, fellow church member Diane died on Holy Saturday, the day before Easter. Most people would have spent the next day at home grieving, but Diane's husband Gary took his grief and children to Easter worship. Tears and all, their presence preached one of the most sincere Easter sermons I've ever heard.

Walking into church another time, I saw Betty. She had just buried her husband Norman. What a friend and gift of God Norm was! So I greeted Betty and said, "I know how hard it is for you to come to church today." It's true, how hard to return to the place you and your spouse worshipped together, where you greeted friends week after week, where you now have to sit alone. "I know," she said. "I have to do this." She affirmed that friends and followers of Jesus come together, even when it is unimaginably hard.

I won't soon forget Everett walking up for Communion. His wife Louise had died the day before but there he was, kneeling to receive the Body and Blood of Christ. He heard the words familiar to many of us, "May this strengthen and preserve you steadfast in the true faith unto life everlasting. Depart in peace. Amen." I trust he did.

There are threads through these thoughts. One is having a point of reference. When death has ended life as you've lived and loved for so many years, church is that stable and safe place to keep you anchored in the storm. Another thread through this *Reflection* is *why*. "For since we believe that Jesus died and rose again, even so, through Jesus, God will bring with him those who have fallen asleep. … and so we will always be with the Lord. Therefore encourage one another with these words" (1 Thessalonians 4:14, 17-18). Sometimes I get weary of the institutional church, but I'll stick with it because of my friends. More than you know, you're helping me.

For further reflection: Hebrews 10:19-25 – "Blest be the tie that binds"[1]

Life eternal! Heav'n rejoices: / Jesus lives who once was dead.
Shout with joy, O deathless voices! / Child of God, lift up your head!
Life eternal! Oh, what wonders / Crowd on faith; what joy unknown,
When, amid earth's closing thunders, / Saints shall stand before the throne.[2]

November 16

Reconciling Our Differences

Permit me to reach back some years. In 2002, Lisa Marie Presley announced she was divorcing husband Nicolas Cage. "I'm sad about this," she said. "We shouldn't have married in the first place … it was a big mistake."[1] Citing irreconcilable differences, she came to this decision after only four months of marriage.

Diane and I were married over 40 years ago and still have plenty of irreconcilable differences! Some come from two different personalities. I'm OK with clutter; she's not. She does things ASAP; I take plenty of time. Other differences come because she puts things on my "honey do" list that I don't want to do. Funny thing, though, about our "irreconcilable differences" over all these years: Living with acknowledged differences, we imperceptibly change to be more and more like one another, and that "honey do" list has quietly turned into a "bucket list." Each difference between us becomes sweeter as our remaining years together become fewer.

In just a couple weeks, the season of Advent will begin. Advent is a time of personal reflection upon our irreconcilable differences with God, our self-willed thoughts and actions, our sins. But like a groom who promises to love and cherish his bride "till death us do part," God's Son came into our world and went into death for His bride the Church. Now He lives and woos us with His love and promises to come and take us home. Any irreconcilable differences between us and God disappear when we embrace Jesus' loving forgiveness. "A threefold cord is not quickly broken" (Ecclesiastes 4:12). "Count the patience of our Lord as salvation" (2 Peter 3:15). What if God only gave you and me four months to work out our differences?

For further reflection: In traditional wedding vows, both bride and groom commit themselves to each other, "to have and to hold from this day forward, for better, for worse, for richer, for poorer, in sickness and in health, to love and to cherish, till death us do part, according to God's holy will; and I pledge to you my faithfulness."[2]

Except You build it, Father, / The house is built in vain;
Unless You, Savior, bless it, / The joy will turn to pain.
But nothing breaks the union / Of hearts in You made one;
The love Your Spirit hallows / Is endless love begun.[3]

November 17

"The Battle Is the LORD's"[1]

Do you ever feel we Christians are like little David going up against the big Goliaths of evil? I hope so! Even when our personal lives are going well, evil in the world should lie heavy on our hearts. Review history, the genocides committed by Hitler and Stalin and Pol Pot and others. Follow the news; so many gruesome reports of murders, abuse, rapes, gang shootings, that we're numb to the sin. Our fellow believers in Jesus are being persecuted and killed in the Middle East and elsewhere. Raised in a safe home, little and clueless, I went to Sunday School, maybe you did too, but growing into adulthood youthful idealism is knocked out of us. Big braggart Goliath, evil in our world.

The youth said to the king:

> "Let no man's heart fail because of him. Your servant will go and fight with this Philistine." And Saul [Saul, the king – worldly, wise, and allegedly mature…] said to David, "You are not able to go against this Philistine to fight with him, for you are but a youth, and he has been a man of war from his youth." … And David said, "The LORD who delivered me from the paw of the lion and from the paw of the bear will deliver me from the hand of this Philistine." (1 Samuel 17:32-33, 37)

That's exactly what the Lord did. You know how the story turned out.

Intimidated by the evil of our time, you and I are staking our lives on another David, on the ultimate Victor in God's relentless war against the evils of this world. Here's our hope – Jesus – "descended from David according to the flesh and … declared to be the Son of God in power according to the Spirit of holiness by his resurrection from the dead" (Romans 1:3-4). Jesus will have His day! "A bruised reed he will not break, and a faintly burning wick he will not quench; he will faithfully bring forth justice. / He will not grow faint or be discouraged till he has established justice in the earth" (Isaiah 42:2-4).

For further reflection: Psalm 7 – "God … saves the upright in heart"

Amen, Lord Jesus, grant our prayer; / Great Captain, now Thine arm make bare,
Fight for us once again! / So shall Thy saints and martyrs raise
A mighty chorus to Thy praise / Forevermore. Amen.[2]

November 18

What Do You Call God?

With what word do you address God? With that word – God? Nothing wrong with that, or do you have other words to name Him?

Call God "Eternal" and you remind yourself of our mortality in contrast to His never-ending life. Call God "Almighty" and you remind yourself that He can do all things, that He can bring worlds into being and help you in your need. Call God "Judge" and you remind yourself that you must give account, but call God "gracious" and you remind yourself that He does not deal with us according to our sins. Call Him "Father" and you've got the dearest picture of all.

And Jesus? Jesus is His name, which means "Savior." Call Him "Savior" and you remind yourself that you need deliverance from sin and so many other evils in this world. Christ is His title. Call Him "Christ" and you are reminded that this man from Nazareth is God's anointed one. Call Him "Lord" and acknowledge your submission to Him.

Although not as common, address some of your prayers to the Holy Spirit. The "Spirit" is the third person in the Trinity who proceeds from the Father and the Son, as the Nicene Creed teaches us. Call Him "holy" because He is far different than our human spirit – small letter "s."

When you invoke God according to His attributes, the Spirit more and more restores you to the divine image. "Then God said, 'Let us make man in our image, after our likeness'" (Genesis 1:26). But since the fall into sin it's the other way around, humans imagine God after our own likeness (see Genesis 5:3). To this true God, the Triune God we pray, until in heaven His image is fully restored in us.

For further reflection: Acts 17:22-31 – The unknown God revealed

Triune God, be Thou our stay; / O let us perish never!
Cleanse us from our sins, we pray, / And grant us life forever.
Keep us from the evil one; / Uphold our faith most holy;
Grant us to trust Thee solely / With humble hearts and lowly.
Let us put God's armor on, / With all true Christians running
Our heav'nly race and shunning / The devil's wiles and cunning.
Amen, amen! This be done; / So sing we, "Alleluia!"[1]

November 19

Simple Truths

Today marks the date, November 19, 1863, when President Abraham Lincoln delivered the Gettysburg Address. What a profound speech that is! Fittingly, Garry Wills wrote a book entitled, *Lincoln at Gettysburg: The Words that Remade America.*[1]

The Gettysburg Address has only 272 words. When the disciples asked Jesus to teach us to pray, He gave us the Lord's Prayer. The Lord's Prayer translated into English has several versions, but the most common version has only 70 words. In our complicated and confusing times, those 70 words give guidance and offer profound impact.

It's the same with commandments. Ancient rabbis identified 613 commandments in the Bible which they ultimately boiled down to three: "He has told you, O man, what is good; and what does the LORD require of you / but to do justice, and to love kindness, and to walk humbly with your God?" (Micah 6:8).

Lincoln's brevity reminds us that living comes down to simple truths but oh, how we paralyze ourselves by constant analysis! Many topics merit dissertations, but "of making many books there is no end, and much study is a weariness of the flesh" (Ecclesiastes 12:12). How often do we disobey God's simple truths to us because we philosophize or theologize over this or that? Daily life, our beliefs and conducts, come down to simple truths.

"I thank you, Father, Lord of heaven and earth," Jesus prayed, "that you have hidden these things from the wise and understanding and revealed them to little children" (Matthew 11:25).

For further reflection: Ecclesiastes 10:5-14 – "A fool multiplies words"

Wisdom's highest, noblest treasure, / Jesus, is revealed in You.
Let me find in You my pleasure, / And my wayward will subdue,
Humility there and simplicity reigning, / In paths of true wisdom my steps ever training.
If I learn from Jesus this knowledge divine, / The blessing of heavenly wisdom is mine.[2]   *Amen.*

November 20

Serving God in Our Routines

Going to airports is routine for me, and routine means we don't always pay as much attention as we should. So, I was in line for a flight to Dallas and found myself standing behind two Army captains. As they were talking with each other, I silently wondered where they might be going, what their duties are, and in my musing I realized how different their routines are from mine. I haven't walked in their shoes, nor have they walked in mine.

Another time I was waiting for a flight in Chicago. At a nearby gate, passengers were getting off their plane and among them was a man with two prosthetic legs. He was dressed as a civilian but I assumed his prostheses were because of a war injury. I didn't stare, but thought how his routine was changed by the war. Seeing him reminded me that I haven't walked in his shoes – literally – but he would probably like to walk in mine.

Routine is not only where we live our lives but it is where God put us, where He calls us to serve Him in society. "For we are his workmanship, created in Christ Jesus for good works, which God prepared beforehand, that we should walk in them" (Ephesians 2:10). So, "whatever your hand finds to do, do it with all your might" (Ecclesiastes 9:10 NIV). Yes, even the little things of your daily routine, because our Lord gives us this promise: "one who is faithful in a very little is also faithful in much" (Luke 16:10).

In these days between Veterans Day and Thanksgiving, our routines should include due thanks and humble gratitude to God for the military personnel who in their own daily routines have served us, and those today who continue to serve us.

For further reflection: 1 Kings 8:54-61 – A benediction upon the nation

Yea, Lord, 'twas Thy rich bounty gave / My body, soul, and all I have
In this poor life of labor.
Lord, grant that I in ev'ry place / May glorify Thy lavish grace
And help and serve my neighbor.[1]   *Amen.*

November 21

Family Meals, a Time of Blessing

I fondly remember evening meals when I was growing up near Chicago. Every meal started with grace, and then we dug into whatever Mom had prepared. And we also dug into conversation. Most of the table talk was mundane, quickly forgotten. But you know, that's when God did – and still does – some of His best for a family. Those were times when we kids learned how Christian adults deal with life, although we didn't realize that we were being schooled. Gathered around a meal, talking about everyday things, there was and still is opportunity to share a good word with one another from God.

Today many families seldom eat together because of the press of busy schedules. Diane and I experienced that some evenings when our children were growing up but that was the exception, not the rule. With the holiday season upon us, you have many opportunities to strengthen your family's bonds of affection by sitting around the table and talking. For your family's sake, please do. TV, you're off! Phones and tablets, you're so out of here!

Jesus used meals together to relax and teach (Mark 2:15-17). He used meals together to show His care and compassion for people (Mark 6:30-44; 8:1-10). Jesus used meals together to deal with serious issues; "one of you will betray me" (Mark 14:18). Jesus used a meal together to give us that most special meal we share in His name on Sundays, the Lord's Supper (Mark 14:22-25), "a foretaste of the feast to come."[1]

You'll find meals together one of the most effective tools for good parenting and better marriages. Awaiting you is more than the grace of the mealtime prayer. The greatest grace awaiting you in family meals is that, in the midst of everyday talk, you can share with one another God's words of help and hope.

Come, Lord Jesus, be our guest and let Thy gifts to us be blest.[2] Amen.

For further reflection: Mark 2:13-22 – God in dinner conversation

Heavenly Father, we thank You for the gift of food You have provided and for all those whose labor brings Your blessings to our table. We pray that at this meal we may be strengthened for Your service and together may await with joy the feast You have prepared for all the faithful in Your eternal kingdom; through Jesus Christ, our Lord.[3] Amen.

November 22

Christ the King ... My King

Is Christ your king? Come the end of November, many churches observe "Christ the King" Sunday. One Gospel reading for Christ the King comes from John 18, with Pontius Pilate interrogating Jesus. "So Pilate entered his headquarters again, summoned Jesus, and called Jesus and said to him, 'Are you the King of the Jews?' Jesus answered, 'Do you say this of your own accord, or did others say it to you about me?'" (John 18:33-34).

Take that question personally. Do you say Christ is King on your own or do you say it because the people around you are saying it? Do you say Christ is King on your own or do you say it because everyone else is singing, "Crown Him with Many Crowns" and you enjoy the sing-along? Am I a Christian when it is convenient or am I a convicted follower of Jesus Christ?

C.S. Lewis put it this way:

> Christ says, *Give me* all. *I don't want so much of your money and so much of your work – I want* you. *I have not come to torment your natural self, but to kill it. No half-measures are any good. I don't want to cut off a branch here and a branch there, I want to have the whole tree down. I don't want to drill the tooth, or crown it, or stop it, but to have it out. Hand over the whole natural self... I will give you a new self instead. In fact I will give you myself, my own will shall become yours.*[1]

"I believe; help my unbelief!" (Mark 9:24).

For further reflection: Luke 18:1-8 – "When the Son of Man comes, will he find faith on earth?"

O Jesus, shepherd, guardian, friend, / My Prophet, Priest, and King,
My Lord, my life, my way, my end, / Accept the praise I bring.[2]   *Amen.*

November 23

"... Read, Mark, Learn, and Inwardly Digest ..."

In 2011, we celebrated the 400th anniversary of the King James Bible. A monument of the English language, the KJB is the medium by which God worked faith in Jesus Christ in countless millions, including me and perhaps you.

That said, early editions of the King James Bible had some amusing typos. For example, the translators got the Sixth Commandment right but the printer left out the word "not" – "Thou shalt commit adultery." That edition came to be known as the "Wicked Bible."

Another amusing printer error: In Luke 14:26, Jesus says that following Him even means hating our own life. Again, the translators got that right but the printer published that we should hate our wife. That edition came to be known as the "Wife-hater Bible."

In another marriage misprint, "hate" came out "ate." A 1682 edition from Amsterdam: "If the latter husband ate her (for 'hate her') ... her former husband ... may not take her again" (Deuteronomy 24:3-4).

And here's a typo for dog lovers. An 1805 edition had this heading: "How we muts love our enemies."

So many things can get in the way of communicating the Word. The Bereans examined the Scriptures to make sure they were getting it right (Acts 17). May we also understand Scripture correctly!

For further reflection: Judges 12:4-6 – Language mistake: "Shibboleth"

Blessed Lord, You have caused all Holy Scriptures to be written for our learning. Grant that we may so hear them, read, mark, learn, and inwardly digest them that, by patience and comfort of Your holy Word, we may embrace and ever hold fast the blessed hope everlasting life; through Jesus Christ, our Lord.[1]   *Amen.*

November 24

"Who Can Discern His Errors?"

Shortly before every Thanksgiving, the President pardons the National Thanksgiving Turkey. If the turkey could think, it would wonder what it had done that needed forgiveness. Simple answer: It's not what you did but who you are. You're a turkey!

How do you determine what you need forgiveness for? "Who can discern his errors?" (Psalm 19:12). Dietrich Bonhoeffer suggests a way to lead us to a better understanding of our need for forgiveness. "The guilt we must acknowledge is not the occasional mistake or going astray, not the breaking of an abstract law, but falling away from Christ, from the form of the One who would take form in us and lead us to our true form."[1]

For example, it's not that I cussed but that even my civil speech often falls short of Christ's pureness. Again, our good deeds often include some selfish calculation whereas Christ's love is totally selfless. Keep thinking like this and you'll understand St. Paul: "The saying is trustworthy and deserving of full acceptance, that Christ Jesus came into the world to save sinners, of whom I am the foremost" (1 Timothy 1:15).

Bonhoeffer: "Genuine acknowledgment of guilt does not grow from experiences … but, for us who have encountered Christ, only by looking at the form Christ has taken."[1] It's a rare turkey who gets pardoned!

> To Jesus we for refuge flee,
> Who from the curse has set us free,
> And humbly worship at His throne,
> Saved by His grace through faith alone.[2]

For further reflection: Matthew 5:2-12 – The form of blessedness

O keep me watchful, then, and humble; / Permit me nevermore to stray.
Uphold me when my feet would stumble, / And keep me on the narrow way.
Fill all my nature with Thy light, / O Radiance strong and bright![3]   *Amen.*

November 25

Always Reason to Be Thankful

How bad would things have to get for you to stop giving thanks? Might the loss of your health stop your thanksgiving? Family problems? Unemployment? The death of a loved one?

An Old Testament prophet named Habakkuk – would you be thankful for a name like that? – lived in a terrible time. His country was under the thumb of a foreign power. Injustice and violence were widespread. Godliness was nowhere to be seen. Nothing was going well and yet Habakkuk said this: "Though the fig tree should not blossom, nor fruit be on the vines, / the produce of the olive fail and the fields yield no food, / the flock be cut off from the fold and there be no herd in the stalls, / yet I will rejoice in the LORD; I will take joy in the God of my salvation" (Habakkuk 3:17-18).

What was it that made Habakkuk joyful? It was God's promise that all would one day be well. Yes, you and I are thankful for things and for people, but all that can and someday will be taken from us. Why can we still give thanks? Because of the promises of good that God has made to us in Jesus Christ. He will never take those promises away. Sooner or later He will fulfill those good promises to us who believe. And so you and I have reason to be thankful, always reason to be thankful – always.

"Oh give thanks to the LORD, for he is good; for his steadfast love endures forever!" (Psalm 118:1). Amen.

For further reflection: 2 Corinthians 1:15-24 – Yes!

O all-embracing Mercy, / O ever-open Door,
What shall I do without You / When heart and eye run o'er?
When all things seem against us, / To drive us to despair,
We know one gate is open, / One ear will hear our prayer.[1]   *Amen.*

November 26

A Prayer of Gratitude

O God, who sets the lonely in families, we thank You for our family and home (Psalm 68:6). Unless You build the house, we labor to build it in vain (cf. Psalm 127:1).

Renew the love of husbands and wives. Turn the hearts of parents to children and children to parents (cf. Malachi 4:6). Bless those who live alone with caring relationships. As John took Jesus' mother Mary into his home, may our home know no stranger, may no one feel alienated (John 19:27).

For family members far from home, may Your righteousness and mercy watch between us while we are away from one another (Genesis 31:49).

For those fretting over hardships of life, give the promise You gave the widow of Zarephath, that the oil and flour will not fail (1 Kings 17:14). If we are bitter, as Naomi was long ago, may our time at home put peace and praise on our mouths as it did on hers (Ruth 1:21; 4:15).

May any place made empty by death turn our hearts to that place where there "is fullness of joy; at your right hand are pleasures forevermore" (Psalm 16:11).

O God, our Father and Father of our Lord Jesus, may we glimpse in our home this Thanksgiving our eternal house in heaven, knowing now by faith what ear has not heard nor eye seen, the good things You have prepared for those who love You and wait on Your Word (cf. 2 Corinthians 5:1; 1 Corinthians 2:9; Isaiah 64:4). Amen.

For further reflection: Psalm 136 – God's people give thanks

Lord, only one leper returned to give thanks to Your Son. How many times this past year have I received your mercies only to go my own way? I thank You for Your patience and for Your Spirit who guides me now to come to You and say, "Thank You." Increase my faith so that this thanksgiving becomes ongoing thanks-living. For Jesus' sake. Amen. (see Luke 17:11-19)

November 27

"Give Thanks in All Circumstances"

You're thankful for the good things you have in life. Of course you are, that's natural, but what about the bad things? For example, who likes getting drawn into other peoples' problems? Who on Thanksgiving Day would say, "We thank You, Lord, that we're stressed out trying to take care of our infirm … parent … spouse … other relative," or, "We thank You, Lord, for the anguish that comes from being in difficult interpersonal relationships," or, "We thank You, Lord, that we get so drawn into activities at church, charity, or club that we have little time for ourselves."

Yet that's exactly what the Bible says: "give thanks in all circumstances; for this is the will of God in Christ Jesus for you" (1 Thessalonians 5:18). That command is not naïve; think it through. When you're into the down and dirty of another person's problems, in the messiness that comes with people, taut with stress and strain, it's then that God teaches us, if only we'll take the time to reflect on it. Then God teaches the supreme importance of the faith, hope, and love that come in Christ Jesus. It's the bad times that make us yearn for the graces of God and thankful for them. "Give thanks in all circumstances," not despite unwelcome circumstances but because of them. Can you get yourself into a frame of mind that sees your heavenly Father working through the bad for your good?

For further reflection: 2 Corinthians 1:3-7 – Comfort shared

O Spirit of God, where we are bothered by the needs of people, give us grace to help. Where we are stressed and strained by problems, help us see occasions for Your mercies. When we are fickle in our thanksgivings, help us to give thanks in all circumstances. In Jesus' name. Amen.

November 28

Remember, God Is with Them!

"Parting is such sweet sorrow," wrote Shakespeare.[1] Many families gathered for Thanksgiving are once again scattered.

When his son-in-law Jacob left, Laban said, "The LORD watch between you and me, when we are out of one another's sight" (Genesis 31:49). God's watching, said Laban. Though separated by distance, God watches that we all act justly, mercifully, and walk humbly with Him (Micah 6:8).

For his part, Jacob had learned that God traveled with him. "Surely the LORD is in this place," he said on an earlier journey (Genesis 28:16). Your loved ones are not alone out there; God's with them…

…with His mercies. As Jacob once prayed, "I am not worthy of all the deeds of steadfast love that you have shown to your servant" (Genesis 32:10). Taking time in daily prayer to ask continuing mercies upon your family will bless them… and it will calm your worries.

> Before our Father's throne / We pour our ardent prayers;
> Our fears, our hopes, our aims are one, / Our comforts and our cares.
> When here our pathways part, / We suffer bitter pain;
> Yet, one in Christ and one in heart, / We hope to meet again.[2]

For further reflection: Matthew 6:9-13 – "Our Father" - pray it as an intercessory prayer for your absent family members

Lord, with gentle mercies to remind us all of Your presence, watch over our family while we are apart from one another. Amen.

November 29

Is Jesus in Your Heart?

Here's a conversation between Diane and the grandsons. Diane was reading to the boys one of their favorite books, about how Superman rescued Metropolis from the evil Lex Luthor.

Christian asked, "Oma, do they have hearts?" Connor pointed to his chest, as if to say, *Of course they have hearts – right here.* But this conversation was going deeper than that. Diane asked Christian, "Does who have hearts?" He said, "Does Lex Luthor have a heart?" "Yes, he has a heart." Then Christian, 4½ years old, revealed his line of thinking. "But Jesus lives in our hearts. How can Lex Luthor be so bad?" Oma said, "Lex Luthor has an evil heart because Jesus isn't in his heart."

Jesus says, "What comes out of a person is what defiles him. For from within, out of the heart of man, come evil thoughts, sexual immorality, theft, murder, adultery, coveting, wickedness, deceit, sensuality, envy, slander, pride, foolishness. All these evil things come from within, and they defile a person" (Mark 7:20-23).

It's true to say that Jesus doesn't live in the hearts of evil people, but it's also easy to say that and move on. *Well, we've taken care of that question. Those evil people!* Christian's simple question opens up a more soul-searching question for us who do have Jesus in our hearts. How is it that *we* do bad, sinful things? That question is timely as Advent begins, time to point to our hearts and ask, *Why do I do some of the things I do... why do I think some of the things I think... if Jesus lives in me?*

> Fling wide the portals of your heart; / Make it a temple set apart
> From earthly use for heav'n's employ, / Adorned with prayer and love and joy.
> So shall your Sov'reign enter in / And new and nobler life begin.
> To God alone be praise / For word and deed and grace![1]

For further reflection: Galatians 2:15-21 – Is your heart a single-Savior dwelling or a duplex?

> *Prepare my heart, Lord Jesus; / Turn not from me aside,*
> *And help me to receive You / This blessed Advent-tide.*
> *From stall and manger low / Come now to dwell within me;*
> *I'll sing Your praises gladly / And forth Your glory show.*[2]

November 30

It's About Jesus!

Today the Church honors Andrew, a saint who knew it wasn't about him. Saints increasingly learn it's all about Jesus. One ancient father of the Church called Andrew the "Introducer" because he humbly brought people to Jesus. When Andrew faced martyrdom, tradition ascribes these words to him: "Hail, precious cross, that has been consecrated by the body of my Lord."

How could Andrew face such a horrifying future? We saints know lesser fears; so many fears haunt us! Unlike Andrew, you may fear talking about your faith, you're no "Introducer," and you may fear death. True, "The LORD is my light and my salvation; whom shall I fear?" (Psalm 27:1), but how can you put that into practice?

Look more and more to Jesus. Hubert Beck writes:

> A basic reason Jesus could never really be cowed by those who threatened Him was that He never claimed to own His own life in the first place. You threaten a person by telling him/her that you will take away some comfort, some money, some possession or life itself if he/she does not do your bidding. But how do you threaten a person who claims to own nothing?[1]

Christ in you, that's how Andrew could hail the cross; and that's the goal of Advent, to be introduced even more deeply to Jesus. "If we live, we live to the Lord, and if we die, we die to the Lord. So then, whether we live or whether we die, we are the Lord's" (Romans 14:8).

For further reflection: John 1:35-42 – Andrew: *It's about Jesus*

All praise, O Lord, for Andrew, / The first to welcome You,
Whose witness to his brother / Named You Messiah true.
May we, with hearts kept open / To You throughout the year,
Confess to friend and neighbor / Your advent ever near.[3]   Amen.

December 1

The Blessings of Family

The house is quiet now, except for an occasional bark from our dog Ferdie. The five grandsons and their wardens have gone home but *wow*, when they were here! Friday night was raucous. I called the zoo to see if they would take them, but the zookeeper declined, saying they don't take undomesticated wild things. I called the police to see if the SWAT team could restore order, but the commander suggested I call the governor to send out the National Guard. The governor didn't answer my call. So Diane and I just sat there and watched the boys, enjoying every minute of it. No, loving every one of them as they played.

It's in the family that we see the reality of sin. "Give that back to me. That's mine!" We see apologies urged on the little sinners. "Give that back to your brother and tell him you're sorry." And in the family, sinners and saints wrestling together, we see genuine love and care for one another. The boys not only squabbled but they also showed care for one another. Children learn, or should learn, basic conducts that will grow into more mature faith in God and love toward one another. "When I was a child, I spoke like a child, I thought like a child, I reasoned like a child. When I became a man, I gave up childish ways" (1 Corinthians 13:11). Family life, with its noise and rare calm, with its spats and love, is from the goodness of God, who "settles the solitary in a home" (Psalm 68:6).

For further reflection: Luke 2:41-52; Mark 6:3 – In Advent we await Someone who knows family

O Christ, Thyself a child / Within an earthly home,
With heart still undefiled, / Thou didst to manhood come;
Our children bless in ev'ry place / That they may all behold Thy face,
And knowing Thee may grow in grace.[1]   *Amen.*

December 2

A Heavenly Reunion Awaits

Some years ago, it was the last Sunday in the church year, I saw several friends who had lost family members that year. How hard these weeks are for people grieving the death of a loved one! Grief is always hard, but the very first Thanksgiving and Christmas have to be the hardest of all. Cruel death hollowed loving hearts, and the empty place at the table or around the Christmas tree makes the hurt painfully fresh. "Rachel is weeping for her children; she refuses to be comforted for her children, because they are no more," says Jeremiah 31:15. That captures it well.

So Advent needs to be appreciated in all its depth. There's plenty of shallowness these days. Shopping, cards, parties, wondering if "Black Friday" was black enough to lift retailers out of the red… Such things are not to be despised but who cares about that when a loved one is gone? For church kids, Advent means getting ready to celebrate Jesus' birth – along with the presents – but Advent offers adults a deeper spiritual experience because it also focuses on Jesus' coming now in the Word and Sacraments, and His return on Judgment Day. Both speak to those grieving with faith. There will be a joyous heavenly reunion: "The dead in Christ will rise first. Then we who are alive, who are left, will be caught up together with them in the clouds to meet the Lord in the air, and so we will always be with the Lord" (1 Thessalonians 4:16-17). Until then, the Spirit of Jesus gives strength and hope.

> Jesus comes in joy and sorrow, shares alike our hopes and fears;
> Jesus comes, whate'er befalls us, cheers our hearts and dries our tears;
> Alleluia! Alleluia! Comforts us in failing years.[1]

For further reflection: John 19:26-27; Acts 1:12-14 – Mother Mary knew the death of a loved one, and knew His resurrection

Spirit of Jesus, mercifully sit with those who are facing the holidays without a loved one. When our human words and love cannot mend their broken hearts, enter in with Your loving kindness. Put the glisten of hope into the tears they shed. Amen.

December 3

Guilt, the Unwanted Guest

"I'll be home for Christmas; you can count on me,"[1] promises the popular song. Who'll be coming to your home in a couple weeks, hauling in suitcases, hugging you, and embracing your heart?

Guilt promises to come.

> *Remember how you hurt that family member? Don't imagine that you can ever repair the damage you've done! Your husband, your wife, your child, died this year, not home for the holidays. Don't you feel guilty for the times you weren't loving? So dedicated to your career, to your corporate climb, you've shut others out, Mr. Scrooge!*

That's not all bad! It's a naïve preacher who imagines that guilt leaves when he preaches about Christ's forgiveness for our sins. True, God does forgive when we're sorry we've disobeyed Him and messed up in life, but any honest believer can't forget some things he or she has done. Guilt is hard-wired into our feelings… and only an outside word from God is able to deal with guilty feelings, take the edge off it, and sometimes remove the feeling altogether. "Whenever our heart condemns us, God is greater than our heart" (1 John 3:20).

This is one reason why followers of Jesus try to get to church every weekend. You hear the word of forgiveness on Sunday but during the week, here comes guilt with all its baggage! You simply can't shut off your feelings; one word of forgiveness is eternally good but on this side of eternity that wonderful word easily gets overwhelmed. That's why we keep going back to church. The Word keeps assuring: *You are indeed forgiven!*

"I'll be home for Christmas; you can count on me." Advent promises coming, not only the coming of guilt but especially the One who keeps coming to you with forgiveness.

For further reflection: Psalm 32 – Instead of groveling in guilt…

> *I, a sinner, come to Thee / With a penitent confession.*
> *Savior, mercy show to me; / Grant for all my sins remission.*
> *Let these words my soul relieve: / Jesus sinners doth receive.*[2]   *Amen.*

December 4

Bigger Than Life

How it happens I have no clue, but there is hidden heavenly knowledge revealed only to my wife, who in turn lays it on me. It has been revealed to her that this Saturday we must buy the family Christmas tree.

My mom once let my dad buy the tree all by himself. Great tree he got. You could see right through it. He probably liked the price but Mom wasn't happy, and when Mom's not happy…

In my own marriage there were some years when I wanted a big tree and I pushed to get it. Great trees all right, but no space left in the living room. Now the divine revelation has taught me to say, "Oh, Diane, I love that tree you've picked!"

There are Sacraments, Baptism and the Eucharist, divine ways God gives and strengthens faith. There are also sacramentals – human rituals or objects that point us to the Gospel and grace God gives us sinners in the Word and Sacraments of Christ. I think Christmas trees serve that function. As a kid growing up, I stood with open-mouthed wonder at the huge Christmas trees in church. Two of them, one on each side of the chancel, reached from the main floor up to the level of the balcony. Those great trees made a lasting impression. I sensed there's something bigger than normal life here, something that puts even grown-ups in awe.

That's still true today. God's grace is coming down in Jesus. Happy tree-hunting!

For further reflection: Psalm 96 – This psalm for Christmas Eve says "the trees of the forest sing for joy"

God of all creation, the Christmas tree! The familiar carol sings to it, "O Christmas tree, O Christmas tree, / Your branches green delight us!"[1] We pray to You, heavenly Father, that in this time of holiday preparation, You give us Your Spirit so that our Christmas trees and all the other decorations we put up will lift our eyes to the heavenly message You reveal to us in Jesus. Amen.

December 5

Oil for Your Lamp[1]

Ever feel that you don't have what it takes? That's when God is ready to do a miracle.

In the second century before Christ, a foreign ruler named Antiochus Epiphanes attempted to eradicate the Jewish religion. To that end, he offered offensive pagan sacrifices on the altar of the temple in Jerusalem. Led by the Maccabees, the Jews rebelled. After a two-year struggle, the Syrians were driven out. The desecrated altar was destroyed, a new altar was built, and eight days of festival declared. But the story goes that there was only enough pure oil to burn candles for one of the eight days. Even so, the priests took the little oil they had and lit the first candle. The first miracle of Hanukkah: that little oil lasted for the full eight days.

Ancient commentators said that the greater miracle was that the priests trusted God to provide, even though it appeared they didn't have enough oil for the eight days. Sometimes God waits for all our hopes to grow dim so He might kindle in us the one hope that will not go out – hope in Him. Hasn't He said, "My grace is sufficient for you, for my power is made perfect in weakness" (2 Corinthians 12:9)? Hasn't He said, "call upon me in the day of trouble; I will deliver you, and you shall glorify me" (Psalm 50:15)? Trust God. He will answer your prayer in the way He knows best. "God is His own interpreter, / And He will make it plain."[2]

Whether the oil miracle happened or not, I don't know. As our Jewish friends observe Hanukkah, you and I are reminded as followers of Jesus to trust God's promises. In Christ Jesus, He "is able to do far more abundantly than all that we ask or think" (Ephesians 3:20). So then, "What more can He say than to you He has said / Who unto the Savior for refuge have fled?"[3]

For further reflection: Mark 6:30-44; 8:1-10 – Insufficient resources?

Amen, that is, so shall it be. / Make strong our faith in You, that we
May doubt not but with trust believe / That what we ask we shall receive.
Thus in Your name and at Your Word / We say, "Amen, O hear us, Lord!"[4]

December 6

Be Holy

In Advent we hear about John the Baptist, "The voice of one crying in the wilderness: 'Prepare the way of the Lord'" (Luke 3:4; cf. Isaiah 40:3). But whose voice is really calling? It is God's, God calling you and God calling me. Calling us to what? Repentance is the obvious answer because Advent is a penitential season and repentance is what we *do* in penitential seasons.

But repentance can be superficial; *doing* is not enough. "As he who called you *is* holy, you also *be* holy in all your conduct, since it is written, 'You shall *be* holy, for I *am* holy.' And if you call on him as Father who judges impartially according to each one's deeds, conduct yourselves with fear through the time of your exile" (1 Peter 1:15-17, italics mine). So the call of Advent is to *be* holy, not just to content yourself with *doing* things that appear holy. How?

Holiness describes the inmost nature of God, His transcendent perfection. God's being, His holiness, is not simply an intellectual concept to be grasped. It can't be anyway. What God's holiness should produce in us is an emotional reaction – fear. This is not slavish fear. This is not cowering fear. Nor should His coming lead to the opposite extreme, flip familiarity before God. Advent fear is an awe, a reverence, a shut-me-up stillness at both the holiness of God and especially that the Holy One comes to us in His Son and teaches us to call Him "Father." We will come before God at our last heartbeat, a fearful thought, but the fear of Advent is our amazement that He already is coming to greet us, coming to us on the heavenward way, coming to us in Jesus. "Teach us to know our God aright / And call Him Father with delight."[1]

For further reflection: Isaiah 6:1-7 – "Woe is me!"

Stir up our hearts, O Lord, to make ready the way of Your only-begotten Son, that by His coming we may be enabled to serve You with pure minds; through the same Jesus Christ, our Lord, who lives and reigns with You and the Holy Spirit, one God, now and forever.[2]   Amen.

December 7

Freedom to Confess

"'Tis the season to be jolly," so let's have some fun with the nonsense du jour, the effort to turn Christmas into a totally secular holiday.

Yesterday, December 6th, was St. Nicholas Day. Nicholas lived in the fourth century and, according to tradition, was imprisoned by the emperor Diocletian, a fierce persecutor of Christians. Nicholas was released, served as the bishop of Myra, and, tradition also says, was a great confessor of Jesus Christ.

The story goes that Nicholas heard of an extremely poor family in his town, so poor that the family's only hope for survival would be to sell their three daughters, a prospect they hated. To save the girls from such a life, Nicholas went secretly to that home in the middle of the night and left a bag of gold coins. Hence the remembrance of this confessor of Christ, Santa Claus, has come to include the giving of gifts.

The First Amendment promises freedom of speech and free exercise of religion to people of all faiths. There are some wannabe Diocletians among us, people who would eliminate the sounding of any Christian themes in public, but they're doomed to frustration and failure. Ho, ho, ho! See Santa, give gifts motivated by the giving love of Jesus Christ to you, and you're in the spirit of that confessor of Jesus Christ, Saint Nicholas!

For further reflection: "Congress shall make no law respecting an establishment of religion, or prohibiting the free exercise thereof; or abridging the freedom of speech, or of the press; or the right of the people peaceably to assemble, and to petition the Government for a redress of grievances." (The First Amendment to the Constitution of the United States) It's not the Bible, but it's a blessing to us. Just practice it with 1 Peter 3:15 in mind.

> *By all Your saints in warfare, / For all Your saints at rest,*
> *Your holy name, O Jesus, / Forevermore be blest!*
> *For You have won the battle / That they might wear the crown;*
> *And now they shine in glory / Reflected from Your throne.*[1]   *Amen.*

December 8

Ten Cultural Commandments for the Season

I.   Thou shalt not pause to plan thy ways, so that thy only goal will be to make it to the 26th.

II. Thou shalt feel obligated to blanket the world with thy Christmas cards, much as snow covereth the earth.

III. Thou shalt deny the simplicity of Christ's stable by impressing guests with thy holiday house.

IV. Thou shalt not be like the shepherds and show up in the same old clothes.

V.   Thou shalt think thyself a wise man or woman by searching far and wide for gifts.

VI. Thou shalt blow the budget, imagining that thus it will go well with thee.

VII. Thou shalt so stress thyself that thy family calleth thee Scrooge.

VIII. Thou shalt be so busy that thou sittest not long by the Christmas tree with family and friends.

IX. Thou shalt not lay aside old grudges, even while singing of peace and good will for all.

X.   Thou shalt forget the Reason for the Season.

For further reflection: Luke 2:19, 51 – It's just that simple

Lord, give us the courage to leave some things undone. Amen.

December 9

More Men like This!

He let faith guide his major life decisions (see Matthew 1:19).

He stood by his wife when she was going through a tough time (see Matthew 1:20, 24-25).

He became a refugee rather than expose her son to danger (see Matthew 2:14).

He seemed ready to settle in the big city so that her son would benefit but to protect the child he chose a small town (see Matthew 2:19-22).

He regularly led his family to worship (see Luke 2:41).

He seems to have died early, perhaps when the son was a teenager or in his early 20s (see John 19:26-27).

He was Joseph, "stepfather," "guardian" of Jesus and husband to the Virgin Mary. What would happen today if more husbands and fathers demonstrated these qualities of Joseph, commitment to faith and family, even to the point of personal sacrifice?

For further reflection: Ephesians 5:25; 6:4; 1 Peter 3:7 – Dad duty

Jesus, we pray for more heroes like Joseph, Your faithful guardian and an example to us. Because Your presence makes for a holy family, help today's husbands and fathers sanctify their families by demonstrating Your presence in their lives. Amen.

December 10

Blessing Others without Losing Yourself

"For everything there is a season," says Ecclesiastes 3:1, and some seasons are harder than others, like Christmas. You have the normal routines of your life, which probably keep you busy enough. Now more gets piled on, putting up Christmas decorations, shopping, holiday parties, and heavy on you is the anxiety of getting it all done and paying for it.

I once heard Father Ronald Rolheiser of San Antonio, Texas, say these are often the times – these overwhelming, stressful times – that your loved ones and friends will most appreciate about you. Remember how wonderful Christmas was when you were a child? Santa got the credit but Mom and Dad were Santa's stressed helpers!

For everything a season. There are people who will deeply appreciate what you are now struggling to accomplish. Get that? There are people who will deeply appreciate what you are now struggling to accomplish! In this season we need grace, grace that gives us the strength to get through it all, and even more we need grace to fill us with wonder at what God does for us this Christmas season. Some years ago I came across a prayer, I don't remember where, but it was written by Robert Hershey. It captures our need for inner calm amidst the whir, the activity, the frenetic rush of this season.

> Dear Father, I want so much to recapture the wonder of Christmas. Every year I get nervous, irritable, and bogged down with the rush of Christmas, and every year I say, "Never again!" This year, dear Lord, help me to make little islands of quiet for myself where I can recapture the wonder. Amen.

For further reflection: Isaiah 26:3 – Give yourself a gift: memorize this verse

Merciful Father, through Holy Baptism You called us to be Your own possession. Grant that our lives may evidence the working of your Holy Spirit in love, joy, peace, patience, kindness, goodness, faithfulness, gentleness, and self-control, according to the image of Your only-begotten Son, Jesus Christ, our Savior.[1]   Amen.

December 11

How Many Times Are You Going to Hit the Spiritual Snooze Button?

Did you wake up thinking today might be Judgment Day?

Most of us didn't. We wake up some mornings and think that our own personal world is coming to an end. Maybe a loved one has just died, our financial house is caving in, we've been laid off, or some such personal disaster. But awake and think that Jesus might come back today? Probably not.

We get all kinds of smoke about the purposes of Advent, but the fire of it all is supposed to be Jesus. He's the One whom God has appointed to "judge the world in righteousness" (Acts 17:31). The earliest Christians thought the interval between Jesus' Ascension and Judgment Day would be short. It's gotten a lot longer than they expected; so it's understandable that we don't wake up thinking that this might be That Day.

Here's a motivator to be more Jesus-minded. "If you call on him as Father who judges impartially according to each one's deeds, conduct yourself with fear" (1 Peter 1:17). This is not cowering fear. This does not mean you should be a fearful person. It does mean that in today's interactions with other people, you should be restrained by the constant awareness that you're not entitled to any special consideration this day or on Judgment Day. Your judge is impartial. Uh-oh! We're in trouble; hence Advent is a season of repentance.

"It should be observed that this is no contradiction of the doctrine that we are saved by grace through faith; it is, in fact, the necessary complement of that doctrine; for the life of faith, and that alone, will issue in the 'work' that God can approve, with partiality"[1] (see John 6:29). "Jesus, Thy blood and righteousness"![2] That's why the Bible couples the fear of God with the love of God.

Christmas trees and lights, special church services, get-togethers… all means to the goal, and the goal is Jesus. As you reflect on this year's walk to Christmas, "Did not our hearts burn within us while he talked to us … ?" (Luke 24:32).

For further reflection: Zechariah 3 – A vision of judgment

O Jesus Christ, do not delay, / But hasten our salvation; / We often tremble on our way / In fear and tribulation. / O hear and grant our fervent plea: / Come, mighty judge, and make us free / From death and ev'ry evil.[3]   Amen.

December 12

Forgiveness, an Advent Blessing

"Jesus came into Galilee, proclaiming the gospel of God" (Mark 1:14). Advent's theme is Jesus' coming – present tense – a coming that brings you forgiveness because of His passion but also lays on you the tough task of forgiving anyone who has wronged you. "Should not you have had mercy on your fellow servant, as I had mercy on you?" (Matthew 18:33). Of course, that's not easy to do. A slight we can forgive, but a deep wound hurts and is harder to forgive. If you brood on an injustice you've suffered, if you let the wound fester, more damage to your soul results. Being unforgiving is toxic to you, and not just spiritually. It can also be toxic physically.

> The physical costs of unforgiveness may include hypertension, chronic headaches, high blood pressure, cardiovascular ailments, and gastro-intestinal disorders, to name just a handful. Because negative emotions have a depressive effect and can suppress immune function, unforgiveness may even have an indirect link to major and severe disorders like rheumatoid arthritis and cancer.

> It's time to consider the great cost we're paying when we don't learn what Jesus came to teach about the miracle of forgiving.[1]

When Jesus began His visible ministry, He "came into Galilee, proclaiming the gospel of God, and saying, 'The time is fulfilled, and the kingdom of God is at hand; repent and believe in the gospel'" (Mark 1:14-15). Jesus' ministry continues today, now. He comes to you in Word and Sacrament, now. Our focus these days isn't just His birth but all the challenges and blessings He brings because of His life, death, and resurrection. That means that repentance is an Advent theme, now. Forgiving others is an Advent blessing awaiting you, now.

For further reflection: Colossians 3:12-17 – Dressed for Advent

Our Father who art in heaven, forgive us our trespasses and give us the willpower to forgive those who trespass against us. Amen.

December 13

Are We Too Good at Hiding Our Sin?

Here's a peek inside the classroom as I was speaking to seminarians in their final year before going out to lead churches.

I shared that over the years I have come to realize how impure I am, that I really am the chief of sinners because of what goes on within me. They watch closely. Is he going to reveal something scandalous? No, there's no scandal. I've been a reasonably good Sunday school, parochial school, seminary, religious person. What's shameful in me is on the inside. "For from within, out of the heart of man, come…" and then Jesus lists 13 really bad, sinful things (Mark 7:21-22). That said, I move closer toward my point. Each of you is just as impure on the inside as I am. Getting closer to my point, and now it's time to deliver it.

The church and seminary teach us how to hide our sin. The hearts of seminarians and pastors are as impure as they come and – what we don't recognize unless we probe our inner thoughts and feelings in light of God's commands – we unconsciously learn from the patterns of seminary and church how to conceal from ourselves and others the shame of our own impurity. "Who can discern his errors?" (Psalm 19:12). The same is true for laypeople. Go to church, go through the motions, maybe even mechanically do daily devotion… Satan works subtly in our church systems to mute our individual realization that I desperately need a Savior, that you need Jesus. "The pious fellowship permits no one to be a sinner. So everybody must conceal his sin from himself and from the fellowship. We dare not be sinners."[1]

The church establishment tells us that Advent is a time of repentance. If we're serious, Advent will be soul-wrenching. "Nothing is hidden except to be made manifest; nor is anything secret except to come to light" (Mark 4:22). "Declare me innocent from hidden faults" (Psalm 19:12)!

For further reflection: Psalm 53 – "There is none who does good"

'Tis Thine to cleanse the heart, / To sanctify the soul, / To pour fresh life on every part, / And new create the whole. / Dwell, therefore, in our hearts; / Our minds from bondage free: / Then shall we know and praise and love / The Father, Son, and Thee. Amen.[2]

December 14

Recapturing That Childlike Joy

Greeting people at the church door, I'm in the habit these days of stooping down and asking the little children if Santa is coming to their house. Their eyes light up, they beam a smile from ear to ear, and these little children, who are usually silent when the big old minister talks to them, now shake their heads and say "yes." Sometimes they'll tell me what they've asked Santa for, but the church line is long, so old Scrooge moves them on. Their unbounded excitement for Christmas is one of the dearest memories I have of raising our children. When they were four, five, and six, God's great big universe was too small to contain their excitement.

Things change. You parents have seen your children get older and become more adult about Christmas. They become like us. Jesus once told adults, "Truly, I say to you, unless you turn and become like children, you will never enter the kingdom of heaven" (Matthew 18:3). Thanks, little children, for reminding us. "Create in me a clean heart, O God … Restore to me the joy of your salvation" (Psalm 51:10, 12). Christmas was made for children, for children like you and me.

> O blest the land, the city blest, / Where Christ the Ruler is confessed!
> O happy hearts and happy homes / To whom this King in triumph comes!
> The cloudless Sun of joy He is, / Who bringeth pure delight and bliss.
> We praise Thee, Spirit, now, / Our Comforter art Thou![1]

For further reflection: Matthew 11:25-30 – "The wisdom of their wise men shall perish" (Isaiah 29:14)

O Lord, how shall I meet You, / How welcome You aright?
Your people long to greet You, / My hope, my heart's delight!
O kindle, Lord most holy, / Your lamp within my breast
To do in spirit lowly / All that may please You best.[2]   Amen.

December 15

Dwelling Together in Peace

This is for the women trying to get everything done for Christmas. Many years ago I asked Diane if I could help her. "If you have to ask, you don't care," she said. In the most recent installment of trying to help unasked, I went Christmas shopping with her last Sunday.

When she suggested we might go to the mall, I said, "No, all the benches are already filled with old men."

When she was looking at a possible gift, I said, "Don't we have one of those at home we're not using?" She didn't like my money-saving idea.

When we got separated in one store, a clerk asked, "Sir, can I help you?" "Yes, find my wife and get me out of here."

When a new checkout line opened in our last store, I started to believe again in God. When we got home, I turned on football and settled into my easy chair. As I fell asleep (that's what Sunday football games are for), I had a big smile on my face. Without asking, I had helped her out! I dozed off quite pleased with myself. Diane probably looked at me napping and thought, *He doesn't have a clue.* But you're wrong, Diane. I do have a clue. That you've put up with me for over 40 years proves that there is a God, a very good God.

> Perhaps we miss some silver notes from out our household song;
> But sweet and full the echo floats from where the ransomed throng.
> Perhaps an angel crossed the sill and left a shadow there,
> But that was by our Father's will and of our Father's care.[1]

For further reflection: "Daily bread [in the Lord's Prayer] includes everything that has to do with the support and needs of the body, such as food, drink, clothing, shoes, house, home, land, animals, money, goods, *a devout husband or wife, devout children…*"[2] (italics mine)

Visit, O Lord, the homes in which Your people dwell, and keep all harm and danger far from them. Grant that we may dwell together in peace under the protection of Your holy angels, sharing eternally in Your blessings; through Jesus Christ, our Lord.[3] Amen.

December 16

Do You Have Room for Him?

"There was no place for them in the inn" (Luke 2:7). And no room in Dale and Diane's house either. Joseph and pregnant Mary came to our front door looking for a place to stay but we shooed them off.

Las Posadas is one of many Christmas customs at Concordia Seminary. Las Posadas began in 1587 in Mexico and continues today in many countries. Under the leadership of the seminary's Center for Hispanic Studies, adults and children – especially children! – walk from place to place looking for lodging, just as Mary and Joseph sought a place to stay. *Posada* means "inn" or "place of lodging." At each home, someone dressed in ancient garb acts as the homeowner and chases them away. With each rejection, a Bible verse is read. At our house it's from John 1:9-12:

> The true light, which gives light to everyone, was coming into the world. He was in the world, and the world was made through him, yet the world did not know him. He came to his own, and his own people did not receive him. But to all who did receive him, who believed in his name, he gave the right to become children of God.

Chased away, the pilgrims pray and journey on, trusting God to finally lead them to a place to stay. There indeed is room in the inn and in your house for Jesus to come. Is there room in your heart?

> Once in royal David's city / Stood a lowly cattle shed,
> Where a mother laid her baby / In a manger for His bed:
> Mary was that mother mild, / Jesus Christ her little child.[1]

For further reflection: Galatians 2:19-20 – I used to live in my heart...

Ah, dearest Jesus, holy Child, / Make Thee a bed, soft, undefiled,
Within my heart, that it may be / A quiet chamber kept for Thee.[2]   Amen.

December 17

Hoping for the Perfect Christmas?

When comes the perfect Christmas? In a few days?

For some we know this Christmas will be spent in a hospital bed, hopefully with some family sitting close by. For some we know this Christmas will be spent in the loneliness of a nursing home. For some we know the circle has been broken because that enemy death has robbed the family circle of a dear one. For some we know the absence around the tree is because of love – a family member offering himself, herself in defense of our country, perhaps laying it on the line in the Middle East. There are other circumstances for some, less spectacular, but still they prevent the whole family from gathering. And even if all will gather and things appear well outwardly, worries and fears and angers within make the holiday less than perfect.

When comes the perfect Christmas? If conditions are all well for you and yours, see these days as a dim reflection of the better celebration still to come. And if the next days will be less than perfect, trust God's promises to you, look ahead, look beyond the horizon.

> They are before the throne of God, and serve him day and night in his temple; and he who sits on the throne will shelter them with his presence. They shall hunger no more, neither thirst anymore; the sun shall not strike them, nor any scorching heat. For the Lamb in the midst of the throne will be their shepherd, and he will guide them to springs of living water, and God will wipe away every tear from their eyes. (Revelation 7:15-17)
>
> Now through His Son doth shine / The Father's grace divine.

Death was reigning o'er us / Through sin and vanity

Till He opened for us / A bright eternity.

May we praise Him there! / May we praise Him there![1]

For further reflection: 2 Corinthians 4:16-18 – "We do not lose heart"

O Christ, do Thou my soul prepare / For that bright home of love
That I may see Thee and adore / With all Thy saints above.[2]   *Amen.*

December 18

Freedom from Our Imprisonment

They finally let me out, but for many years I did time at an Illinois state prison. I've been in other prisons... I guess I'm supposed to say "correctional facilities," whatever. I especially remember Fort Leavenworth. That was one tough place! Anyway, I did most of my time in Illinois, in Centralia. There I had time to read the Bible, and I read Jesus say, "He has sent me to proclaim liberty to the captives" (Luke 4:18). Huh?

That means more than getting out from behind bars. There are business people who seem free but are imprisoned in their big deals: *If I can pull this off, I'll be set for life!* There's no lack of folks caught in career-climbing: *I'll do whatever it takes to get that promotion.* How many people are imprisoned by something in their past? Are you? The past won't let you out. People "on the outside" are imprisoned by all sorts of things... to addictions... to fear and anger and guilt... to meaningless lives. A few of them end up here but most of them stay on the streets, looking free but not really being free. Chaplain tells me what freedom is. It's God forgiving me, God helping me wherever I am, God giving me hope for a better tomorrow.

"For freedom Christ has set us free; stand firm therefore, and do not submit again to a yoke of slavery" (Galatians 5:1).

>He comes the pris'ners to release, / In Satan's bondage held.
>
>The gates of brass before Him burst, / The iron fetters yield.[1]

Oh, I forgot to say that the jail time I'm talking about is the privilege I had for many years to take a Christmas message to that Illinois facility. I count myself blessed to have done that time.

For further reflection: Isaiah 42:1-7 – Incarnation and incarceration

Heavenly Father, Your Son Jesus offers freedom to all sinners. Help us who are outside to live in responsible freedom through faith in Christ. Help us who are inside to know the spiritual freedom Jesus brings and to witness to the faith, hope, and love You give us in Him. Amen.

December 19

Distracted Parents, Lost Opportunities

Here's how Jesus presents Himself in Hebrews 2:13: "Behold, I and the children God has given me." Can parents say that of themselves and their children? Can the church come before God and say it? Here we are, parents and congregation, with the children You, our God, have given us?

When he was a seminarian, Rev. Clayton Sellers shared a disturbing observation about modern parenting. "Sometime shortly before Christmas we – my wife, our son, and I – were standing in line to see Santa at the mall. While we were in line, 85% of the parents were looking at their phone, at very important Facebook updates at 10 A.M. on a Saturday while their children tugged at their parents' pant legs, begging for attention. A time to be family is now."

When the commandment says that children should honor their parents, it is obviously implied that parents be worthy of honor. Why would a parent choose a screen over participating in a child's flesh-and-blood anticipation of Santa? And what does that neglect teach the child? When the first commandment tells us to love the Lord our God with all our heart, soul, and mind, it follows that parents, indeed all adults, need times away from society, time away from our connectedness, to be in solitude – away from our devices – to be in stillness before God. Why would we not choose quiet quantity time with our heavenly Father? And if we can't be in silence with God, how will we instill in our children the peace that passes understanding (cf. Philippians 4:7)?

Dietrich Bonhoeffer: "Let him who cannot be alone beware of community. Let him who is not in community beware of being alone."[1]

Here I am, and the children God has given me?

For further reflection: Mark 10:13-16 – We're like those disciples; we do it with our devices

O Jesus so sweet, O Jesus so mild! / Joy fills the world which sin defiled.
Whate'er we have belongs to You; / O keep us faithful, strong, and true.
O Jesus so sweet, O Jesus so mild![2]

December 20

Slower Than Christmas

"The cashiers were slower than Christmas."

"Slower than Christmas?" I asked.

My son-in-law Darren explained. "Just an expression I picked up. Christmas comes so slow when you're a kid."

In these busy, busy, busy days, when time is flying, flying, flying, we adults forget how slow Christmas comes when you're a kid. Yet in our adult world, there is something we still yearn for that is oh, so slow in coming. Have you ever wished that everything would be laid bare, that people would stop justifying themselves, stop making excuses, even admit their wrongs? Have you ever wished that God would reveal Himself to us in a very visible way, a way that would make us say honestly yet comfortably, *Yes, I am Your creature. Have mercy on me!* The celebration of Christ's birth long ago rushes quickly at us, quickly past us, and quickly behind us, yet our yearning for the perfect bliss He will bring at the end of time, oh, that seems to be coming so, so slowly.

The presents given these days will satisfy, being with family and friends will satisfy, the food and drink will satisfy… and then some! But I hope that you sense that something is still missing, something good still needs to come, and it's coming "slower than Christmas."

> If then you have been raised with Christ, seek the things that are above, where Christ is, seated at the right hand of God. Set your minds on things that are above, not on things that are on earth. For you have died, and your life is hidden with Christ in God. When Christ who is your life appears, then you also will appear with him in glory. (Colossians 3:1-4)

For further reflection: Isaiah 64 – "Oh that you would rend the heavens and come down"!

Come, then, O Lord Jesus, / From our sins release us.
Keep our hearts believing, / That we, grace receiving,
Ever may confess You / Till in heav'n we bless You.[1]   *Amen.*

December 21

Heaven and Earth United in Song

"Oh, come, all ye faithful, / Joyful and triumphant!"[1]

We come to Bethlehem these next days, bowing our hearts before the Son of God born into human flesh. Not all the faithful will come joyful. For many Christians this will be the first Christmas without a beloved spouse, a dear child, a parent. For many the familiar presence of a loved one will be replaced by a tear. As someone in my extended family wrote, "This has been the saddest year of my life."

"Sing, choirs of angels," continues the hymn, "Sing in exultation, / Sing, all ye citizens of heaven above!"[2] "All ye citizens of heaven above" means our loved ones who have died trusting that this baby of Bethlehem is the One who paid the price for our sins and who gives hope by His resurrection from the dead. Those citizens of heaven, absent from us, sing along with the angels this Christmas.

Therefore, when we sing, when we worship this Christmas, we are mysteriously united with our loved ones who have died in the faith. There is only one Church of Jesus Christ. Some of its members are in heaven; we are here. It's this one Church, the citizens of heaven along with us on earth… this one Church that worships this Christmas.

> Then let our songs abound, / And ev'ry tear be dry;
> We're marching through Emmanuel's ground, / We're marching through Emmanuel's ground
> To fairer worlds on high, / To fairer worlds on high.
> We're marching to Zion, / Beautiful, beautiful Zion;
> We're marching upward to Zion, / The beautiful city of God.[3]

For further reflection: Psalm 48 – "O come, let us adore Him"![4]

It is truly good, right, and salutary that we should at all times and in all places give thanks to You, holy Lord, almighty Father, everlasting God. In the communion of all Your saints gathered into the one body of Your Son, You have surrounded us with so great a cloud of witnesses that we, encouraged by their faith and strengthened by their fellowship, may run with perseverance the race that is set before us and, together with them, receive the crown of glory that does not fade away. Therefore with angels and archangels and with all the company of heaven we laud and magnify Your glorious name.[5]   Amen.

December 22

Would You Have Done Better?

The news tends to become bland these days before Christmas but you can count on economic reports filling the void. How do same-store sales compare to last year? How are people handling credit? How is the economy performing? Congregations and charitable institutions hope for strong donations to close out the year.

Martin Luther:

> Many become inflamed with dreamy devotion when they hear about how impoverished Christ was when He was born. They grow furious at the people of Bethlehem and criticize their blindness and ingratitude. They think that if they had been there, they would have served the Lord and His mother. They wouldn't have allowed them to be so miserable. But these people don't even notice their own neighbors who are nearby and need their help. They ignore them and leave them as they are. Who on earth doesn't have miserable, sick, blundering or sinful people around them? Why don't they show their love to these people? Why don't they do for their neighbors what Christ did for them?[1]

Puts economic news in perspective, doesn't it? Jesus: "Do not lay up for yourselves treasures on earth, where moth and rust destroy and where thieves break in a steal, but lay up for yourselves treasures in heaven, where neither moth nor rust destroys and where thieves do not break in and steal. For where your treasure is, there your heart will be also" (Matthew 6:19-21). We can say in the reverie of Christmas worship that our hearts are focused on heaven, but look at your expenditures and your charitable contributions. Where we spend our money gives a clue where our hearts really are.

For further reflection: Mark 12:41-44 – It's not the amount but the proportion

Ah, Lord, though You created all, / How weak You are, so poor and small,
That You should choose to lay Your head / Where lowly cattle lately fed!
And so it pleases You to see / This simple truth revealed to me:
That worldly honor, wealth, and might / Are weak and worthless in Your sight.[2]
Amen.

December 23

"What Child Is This?"

"What child is this, who, laid to rest, / On Mary's lap is sleeping?"[1] William Dix's question challenges you to ask what you really believe about Jesus Christ.

Do we realize how breathtaking the claims of the Christmas story are upon our life and belief? "My Lord and my God!" said doubting Thomas (John 20:28). Lest you romanticize the birth of Jesus, reducing Him to cute baby and not God and Lord: "Whoever is ashamed of me and of my words in this adulterous and sinful generation, of him will the Son of Man also be ashamed when he comes in the glory of his Father with the holy angels" (Mark 8:38). You know what? That's Law, you can't do it, and the cost would be terrible.

C.F.W. Walther wrote: "While the Law tells us what to do, it does not give us the strength to keep the Law."[2] "The Gospel issues no orders. Rather it changes people. It demands nothing but gives all."[3]

Children get onto a school bus to be taken to learn lessons for life. The Law is like a school bus that brings us to realize we need the Gospel (see Galatians 3:24). So let's take ourselves to church with childlike anticipation of the message of faith, that our God and Lord has come not to condemn but to save you and me (see John 3:17).

> This, this is Christ the king, / Whom shepherds guard and angels sing;
> Haste, haste to bring Him laud, / The babe, the son of Mary![1]

Jesus, I am not ashamed of You! You are my Lord and God!

For further reflection: "I believe that I cannot by my own reason or strength believe in Jesus Christ, my Lord, or come to Him; but the Holy Spirit has called me by the Gospel"[4]

Dear Jesus, You say that You have come "not to call the righteous, but sinners" (Mark 2:17). I cannot fulfill the demands of the Law. Only Your Spirit can replace my futile reliance upon my religious efforts with faith in the salvation You bring. My God and my Lord, increase this sinner's faith! Amen.

December 24

Christmas Memories

Like every kid, I wondered how Santa could get to all the homes in one night. Santa came to our house early on Christmas Eve. I knew that somehow or other he had to get to other homes so those kids could open their presents on Christmas Day. My conclusion was that he had a lot of work to do and if we just happened to be higher on his list of visits, great! Another thing that puzzled me was that he always came to our house during that little hour on Christmas Eve when we were in church. Lots of people are in church during the same hour, but somehow Santa gets to us? This guy, I thought, is really good!

Why couldn't my dad be so punctual? Every year we kids sat impatiently in the car with Mom, waiting for him to come out and drive us to Christmas Eve church. We'd complain about Father being late; Mother would kind of agree with us. Eventually he came out, we went to church, and then hurried home to open presents. As sure as Jesus being born and Santa coming, on Christmas Eve Dad was always late.

Finally I figured out what was happening while we waited in the car. This guy really is good!

Today's a memory-making day for you and your loved ones. Faith and good works are lived out in the real stuff of our daily lives. Nurture your traditions; let them reflect the radiance of God's love. "Mary treasured up all these things, pondering them in her heart" (Luke 2:19). Holy families treasure Christmas memories.

My wife Diane, who has so ably helped me for many years in putting out these *Meyer Minutes*, joins me in wishing you and your loved ones a blessed Christmas. From our home to yours, best wishes for a blessed celebration of the Savior's birth!

For further reflection: Just enjoy the day. God is good!

O God, You make this most holy night to shine with the brightness of the true Light. Grant that as we have known the mysteries of that Light on earth we may also come to the fullness of His joys in heaven; through the same Jesus Christ, Your Son, our Lord, who lives and reigns with You and the Holy Spirit, one God, now and forever.[1] Amen.

December 25

God with Us – Who Would Have Thought?

"It came to pass in those days …" Who would have thought that God works through the mundane things of daily life?

"… that there went out a decree from Caesar Augustus …" Who would have thought that God uses government for His great purposes?

"… And Joseph also went up … with Mary his espoused wife, being great with child …" Who would have thought that God works blessings though our inconveniences?

"… She brought forth her firstborn son …" Who would have thought birth is the way God chooses to come into our world?

"… and laid him in a manger …" God in a feed box?

And who would have thought the birth announcement would go first to below minimum wage workers on the night shift? Who would have thought that the shepherds were hurrying on the streets because God had quickened their steps? "… Let us now go even unto Bethlehem, and see this thing which is come to pass …"

Who thought back "in those days" that God is in the mundane things of daily life? "… Mary kept all these things, and pondered them in her heart" (Luke 2:1-19 KJV). And today, it is still true. God bless you today as you celebrate the birth of God's Son, Immanuel, God with us. Routine made divine. "This is the day that the LORD has made" (Psalm 118:24)! Who would think it? You!

For further reflection: Psalm 98:1-4 – "To us a child is born" (Isaiah 9:6)

O holy Child of Bethlehem, / Descend to us, we pray;
Cast out our sin, and enter in, / Be born in us today.
We hear the Christmas angels / The great glad tidings tell;
O come to us, abide with us, / Our Lord Immanuel![1]   *Amen.*

December 26

From Calm to Cross

One of history's most inspiring stories is also one of its saddest. The setting is Europe. The date is December 24, 1914. World War I is raging. But it's Christmas Eve and the soldiers don't want to fight each other. The French heard their German enemies singing "Silent Night, Holy Night" across the field. So they joined their enemies in singing the famous carol. Peace broke out, a spontaneous truce. For a time that Christmas in 1914, all was calm. What's sad is that they were ordered to return to their fighting.

It's an ironic thing that the Christian Church has selected this day, December 26th, to commemorate the death of Stephen, the first martyr. From the silent, holy night of Christ's birth, we're yanked into the reality of the Christian call to suffer, even to die for Jesus. It's not a contradiction. It's a reminder that Christ came to die so that we might live forever. The Babe of Bethlehem calls us to take up His cross and follow Him.

> A noble army, men and boys, / The matron and the maid,
> Around the Savior's throne rejoice, / In robes of light arrayed.
> They climbed the steep ascent of heav'n / Through peril, toil, and pain.
> O God, to us may grace be giv'n / To follow in their train![1]

"All is calm, all is bright."[2] So it was, and after the cross, in the resurrection, it will be again.

For further reflection: Acts 6-7 – Stephen's story

Heavenly Father, in the midst of our sufferings for the sake of Christ grant us grace to follow the example of the first martyr, Stephen, that we also may look to the One who suffered and was crucified on our behalf and pray for those who do us wrong; through Jesus Christ, our Lord, who lives and reigns with You and the Holy Spirit, one God, now and forever.[3]   Amen.

December 27

Don't Box Up Jesus!

Christmas Day has come and gone. Some people have already packed up nativity scenes. Baby Jesus back in his box.

Today the Church honors "St. John, Apostle and Evangelist." His symbol is the eagle because John's depictions of Christ soar high.

> To him who loves us and has freed us from our sins by his blood and made us a kingdom, priests to his God and Father, to him be glory and dominion forever and ever. Amen. Behold, he is coming with the clouds, and every eye will see him, even those who pierced him, and all tribes of the earth will wail on account of him. Even so. Amen. (Revelation 1:5-7)

Doesn't sound like a baby Jesus you can pack away, does it?

In a sermon for St. John's Day, Martin Luther compared the believer to a young girl.

> The lovely Maggie in scarlet shoes, the little daughter of God, is the believing soul. The soul that trusts may be likened to the maiden who trips fearlessly along in her beautiful scarlet and golden shoes. Paul says (Ephesians 6:15 [KJV]), [having "]your feet shod" – with what? "With the preparation of the gospel of peace." Note that when the heart, through faith, enters the Gospel and lives in the Word, it is … Maggie in her beautiful shoes.[1]

How can you put on happy shoes if you box up Jesus, if you go back to life as normal, if you don't soar on the wings of the Word made flesh?

> For Your belov'd disciple / Exiled to Patmos' shore,
>
> And for his faithful record, / We praise You evermore.
>
> Praise for the mystic vision / Through him to us revealed;
>
> May we, in patience waiting, / With Your elect be sealed.[2]

For further reflection: 1 John 1:1 - 2:2 – "My little children…"

Merciful Lord, cast the bright beams of Your light upon Your Church that we, being instructed in the doctrine of Your blessed apostle and evangelist John, may come to the light of everlasting life; for You live and reign with the Father and the Holy Spirit, one God, now and forever.[3] Amen.

December 28

Enlightened through Affliction

Where's God when pain and wrong have the upper hand? Where's God when tidal waves kill tens of thousands? Where's God when terrorists strike? Where's God when children are slaughtered?

Today the Church remembers the "Holy Innocents."

> Herod, when he saw that he had been tricked by the wise men, became furious, and he sent and killed all the male children in Bethlehem and in all that region who were two years old or under ... Then was fulfilled what was spoken by the prophet Jeremiah: "A voice was heard in Ramah, weeping and loud lamentation, Rachel weeping for her children; she refused to be comforted, because they are no more." (Matthew 2:16-18)

"God is good," we say, but does that mean God is present only when we're having good times?

Malcolm Muggeridge:

> Contrary to what might be expected, I look back on experiences that at the time seemed especially desolating and painful with particular satisfaction. Indeed, I can say with complete truthfulness that everything I have learned in my 75 years in this world, everything that has truly enhanced and enlightened my existence, has been through affliction and not through happiness. In other words, if it ever were to be possible to eliminate affliction from our earthly existence ... the result would not be to make life delectable, but to make it too banal and trivial to be endurable. This, of course, is what the Cross signifies. And it is the Cross, more than anything else, that has called me inexorably to Christ.[1]

For further reflection: Jeremiah 31:15-17 – From weeping and tears to hope

Almighty God, the martyred innocents of Bethlehem showed forth Your praise not by speaking but by dying. Put to death in us all that is in conflict with Your will that our lives may bear witness to the faith we profess with our lips; through Jesus Christ, our Lord, who lives and reigns with You and the Holy Spirit, one God, now and forever.[2]   Amen.

December 29

Take Time to Ponder

Quiet time.

After a 90 mile journey on foot or donkey while she was pregnant…

After giving birth in a strange place…

After unexpected visitors…

After Lord only knows what else…

After all that, Mary grabbed some quiet time.

"Mary treasured up all these things, pondering them her heart" (Luke 2:19).

Why don't you take some quiet time in these down days between the holidays? With the Book open, ponder the ultimate questions of life. Jesus says, "My mother and my brothers are those who hear the word of God and do it" (Luke 8:21). Another place He says, "Blessed … are those who hear the word of God and keep it!" (Luke 11:28). So don't just do something! Sit there … and ponder.

How silently, how silently / The wondrous gift is giv'n!

So God imparts to human hearts / The blessings of His heav'n.

No ear may hear His coming; / But in this world of sin,

Where meek souls will receive Him, still / The dear Christ enters in.[1]

God! I don't have to work all the time. This quiet time between the holidays is not wasted if I do what Mary did and ponder what You are doing in my life. Amen.

For further reflection: Psalm 119, as far as you want to read – Every verse ponders God's Word

Almighty God, our heavenly Father, without Your help our labor is useless, and without Your light our search is in vain. Invigorate our study of Your holy Word that, by due diligence and right discernment, we may establish ourselves and others in Your holy faith; through Jesus Christ, our Lord.[2] Amen.

December 30

Resolved: an Attitude Readjustment

Here's a New Year's resolution for you to consider. Resolve to interpret your day-in and day-out experiences in a positive light. After all, isn't it the turn that makes many stories so good – the turn from the expected conclusion to the unexpected? Why not resolve to turn your daily attitude from ho-hum… or worse… to a positive outlook? On one hand, it's just common sense. The ancient Greek philosopher Epictetus said, "Men are disturbed not by things that happen, but by their opinions of the things that happen."

On the other hand, you have God's promises to turn your attitude toward the positive.

> He gives power to the faint, and to him who has no might he increases strength. / Even youths shall faint and be weary, and young men shall fall exhausted; / but they who wait for the LORD shall renew their strength; they shall mount up with wings like eagles; / they shall run and not be weary; they shall walk and not faint. (Isaiah 40:29-31)

Especially when your story seems bad and discouraging, God's promises offer you an attitude readjustment. "Be strong and courageous. Do not fear or be in dread of them, for it is the LORD your God who goes with you. He will not leave you or forsake you" (Deuteronomy 31:6). "We know that for those who love God all things work together for good … What then shall we say to these things? If God is for us, who can be against us?" (Romans 8:28, 31).

> Now I will cling forever / To Christ, my Savior true;
> My Lord will leave me never, / Whate'er He passes through.
> He rends death's iron chain; / He breaks through sin and pain;
> He shatters hell's dark thrall; / I follow Him through all.[1]

For further reflection: Romans 12 – What your resolution will look like

Jesus, guard and guide Thy members, / Fill them with Thy boundless grace,
Hear their prayers in ev'ry place. / Fan to flame faith's glowing embers;
Grant all Christians, far and near, / Holy peace, a glad new year!
Joy, O joy, beyond all gladness, / Christ has done away with sadness!
Hence all sorrow and repining, / For the Sun of Grace is shining![2]

December 31

Abide among Us!

A prayer for the New Year:

God of the ages, "As a father shows compassion to his children, so the LORD shows compassion to those who fear Him" (Psalm 103:13). Heavenly Father, I pray Your loving kindnesses be with me and all people in the new year.

For the poor, the unemployed, and the underemployed: "If anyone has the world's goods and sees his brother in need, yet closes his heart against him, how does God's love abide in him?" (1 John 3:17). Motivate me to open my heart in loving kindness.

For the sick: "And they came, bringing to him a paralytic carried by four men" (Mark 2:3). Move me in love to bring the sick to the Great Physician by intercession and by my affirmation of hope.

For the person who is lonely: Let me not forget the blessed tie that binds us all, so that the love of Christ will detour me from my routine way to be with one who is lonely.

For the safety of our armed forces and for the leaders of nations: May they invoke You, "My refuge and my fortress, my God, in whom I trust" (Psalm 91:2).

For public discourse in society and church that is gentle and respectful: Let my speech "always be gracious, seasoned with salt" (Colossians 4:6).

For my own growth in the one, true saving faith: "Lord, to whom shall we go? You have the words of eternal life, and we have believed, and have come to know, that you are the Holy One of God" (John 6:68-69).

Of our many petitions for Your loving kindness, let this be the most earnest: "Hear, O LORD, when I cry aloud; be gracious to me and answer me! / You have said, 'Seek my face.' / My heart says to you, 'Your face, LORD, do I seek'" (Psalm 27:7-8). Amen.

For further reflection: Numbers 6:24-26 – "The LORD bless you and keep you"

Eternal God, we commit to Your mercy and forgiveness the year now ending and commend to Your blessing and love the times yet to come. In the new year, abide among us with Your Holy Spirit that we may always trust in the saving name of our Lord Jesus Christ, who lives and reigns with You and the Holy Spirit, one God, now and forever.[1]   Amen.

392

Dr. Dale A. Meyer Biographical Information

Dale A. Meyer was born in Chicago Heights, Illinois. He completed a B.A. in 1969 at Concordia Senior College, Fort Wayne, Indiana. He is a 1973 graduate of Concordia Seminary, St. Louis, earning a Master of Divinity degree. He earned an M.A. (1974) and a Ph.D. (1986) in classical languages from Washington University in St. Louis. In 1993, Concordia Theological Seminary in Fort Wayne, Indiana awarded him the honorary degree of Doctor of Divinity.

Meyer began his pastoral career serving as pastor of St. Salvator Lutheran Church in Venedy, Illinois and St. Peter Lutheran Church in New Memphis, Illinois from 1974 to 1981. He served on the faculty of Concordia Seminary, St. Louis, Missouri from 1979 to 1981 as a guest instructor and 1981 to 1984 as an assistant professor teaching classes in New Testament and homiletics and as the director of Resident Field Education. From 1984 to 1988, Meyer served as senior pastor at Holy Cross Lutheran Church, Collinsville, Illinois. From 1989 to 2001, Meyer was speaker on the radio program *The Lutheran Hour* and until 2003 he was the host of the television show *On Main Street*.

Meyer joined the faculty at Concordia Seminary, St. Louis again in 2001. He occupied the Gregg H. Benidt Memorial Chair in Homiletics and Literature at Concordia from 2001-2005. He served as the interim president from 2004 to 2005 and became the tenth president of Concordia Seminary, St. Louis in 2005. He also serves as a professor of practical theology.

Meyer has served The Lutheran Church—Missouri Synod (LCMS) and the church-at-large over the years in several capacities. He served as third vice-president of the LCMS from 1995 to 1998. He was a charter board member of ALOA (Association of Lutheran Older Adults), has served as an honorary director of God's Word to the Nations Bible Society and as a member of the Standing Committee on Pastoral Ministry for the LCMS. He was pastoral adviser for the Southern Illinois District of the International Lutheran Laymen's League and has served as first vice-president, second vice-president, secretary, and circuit counselor of the LCMS Southern Illinois District. From 2001 until 2013, he served on the Board of Trustees of American Bible Society.

Meyer has written numerous sermons and columns for Lutheran Hour Ministries, including the booklets "Coping with Cancer" and "Real Men." He coauthored *The Crosses of Lent*, in-depth Bible studies of Matthew and Prophecy in the *LifeLight* series, and authored "The Place of the Sermon in the Order of Service" in *Liturgical Preaching* for Concordia Publishing House. He has contributed to the *Concordia Journal* and *Issues in Christian Education.* His articles include "A Church Caught in the Middle," "An Urban Seminary," and "Why Go to Church?" In 2014, Meyer wrote *Timely Reflections: A Minute a Day with Dale Meyer*, a compilation of 365 daily devotions from his long-running online series, *The Meyer Minute*. This book was published by Tri-Pillar Publishing in conjunction with Concordia Seminary, St. Louis.

Meyer has been speaking and preaching on the road for over 25 years and continues to do so. His areas of interest and study include: 1 Peter, the Church in a changing culture, and the Sabbath applied to life today. He resides in St. Louis with his wife Diane. They have two grown daughters: Elizabeth (Darren) Pittman and Catharine (Charles) Bailey, and five grandsons: Christian, Connor, Drew, Jacob, and Nicholas.

Dr. Meyer's Recommended Reading List

I live in a world of books. The Concordia Seminary Library has some 270,000 volumes, all related in some way to the study of theology, and my personal library has several thousand volumes. If you could read them all, it still comes down to faith. "Of making many books there is no end, and much study is a weariness of the flesh" (Ecclesiastes 12:12). Faith seeks understanding, as St. Augustine reminds us, and reading helps illuminate faith. The few books listed below are sources quoted in *Timely Reflections* or are volumes that have especially shaped my understanding of discipleship.

Dietrich Bonhoeffer, *Life Together: The Classic Exploration of Christian Community*

Dietrich Bonhoeffer, *The Cost of Discipleship*

> Bonhoeffer is the well-known German theologian whose opposition to Hitler cost him his life. *The Cost of Discipleship* is a classic. *Life Together* is about community in Seminary but its insights also speak to congregational life. Bonhoeffer makes you think; you don't flip through his pages quickly.

Oswald Chambers, *My Utmost for His Highest: Selections for the Year*

> Chambers grew up in the British Empire and spent his short ministry traveling and teaching around the world. He died at age 43 in 1917. *My Utmost for His Highest* is perennially popular because Chambers cuts through our human self-importance to the reality of following God.

Abraham Heschel, *The Sabbath*

> Heschel was a twentieth century Jewish philosopher and theologian. Although not a Christian, his numerous writings give us much to think about from our perspective as followers of Jesus Christ. *The Sabbath* is a classic about time and eternity.

Horace, *Satires.*

> Horace was a Roman poet who lived in the first century before Christ. His *Satires*, some of the most enduring works of antiquity, suggest that we can use humor, specifically satire, to convey God's Law in a gentle but still effective way that does not repel listeners with a preacher's thunder.

David Kinnaman and Gabe Lyons, *unChristian: What a New Generation Really Thinks about Christianity... and Why It Matters*

David Kinnaman, *You Lost Me: Why Young Christians Are Leaving Church... and Rethinking Faith*

> David Kinnaman is president of the Barna Group and Gabe Lyons is the founder of Q Ideas. Based on surveys of 18- to 29-year-olds, these two books are must reading for any pastor or layperson concerned about young people and the church. Both books read easily and offer suggestions.

C.S. Lewis, *Beyond Personality*

C.S. Lewis, *A Grief Observed*

C.S. Lewis, *The Problem of Pain*

> These books are used in *Timely Reflections* but Lewis wrote far, far more and will not disappoint you. The titles *Beyond Personality* and *The Problem of Pain* are self-explanatory. *A Grief Observed* is about the death of his wife. Lewis is most popularly known for *The Chronicles of Narnia*. In youth he had been disenchanted with Christianity, but came to be an eloquent and insightful apologist for the faith.

Abraham Lincoln, *The Second Inaugural Address*

> Lincoln remains a commanding personality. His *Second Inaugural* is quoted and cited here for its brief but profound exploration of Christians disagreeing to the point of war.

Martin Luther, *The Small Catechism*

Martin Luther, *Sermon for the Third Sunday after Epiphany, 1528*

Martin Luther, *A Simple Way to Pray (...for Master Peter the Barber)*

> *Timely Reflections,* written by a Lutheran, will obviously quote the prolific Luther often but three deserve mention. *The Small Catechism,* often quoted throughout this book, summarizes biblical teaching in a simple way. Luther's short Epiphany sermon offers an in-depth discussion of Baptism, including the practice of baptizing infants. His advice to *Peter the Barber* is an excellent guide for how to go about daily personal devotion.

Johann Friedrich Starck, *Starck's Prayer Book*

> Starck was an eighteenth century German pastor in the era of Pietism. His *Prayer Book* has endured through the centuries, and is rich with pastoral guidance and copious in quoting Scripture and hymnody. His style is different than twenty-first century tastes, but well worth quiet reading.

Peter L. Steinke, *A Door Set Open: Grounding Change in Mission and Hope*

> Quoted in *Timely Reflections* and a must read for pastors and church leaders. Steinke has consulted with hundreds of congregations and offers practical insights for navigating changed times for the church in America.

C.F.W. Walther, *Law and Gospel: How to Read and Apply the Bible*

> Walther was a nineteenth century American Lutheran theologian and the first president of Concordia Seminary. *Law and Gospel* is invaluable because it explains the complex interaction of God's commands and God's grace in forgiveness.

Lutheran Service Book

> This is the hymnal currently used in the chapel of Concordia Seminary and throughout The Lutheran Church—Missouri Synod. Its hymns are quoted on almost every page of *Timely Reflections,* and it is listed here because a good hymnal is itself a book for personal devotion.

Calendars

2015 Dates

New Year's Day_____Thursday, January 1

Epiphany_____Tuesday, January 6

The Baptism of Our Lord_____Sunday, January 11

The Confession of St. Peter_____Sunday, January 18

Martin Luther King, Jr. Day_____Monday, January 19

The Conversion of St. Paul_____Sunday, January 25

National Lutheran Schools Week_____January 25-31

Lincoln's Birthday_____Thursday, February 12

Valentine's Day_____Saturday, February 14

The Transfiguration of Our Lord_____Sunday, February 15

Presidents' Day (Washington's Birthday)_____Monday February 16

Shrove Tuesday_____Tuesday, February 17

Ash Wednesday_____Wednesday, February 18

LENT 2015_____February 18 – April 4

St. Patrick's Day_____Tuesday, March 17

St. Joseph, Guardian of Jesus_____Thursday, March 19

Palm Sunday_____Sunday, March 29

Maundy Thursday_____Thursday, April 2

Good Friday_____Friday, April 3

Easter_____Sunday, April 5

Earth Day_____Wednesday, April 22

St. Mark, Evangelist_____Saturday, April 25

Concordia Seminary Call Day (CTS)_____Tuesday, April 28

Concordia Seminary Call Day (CSL)_____Wednesday, April 29

National Day of Prayer_____Thursday, May 7

Mother's Day_____Sunday, May 10

Ascension Day_____Thursday, May 14

Armed Forces Day_____Saturday, May 16

Ascension Sunday_____Sunday, May 17

Concordia Seminary Graduation (CTS and CSL)_____Friday, May 22

Pentecost_____Sunday, May 24

Memorial Day_____Monday, May 25

Flag Day_____Sunday, June 14
Father's Day_____Sunday, June 21
Independence Day_____Saturday, July 4
St. James the Elder, Apostle_____Saturday, July 25
St. Mary, Mother of Our Lord_____Saturday, August 15
Labor Day_____Monday, September 7
Patriot Day_____Friday, September 11
Grandparents Day_____Sunday, September 13
St. Matthew, Apostle and Evangelist_____Monday, September 21
St. Michael and All Angels_____Tuesday, September 29
Columbus Day_____Monday, October 12
St. Luke, Evangelist_____Sunday, October 18
Reformation Sunday_____Sunday, October 25
Reformation Day_____Saturday, October 31
All Saints' Day_____Sunday, November 1
Election Day_____Tuesday, November 3
Veterans Day_____Wednesday, November 11
Christ the King Sunday_____Sunday, November 22
Thanksgiving_____Thursday, November 26
First Sunday in Advent_____Sunday, November 29
ADVENT 2015_____November 29 – December 24
St. Andrew, Apostle_____Monday, November 30
Christmas Eve_____Thursday, December 24
Christmas Day_____Friday, December 25
St. Stephen, First Martyr_____Saturday, December 26
St. John, Apostle and Evangelist_____Sunday, December 27
The Holy Innocents, Martyrs_____Monday, December 28
New Year's Eve_____Thursday, December 31

2016 Dates and [Date of *Minute* in the Book]

New Year's Day_____Friday, January 1 [January 1]

Epiphany_____Wednesday, January 6 [January 6]

The Baptism of Our Lord_____Sunday, January 10 [January 11]

The Confession of St. Peter_____Monday, January 18 [January 18]

Martin Luther King, Jr. Day_____Monday, January 18 [January 19]

National Lutheran Schools Week_____January 24-30 [January 25-31]

The Conversion of St. Paul_____Monday, January 25 [January 25]

The Transfiguration of Our Lord_____Sunday, February 7 [February 15]

Shrove Tuesday_____Tuesday, February 9 [February 17]

Ash Wednesday_____Wednesday, February 10 [February 18]

LENT 2016_____February 10 – March 26 [February 18 – April 4]

Lincoln's Birthday_____Friday, February 12 [February 12]

Valentine's Day_____Sunday, February 14 [February 14]

Presidents' Day (Washington's Birthday)___Monday February 15 [February 16]

St. Patrick's Day_____Thursday, March 17 [March 17]

St. Joseph, Guardian of Jesus_____Saturday, March 19 [March 19]

Palm Sunday_____Sunday, March 20 [March 29]

Maundy Thursday_____Thursday, March 24 [April 2]

Good Friday_____Friday, March 25 [April 3]

Easter_____Sunday, March 27 [April 5]

Earth Day_____Friday, April 22 [April 22]

St. Mark, Evangelist_____Monday, April 25 [April 25]

National Day of Prayer_____Thursday, May 5 [May 7]

Ascension Day_____Thursday, May 5 [May 14]

Ascension Sunday_____Sunday, May 8 [May 17]

Mother's Day_____Sunday, May 8 [May 10]

Pentecost_____Sunday, May 15 [May 24]

Armed Forces Day_____Saturday, May 21 [May 16]

Memorial Day_____Monday, May 30 [May 25]

Flag Day_____Tuesday, June 14 [June 14]

Father's Day_____Sunday, June 19 [June 21]

Independence Day_____Monday, July 4 [July 4]

St. James the Elder, Apostle_____Monday, July 25 [July 25]

St. Mary, Mother of Our Lord_____Monday, August 15 [August 15]

Labor Day_____Monday, September 5 [September 7]

Patriot Day_____Sunday, September 11 [September 11]

Grandparents Day_____Sunday, September 11 [September 13]

St. Matthew, Apostle and Evangelist_____Wed., September 21 [September 21]

St. Michael and All Angels_____Thursday, September 29 [September 29]

Columbus Day_____Monday, October 10 [October 12]

St. Luke, Evangelist_____Tuesday, October 18 [October 18]

Reformation Sunday_____Sunday, October 30 [October 25]

Reformation Day_____Monday, October 31 [October 31]

All Saints' Day_____Tuesday, November 1 [November 1]

Election Day_____Tuesday, November 8 [November 3]

Veterans Day_____Friday, November 11 [November 11]

Christ the King Sunday_____Sunday, November 20 [November 22]

Thanksgiving_____Thursday, November 24 [November 26]

First Sunday in Advent_____Sunday, November 27 [November 29]

ADVENT 2016___November 27 – December 24 [November 29 – December 24]

St. Andrew, Apostle_____Wednesday, November 30 [November 30]

Christmas Eve_____Saturday, December 24 [December 24]

Christmas Day_____Sunday, December 25 [December 25]

St. Stephen, First Martyr_____Monday, December 26 [December 26]

St. John, Apostle and Evangelist_____Tuesday, December 27 [December 27]

The Holy Innocents, Martyrs_____Wednesday, December 28 [December 28]

New Year's Eve_____Saturday, December 31 [December 31]

2017 Dates and [Date of *Minute* in the Book]

New Year's Day_____Sunday, January 1 [January 1]

Epiphany_____Friday, January 6 [January 6]

The Baptism of Our Lord_____Sunday, January 8 [January 11]

Martin Luther King, Jr. Day_____Monday, January 16 [January 19]

The Confession of St. Peter_____Wednesday, January 18 [January 18]

The Conversion of St. Paul_____Wednesday, January 25 [January 25]

Lincoln's Birthday_____Sunday, February 12 [February 12]

Valentine's Day_____Tuesday, February 14 [February 14]

Presidents' Day (Washington's Birthday)___Monday February 20 [February 16]

The Transfiguration of Our Lord_____Sunday, February 26 [February 15]

Shrove Tuesday_____Tuesday, February 28 [February 17]

Ash Wednesday_____Wednesday, March 1 [February 18]

LENT 2017_____March 1 – April 15 [February 18 – April 4]

St. Patrick's Day_____Friday, March 17 [March 17]

St. Joseph, Guardian of Jesus_____Sunday, March 19 [March 19]

Palm Sunday_____Sunday, April 9 [March 29]

Maundy Thursday_____Thursday, April 13 [April 2]

Good Friday_____Friday, April 14 [April 3]

Easter_____Sunday, April 16 [April 5]

Earth Day_____Saturday, April 22 [April 22]

St. Mark, Evangelist_____Tuesday, April 25 [April 25]

National Day of Prayer_____Thursday, May 4 [May 7]

Mother's Day_____Sunday, May 14 [May 10]

Armed Forces Day_____Saturday, May 20 [May 16]

Ascension Day_____Thursday, May 25 [May 14]

Ascension Sunday_____Sunday, May 28 [May 17]

Memorial Day_____Monday, May 29 [May 25]

Pentecost_____Sunday, June 4 [May 24]

Flag Day_____Wednesday, June 14 [June 14]

Father's Day_____Sunday, June 18 [June 21]

Independence Day_____Tuesday, July 4 [July 4]

St. James the Elder, Apostle_____Tuesday, July 25 [July 25]

St. Mary, Mother of Our Lord_____Tuesday, August 15 [August 15]

Labor Day_____Monday, September 4 [September 7]

Grandparents Day_____Sunday, September 10 [September 13]

Patriot Day_____Monday, September 11 [September 11]

St. Matthew, Apostle and Evangelist__Thursday, September 21 [September 21]

St. Michael and All Angels_____Friday, September 29 [September 29]

Columbus Day_____Monday, October 9 [October 12]

St. Luke, Evangelist_____Wednesday, October 18 [October 18]

Reformation Sunday_____Sunday, October 29 [October 25]

Reformation Day_____Tuesday, October 31 [October 31]

All Saints' Day_____Wednesday, November 1 [November 1]

Election Day_____Tuesday, November 7 [November 3]

Veterans Day_____Saturday, November 11 [November 11]

Thanksgiving_____Thursday, November 23 [November 26]

Christ the King Sunday_____Sunday, November 26 [November 22]

St. Andrew, Apostle_____Thursday, November 30 [November 30]

First Sunday in Advent_____Sunday, December 3 [November 29]

ADVENT 2017____December 3 – December 24 [November 29 – December 24]

Christmas Eve_____Sunday, December 24 [December 24]

Christmas Day_____Monday, December 25 [December 25]

St. Stephen, First Martyr_____Tuesday, December 26 [December 26]

St. John, Apostle and Evangelist_____Wednesday, December 27 [December 27]

The Holy Innocents, Martyrs_____Thursday, December 28 [December 28]

New Year's Eve_____Sunday, December 31 [December 31]

Topical Index

November 24
December 1
December 3
December 12

Freedom
March 20
June 4
July 3
July 6
July 15
October 7
November 9
December 7
December 18

Friendliness
August 1

Friends
November 15

Fruit of the Spirit
July 9
July 25
September 20

Future
May 30
October 12
October 16
November 25

Generosity
October 11

Gentiles
January 6

Gentle
January 11

George Washington
February 16

July 5

Giving
December 7
December 22

God's Acceptance
August 9

God's Blessing
December 31

God's Call
March 14
April 28
April 29
June 8
December 6

God's Comfort
June 13
July 23

God's Compassion
September 2
November 21
December 31

God's Discipline
February 6

God's Glory
December 27

God's Guidance
April 11
May 1
June 8
October 4
November 13

God's Law
March 4
May 1

July 21

God's Love
April 24
May 10
October 18

God's Peace
April 10
July 6
September 18

God's Presence
April 27
August 30
October 6
November 14

God's Promises
January 31
March 11
April 5
April 18
April 21
April 27
May 14
May 17
May 27
May 30
June 3
June 22
July 5
July 19
August 7
August 17
August 30
October 5
October 13
October 21
October 22
October 24
October 28
November 2
November 13

Scripture Passage Index

Micah 6:8
July 1
September 12
September 20
November 19
November 28

Habakkuk 1:2-3
June 3

Habakkuk 2:3
February 10

Habakkuk 2:4
June 3

Habakkuk 2:20
February 5

Habakkuk 3:17-18
August 20
November 25

Habakkuk 3:17-19
October 2

Zephaniah
July 22

Zephaniah 3:14-20
June 30

Zechariah 3
November 7
December 11

Zechariah 3:1-2
October 19

Zechariah 3:1-5
September 23

Zechariah 9:9
May 2

Zechariah 14:1-9
October 24

Malachi 3:3
March 3

Malachi 3:6
January 22

Malachi 3:6-12
August 7

Malachi 4:6
November 26

Matthew 1:19-20
December 9

Matthew 1:20
March 19

Matthew 1:24-25
December 9

Matthew 2
January 6

Matthew 2:10
January 8

Matthew 2:12
January 7

Matthew 2:13-23
March 19
August 23

Matthew 2:14
December 9

Matthew 2:16-18
December 28

Matthew 2:19-22
December 9

Matthew 3:13-17
January 11

Matthew 4:1-11
September 10
October 29

Matthew 5-7
January 7

Matthew 5:1
February 7
April 6

Matthew 5:2-12
November 24

Matthew 5:10
March 14

Matthew 5:22
July 28

Matthew 5:37
August 6

Matthew 5:43-48
November 9

Matthew 5:44
September 24

Matthew 6:1
February 25

Matthew 6:1-16
July 11

Matthew 6:5-8
April 17

Romans 13:4
April 15
April 27

Romans 13:14
August 10

Romans 14:8
November 30

Romans 14:19
July 30

Romans 15:1-7
May 31

Romans 15:4
January 7
March 7
May 18

Romans 15:13
January 14

Romans 16:1-16
November 1

Romans 16:22
August 2

1 Corinthians 1:12-13
July 30

1 Corinthians 1:24
August 8

1 Corinthians 2:9
November 26

1 Corinthians 2:9-10
March 12
April 26

1 Corinthians 5:7-8
April 2

1 Corinthians 6:1-11
March 6

1 Corinthians 6:11
January 26
March 15

1 Corinthians 6:20
January 27

1 Corinthians 7
June 27

1 Corinthians 10:12
January 17

1 Corinthians 10:13
March 7

1 Corinthians 10:31
October 3

1 Corinthians 11:23-34
June 8

1 Corinthians 12:3
January 1

1 Corinthians 12:4-7, 12-13
June 18

1 Corinthians 12:24-27
June 28

1 Corinthians 12:26
October 10

1 Corinthians 13
February 14

1 Corinthians 13:1
November 14

1 Corinthians 13:4, 7
July 18

1 Corinthians 13:5, 7
July 1

1 Corinthians 13:8
July 10
July 14

1 Corinthians 13:11
December 1

1 Corinthians 13:12
March 3
August 21
October 21

1 Corinthians 13:13
April 12
July 10
October 28

1 Corinthians 15:3
March 20

1 Corinthians 15:12-20
May 18

1 Corinthians 15:17
April 7

1 Corinthians 15:25-26
March 27

1 Corinthians 15:26
June 3

1 Corinthians 15:58
January 31
August 27

Endnotes

Acknowledgments
[1] "Divine Service: Setting Two," *Lutheran Book of Worship*: Prepared by the churches participating in the Inter-Lutheran Commission on Worship (Minneapolis: Augsburg Publishing House, 1978), 261

Forewords
[1] Date of this original *Meyer Minute* is October 3, 2014; date in this book of a revised version of this *Minute* is February 8

Introduction
[1] Paul McCartney and John Lennon, "Getting Better," recorded by The Beatles, 1967
[2] Philipp Melanchthon, *Loci Communes, 1543*, tr. J.A.O. Preus, (St. Louis: Concordia Publishing House, 1992)
[3] C.F.W. Walther, *The Proper Distinction between Law and Gospel: Thirty-Nine Evening Lectures*, ed. W.H.T. Dau (St. Louis: Concordia Publishing House, 1929), 313
[4] Martin Luther, "Heidelberg Disputation, 1518," in *Career of the Reformer I*, ed. Harold J. Grimm, vol. 31 of *Luther's Works*, ed. Jaroslav Pelikan and Helmut T. Lehman (Philadelphia: Muhlenberg/Fortress; St. Louis: Concordia Publishing House, 1957), 40
[5] Neumeister, "I Know My Faith Is Founded," tr. *The Lutheran Hymnal*, 1941, *Lutheran Service Book* (St. Louis: Concordia Publishing House, 2006), 587, 1

January 1
[1] Nicolas Berdyaev, *Solitude and Society* (London: Geoffrey Bless: The Centenary Press, 1938), 134
[2] Bridges, "Crown Him with Many Crowns," *Lutheran Worship* (St. Louis: Concordia Publishing House, 1982), 278, 5

January 2
[1] Elliott, "Just as I Am, without One Plea," *Lutheran Service Book* (St. Louis: Concordia Publishing House, 2006), 570, 1
[2] Watts, "Oh, That the Lord Would Guide My Ways," *Lutheran Service Book* (St. Louis: Concordia Publishing House, 2006), 707, 1

January 4
[1] "How Firm a Foundation," *Lutheran Service Book* (St. Louis: Concordia Publishing House, 2006), 728, 2

January 5
[1] Seneca, "Letter VII," in *Selected Letters of Seneca*, edited by Walter C. Summers (New Rochelle, NY: Caratzas Publishing Co., 1983), 5-6
[2] Martin Chemnitz, *Loci Theologici*, tr. J.A.O. Preus (St. Louis: Concordia Publishing House, 2008), 716-717

January 6

[1] "The Epiphany of Our Lord: Collect of the Day," *Lutheran Service Book: Altar Book* (St. Louis: Concordia Publishing House, 2006), 566

January 7

[1] von Hessen-Darmstadt, "Speak, O Lord, Your Servant Listens," tr. Rygh, *Lutheran Service Book* (St. Louis: Concordia Publishing House, 2006), 589, 2

January 9

[1] Ringwaldt, "O Holy Spirit, Grant Us Grace," tr. Smeby, *Lutheran Service Book* (St. Louis: Concordia Publishing House, 2006), 693, 2

January 10

[1] Juliane, "The Lord hath Helped Me Hitherto," tr. Crull, *The Lutheran Hymnal* (St. Louis: Concordia Publishing House, 1941), 33, 1, 3

January 12

[1] Scriven, "What a Friend We Have in Jesus," *Lutheran Service Book* (St. Louis: Concordia Publishing House, 2006), 770, 1

[2] Martin Luther, "A Simple Way to Pray, 1535," in *Devotional Writings II*, ed. Gustav K. Wiencke, vol. 43 of *Luther's Works*, ed. Jaroslav Pelikan and Helmut T. Lehmann (Philadelphia: Muhlenberg/Fortress; St. Louis: Concordia Publishing House,1968), 194

[3] Dix, "Come unto Me, Ye Weary," *Lutheran Service Book* (St. Louis: Concordia Publishing House, 2006), 684, 1

January 13

[1] Dietrich Bonhoeffer, *The Cost of Discipleship* (New York: Macmillan, 1959), 35-36

[2] Bonar, "Thy Works, Not Mine, O Christ," *Lutheran Service Book* (St. Louis: Concordia Publishing House, 2006), 565, 1 and refrain

January 14

[1] Peter Marshall, *The Senate Prayers of Peter Marshall* (Sandwich, MA: Chapman Billies, 1996), 58

[2] "Hope of Eternal Life in Christ: Collect 222," *Lutheran Service Book* (St. Louis: Concordia Publishing House, 2006), 313

January 15

[1] "Holy Matrimony," *Lutheran Service Book* (St. Louis: Concordia Publishing House, 2006), 275

January 16

[1] *Fuller's Church History*, ed. 1655, book x., 21

[2] Erroll F. Rhodes and Liana Lupas, eds., *The Translators to the Reader: The Original Preface to the King James Version of 1611 Revisited* (New York: American Bible Society, 1997), 68-69

January 17
[1] Brorson, "I Walk in Danger All the Way," tr. Ristad, *Lutheran Service Book* (St. Louis: Concordia Publishing House, 2006), 716, 1
[2] Scheffler, "Thee Will I Love, My Strength, My Tower," tr. Winkworth, *Lutheran Service Book* (St. Louis: Concordia Publishing House, 2006), 694, 4

January 18
[1] Johann Friedrich Starck, *Starck's Prayer Book*, ed. W.H.T. Dau (St. Louis: Concordia Publishing House, 1921), 387

January 19
[1] Frederick J. Schumacher and Dorothy A. Zelenko, eds., *For All the Saints: A Prayer Book For and By the Church*, vol. 3 (Delhi, NY: The American Lutheran Publicity Bureau, 1995), 978-979

January 20
[1] *Die Losungen*, February 18, 2008
[2] Synesius of Cyrene, "Lord Jesus, Think on Me," tr. Chatfield, *Lutheran Service Book* (St. Louis: Concordia Publishing House, 2006), 610, 1

January 21
[1] "Collect for Grace," *Lutheran Service Book* (St. Louis: Concordia Publishing House, 2006), 228
[2] Luther, "A Mighty Fortress Is Our God," tr. composite, *Lutheran Service Book* (St. Louis: Concordia Publishing House, 2006), 656
[3] Brorson, "I Walk in Danger All the Way," tr. Ristad, *Lutheran Service Book* (St. Louis: Concordia Publishing House, 2006), 716, 1
[4] "Collect for Grace," *Lutheran Service Book* (St. Louis: Concordia Publishing House, 2006), 228

January 22
[1] Gerhardt, "Why Should Cross and Trial Grieve Me," tr. *Christian Worship*, *Lutheran Service Book* (St. Louis: Concordia Publishing House, 2006), 756, 3

January 23
[1] Oswald Chambers, "January 3," *My Utmost for His Highest: Selections for the Year* (New York: Dodd, Mead & Company, 1935)
[2] Held, "Come, Oh, Come, Thou Quickening Spirit," tr. Schaeffer, *The Lutheran Hymnal* (St. Louis: Concordia Publishing House, 1941), 226, 4

January 24
[1] March, "Hark, the Voice of Jesus Crying," *The Lutheran Hymnal* (St. Louis: Concordia Publishing House, 1941), 496, 2

January 25
[1] Martin Luther, "On the Sum of the Christian Life," 1532, in *Sermons I*, ed. John W. Doberstein, vol. 51 of *Luther's Works*, ed. Jaroslav Pelikan and Helmut T. Lehmann (Philadelphia: Muhlenberg/Fortress; St. Louis: Concordia Publishing House, 1959), 276

January 27
[1] von Pfeil, "Oh, Blest the House," tr. *Evangelical Lutheran Hymnal*, Columbus, 1880, *Lutheran Service Book* (St. Louis: Concordia Publishing House, 2006), 862, 3
[2] Schröder, "One Thing's Needful," tr. Cox, *Lutheran Service Book* (St. Louis: Concordia Publishing House, 2006), 536, 3

January 28
[1] Daniel O. Aleshire, *Earthen Vessels: Hopeful Reflections on the Work and Future of Theological Schools* (Grand Rapids, MI: Eerdmans, 2008), 145

January 29
[1] Watts, "Let Children Hear the Mighty Deeds," *Lutheran Service Book* (St. Louis: Concordia Publishing House, 2006), 867, 3

January 30
[1] Newton, "Amazing Grace," *Lutheran Service Book* (St. Louis: Concordia Publishing House, 2006), 744, 3
[2] Toplady, "Rock of Ages, Cleft for Me," *Lutheran Service Book* (St. Louis: Concordia Publishing House, 2006), 761, 1

January 31
[1] From the Latin phrase: *repetitio est mater studiorum*
[2] Wesley, "Forth in Thy Name, O Lord, I Go," *Lutheran Service Book* (St. Louis: Concordia Publishing House, 2006), 854, 1-2

February 1
[1] "Six Reasons Young Christians Leave Church," *Barna Group*, Sept. 28, 2011, https://www.barna.org/teens-next-gen-articles/528-six-reasons-young-christians-leave-church
[2] Frederick J. Schumacher and Dorothy A. Zelenko, eds., *For All the Saints: A Prayer Book For and By the Church*, vol. 1 (Delhi, NY: The American Lutheran Publicity Bureau, 1994), 286
[3] Graham Nash, "Teach Your Children," recorded by Crosby, Stills, Nash & Young, 1970

February 2
[1] Wesley, "Love Divine, All Loves Excelling," *Lutheran Service Book* (St. Louis: Concordia Publishing House, 2006), 700, 2
[2] "Holy Matrimony: Collect 526," *Lutheran Service Book: Agenda* (St. Louis: Concordia Publishing House, 2006), 74

February 3
[1] Montgomery, "Come to Calvary's Holy Mountain," *Lutheran Service Book* (St. Louis: Concordia Publishing House, 2006), 435, 2
[2] Neumeister, "Jesus Sinners Doth Receive," tr. *The Lutheran Hymnal*, 1941, *Lutheran Service Book* (St. Louis: Concordia Publishing House, 2006), 609, 4

February 4
[1] Ronald C. White, Jr., *Lincoln's Greatest Speech: The Second Inaugural Address* (New York: Simon & Schuster Lincoln Library, 2006), 23
[2] "The Litany," *Lutheran Service Book* (St. Louis: Concordia Publishing House, 2006), 289

February 5
[1] Newton, "Come, My Soul, with Every Care," *Lutheran Service Book* (St. Louis: Concordia Publishing House, 2006), 779, 2
[2] William Walford, "Sweet Hour of Prayer," 1845
[3] Schmolck, "Open Now Thy Gates of Beauty," tr. Winkworth, *Lutheran Service Book* (St. Louis: Concordia Publishing House, 2006), 901, 5

February 6
[1] "For Divine Guidance: Collect 187," *Lutheran Service Book* (St. Louis: Concordia Publishing House, 2006), 310

February 7
[1] Doane, "You Are the Way; through You Alone," *Lutheran Service Book* (St. Louis: Concordia Publishing House, 2006), 526, 2

February 8
[1] "For the Mission of the Church: Collect 104," *Lutheran Service Book* (St. Louis: Concordia Publishing House, 2006), 305

February 9
[1] von Hayn, "I Am Jesus' Little Lamb," tr. *The Lutheran Hymnal*, 1941, *Lutheran Service Book* (St. Louis: Concordia Publishing House, 2006), 740, 1
[2] "Savior, like a Shepherd Lead Us," *Lutheran Service Book* (St. Louis: Concordia Publishing House, 2006), 711, 4

February 10
[1] Gerhardt, "If God Himself Be for Me," tr. *Evangelical Lutheran Hymn-Book*, 1907, *Lutheran Service Book* (St. Louis: Concordia Publishing House, 2006), 724, 10
[2] Maude, "Thine Forever, God of Love," *Lutheran Service Book* (St. Louis: Concordia Publishing House, 2006), 687, 2, 5

February 11
[1] Savanarola, "Jesus, Refuge of the Weary," tr. Wilde, *Lutheran Service Book* (St. Louis: Concordia Publishing House, 2006), 423, 3
[2] Schalling, "Lord, Thee I Love with All My Heart," tr. Winkworth, *Lutheran Service Book* (St. Louis: Concordia Publishing House, 2006), 708, 1

February 12
[1] James C. Humes, *The Wit and Wisdom of Abraham Lincoln: A Treasury of Quotations, Anecdotes, and Observations* (New York: Gramercy Books, 1996), 130
[2] Ibid., 155

February 13
[1] Plumptre, "Your Hand, O Lord, in Days of Old," *Lutheran Service Book* (St. Louis: Concordia Publishing House, 2006), 846, 3

February 14
[1] Schultz, "Love in Christ Is Strong and Living," *Lutheran Service Book* (St. Louis: Concordia Publishing House, 2006), 706, 1

February 15
[1] Lyte, "Abide with Me," *Lutheran Service Book* (St. Louis: Concordia Publishing House, 2006), 878, 4
[2] Robinson, "'Tis Good, Lord, to Be Here," *Lutheran Service Book* (St. Louis: Concordia Publishing House, 2006), 414, 5

February 16
[1] Robert V. Remini, *The House: The History of the House of Representatives* (New York: Smithsonian Books, 2006), 20-23

February 17
[1] Stephanie Simon, "Status: Dad Wonders If He Can Last All of Lent Without Facebook," *The Wall Street Journal*, Feb. 20, 2009

February 18
[1] Samuel Moor Shoemaker, "I Stand by the Door: An Apologia of My Life," in Helen Smith Shoemaker, *I Stand by the Door* (New York: Harper & Row, 1967)

February 19
[1] Spafford, "When Peace, Like a River," *Lutheran Service Book* (St. Louis: Concordia Publishing House, 2006), 763, 1

February 20
[1] Pollock, "Jesus, in Your Dying Woes," *Lutheran Service Book* (St. Louis: Concordia Publishing House, 2006), 447:1-3

February 21
[1] Oswald Chambers, "April 27," *My Utmost for His Highest: Selections for the Year* (New York: Dodd, Mead & Company, 1935)
[2] Dietrich Bonhoeffer, *Discipleship*, vol. 4 of *Dietrich Bonhoeffer Works*, ed. Geffery B. Kelley and John D. Godsey, tr. Barbara Green and Reinhard Krauss (Minneapolis: Fortress Press, 2001), 167

February 22
[1] Johann Friedrich Starck, *Starck's Prayer Book*, ed. W.H.T. Dau (St. Louis: Concordia Publishing House, 1921), 225
[2] von Birken, "Jesus, I Will Ponder Now," tr. Crull, *Lutheran Service Book* (St. Louis: Concordia Publishing House, 2006), 440, 4

February 23
[1] Schröder, "One Thing's Needful," tr. Cox, *Lutheran Service Book* (St. Louis: Concordia Publishing House, 2006), 536, 5

February 24
[1] Sinclair Lewis in Ashley Halsey, "Do Weather Gripes Leave You Cold?" *The Washington Post* (Washington, D.C.) Feb. 7, 2007
[2] Olearius, "The Lord, My God, Be Praised," tr. Crull, *Lutheran Service Book* (St. Louis: Concordia Publishing House, 2006), 794, 1

February 25

[1] Kingo, "On My Heart Imprint Your Image," tr. Stromme, *Lutheran Service Book* (St. Louis: Concordia Publishing House, 2006), 422

February 26

[1] Dietrich Bonhoeffer, *Life Together: The Classic Exploration of Christian Community*, tr. Doberstein (New York: Harper & Row Publishers, 1954), 54

February 27

[1] Martin Chemnitz, *Loci Theologici*, tr. J.A.O. Preus (St. Louis: Concordia Publishing House, 2008), 739-740

[2] Oswald Chambers, "January 9," *My Utmost for His Highest: Selections for the Year* (New York: Dodd, Mead & Company, 1935)

[3] Ken, "Awake, My Soul, and with the Sun," *Lutheran Service Book* (St. Louis: Concordia Publishing House, 2006), 868, 4-5

February 28

[1] Robinson, "Come, Thou Fount of Every Blessing," *Lutheran Service Book* (St. Louis: Concordia Publishing House, 2006), 686, 3

March 1

[1] "Good Friday: Collect of the Day," *Lutheran Service Book: Altar Book*, prepared by the Commission on Worship of The Lutheran Church–Missouri Synod (St. Louis: Concordia Publishing House, 2006), 592

March 2

[1] Robin Pogrebin "Inside the Music: A Cellist's Perspective," *The New York Times*, February 21, 2003

[2] Westendorf, "Sent Forth by God's Blessing," *Lutheran Service Book* (St. Louis: Concordia Publishing House, 2006), 643, 2

[3] Franzmann, "O God, O Lord of Heaven and Earth," *Lutheran Service Book* (St. Louis: Concordia Publishing House, 2006), 834, 4

[4] "Holy God, We Praise Thy Name," tr. Walworth, *Lutheran Service Book* (St. Louis: Concordia Publishing House, 2006), 940, 3

[5] "Grace To Use Our Gifts: Collect 192," *Lutheran Service Book* (Saint: Louis: Concordia Publishing House, 2006), 311

March 3

[1] "How Firm a Foundation," *Lutheran Service Book* (St. Louis: Concordia Publishing House, 2006), 728, 4

[2] Luther, "Our Father, Who from Heaven Above," tr. *The Lutheran Hymnal*, 1941, *Lutheran Service Book* (St. Louis: Concordia Publishing House, 2006), 766, 8

March 4

[1] *Rocky Balboa*. Dir. Sylvester Stallone. Perf. Sylvester Stallone, Antonio Tarver, and Milo Ventimiglia. Metro-Goldwyn-Mayer, Columbia Pictures, and Revolution Studios, 2006

March 5

[1] Spengler, "All Mankind Fell in Adam's Fall," tr. Loy, *Lutheran Service Book* (St. Louis: Concordia Publishing House, 2006), 562, 3, 6

March 7

[1] Johann Sebastian Bach, *Jauchzet Gott in allen Landen* (*Let Praise Arise to God in Every Land*), BWV 51

[2] Neumeister, "I Know My Faith Is Founded," tr. *The Lutheran Hymnal*, 1941, *Lutheran Service Book* (St. Louis: Concordia Publishing House, 2006), 587, 3

March 8

[1] da Siena, "Come Down, O Love Divine," tr. Littledale, *Lutheran Service Book* (St. Louis: Concordia Publishing House, 2006), 501, 1-2

March 9

[1] Michael Downing, *Spring Forward: The Annual Madness of Daylight Saving Time* (Washington, D.C.: Shoemaker and Hoard, 2005)

[2] Watts, "O God, Our Help in Ages Past," *Lutheran Service Book* (St. Louis: Concordia Publishing House, 2006), 733, 1, 5-6

March 10

[1] "How Firm a Foundation," *Lutheran Service Book* (St. Louis: Concordia Publishing House, 2006), 728, 2

[2] *Luther's Small Catechism with Explanation* (St. Louis: Concordia Publishing House, 1991), 30-31

March 11

[1] Vicki Baum quoted in Susan Wales, *Standing on the Promises: A Woman's Guide for Surviving the Storms of Life* (Sisters, OR: Multnomah Publishers, 2001), 138

[2] Neander, "Praise to the Lord, the Almighty," tr. Winkworth, *Lutheran Service Book* (St. Louis: Concordia Publishing House, 2006), 790, 3

[3] "How Firm a Foundation," *Lutheran Service Book* (St. Louis: Concordia Publishing House, 2006), 728, 1

March 12

[1] Bernard of Cluny, "Jerusalem the Golden," tr. Neale, *Lutheran Service Book* (St. Louis: Concordia Publishing House, 2006), 672, 1

[2] Ibid., 4

March 13

1 Kathleen Norris, *Amazing Grace: A Vocabulary of Faith* (New York: Riverhead Books, 1998), 19-20

2 W. Bauer, F.W. Danker, W.F. Arndt, and F.W. Gingrich. *Greek-English Lexicon of the New Testament and Other Early Christian Literature*. 3rd ed. (Chicago: University of Chicago Press, 1999)

3 J.A.O. Preus, *Just Words: Understanding the Fullness of the Gospel* (St. Louis: Concordia Publishing House, 2000), 190

4 Luther, "A Mighty Fortress Is Our God," tr. composite, *Lutheran Service Book* (St. Louis: Concordia Publishing House, 2006), 656, 1

5 Brorson, "I Walk in Danger All the Way," tr. Ristad, *Lutheran Service Book* (St. Louis: Concordia Publishing House, 2006), 716, 5

March 14

1 Green, "How Clear Is Our Vocation, Lord," *Lutheran Service Book* (St. Louis: Concordia Publishing House, 2006), 853, 1

March 15

1 Barbara Brown Taylor, "Hands and Feet," in *Home by Another Way* (Cambridge and Boston: Cowley, 1999), 123

2 Johann Friedrich Starck, *Starck's Prayer Book*, ed. W.H.T. Dau (St. Louis: Concordia Publishing House, 1921), 460

3 Lyte, "Abide with Me," *Lutheran Service Book* (St. Louis: Concordia Publishing House, 2006), 878, 4

March 16

1 Brackett, "Simple Gifts," 1848

2 Franck, "Jesus, Priceless Treasure," tr. Winkworth, *Lutheran Service Book* (St. Louis: Concordia Publishing House, 2006), 743, 4

March 17

1 Heermann, "Jesus, Grant That Balm and Healing," tr. composite, *Lutheran Service Book* (St. Louis: Concordia Publishing House, 2006), 421, 4

March 18

1 Allen, "Today Your Mercy Calls Us," *Lutheran Service Book* (St. Louis: Concordia Publishing House, 2006), 915, 4

March 19

1 "St. Joseph, Guardian of Jesus: Collect of the Day," *Lutheran Service Book: Altar Book* (St. Louis: Concordia Publishing House, 2006), 959

March 20

1 "Collect for Grace," *Lutheran Service Book* (St. Louis: Concordia Publishing House, 2006), 228

March 21
[1] Eli Kintisch, "Spring's Secrets Bloom Slowly," *St. Louis Post-Dispatch*, Mar. 19, 2004
[2] Babcock, "This Is My Father's World," *Lutheran Book of Worship*: Prepared by the churches participating in the Inter-Lutheran Commission on Worship (Minneapolis: Augsburg Publishing House, 1978), 554, 3

March 22
[1] Thring, "O God of Mercy, God of Might," *Lutheran Service Book* (St. Louis: Concordia Publishing House, 2006), 852, 3

March 23
[1] Franzmann, "Thy Strong Word," *Lutheran Service Book* (St. Louis: Concordia Publishing House, 2006), 578, 4
[2] Irons, "Drawn to the Cross, Which Thou Hast Blessed," *Lutheran Service Book* (St. Louis: Concordia Publishing House, 2006), 560, 1

March 24
[1] *Luther's Small Catechism with Explanation* (St. Louis: Concordia Publishing House, 1991), 25
[2] Eber, "When in the Hour of Deepest Need," tr. Winkworth, *Lutheran Service Book* (St. Louis: Concordia Publishing House, 2006), 615, 3, 6

March 25
[1] von Spee, "O Darkest Woe," tr. Winkworth, *Lutheran Service Book* (St. Louis: Concordia Publishing House, 2006), 448, 1
[2] "At the Lamb's High Feast We Sing," tr. Campbell, *Lutheran Service Book* (St. Louis: Concordia Publishing House, 2006), 633, 6

March 26
[1] "Were You There," *Lutheran Service Book* (St. Louis: Concordia Publishing House, 2006), 456, 1-2
[2] Richard I. Abrams and Warner A. Hutchinson, *An Illustrated Life of Jesus: From the National Gallery of Art Collection* (Nashville: Abingdon Press, 1982), 118
[3] "The Resurrection of Our Lord: Collect of the Day," *Lutheran Service Book: Altar Book* (St. Louis: Concordia Publishing House, 2006), 595

March 27
[1] *Luther's Small Catechism with Explanation* (St. Louis: Concordia Publishing House, 1991), 14
[2] Homburg, "Christ, the Life of All the Living," tr. Winkworth, *Lutheran Service Book* (St. Louis: Concordia Publishing House, 2006), 420, 1

March 28
[1] Savonarola, "Jesus, Refuge of the Weary," tr. Wilde, *Lutheran Service Book* (St. Louis: Concordia Publishing House, 2006), 423, 2

March 29
[1] "Palm Sunday: Collect of the Day," *Lutheran Service Book: Altar Book* (St. Louis: Concordia Publishing House, 2006), 586

March 30

[1] Thring, "O God of Mercy, God of Might," *Lutheran Service Book* (St. Louis: Concordia Publishing House, 2006), 852, 4

March 31

[1] von Birken, "Jesus, I Will Ponder Now," tr. Crull, *Lutheran Service Book* (St. Louis: Concordia Publishing House, 2006), 440, 1

[2] "Tuesday in Holy Week: Collect of the Day," *Lutheran Service Book: Altar Book* (St. Louis: Concordia Publishing House, 2006), 588

April 1

[1] Luther, "Our Father, Who from Heaven Above," tr. *The Lutheran Hymnal*, 1941, *Lutheran Service Book* (St. Louis: Concordia Publishing House, 2006), 766, 9

April 2

[1] George Robinson, *Essential Judaism: A Complete Guide to Beliefs, Customs, and Rituals* (New York: Pocket Books, 2000), 120

[2] "The Litany," *Lutheran Service Book* (St. Louis: Concordia Publishing House, 2006), 288-289

[3] "Holy (Maundy) Thursday: Collect of the Day," *Lutheran Service Book: Altar Book* (St. Louis: Concordia Publishing House, 2006), 590

April 3

[1] Pollock, "Jesus, in Your Dying Woes," *Lutheran Service Book* (St. Louis: Concordia Publishing House, 2006), 447, 21

April 4

[1] Rambach, "Baptized into Your Name Most Holy," tr. Winkworth, *Lutheran Service Book* (St. Louis: Concordia Publishing House, 2006), 590, 1

April 5

[1] Rinckhart, "Now Thank We All Our God," tr. Winkworth, *Lutheran Service Book* (St. Louis: Concordia Publishing House, 2006), 895, 1

[2] Gerhardt, "Awake, My Heart, with Gladness," tr. Kelly, *Lutheran Service Book* (St. Louis: Concordia Publishing House, 2006), 467, 6

April 6

[1] Medley, "I Know That My Redeemer Lives," *Lutheran Service Book* (St. Louis: Concordia Publishing House, 2006), 461, 5

April 7

[1] "O Christ, Our Hope, Our Hearts' Desire," tr. Chandler, *Lutheran Service Book* (St. Louis: Concordia Publishing House, 2006), 553, 5

April 8

[1] von Zinzendorf, "Jesus, Lead Thou On," tr. Borthwick, *Lutheran Service Book* (St. Louis: Concordia Publishing House, 2006), 718, 4

April 9
[1] Rinckhart, "Now Thank We All Our God," tr. Winkworth, *Lutheran Service Book* (St. Louis: Concordia Publishing House, 2006), 895, 1

April 11
[1] Lyte, "Abide with Me," *Lutheran Service Book* (St. Louis: Concordia Publishing House, 2006), 878, 4
[2] Newton, "Amazing Grace," *Lutheran Service Book* (St. Louis: Concordia Publishing House, 2006), 744, 3
[3] Lyte, "Abide with Me," *Lutheran Service Book* (St. Louis: Concordia Publishing House, 2006), 878, 2

April 12
[1] Frederick J. Schumacher and Dorothy A. Zelenko, eds., *For All the Saints: A Prayer Book For and By the Church*, vol. 3 (Delhi, NY: American Lutheran Publicity Bureau, 1995), 1049
[2] Alford, "We Walk by Faith and Not by Sight," *Lutheran Service Book* (St. Louis: Concordia Publishing House, 2006), 720, 5

April 13
[1] cf. Hebrews 4:12
[2] Kua Wee Seng, "50 Million and Counting," *American Bible Society Record*, Spring/Summer 2008, 7-8

April 14
[1] Ralph Nader, *Unsafe at Any Speed: The Designed-In Dangers of the American Automobile* (New York: Grossman Publishers, 1965)
[2] Allen, "Today Your Mercy Calls Us," *Lutheran Service Book* (St. Louis: Concordia Publishing House, 2006), 915, 4

April 16
[1] Martin Luther, "Easter Sunday: Second Sermon, Mark 16:1-8," vol. II of *Sermon's of Martin Luther: The Church Postils*, ed. John Nicholas Lenker (Grand Rapids MI: Baker Books, 1995), 252
[2] Ibid., 253
[3] Reusner, "In Thee, Lord, have I Put My Trust," tr. Winkworth, *The Lutheran Hymnal* (St. Louis: Concordia Publishing House, 1941), 524, 1

April 17
[1] Newton, "On What Has Now Been Sown," *Lutheran Service Book* (St. Louis: Concordia Publishing House, 2006), 921, 2

April 18
[1] "Who Trusts in God a Strong Abode," tr. Kennedy, *Lutheran Service Book* (St. Louis: Concordia Publishing House, 2006), 714, 3

April 19
[1] Spafford, "When Peace, Like a River," *Lutheran Service Book* (St. Louis: Concordia Publishing House, 2006), 763, 4

April 20
[1] Juliane, "The Lord Hath Helped Me Hitherto," tr. Crull, *The Lutheran Hymnal* (St. Louis: Concordia Publishing House, 1941), 33, 3
[2] von Zinzendorf, "Jesus, Thy Blood and Righteousness," tr. Wesley, *Lutheran Service Book* (St. Louis: Concordia Publishing House, 2006), 563, 1
[3] *Luther's Small Catechism with Explanation* (St. Louis: Concordia Publishing House, 1991), 31

April 21
[1] Allen, "Today Your Mercy Calls Us," *Lutheran Service Book* (St. Louis: Concordia Publishing House, 2006), 915, 4
[2] Johann Friedrich Starck, *Starck's Prayer Book*, ed. W.H.T. Dau (St. Louis: Concordia Publishing House, 1921), 397

April 22
[1] Gerhardt, "Awake, My Heart, with Gladness," tr. Kelly, *Lutheran Service Book* (St. Louis: Concordia Publishing House, 2006), 467, 5
[2] "Te Deum," *Lutheran Service Book* (St. Louis: Concordia Publishing House, 2006) 223

April 23
[1] "Confirmation," *Lutheran Service Book* (St. Louis: Concordia Publishing House, 2006), 272-273
[2] Eric Metaxas, *Bonhoeffer: Pastor, Martyr, Prophet, Spy* (Nashville, TN: Thomas Nelson, 2010), 309
[3] "Holy Baptism," *Lutheran Service Book* (St. Louis: Concordia Publishing House, 2006), 268
[4] Maude, "Thine Forever, God of Love," *Lutheran Service Book* (St. Louis: Concordia Publishing House, 2006), 687, 1, 4

April 24
[1] Smith, "Immortal, Invisible, God Only Wise," *Lutheran Service Book* (St. Louis: Concordia Publishing House, 2006), 802, 1

April 25
[1] Nelson, "By All Your Saints in Warfare," *Lutheran Service Book* (St. Louis: Concordia Publishing House, 2006), 518, 15

April 26
[1] Hopper, "Jesus, Savior, Pilot Me," *Lutheran Service Book* (St. Louis: Concordia Publishing House, 2006), 715, 3

April 27
[1] James Madison, "The Federalist No. 51," in Alexander Hamilton, James Madison, and John Jay, *The Federalist: A Commentary on the Constitution of the United States being a Collection of Essays Written in Support of the Constitution Agreed upon September 17, 1787, by The Federal Convention*, ed. Sherman F. Mitchell (Washington: National Home Library Foundation, 1937), 337
[2] *Luther's Small Catechism with Explanation* (St. Louis: Concordia Publishing House, 1991), 18-19

April 28
[1] Wesley, "Forth in Thy Name, O Lord, I Go," *Lutheran Service Book* (St. Louis: Concordia Publishing House, 2006), 854, 1

April 29
[1] "For Guidance in Our Calling: Collect 193," *Lutheran Service Book* (St. Louis: Concordia Publishing House, 2006), 311

May 1
[1] Leeson, "Gracious Savior, Gentle Shepherd," *The Lutheran Hymnal* (St. Louis: Concordia Publishing House, 1941), 627, 2

May 3
[1] Fick, "Rise, Thou Light of Gentile Nations," tr. composite, *The Lutheran Hymnal* (St. Louis: Concordia Publishing House, 1941), 498, 6

May 4
[1] LC 1.2 in *The Book of Concord: The Confessions of the Evangelical Lutheran Church*, tr. and ed. Theodore Tappert, in collaboration with Jaroslav Pelikan, Robert H. Fischer, and Arthur C. Piepkorn (Philadephia: Fortress Press, 1959), 365
[2] Ruopp, "Renew Me, O Eternal Light," tr. Crull, *Lutheran Service Book* (St. Louis: Concordia Publishing House, 2006), 704, 4

May 5
[1] "Grace To Receive the Word: Collect 148," *Lutheran Service Book* (St. Louis: Concordia Publishing House, 2006), 308

May 6
[1] Newton, "Amazing Grace," *Lutheran Service Book* (St. Louis: Concordia Publishing House, 2006), 744, 3
[2] Toplady, "Rock of Ages, Cleft for Me," *Lutheran Service Book* (St. Louis: Concordia Publishing House, 2006), 761, 2

May 7
[1] Watts, "Joy to the World," *Lutheran Service Book* (St. Louis: Concordia Publishing House, 2006), 387, 4

May 8
[1] Mote, "My Hope Is Built on Nothing Less," *Lutheran Service Book* (St. Louis: Concordia Publishing House, 2006), 575, 3 and refrain

May 9
[1] Grigg, "Jesus, and Shall It Ever Be," *The Lutheran Hymnal* (St. Louis: Concordia Publishing House, 1941), 346, 4

May 10
[1] Rinckhart, "Now Thank We All Our God," tr. Winkworth, *Lutheran Service Book* (St. Louis: Concordia Publishing House, 2006), 895, 1

May 11

[1] LC 1.107-108 in *The Book of Concord: The Confessions of the Evangelical Lutheran Church*, tr. and ed. Theodore Tappert, in collaboration with Jaroslav Pelikan, Robert H. Fischer, and Arthur C. Piepkorn (Philadephia: Fortress Press, 1959), 379

[2] Helmbold, "Lord, Help Us Ever to Retain," tr. Loy, *Lutheran Service Book* (St. Louis: Concordia Publishing House, 2006), 865, 1

May 14

[1] Doane, "You Are the Way; through You Alone," *Lutheran Service Book* (St. Louis: Concordia Publishing House, 2006), 526, 4

May 15

[1] C.F.W. Walther, *Law and Gospel: How to Read and Apply the Bible*, ed. Charles P. Schaum, John P. Hellwege, Jr., and Thomas E. Manteufel, tr. Christian C. Tiews (St. Louis: Concordia Publishing House, 2010) 458-459

[2] Reusner, "In Thee, Lord, Have I Put My Trust," tr. Winkworth, *The Lutheran Hymnal* (St. Louis: Concordia Publishing House, 2006), 524, 1

[3] Fischer, "Lord Jesus, Who Art Come," tr. composite, *The Lutheran Hymnal* (St. Louis: Concordia Publishing House, 2006), 485, 5

May 16

[1] Abraham Lincoln, *Second Inaugural Address*, 1865

May 17

[1] Allen, "Today Your Mercy Calls Us," *Lutheran Service Book* (St. Louis: Concordia Publishing House, 2006), 915, 4

[2] Gellert, "Jesus Lives! The Victory's Won," tr. Cox, *Lutheran Service Book* (St. Louis: Concordia Publishing House, 2006), 490, 5

[3] Havergal, "I Am Trusting Thee, Lord Jesus," *Lutheran Service Book* (St. Louis: Concordia Publishing House, 2006), 729, 6

May 18

[1] Gerhardt, "Awake, My Heart, with Gladness," tr. Kelly, *Lutheran Service Book* (St. Louis: Concordia Publishing House, 2006), 467, 3

May 19

[1] Leeson, "Gracious Savior, Gentle Shepherd," *The Lutheran Hymnal* (St. Louis: Concordia Publishing House, 1941), 627, 5

May 20

[1] Juliane, "Who Knows When Death May Overtake Me," tr. composite, *The Lutheran Hymnal* (St. Louis: Concordia Publishing House, 1941), 598, 3

May 21

[1] Schröder, "One Thing's Needful," tr. Cox, *Lutheran Service Book* (St. Louis: Concordia Publishing House, 2006), 536, 3

May 22
[1] Wortman, "God of the Prophets, Bless the Prophets' Sons," *Lutheran Service Book* (St. Louis: Concordia Publishing House, 2006), 682, 1

May 23
[1] Havergal, "Now the Light Has Gone Away," *Lutheran Service Book* (St. Louis: Concordia Publishing House, 2006), 887, 2-3

May 24
[1] Albert S. Cook, "The 'Authorized Version' and Its Influence," in Adolphus William Ward and A.R. Waller, *The Cambridge History of English Literature*, vol. 4 (New York: G.P. Putnam's Sons, 1910), 48
[2] "For the Holy Spirit: Collect 183" *Lutheran Service Book* (St. Louis: Concordia Publishing House, 2006), 310

May 25
[1] "In Times of War: Collect 228," *Lutheran Service Book* (St. Louis: Concordia Publishing House, 2006), 313

May 26
[1] C.S. Lewis, *The Problem of Pain* (New York: Macmillan, 1962), 83-84
[2] "O Christ, Our Hope, Our Hearts' Desire," tr. Chandler, *Lutheran Service Book* (St. Louis: Concordia Publishing House, 2006), 553, 4

May 27
[1] von Zinzendorf, "Jesus, Lead Thou On," tr. Borthwick, *Lutheran Service Book* (St. Louis: Concordia Publishing House, 2006), 718, 3-4

May 29
[1] "Collect 441," *Lutheran Service Book* (St. Louis: Concordia Publishing House, 2006), 295

May 31
[1] "Grace To Receive the Word: Collect 148," *Lutheran Service Book* (St. Louis: Concordia Publishing House, 2006), 308

June 1
[1] Mentzer, "Oh, That I Had a Thousand Voices," tr. *The Lutheran Hymnal*, *Lutheran Service Book* (St. Louis: Concordia Publishing House, 2006), 811, 3

June 2
[1] Lee Kwan Yew in Peggy Noonan, "A Statesman's Friendly Advice: Singapore's Lee Kwan Yew on What Makes America Great – and What Threatens Its Greatness," *The Wall Street Journal* (New York) April 4, 2013
[2] Cawood, "Almighty God, Your Word Is Cast," *Lutheran Service Book* (St. Louis: Concordia Publishing House, 2006), 577, 4

June 3
[1] C.S. Lewis, *A Grief Observed* (New York: Seabury Press, 1961)
[2] Alford, "We Walk by Faith and Not by Sight," *Lutheran Service Book* (St. Louis: Concordia Publishing House, 2006), 720, 1, 3

June 4
[1] Whiting, "Eternal Father, Strong to Save," *Lutheran Service Book* (St. Louis: Concordia Publishing House, 2006), 717, 4

June 5
[1] Gerhardt, "Rejoice, My Heart, Be Glad and Sing," tr. Kelly, *Lutheran Service Book* (St. Louis: Concordia Publishing House, 2006), 737, 1-2
[2] Luther, "May God Bestow on Us His Grace," tr. Massie, *Lutheran Service Book* (St. Louis: Concordia Publishing House, 2006), 823, 3

June 6
[1] Franklin D. Roosevelt, "D-Day Prayer," The History Place Great Speeches Collection, accessed December 8, 2014, http://www.historyplace.com/speeches/fdr-prayer.htm
[2] "In Times of War: Collect 228," *Lutheran Service Book* (St. Louis: Concordia Publishing House, 2006), 313

June 7
[1] Reusner, "I Trust, O Lord, Your Holy Name," tr. Winkworth, *Lutheran Service Book* (St. Louis: Concordia Publishing House, 2006), 734, 4

June 8
[1] "For Divine Guidance: Collect 188," *Lutheran Service Book* (St. Louis: Concordia Publishing House, 2006), 310

June 9
[1] Robinson, "Come, Thou Fount of Every Blessing," *Lutheran Service Book* (St. Louis: Concordia Publishing House, 2006), 686, 3

June 11
[1] Ellerton, "O Father, All Creating," *Lutheran Service Book* (St. Louis: Concordia Publishing House, 2006), 858, 3

June 12
[1] Oswald Chambers, "March 8," *My Utmost for His Highest: Selections for the Year* (New York: Dodd, Mead & Company, 1935)
[2] Havergal, "Now the Light Has Gone Away," *Lutheran Service Book* (St. Louis: Concordia Publishing House, 2006), 887, 2
[3] *Luther's Small Catechism with Explanation* (St. Louis: Concordia Publishing House, 1991), 31

June 13
[1] Medley, "I Know That My Redeemer Lives," *Lutheran Service Book* (St. Louis: Concordia Publishing House, 2006), 461, 5, 8

June 14
[1] Key, "The Star-Spangled Banner," 1814
[2] Key, "Before You, Lord, We Bow," *Lutheran Service Book* (St. Louis: Concordia Publishing House, 2006), 966, 5

June 15
[1] Johann Friedrich Starck, *Starck's Prayer Book*, ed. W.H.T. Dau (St. Louis: Concordia Publishing House, 1921), 263

June 17
[1] Dietrich Bonhoeffer, *Life Together: The Classic Exploration of Christian Community*, tr. Doberstein (New York: Harper & Row Publishers), 50
[2] Ibid., 57
[3] Ibid., 50-51

June 19
[1] Eric Morath, "Aging Americans Sleep More, Work Less, Survey Finds," *The Wall Street Journal* (New York), June 19, 2014

June 20
[1] *Luther's Small Catechism with Explanation* (St. Louis: Concordia Publishing House, 1991), 22
[2] "Six Reasons Young Christians Leave Church," *Barna Group*, Sept. 28, 2011, https://www.barna.org/teens-next-gen-articles/528-six-reasons-young-christians-leave-church
[3] Johann Friedrich Starck, *Starck's Prayer Book*, ed. W.H.T. Dau (St. Louis: Concordia Publishing House, 1921), 240

June 21
[1] von Pfeil, "Oh, Blest the House," tr. Winkworth, *Lutheran Service Book* (St. Louis: Concordia Publishing House, 2006), 862, 4

June 22
[1] Numbers 6:25

June 23
[1] "For Patience: Collect 217," *Lutheran Service Book* (St. Louis: Concordia Publishing House, 2006), 312

June 24
[1] Dorothy Frances Gurney, "God's Garden."
[2] "Jerusalem, My Happy Home," *Lutheran Service Book* (St. Louis: Concordia Publishing House, 2006), 673, 2, 6

June 25

[1] Cathy Lynn Grossman, "For Many, 'Losing My Religion' Isn't Just a Song: It's Life," *USA Today* (McLean, VA), Jan. 3, 2012

[2] *Luther's Small Catechism with Explanation* (St. Louis: Concordia Publishing House, 1991), 42

[3] Hastings, "Delay Not, Delay Not, O Sinner, Draw Near," *The Lutheran Hymnal* (St. Louis: Concordia Publishing House, 1941), 278, 5

June 26

[1] Paul Wilkes, "The Hands That Would Shape Our Souls," *The Atlantic Monthly*, vol. 266, no. 6 (December 1990), 59

[2] Osler, "Lord of the Church, We Humbly Pray," *The Lutheran Hymnal* (St. Louis: Concordia Publishing House, 2006), 489, 1

June 27

[1] Roland H. Bainton, *Here I Stand: A Life of Martin Luther* (New York: Abingdon-Cokesbury Press, 1950), 290

[2] Ibid., 289

June 28

[1] Chaeyoon Lim and Robert D. Putnam, "Religion, Social Networks, and Life Satisfaction," *American Sociological Review* 75 (December 2010): 914-933

[2] Jacobs, "Lord Jesus Christ, We Humbly Pray," *Lutheran Service Book* (St. Louis: Concordia Publishing House, 2006), 623, 4-5

June 29

[1] Ken, "All Praise to Thee, My God, This Night," *Lutheran Service Book* (St. Louis: Concordia Publishing House, 2006), 883, 5, 4

[2] Gerhardt, "Now Rest Beneath Night's Shadow," *The Lutheran Hymnal* (St. Louis: Concordia Publishing House, 1941), 554, 5

June 30

[1] Iona Opie and Peter Opie, *The Oxford Dictionary of Nursery Rhymes* (Oxford University Press, 1997), 213-215

[2] Ellerton, "Savior, Again to Thy Dear Name We Raise," *Lutheran Service Book* (St. Louis: Concordia Publishing House, 2006), 917, 4

July 1

[1] James Madison, "The Federalist No. 51," in Alexander Hamilton, James Madison, and John Jay, *The Federalist: A Commentary on the Constitution of the United States being a Collection of Essays Written in Support of the Constitution Agreed upon September 17, 1787, by The Federal Convention*, ed. Sherman F. Mitchell (Washington: National Home Library Foundation, 1937), 340

[2] Key, "Before You, Lord, We Bow," *Lutheran Service Book* (St. Louis: Concordia Publishing House, 2006), 966, 3

July 2
1   "A Confederate Soldier's Prayer."
2   Franck, "Jesus, Priceless Treasure," tr. Winkworth, *Lutheran Service Book* (St. Louis: Concordia Publishing House, 2006), 743, 4

July 3
1   David McCullough, *John Adams* (New York: Touchstone, 2002), 127
2   Ibid., 130

July 4
1   Maya Jasanoff, "Loyal to a Fault," *The New York Times Magazine*, Jul. 1, 2007, 20
2   Fosdick, "God of Grace and God of Glory," *Lutheran Service Book* (St. Louis: Concordia Publishing House, 2006), 850, 4

July 5
1   Anonymous

July 6
1   Johann Friedrich Starck, *Starck's Prayer Book*, ed. W.H.T. Dau (St. Louis: Concordia Publishing House, 1921), 217

July 7
1   From the Latin phrase: *repetitio est mater studiorum*
2   Oswald Chambers, "July 4," *My Utmost for His Highest: Selections for the Year* (New York: Dodd, Mead & Company, 1935)
3   Gerhardt, "Rejoice, My Heart, Be Glad and Sing," tr. Kelly, *Lutheran Service Book* (St. Louis: Concordia Publishing House, 2006), 737, 6
4   *Luther's Small Catechism with Explanation* (St. Louis: Concordia Publishing House, 1991), 30-31

July 8
1   Richard Baxter, *The Saints Everlasting Rest*, abridged by Benjamin Fawcett (New York: American Tract Society, 1850), 122-123
2   Ringwaldt, "The Day Is Surely Drawing Near," tr. Peter, *Lutheran Service Book* (St. Louis: Concordia Publishing House, 2006), 508, 1
3   Johann Gerhard, *Loci*, "De Inferno," Section (§) 69
4   Richard Baxter, *The Saints Everlasting Rest*, abridged by Benjamin Fawcett (New York: American Tract Society, 1850), 80
5   Ringwaldt, "The Day Is Surely Drawing Near," tr. Peter, *Lutheran Service Book* (St. Louis: Concordia Publishing House, 2006), 508, 6

July 9
1   Denicke, "How Can I thank You, Lord," tr. Crull, *Lutheran Service Book* (St. Louis: Concordia Publishing House, 2006), 703, 1

July 10
1 *Lutheran Service Book* (St. Louis: Concordia Publishing House, 2006), 268
2 For further information about Enoch, read Genesis 4:17-18, Genesis 5:24, and Hebrews 11:5
3 McComb, "Chief of Sinners Though I Be," *Lutheran Service Book* (St. Louis: Concordia Publishing House, 2006), 611, 3

July 11
1 Frank B. St. John, "I Do Not Come Because My Soul," *The Lutheran Hymnal* (St. Louis: Concordia Publishing House, 1941), 379, 1, 4

July 12
1 Thomas G. Long, *The Witness of Preaching*, 2nd ed., (Louisville, KY: Westminster John Knox Press, 2005), 49
2 Ibid., 48

July 13
1 Schalling, "Lord, Thee I Love with All My Heart," tr. Winkworth, *Lutheran Service Book* (St. Louis: Concordia Publishing House, 2006), 708, 1

July 15
1 Luke 11:1
2 Heermann, "O God, My Faithful God," tr. Winkworth, *Lutheran Service Book* (St. Louis: Concordia Publishing House, 2006), 696, 2

July 16
1 Thomas J. DiLorenzo, *The Real Lincoln: A New Look at Abraham Lincoln, His Agenda, and an Unnecessary War* (New York: Three Rivers Press, 2003), 38
2 "Alleluia, Song of Gladness," tr. Neale, *Lutheran Service Book* (St. Louis: Concordia Publishing House, 2006), 417, 3
3 Ibid., 4

July 17
1 Grant, "O Worship the King," *Lutheran Service Book* (St. Louis: Concordia Publishing House, 2006), 804, 6

July 19
1 Moore, "Come, Ye Disconsolate," *The Lutheran Hymnal* (St. Louis: Concordia Publishing House, 1941), 531, 2
2 Schmolck, "Open Now Thy Gates of Beauty," tr. Winkworth, *Lutheran Service Book* (St. Louis: Concordia Publishing House, 2006), 901, 5

July 20
1 Psalm 19:1
2 Neander, "Praise to the Lord, the Almighty," tr. Winkworth, *Lutheran Service Book* (St. Louis: Concordia Publishing House, 2006), 790, 5

July 21
[1] "Forever Left Untold," *St. Louis Post-Dispatch* (St. Louis, MO), October 27, 2014, B1
[2] Clare Booth Luce in Letitia Baldrige, *Roman Candle* (Boston: Houghton Mifflin, 1956), 129
[3] Schütz, "Sing Praise to God, the Highest God," tr. Cox, *Lutheran Service Book* (St. Louis: Concordia Publishing House, 2006), 819, 2
[4] Luther, "These Are the Holy Ten Commands," tr. *Christian Worship*, 1928, *Lutheran Service Book* (St. Louis: Concordia Publishing House, 2006), 581, 12

July 22
[1] von Zinzendorf, "Jesus, Thy Blood and Righteousness," tr. Wesley, *Lutheran Service Book* (St. Louis: Concordia Publishing House, 2006), 563, 1-2

July 23
[1] "How Firm a Foundation," *Lutheran Service Book* (St. Louis: Concordia Publishing House, 2006), 728, 3
[2] Havergal, "I Am Trusting Thee, Lord Jesus," *Lutheran Service Book* (St. Louis: Concordia Publishing House, 2006), 729, 4, 6

July 24
[1] Wismar, "In Holy Conversation," *Lutheran Service Book* (St. Louis: Concordia Publishing House, 2006), 772, 2
[2] Havergal, "Now the Light Has Gone Away," *Lutheran Service Book* (St. Louis: Concordia Publishing House, 2006), 887, 1-3

July 25
[1] C.F.W. Walther, *Law and Gospel: How to Read and Apply the Bible*, ed. Charles P. Schaum, John P. Hellwege, Jr., and Thomas E. Manteufel, tr. Christian C. Tiews (St. Louis: Concordia Publishing House, 2010), 350
[2] Nelson, "By All Your Saints in Warfare," *Lutheran Service Book* (St. Louis: Concordia Publishing House, 2006), 518, 21

July 26
[1] Scriven, "What a Friend We Have in Jesus," *Lutheran Service Book* (St. Louis: Concordia Publishing House, 2006), 770, 2
[2] Newton, "Glorious Things of You Are Spoken," *Lutheran Service Book* (St. Louis: Concordia Publishing House, 2006), 648, 1

July 27
[1] Ken, "Awake, My Soul, and with the Sun," *Lutheran Service Book* (St. Louis: Concordia Publishing House, 2006), 868, 1, 3

July 28
[1] Heermann, "O God, My Faithful God," tr. Winkworth, *Lutheran Service Book* (St. Louis: Concordia Publishing House, 2006), 696, 4

July 29

[1] Watts, "O God, Our Help in Ages Past," *Lutheran Service Book* (St. Louis: Concordia Publishing House, 2006), 733, 1

[2] Monsell, "Fight the Good Fight," *Lutheran Service Book* (St. Louis: Concordia Publishing House, 2006), 664, 4

[3] "For Pardon, Growth in Grace, and Divine Protection: Collect 159," *Lutheran Service Book* (St. Louis: Concordia Publishing House, 2006), 309

July 30

[1] Peter L. Steinke, *A Door Set Open: Grounding Change in Mission and Hope* (Herndon, VA: The Alban Institute, 2010), 2

[2] James Davidson Hunter, *To Change the World: The Irony, Tragedy, and Possibility of Christianity in the Late Modern World* (Oxford: Oxford University Press, 2010), 105

[3] Rees, "Holy Spirit, Ever Dwelling," *Lutheran Service Book* (St. Louis: Concordia Publishing House, 2006), 650, 2

July 31

[1] Havergal, "Take My Life and Let It Be," *Lutheran Service Book* (St. Louis: Concordia Publishing House, 2006), 784, 1, 4

August 1

[1] Amy Gamerman, "The Porch Is Making a Comeback," *The Wall Street Journal*, July 24, 2014, M8

[2] Mark Dunkelman, *The Vanishing Neighbor: The Transformation of American Community* (New York: W.W. Norton & Company, 2014), xi-xii

August 2

[1] Martin Luther, "Preface to the Epistle of St. Paul to the Romans," in *Word and Sacrament I*, ed. E. Theodore Bachmann, vol. 35 of *Luther's Works*, ed. Jaroslav Pelikan and Helmut T. Lehmann (Philadelphia: Muhlenberg/Fortress Press; St. Louis: Concordia Publishing House, 1960), 370-371

[2] Rambach, "Baptized into Your Name Most Holy," tr. Winkworth, *Lutheran Service Book* (St. Louis: Concordia Publishing House, 2006), 590, 4

August 3

[1] *Lutheran Service Book* (St. Louis: Concordia Publishing House, 2006), 151

[2] Franck, "O God, Forsake Me Not," tr. Crull, *Lutheran Service Book* (St. Louis: Concordia Publishing House, 2006), 731, 2

August 4

[1] Elinor Markgraf, "Being Sick Is Worthwhile If We've Not Run Out of Milk," *The Oregonian* (Portland, OR), May 15, 2004

[2] Thring, "O God of Mercy, God of Might," *Lutheran Service Book* (St. Louis: Concordia Publishing House, 2006), 852, 1, 5

August 7

[1] Schröder, "One Thing's Needful," tr. Cox, *Lutheran Service Book* (St. Louis: Concordia Publishing House, 2006), 536, 1

August 8

1 Allen, "Today Your Mercy Calls Us," *Lutheran Service Book* (St. Louis: Concordia Publishing House, 2006), 915, 2

2 Doane, "You Are the Way; through You Alone," *Lutheran Service Book* (St. Louis: Concordia Publishing House, 2006), 526, 4

August 9

1 Dix, "Come unto Me, Ye Weary," *Lutheran Service Book* (St. Louis: Concordia Publishing House, 2006), 684, 3

2 Ibid., 4

3 Havergal, "O Savior, Precious Savior," *Lutheran Service Book* (St. Louis: Concordia Publishing House, 2006), 527, 2

August 10

1 Gerhardt, "Jesus, Thy Boundless Love to Me," tr. Wesley, *Lutheran Service Book* (St. Louis: Concordia Publishing House, 2006), 683, 2

August 11

1 Ken, "All Praise to Thee, My God, This Night," *Lutheran Service Book* (St. Louis: Concordia Publishing House, 2006), 883, 2, 4, 5

August 12

1 *Lutheran Service Book* (St. Louis: Concordia Publishing House, 2006), 151

August 13

1 Thring, "O God of Mercy, God of Might," *Lutheran Service Book* (St. Louis: Concordia Publishing House, 2006), 852, 4

August 14

1 St. Patrick, "I Bind unto Myself Today," tr. Alexander, *Lutheran Service Book* (St. Louis: Concordia Publishing House, 2006), 604, 3-5

2 "For the Holy Spirit: Collect 183," *Lutheran Service Book* (St. Louis: Concordia Publishing House, 2006), 310

August 15

1 Bridges, "Crown Him with Many Crowns," *Lutheran Service Book* (St. Louis: Concordia Publishing House, 2006), 525, 2

2 Nelson, "By All Your Saints in Warfare," *Lutheran Service Book* (St. Louis: Concordia Publishing House, 2006), 518, 22

August 16

1 "Tryst" – An agreement, as between lovers, to meet at a certain time and place: *The American Heritage Dictionary of the English Language* (Boston: Houghton Mifflin, 2000)

2 MacKellar, "Come Ye Apart and Rest a While," 4-6, in Johann Friedrich Starck, *Starck's Prayer Book*, tr. W.H.T. Dau (St. Louis: Concordia Publishing House, 1921), 14-15

August 17
1 Oswald Chambers, "August 17," *My Utmost for His Highest: Selections for the Year* (New York: Dodd, Mead & Company, 1935)
2 "For Divine Guidance: Collect 188," *Lutheran Service Book* (St. Louis: Concordia Publishing House, 2006), 310

August 18
1 David Kinnaman and Gabe Lyons, *unChristian: What a New Generation Really Thinks About Christianity... and Why It Matters* (Grand Rapids, MI: Baker Books, 2007), 24
2 Ibid., 29
3 Ibid., 42
4 Ibid., 60
5 Heermann, "O God, My Faithful God," tr. Winkworth, *Lutheran Service Book* (St. Louis: Concordia Publishing House, 2006), 696, 4

August 19
1 "Proper 21: Collect of the Day," *Lutheran Service Book: Altar Book* (St. Louis: Concordia Publishing House, 2006), 638

August 20
1 Newton, "Amazing Grace," *Lutheran Service Book* (St. Louis: Concordia Publishing House, 2006), 744, 2
2 Spafford, "When Peace, Like a River," *Lutheran Service Book* (St. Louis: Concordia Publishing House, 2006), 763, 1

August 21
1 Monsell, "Fight the Good Fight," *Lutheran Service Book* (St. Louis: Concordia Publishing House, 2006), 664, 2, 4

August 22
1 Thomas G. Long, *The Witness of Preaching*, 2nd ed. (Louisville, KY: Westminster John Knox Press, 2005), 48
2 *The Augsburg Confession, Article 5.3* in *The Book of Concord: The Confessions of the Evangelical Lutheran Church*, ed. Robert Kolb and Timothy J. Wengert, tr. Charles Arand, Eric Ritsch, Robert Kolb, William Russell, James Schaaf, Jane Strohl, and Timothy J. Wengert (Minneapolis: Fortress Press, 2000), 40
3 Ibid., *Article 4.1-3*, 39, 41
4 Maurus, "Come, Holy Ghost, Creator Blest," tr. Caswall, *Lutheran Service Book* (St. Louis: Concordia Publishing House, 2006), 498, 6

August 23
1 "Holy Matrimony," *Lutheran Service Book* (St. Louis: Concordia Publishing House, 2006), 276

August 24
1 Robert V. Remini, *The House: The History of the House of Representatives* (New York: Smithsonian Books, 2006), 98

August 25
[1] von Hayn, "I Am Jesus' Little Lamb," tr. *The Lutheran Hymnal*, 1941, *Lutheran Service Book* (St. Louis: Concordia Publishing House, 2006), 740, 2

August 26
[1] Smith, "Immortal, Invisible, God Only Wise," *Lutheran Service Book* (St. Louis: Concordia Publishing House, 2006), 802, 1, 4

August 27
[1] Saint Augustine, *Confessions*, tr. Albert C. Outler (New York: Barnes and Noble Books, 2007), 21
[2] Scriven, "What a Friend We Have in Jesus," *Lutheran Service Book* (St. Louis: Concordia Publishing House, 2006), 770, 2

August 28
[1] Frederick J. Schumacher and Dorothy A. Zelenko, eds., *For All the Saints: A Prayer Book For and By the Church*, vol. 2 (Delhi, NY: American Lutheran Publicity Bureau, 1995)
[2] Thring, "O God of Mercy, God of Might," *Lutheran Service Book* (St. Louis: Concordia Publishing House, 2006), 852, 4

August 29
[1] Adapted from *Luther's Small Catechism with Explanation* (St. Louis: Concordia Publishing House, 1991), 14

August 30
[1] Gerhardt, "Awake, My Heart, with Gladness," tr. Kelly, *Lutheran Service Book* (St. Louis: Concordia Publishing House, 2006), 467, 3
[2] Gerhardt, "Why Should Cross and Trial Grieve Me," tr. *Christian Worship*, *Lutheran Service Book* (St. Louis: Concordia Publishing House, 2006), 756, 3

August 31
[1] Olearius, "Lord, Open Now My Heart," tr. Loy, *Lutheran Service Book* (St. Louis: Concordia Publishing House, 2006), 908, 1
[2] "Grace To Receive the Word: Collect 148," *Lutheran Service Book* (St. Louis: Concordia Publishing House, 2006), 308

September 2
[1] Logan, "O God of Jacob, by Whose Hand," *The Lutheran Hymnal* (St. Louis: Concordia Publishing House, 1941), 434, 5

September 3
[1] Gerhardt, "Rejoice, My Heart, Be Glad and Sing," tr. Kelly, *Lutheran Service Book* (St. Louis: Concordia Publishing House, 2006), 737, 3
[2] "All Depends on Our Possessing," tr. Winkworth, *Lutheran Service Book* (St. Louis: Concordia Publishing House, 2006), 732, 3

September 4

[1] From Dallas Willard, *The Divine Conspiracy: Rediscovering Our Hidden Life in God* (San Francisco: Harper San Francisco, 1998), in Patrick Kampert, "Has the Faith Race Passed You By?" *Chicago Tribune,* January 29, 2006

[2] Patrick Kampert, "Has the Faith Race Passed You By?" *Chicago Tribune,* January 29, 2006

[3] "What Wondrous Love Is This," *Lutheran Service Book* (St. Louis: Concordia Publishing House, 2006), 543, 1

September 5

[1] Heber, "God, Who Made the Earth and Heaven," *Lutheran Service Book* (St. Louis: Concordia Publishing House, 2006), 877, 1

September 6

[1] *The Meditations of Marcus Aurelius Antoninus: With the Manual of Epictetus, and a Summary of Christian Morality* (Longman, Brown, Green, and Longmans, 1844), 55

[2] Bonar, "I Heard the Voice of Jesus Say," *Lutheran Service Book* (St. Louis: Concordia Publishing House, 2006), 699, 1

[3] Lyte, "Abide with Me," *Lutheran Service Book* (St. Louis: Concordia Publishing House, 2006), 878, 4

September 7

[1] Elliott, "Just as I Am, without One Plea," *Lutheran Service Book* (St. Louis: Concordia Publishing House, 2006), 570

[2] "In God, My Faithful God," tr. Winkworth, *Lutheran Service Book* (St. Louis: Concordia Publishing House, 2006), 745, 4-5

September 8

[1] James Chace, *1912,* (New York: Simon & Schuster, 2004), 45

[2] "Seminaries and Colleges: Collect 116," *Lutheran Service Book* (St. Louis: Concordia Publishing House, 2006), 306

September 9

[1] Adolph Biewend in *Der Lutheraner*

[2] "When Morning Gilds the Skies," tr. Bridges, *Lutheran Service Book* (St. Louis: Concordia Publishing House, 2006), 807, 1

[3] Ken, "Awake, My Soul, and with the Sun," *Lutheran Service Book* (St. Louis: Concordia Publishing House, 2006), 868, 4-5

September 10

[1] Luther, "A Mighty Fortress Is Our God," tr. composite, *Lutheran Service Book* (St. Louis: Concordia Publishing House, 2006), 656, 2

[2] "Who Trusts in God a Strong Abode," tr. Kennedy, *Lutheran Service Book* (St. Louis: Concordia Publishing House, 2006), 714, 2

September 12

[1] Baker, "O God of Love, O King of Peace," *Lutheran Service Book* (St. Louis: Concordia Publishing House, 2006), 751, 1

September 15
[1] Oswald Chambers, "March 30," *My Utmost for His Highest: Selections for the Year* (New York: Dodd, Mead & Company, 1935)

September 16
[1] Quoted in Harold I. Lessem and George C. MacKenzie, *Fort McHenry National Monument and Historic Shrine, Maryland* (Washington: National Park Service, 1954, reprinted 1961)
[2] Key, "Before You, Lord, We Bow," *Lutheran Service Book* (St. Louis: Concordia Publishing House, 2006), 966, 2

September 17
[1] Ken, "Awake, My Soul, and with the Sun," *Lutheran Service Book* (St. Louis: Concordia Publishing House, 2006), 868, 4

September 18
[1] Franck, "Jesus, Priceless Treasure," tr. Winkworth, *Lutheran Service Book* (St. Louis: Concordia Publishing House, 2006), 743, 6

September 19
[1] Johann Friedrich Starck, *Starck's Prayer Book*, ed. W.H.T. Dau (St. Louis: Concordia Publishing House, 1921), 253

September 20
[1] Olearius, "Comfort, Comfort Ye My People," tr. Winkworth, *Lutheran Service Book* (St. Louis: Concordia Publishing House, 2006), 347, 4
[2] "For Humility: Collect 216," *Lutheran Service Book* (St. Louis: Concordia Publishing House, 2006), 312

September 21
[1] Leroy Barber in David Kinnaman and Gabe Lyons, *unChristian: What a New Generation Really Thinks About Christianity... and Why It Matters* (Grand Rapids, MI: Baker Books, 2007), 24
[2] Bathurst, "Oh, for a Faith That Will Not Shrink," *The Lutheran Hymnal* (St. Louis: Concordia Publishing House, 1941), 396, 6
[3] Nelson, "By All Your Saints in Warfare," *Lutheran Service Book* (St. Louis: Concordia Publishing House, 2006), 518, 25

September 22
[1] Ken, "All Praise to Thee, My God, This Night," *Lutheran Service Book* (St. Louis: Concordia Publishing House, 2006), 883, 4

September 23
[1] von Zinzendorf, "Jesus, Thy Blood and Righteousness," tr. Wesley, *Lutheran Service Book* (St. Louis: Concordia Publishing House, 2006), 563, 3

September 24
[1] Barry Koltnow, "Classic Movie Lines Keep on Coming," *The Orange County Register* (Santa Ana, CA), November 18, 2007
[2] Actual line from *Field of Dreams* is: "If you build it, he will come."
[3] Grundtvig, "God's Word Is Our Great Heritage," tr. Belsheim, *Lutheran Service Book* (St. Louis: Concordia Publishing House, 2006), 582

September 25
[1] Kingo, "All Who Believe and Are Baptized," tr. Rygh, *Lutheran Service Book* (St. Louis: Concordia Publishing House, 2006), 601, 2

September 26
[1] Adapted from *Luther's Small Catechism with Explanation* (St. Louis: Concordia Publishing House, 1991), 20

September 27
[1] Schalling, "Lord, Thee I Love with All My Heart," tr. Winkworth, *Lutheran Service Book* (St. Louis: Concordia Publishing House, 2006), 708, 3

September 28
[1] Newton, "Come, My Soul, with Every Care," *Lutheran Service Book* (St. Louis: Concordia Publishing House, 2006), 779, 2
[2] "For the Sick: Collect 254," *Lutheran Service Book* (St. Louis: Concordia Publishing House, 2006), 316

September 29
[1] Montgomery, "Angels from the Realms of Glory," *Lutheran Service Book* (St. Louis: Concordia Publishing House, 2006), 367, 1
[2] Joseph the Hymnographer, "Stars of the Morning, So Gloriously Bright," tr. Neale, *Lutheran Service Book* (St. Louis: Concordia Publishing House, 2006), 520, 4

September 30
[1] Lyte, "Praise, My Soul, the King of Heaven," *Lutheran Service Book* (St. Louis: Concordia Publishing House, 2006), 793, 3

October 1
[1] C.S. Lewis, *The Problem of Pain* (New York: Macmillan, 1962), 115
[2] Gerhardt, "Why Should Cross and Trial Grieve Me," tr. *Christian Worship*, 1933, *Lutheran Service Book* (St. Louis: Concordia Publishing House, 2006), 756, 1

October 2
[1] Attributed to Alan of Lille, twelfth century
[2] *Luther's Small Catechism with Explanation* (St. Louis: Concordia Publishing House, 1991), 18

October 3
[1] *Luther's Small Catechism with Explanation* (St. Louis: Concordia Publishing House, 1991), 13
[2] Schenck, "Now, the Hour of Worship O'er," tr. Kaiser, *The Lutheran Hymnal* (St. Louis: Concordia Publishing House, 1941), 45, 3

October 4
[1] Conder, "Lord, 'Tis Not That I Did Choose Thee," *Lutheran Service Book* (St. Louis: Concordia Publishing House, 2006), 573, 1

October 5
[1] Peter L. Steinke, *A Door Set Open: Grounding Change in Mission and Hope* (Herndon, VA: The Alban Institute, 2010), 3

October 6
[1] Lyte, "Abide with Me," *Lutheran Service Book* (St. Louis: Concordia Publishing House, 2006), 878, 2
[2] From the Latin phrase: *Memoria est thesaurus omnium rerum e custos* (Cicero – *De Oratore*. I. 5.)
[3] Steele, "Father of Mercies, in Thy Word," *The Lutheran Hymnal* (St. Louis: Concordia Publishing House, 1941), 284, 1, 3, 5-6

October 7
[1] Luther, "Our Father, Who from Heaven Above," tr. *The Lutheran Hymnal*, 1941, *Lutheran Service Book* (St. Louis: Concordia Publishing House, 2006), 766, 6

October 8
[1] Third person: Use of the pronouns "he," "she," or "it" when referring to a person, place, thing, or idea
[2] *St. Augustine's Confessions*, tr. William Watts, Vol. 1 (Cambridge, MA: Harvard University Press, 1912), 3
[3] Second person: Use of the pronouns "you," "your," or "yours," or use of a specific name or title (e.g., Father), when referring to a person or persons
[4] Adapted from *Luther's Small Catechism with Explanation* (St. Louis: Concordia Publishing House, 1991), 17

October 9
[1] Synesius of Cyrene, "Lord Jesus, Think on Me," tr. Chatfield, *Lutheran Service Book* (St. Louis: Concordia Publishing House, 2006), 610, 1

October 10
[1] Robinson, "Come, Thou Fount of Every Blessing," *Lutheran Service Book* (St. Louis: Concordia Publishing House, 2006), 686, 3
[2] Allen, "Today Your Mercy Calls Us," *Lutheran Service Book* (St. Louis: Concordia Publishing House, 2006), 915, 4

October 11
[1] *Luther's Small Catechism with Explanation* (St. Louis: Concordia Publishing House, 1991), 18-19
[2] Arnold Kuntz, "Till Only One Thing Matters," *Devotions for the Chronologically Gifted*, ed. Les Bayer (St. Louis: Concordia Publishing House, 1999), 46
[3] How, "We Give Thee But Thine Own," *Lutheran Service Book* (St. Louis: Concordia Publishing House, 2006), 781, 1

October 12
[1] "For Guidance in Our Calling: Collect 193," *Lutheran Service Book* (St. Louis: Concordia Publishing House, 2006), 311

October 13
[1] Carol Kent, *Tame Your Fears: And Transform Them into Faith, Confidence, and Action* (Carol Stream, IL: NavPress, 2003)
[2] Scriven "What a Friend We Have in Jesus," *Lutheran Service Book* (St. Louis: Concordia Publishing House, 2006), 770, 2

October 14
[1] Dietrich Bonhoeffer, *Life Together: The Classic Exploration of Christian Community*, tr. Doberstein (New York: Harper & Row Publishers), 85
[2] Robinson, "Come, Thou Fount of Every Blessing," *Lutheran Service Book* (St. Louis: Concordia Publishing House, 2006), 686, 3

October 15
[1] Juvenal (Satire 14, 105-106)
[2] Erich Gruen, *Diaspora: Jews amidst Greeks and Romans* (Cambridge, MA: Harvard University Press, 2004), 48
[3] Abbreviated from "Defending the Church from Error: Collect 109," *Lutheran Service Book* (St. Louis: Concordia Publishing House, 2006), 305

October 17
[1] "For the Church: Collect 102," *Lutheran Service Book* (St. Louis: Concordia Publishing House, 2006), 305

October 18
[1] Nelson, "By All Your Saints in Warfare," *Lutheran Service Book* (St. Louis: Concordia Publishing House, 2006), 518, 26

October 19
[1] Neumeister, "Jesus Sinners Doth Receive," tr. *The Lutheran Hymnal*, 1941, *Lutheran Service Book* (St. Louis: Concordia Publishing House, 2006), 609, 5

October 20
[1] Ellerton, "O Father, All Creating," *Lutheran Service Book* (St. Louis: Concordia Publishing House, 2006), 858, 4

October 21
[1] Oswald Chambers, "October 31," *My Utmost for His Highest: Selections for the Year* (New York: Dodd, Mead & Company, 1935)
[2] Neumark, "If Thou But Trust in God to Guide Thee," tr. Winkworth, *Lutheran Service Book* (St. Louis: Concordia Publishing House, 2006), 750, 7

October 22
[1] "How Firm a Foundation," *Lutheran Service Book* (St. Louis: Concordia Publishing House, 2006), 728, 5
[2] Schalling, "Lord, Thee I Love with All My Heart," tr. Winkworth, *Lutheran Service Book* (St. Louis: Concordia Publishing House, 2006), 708, 1

October 23
[1] Fawcett, "Blest Be the Tie That Binds," *Lutheran Service Book* (St. Louis: Concordia Publishing House, 2006), 649, 1-2

October 25
[1] Dietrich Bonhoeffer, *The Cost of Discipleship* (New York: Macmillan, 1959), 35-36
[2] Dee Simmons, *Ultimate Living* (Lake Mary, FL: Siloam Press, 1999), 171
[3] "If Your Beloved Son, O God," tr. *The Lutheran Hymnal*, 1941, *Lutheran Service Book* (St. Louis: Concordia Publishing House, 2006), 568, 5

October 26
[1] "Responsible Citizenship: Collect 225," *Lutheran Service Book* (St. Louis: Concordia Publishing House, 2006), 313

October 27
[1] "Jesus, the Very Thought of Thee," tr. Caswall, *The Lutheran Hymnal* (St. Louis: Concordia Publishing House, 1941), 350, 3, 5

October 28
[1] da Siena, "Come Down, O Love Divine," tr. Littledale, *Lutheran Service Book* (St. Louis: Concordia Publishing House, 2006), 501, 1

October 29
[1] Luther, "A Mighty Fortress Is Our God," tr. composite, *Lutheran Service Book* (St. Louis: Concordia Publishing House, 2006), 656, 3
[2] C.S. Lewis, *The Screwtape Letters* (New York: Macmillan, 1948), 3
[3] Fabricius, "O Little Flock, Fear Not the Foe," tr. Winkworth, *Lutheran Service Book* (St. Louis: Concordia Publishing House, 2006), 666

October 30
[1] Luther, "A Mighty Fortress Is Our God," tr. composite, *Lutheran Service Book* (St. Louis: Concordia Publishing House, 2006), 656, 1-2
[2] Heermann, " O Christ, Our True and Only Light," tr. Winkworth, *Lutheran Service Book* (St. Louis: Concordia Publishing House, 2006), 839, 2

October 31
[1] *Luther's Small Catechism with Explanation* (St. Louis: Concordia Publishing House, 1991), 14
[2] Toplady, "Rock of Ages, Cleft for Me," *Lutheran Service Book* (St. Louis: Concordia Publishing House, 2006), 761, 1-2

November 1
[1] Martin Luther, "Preface to the Epistle of St. Paul to the Romans," in *Word and Sacrament I*, ed. E. Theodore Bachmann, vol. 35 of *Luther's Works*, ed. Jaroslav Pelikan and Helmut T. Lehmann (Philadelphia: Muhlenberg/Fortress Press; St. Louis: Concordia Publishing House, 1960), 370
[2] "All Saints' Day: Collect of the Day," *Lutheran Worship* (St. Louis: Concordia Publishing House, 1982), 116.

November 2
[1] "At the Lamb's High Feast We Sing," tr. Campbell, *Lutheran Service Book* (St. Louis: Concordia Publishing House, 2006), 633, 6

November 3
[1] Abraham Lincoln, *Second Inaugural Address*, 1865
[2] von Preussen, "The Will of God Is Always Best," tr. *The Lutheran Hymnal*, 1941, *Lutheran Service Book* (St. Louis: Concordia Publishing House, 2006), 758, 1
[3] "Responsible Citizenship: Collect 225," *Lutheran Service Book* (St. Louis: Concordia Publishing House, 2006), 313

November 4
[1] Watts, "O God, Our Help in Ages Past," *Lutheran Service Book* (St. Louis: Concordia Publishing House, 2006), 733, 1, 3, 6

November 5
[1] Boberg, "How Great Thou Art," tr. Hine, *Lutheran Service Book* (St. Louis: Concordia Publishing House, 2006), 801, 2
[2] Elizabeth Barrett Browning, "Aurora Leigh" (London: J. Miller, 1864)
[3] Van Dyke, "Joyful, Joyful We Adore Thee," *Lutheran Service Book* (St. Louis: Concordia Publishing House, 2006), 803, 2

November 6
[1] Frederick J. Schumacher and Dorothy A. Zelenko, eds., *For All the Saints: A Prayer Book For and By the Church*, vol. 4 (Delhi, NY: American Lutheran Publicity Bureau, 1996), 501-502
[2] Reusner, "I Trust, O Lord, Your Holy Name," tr. Winkworth, *Lutheran Service Book* (St. Louis: Concordia Publishing House, 2006), 734, 2-3

November 7
[1] "Life as a Baptized Child of God: Collect 175," *Lutheran Service Book* (St. Louis: Concordia Publishing House, 2006), 310

November 8

[1] Don E. Fehrenbacher, *Abraham Lincoln: A Documentary Portrait Through His Speeches and Writings* (Stanford University Press, 1964), 60

November 9

[1] "O Come, O Come, Emmanuel," tr. Neale, *Lutheran Service Book* (St. Louis: Concordia Publishing House, 2006), 357, 7

November 10

[1] Rambach, "Baptized into Your Name Most Holy," tr. Winkworth, *Lutheran Service Book* (St. Louis: Concordia Publishing House, 2006), 590, 3

November 12

[1] Oswald Chambers, "November 20," *My Utmost for His Highest: Selections for the Year* (New York: Dodd, Mead & Company, 1935)

[2] Crossman, "My Song Is Love Unknown," *Lutheran Service Book* (St. Louis: Concordia Publishing House, 2006), 430, 1, 7

November 13

[1] Held, "Come, Oh, Come, Thou Quickening Spirit," tr. Schaeffer, *The Lutheran Hymnal* (St. Louis: Concordia Publishing House, 1941), 226, 4

[2] Löwenstern, "Now Let All Loudly Sing Praise," tr. Winkworth, *The Lutheran Hymnal* (St. Louis: Concordia Publishing House, 1941), 28, 4

[3] Hausmann, "Lord, Take My Hand and Lead Me," tr. *Lutheran Book of Worship*, *Lutheran Service Book* (St. Louis: Concordia Publishing House, 2006), 722, 1

November 14

[1] Frederick J. Schumacher and Dorothy A. Zelenko, eds., *For All the Saints: A Prayer Book For and By the Church*, vol. 4 (Delhi, NY: American Lutheran Publicity Bureau, 1996), 423-424

[2] Grundtvig, "Built on the Rock," tr. Döving, *Lutheran Service Book* (St. Louis: Concordia Publishing House, 2006), 645, 1

[3] Ibid., 5

November 15

[1] Fawcett, "Blest Be the Tie That Binds," *Lutheran Service Book* (St. Louis: Concordia Publishing House, 2006), 649, 1

[2] Irons, "Sing with All the Saints in Glory," *Lutheran Service Book* (St. Louis: Concordia Publishing House, 2006), 671, 3

November 16

[1] Editorial "Don't Cry Daddy," *Chicago Sun-Times*, November 29, 2002

[2] "Holy Matrimony," *Lutheran Service Book: Agenda* (St. Louis: Concordia Publishing House, 2006), 68

[3] Ellerton, "O Father, All Creating," *Lutheran Service Book* (St. Louis: Concordia Publishing House, 2006), 858, 4

November 17
[1] 1 Samuel 17:47
[2] Fabricius, "O Little Flock, Fear Not the Foe," tr. Winkworth, *Lutheran Service Book* (St. Louis: Concordia Publishing House, 2006), 666, 4

November 18
[1] Luther, "Triune God, Be Thou Our Stay," tr. Massie, *Lutheran Service Book* (St. Louis: Concordia Publishing House, 2006), 505, 1

November 19
[1] Garry Wills, *Lincoln at Gettysburg: The Words that Remade America* (New York: Simon and Schuster, 2006)
[2] Schröder, "One Thing's Needful," tr. Cox, *Lutheran Service Book* (St. Louis: Concordia Publishing House, 2006), 536, 3

November 20
[1] Schalling, "Lord, Thee I Love with All My Heart," tr. Winkworth, *Lutheran Service Book* (St. Louis: Concordia Publishing House, 2006), 708, 2

November 21
[1] "Post-Communion Collect: Divine Service, Setting One," *Lutheran Service Book* (St. Louis: Concordia Publishing House, 2006), 166
[2] http://en.wikipedia.org/wiki/Common_table_prayer
[3] "Asking a Blessing at Mealtime: Collect 252," *Lutheran Service Book* (St. Louis: Concordia Publishing House, 2006), 315

November 22
[1] C.S. Lewis, *Beyond Personality* (New York: Macmillan, 1964), 40, quoted in *Sermon Illustrations for the Gospel Lessons* (St. Louis: Concordia Publishing House, 1982), 81
[2] Newton, "How Sweet the Name of Jesus Sounds," *Lutheran Service Book* (St. Louis: Concordia Publishing House, 2006), 524, 4

November 23
[1] "Grace To Receive the Word: Collect 148," *Lutheran Service Book* (St. Louis: Concordia Publishing House, 2006), 308

November 24
[1] Dietrich Bonhoeffer, *Ethics*, vol. 6 of *Dietrich Bonhoeffer Works*, ed. Clifford J. Green, tr. Reinhard Krauss, Douglas W. Stott, and Charles C. West (Minneapolis: Fortress Press, 2005), 135
[2] Loy, "The Law of God Is Good and Wise," *Lutheran Service Book* (St. Louis: Concordia Publishing House, 2006), 579, 6
[3] Scheffler, "Thee Will I Love, My Strength, My Tower," tr. Winkworth, *Lutheran Service Book* (St. Louis: Concordia Publishing House, 2006), 694, 4

November 25
[1] Allen, "Today Your Mercy Calls Us," *Lutheran Service Book* (St. Louis: Concordia Publishing House, 2006), 915, 4

November 28
[1] William Shakespeare, *Romeo and Juliet*, ed. Horace Howard Furness (Philadelphia: J.B. Lippencott Company, 1899), 109
[2] Fawcett, "Blest Be the Tie That Binds," *Lutheran Service Book* (St. Louis: Concordia Publishing House, 2006), 649, 2, 4

November 29
[1] Weissel, "Lift Up Your Heads, Ye Mighty Gates," tr. Winkworth, *Lutheran Service Book* (St. Louis: Concordia Publishing House, 2006), 340, 4
[2] Thilo, "Arise, O Christian People," tr. Russell, *Lutheran Service Book* (St. Louis: Concordia Publishing House, 2006), 354, 4

November 30
[1] Dale A. Meyer and Hubert F. Beck, *The Crosses of Lent Sermon Book: Sermons and Sermonic Studies* (St. Louis: Concordia Publishing House, 1987), 27
[2] C.S. Lewis, *Beyond Personality* (New York: Macmillan, 1964), 40, quoted in *Sermon Illustrations for the Gospel Lessons* (St. Louis: Concordia Publishing House, 1982), 81
[3] Nelson, "By All Your Saints in Warfare," *Lutheran Service Book* (St. Louis: Concordia Publishing House, 2006), 517, 5

December 1
[1] Tucker, "Our Father, by Whose Name," *Lutheran Service Book* (St. Louis: Concordia Publishing House, 2006), 863, 2

December 2
[1] Thring, "Jesus Came, the Heavens Adoring," *Lutheran Service Book* (St. Louis: Concordia Publishing House, 2006), 353, 4

December 3
[1] Walter Kent (Music) and James Gannon (Lyrics), "I'll Be Home for Christmas," recorded by Bing Crosby, 1943
[2] Neumeister, "Jesus Sinners Doth Receive," tr. *The Lutheran Hymnal*, 1941, *Lutheran Service Book* (St. Louis: Concordia Publishing House, 2006), 609, 4

December 4
[1] Ernst Anschütz, "O Tannenbaum," 1824

December 5
[1] Matthew 25:1-13
[2] Cowper, "God Moves in a Mysterious Way," *Lutheran Service Book* (St. Louis: Concordia Publishing House, 2006), 765, 4
[3] "How Firm a Foundation," *Lutheran Service Book* (St. Louis: Concordia Publishing House, 2006), 728, 1
[4] Luther, "Our Father, Who from Heaven Above," tr. *The Lutheran Hymnal*, 1941, *Lutheran Service Book* (St. Louis: Concordia Publishing House, 2006), 766, 9

December 6

[1] Luther, "Come, Holy Ghost, God and Lord," tr. *The Lutheran Hymnal*, 1941, *Lutheran Service Book* (St. Louis: Concordia Publishing House, 2006), 497, 2

[2] "Second Sunday in Advent: Collect of the Day," *Lutheran Service Book: Altar Book* (St. Louis: Concordia Publishing House, 2006), 555

December 7

[1] Nelson, "By All Your Saints in Warfare," *Lutheran Service Book* (St. Louis: Concordia Publishing House, 2006), 518, 1

December 10

[1] "Life as a Baptized Child of God: Collect 175," *Lutheran Service Book* (St. Louis: Concordia Publishing House, 2006), 310

December 11

[1] F.W. Beare, *The First Epistle of Peter*, 3rd ed. (Oxford: Basil Blackwell, 1970), 76

[2] von Zinzendorf, "Jesus, Thy Blood and Righteousness," tr. Wesley, *Lutheran Service Book* (St. Louis: Concordia Publishing House, 2006), 563, 1

[3] Ringwaldt, "The Day Is Surely Drawing Near," tr. Peter, *Lutheran Service Book* (St. Louis: Concordia Publishing House, 2006), 508, 7

December 12

[1] Grace Ketterman and David Hazard, *When You Can't Say "I Forgive You:" Breaking the Bonds of Anger and Hurt* (Colorado Springs, CO: NavPress, 2000), 32

December 13

[1] Dietrich Bonhoeffer, *Life Together: The Classic Exploration of Christian Community*, tr. Doberstein (New York: Harper & Row Publishers, 1954), 110

[2] Johann Friedrich Starck, *Starck's Prayer Book*, ed. W.H.T. Dau (St. Louis: Concordia Publishing House, 1921), 179

December 14

[1] Weissel, "Lift Up Your Heads, Ye Mighty Gates," tr. Winkworth, *The Lutheran Hymnal* (St. Louis: Concordia Publishing House, 1941), 73, 3

[2] Gerhardt, "O Lord, How Shall I Meet You," tr. *The Lutheran Hymnal*, 1941, *Lutheran Service Book* (St. Louis: Concordia Publishing House, 2006), 334, 1

December 15

[1] Johann Friedrich Starck, *Starck's Prayer Book*, ed. W.H.T. Dau (St. Louis: Concordia Publishing House, 1921), 465

[2] *Luther's Small Catechism with Explanation* (St. Louis: Concordia Publishing House, 1991), 18-19

[3] "For Home and Family: Collect 239," *Lutheran Service Book* (St. Louis: Concordia Publishing House, 2006), 315

December 16

[1] Alexander, "Once in Royal David's City," *Lutheran Service Book* (St. Louis: Concordia Publishing House, 2006), 376, 1

[2] Luther, "From Heaven Above to Earth I Come," tr. Winkworth, *The Lutheran Hymnal* (St. Louis: Concordia Publishing House, 1941), 85, 13

December 17

[1] "Now Sing We, Now Rejoice," tr. Russell, *Lutheran Service Book* (St. Louis: Concordia Publishing House, 2006), 386, 3

[2] "Jerusalem, My Happy Home," *Lutheran Service Book* (St. Louis: Concordia Publishing House, 2006), 673, 6

December 18

[1] Doddridge, "Hark the Glad Sound," *Lutheran Service Book* (St. Louis: Concordia Publishing House, 2006), 349, 2

December 19

[1] Dietrich Bonhoeffer, *Life Together: The Classic Exploration of Christian Community*, tr. Doberstein (New York: Harper & Row Publishers, 1954), 77

[2] Thilo, "O Jesus So Sweet, O Jesus So Mild," tr. Pietsch, *Lutheran Service Book* (St. Louis: Concordia Publishing House, 2006), 546, 3

December 20

[1] Horn, "Savior of the Nations, Come," tr. Winkworth, *Lutheran Service Book* (St. Louis: Concordia Publishing House, 2006), 333, 4

December 21

[1] Wade, "O Come, All Ye Faithful," tr. Oakeley, *Lutheran Service Book* (St. Louis: Concordia Publishing House, 2006), 379, 1

[2] Ibid., 3

[3] Watts and Lowry, "Come, We That Love the Lord," *Lutheran Service Book* (St. Louis: Concordia Publishing House, 2006), 669, 4

[4] Wade, "O Come, All Ye Faithful," tr. Oakeley, *Lutheran Service Book* (St. Louis: Concordia Publishing House, 2006), 379, Refrain

[5] "The Proper Preface: All Saints' Day," *Lutheran Service Book: Altar Book* (St. Louis: Concordia Publishing House, 2006), 160

December 22

[1] Martin Luther, "The Gospel for Christmas Eve, Luke 2[:1-14]" in *Sermons II*, ed. Hans J. Hillerbrand, vol. 52 of *Luther's Works*, ed. Jaroslav Pelikan and Helmut T. Lehmann (Philadelphia: Muhlenberg/Fortress Press; St. Louis: Concordia Publishing House, 1974), 26

[2] Luther, "From Heaven Above to Earth I Come," tr. Winkworth, *Lutheran Service Book* (St. Louis: Concordia Publishing House, 2006), 358, 9, 12

December 23
[1] Dix, "What Child Is This," *Lutheran Service Book* (St. Louis: Concordia Publishing House, 2006), 370, 1
[2] C.F.W. Walther, *Law and Gospel: How to Read and Apply the Bible*, ed. Charles P. Schaum, John P. Hellwege, Jr., and Thomas E. Manteufel, tr. Christian C. Tiews (St. Louis: Concordia Publishing House, 2010), 18
[3] Ibid., 20
[4] *Luther's Small Catechism with Explanation* (St. Louis: Concordia Publishing House, 1991), 15

December 24
[1] "The Nativity of Our Lord, Christmas Midnight: Collect of the Day," *Lutheran Service Book: Altar Book* (St. Louis: Concordia Publishing House, 2006), 559

December 25
[1] Brooks, "O Little Town of Bethlehem," *Lutheran Service Book* (St. Louis: Concordia Publishing House, 2006), 361, 4

December 26
[1] Heber, "The Son of God Goes Forth to War," *Lutheran Service Book* (St. Louis: Concordia Publishing House, 2006), 661, 4
[2] Mohr, "Silent Night, Holy Night," tr. Young, *Lutheran Service Book* (St. Louis: Concordia Publishing House, 2006), 363, 1
[3] "St. Stephen, Martyr: Collect of the Day," *Lutheran Service Book: Altar Book* (St. Louis: Concordia Publishing House, 2006), 946

December 27
[1] Martin Luther, "St. John's Day," vol. VI of *Sermon's of Martin Luther: The Church Postils*, ed. John Nicholas Lenker (Grand Rapids MI: Baker Books, 1995), 215
[2] Nelson, "By All Your Saints in Warfare," *Lutheran Service Book* (St. Louis: Concordia Publishing House, 2006), 517, 8
[3] "St. John, Apostle and Evangelist: Collect of the Day," *Lutheran Service Book: Altar Book* (St. Louis: Concordia Publishing House, 2006), 947

December 28
[1] Malcolm Muggeridge in Charles Swindoll, *Hope Again: When Life Hurts and Dreams Fade* (Nashville, TN: Thomas Nelson, 1997)
[2] "The Holy Innocents, Martyrs: Collect of the Day," *Lutheran Service Book: Altar Book* (St. Louis: Concordia Publishing House, 2006), 948

December 29
[1] Brooks, "O Little Town of Bethlehem," *Lutheran Service Book* (St. Louis: Concordia Publishing House, 2006), 361, 3
[2] "Before the Study of God's Word: Collect 203," *Lutheran Service Book* (St. Louis: Concordia Publishing House, 2006), 312

December 30
[1] Gerhardt, "Awake, My Heart, with Gladness," tr. Kelly, *Lutheran Service Book* (St. Louis: Concordia Publishing House, 2006), 467, 6
[2] Keimann, "O Rejoice, Ye Christians, Loudly," tr. Winkworth, *Lutheran Service Book* (St. Louis: Concordia Publishing House, 2006), 897, 4 and refrain

December 31
[1] "New Year's Eve: Collect of the Day," *Lutheran Service Book: Altar Book* (St. Louis: Concordia Publishing House, 2006), 949

Also from Tri-Pillar Publishing

MEETING ANANIAS

AND OTHER EYE-OPENING STORIES OF FAITH

by James Tino
Foreword by Dale A. Meyer

Bring your faith back into focus!

Are you finding it harder to keep your faith energized? Why does the Christian life, initially so exciting and full of promise, often become routine and ordinary? It is easy to get overwhelmed by the concerns of life and to focus on the wrong things, which quickly drains the life out of our faith. We need to have our vision adjusted by the Word of God and the Holy Spirit so we can see the hand of God at work in our lives. In Meeting Ananias, our eyes are opened to see what we sometimes miss: the ordinary and extraordinary ways that God makes Himself known to us as we follow Him.

Rev. Dr. James Tino is Director of Global Lutheran Outreach, a Lutheran mission-sending organization.

$11.95 – Order online at www.tripillarpublishing.com

Life As a Mission Trip

DR. JACOB YOUMANS

Missional Living 101!

Trips to the mission field always bring new spiritual growth and insight to our lives. What if we could learn to see mission not as an event to take part in, but as a lifestyle to embrace? In *Missional U: Life As a Mission Trip*, that's exactly what Dr. Jacob Youmans teaches us as he shows, through Scripture and by personal example, what missional living is all about! If you're looking for a new way to travel, then come along. Missional U is your ticket to an exciting and fulfilling spiritual adventure – one that's sure to last a lifetime!

Dr. Jacob Youmans, a dynamic conference speaker, is Director of the DCE Program at Concordia University in Austin, Texas.

$14.95 – Order online at www.tripillarpublishing.com

MISSIONAL TOO

The Trip of a Lifetime

DR. JACOB YOUMANS

Bon Voyage... Again!

In this second volume of devotions on the joy of missional living, Dr. Jacob Youmans shows us what it means to see the world through redemptive eyes, love the world with an evangelistic heart, and travel the world with the Gospel of peace firmly on our feet. In Missional Too: The Trip of a Lifetime, we discover that when we walk in the footsteps of Jesus, the imprint we leave behind is His, not our own – and that makes all the difference. Our journey here as God's dearly loved people is a Gospel-sharing, disciple-making one.

Dr. Jacob Youmans, a dynamic conference speaker, is Director of the DCE Program at Concordia University in Austin, Texas.

$14.95 – Order online at www.tripillarpublishing.com